American Politics in the Early Republic

American Politics in the Early Republic

The New Nation in Crisis

James Roger Sharp

Yale University Press
New Haven and London

Published with assistance from the Mary Cady Tew Memorial Fund.

Designed by James J. Johnson and set in Baskerville by
Marathon Typography Service, Durham, North Carolina.
Printed in the United States of America

Library of Congress Cataloging-in-Publication Data

Sharp, James Roger, 1936–
   American politics in the early republic : the new nation in crisis / James Roger Sharp.
      p. cm.
   Includes bibliographical references and index.
   ISBN 978-0-300-05530-6 (cloth: alk. paper)
          978-0-300-06519-0 (pbk: alk. paper)

   1. United States—Politics and government—1789–1809.   I. Title.
E310.S48   1993   93-19179
973.4—dc20

A catalogue record for this book is available from the British Library.
The paper in this book meets the guidelines for permanence and durability of
the Committee on Production Guidelines for Book Longevity of the
Council on Library Resources.

8   10   9   7

With love for Sandy and Matt
And, above all, for Nancy

Contents

Acknowledgments

No book is written in isolation, and I am enormously indebted to the many scholars who have worked diligently and creatively to disentangle and decode the events surrounding our nation's origins two centuries ago. The notes and the bibliography reflect the richness of these historians' and others' work and my dependence on their insights.

My questions about how American politics developed were stimulated years ago while I was a graduate student at Berkeley where I benefited immensely from the lively give-and-take in and out of class with my intellectually engaging graduate colleagues. Charles Sellers' influence as mentor and friend then and through the years has been enormous, and I like to think if I have had any success as a teacher and scholar it is because of the example of his own integrity and dedication to our profession.

My research was aided by the generosity of many people. The National Endowment for the Humanities and the American Council of Learned Societies, along with Syracuse University, provided funds that allowed me time off from teaching to do some of the initial research and writing for this book. A number of libraries and their staffs were helpful, and I am especially indebted to Jon McDonough and the staff at the Library of Congress, as well as the staff at the Historical Society of Pennsylvania, the New-York Historical Society, and the New York Public Library. Robert Rupp and Michael Oberg gave me indispensable help in running down sources and checking footnotes. I also want to thank Walda Metcalf for giving me some excellent advice during a critical stage in the development of the book.

A number of scholars unselfishly gave considerable time and effort to reading my work. Joel Silbey, Gerard Clarfield, and Steve Maizlish painstakingly read the entire manuscript and gave me invaluable suggestions. I am also grateful to Ralph Ketcham, Don Meinig, and Simon Newman, who read parts of the manuscript and offered very supportive and constructive advice. In addition, I would like to acknowledge the help of Thomas P. Slaughter for his enthusiasm for the project as well as his unusually perceptive critique.

Thanks also to Chuck Grench and Otto Bohlmann at Yale University Press and, especially, Jane Hedges for her able editorial assistance in preparing the manuscript. Phillip King did an admirable job of preparing the index.

And, most important, as reflected in the dedication, this book could not have been written without the love and support of my family. If I took a bit longer to finish it, it was *not* because of family obligations, but because I did not want to miss out on the growing up of Sandy and Matt and be like the father in Harry Chapin's "The Cat's in the Cradle." Finally, my wife Nancy's imprint is on every page. A lovingly supportive critic and imaginative editor, she labored mightily to convince a sometimes unwilling and sometimes unreceptive author that certain passages needed to be rewritten or sections needed to be reorganized. She was always right and invariably offered creative reformulations. Her love, assistance, and unflagging honesty and courage are responsible for any merit this book might have.

But despite all the help I have received, any errors of commission or omission are of course my sole responsibility.

American Politics in the Early Republic

Introduction

I t was in a hothouse atmosphere of passion, suspicion, and fear that the republican political institutions forged by the American Constitution were put to the test. Indeed, the twelve years from 1789 to 1801 represent a critical era in American history equivalent to that of the Civil War. The new nation was on trial in the 1790s and no one knew what the verdict would be. The overriding question in the minds of all Americans was: Could a people whose identity was born in revolution and divided into thirteen independent and jealous sovereignties create a stable, enduring national authority? And would this be possible amid the swirl of international conflict that threatened to engulf the young nation and plunge it into that great life-and-death struggle between the French Republic and Imperial Britain, an involvement that would imperil American independence?

The nation's first attempt at creating a central government had proved nearly disastrous. The American people, deeply suspicious of political power beyond the state and local level, had fatally crippled the Articles of Confederation government by restricting its authority to deal with the problems facing the nation. Now, for the first time since Independence, Americans were entrusting a central government with considerable power. But it was one thing for a government to be *granted* power and quite another for it to *exercise* it.

As historian Gordon Wood has noted, "Most of us today tend to take the creation of a strong national government for granted, and thus we tend to miss the radicalness of the Constitution." He contends that, "from the vantage point of the late twentieth century, allegiance to the nation, to the union, seems a matter of course; we can scarcely conceive of the United States without a powerful central government. . . . But if we change our vantage point and stand in 1776, then a strong national government is not something we can take for granted."[1]

The ratification of the Constitution in 1788 did seem to promise greater internal stability and international security for the country. Nonetheless, Americans shared a pervasive unease and skepticism about the future. Many judged that the union and the Constitution would be lucky to survive into the nineteenth century, and the events of the 1790s only confirmed their forebodings. As the decade unfolded, the country was beset by civil insurrections, secession threats, a quasi-war, foreign intrigue, and government repression. Even after a decade of government under the Constitution, George Washington was still unsure about the ultimate outcome. Less than a month before his death in 1799, he lamented that the critical political situation he had been observing "with an anxious, and painful eye" appeared "to be moving by hasty strides to some awful crisis."[2]

Americans at the time did *not* realize that the Constitution —although it was to survive, grow, and sustain the economic and political development of the United States for more than two hundred years—was almost fatally flawed at its inception. Reflecting expectations at odds with the political reality, it provided few mechanisms for resolving conflict.[3] And the instruments of government that were provided were inadequate to broker and mediate the increasingly vitriolic sectional suspicions and hostilities that threatened the new republic in the 1790s.

The new frame of government, as ratified in 1788, was influenced by the overly optimistic, classical republican, civic humanist assumption that selfless representatives of the citizenry could and would come together and legislate for the national public good and that this public good somehow could and would be determinable.[4] The Founders believed that political conflict, or the conflict between interests within the community, would be resolved and checked institutionally: first, by the separation of powers on the national level among the legislature, executive, and judiciary, and second, by the federal system with its division of power between the national and state governments. Resolution of conflict, however, was not the major question for the Founding Fathers. Rather, they were more concerned with abuse of power.

In the campaign to ratify the Constitution, Madison in *Federalist* 10 reflected the influence of civic humanist ideas[5] when he promised that Congress would be able to overcome factionalism and "to refine and enlarge the public views by passing them through the medium of a chosen body of citizens, whose wisdom may best discern the true interest of their country and whose patriotism and love of justice will be less likely to sacrifice it to temporary or partial considerations." Therefore, "the public voice [as] pronounced by the representatives of the people, will be more consonant to the public good than if pronounced by the people themselves."[6]

Classical republican ideas steeped in a civic humanist tradition that celebrated "partnership in virtue among all citizens" who would "equally and immediately" participate "in the pursuit of the universal good"[7] were the intellectual crucible that gave form to the political debate and the political expectations of the public men of the 1790s. But it is also clear that expectations of civic harmony, selfless behavior, and consensus upon a national public good did not match the reality of the deep sectional divisions within American society of that era. It was a society characterized by racial and ethnic diversity; beset by provincial, localist biases and antagonisms; separated geographically by vast distances as well as by barriers of mountains, forests, and streams. Furthermore, it was a society in transformation—one that had been recast by a revolution that had politicized large numbers of people and whetted their appetites for greater oversight and popular participation in public affairs. As a result, the authority of the traditional political elite had been eroded.[8] Despite the increasing incongruity between civic humanist ideas and the social, economic, and political realities of American life in the 1790s, however, public men did not abandon their classical republican beliefs. Instead, they interpreted political events in such a way as to reshape their understanding of a public good along sectional and partisan lines. Thus, Americans of differing political persuasions could with great sincerity and conviction argue that they, and they *alone*, reflected the national public good. So, although it is true that classical republican beliefs dominated the political debate of the 1790s, it is also true that the pluralist individualism of liberal republicanism was reflected in the economic, social, and political realities of the period with its many competing interests and divisions.[9] Thus, this classical republicanism, which in many ways became increasingly irrelevant and anachronistic amid the emerging political landscape of the 1790s, aggravated the already deep political and sectional divisions in the country.

Many of the Founding Fathers observed and lamented the contradiction between their civic humanist vision and the rapidly changing, hustling and bustling society in which they lived. Change, they feared, was transforming the United States that they had created into an increasingly alien country. Most of "the Founding Fathers recognized the reality of the self-interested pursuit of happiness by Americans," Wood has argued, "but were unwilling to accept it without regret; indeed, most of them died deeply disillusioned with what they had wrought."[10]

II

This disjunction between the Founders' political ideas and assumptions and the realities they faced, however, was only one of a number of problems the country faced in the years following the adoption of the Constitution. In attempting to assuage the localist-oriented Antifederalist opponents of the Constitution, the Founders had divided sovereignty and power between the states and the national government. But they had not spelled out the exact nature of the relationship. And this proved a serious ambiguity. Not only did it come perilously *close* to causing a civil breakdown in the 1790s, it *did* cause a bloody civil war in the 1860s.

The nature of representation also needed to be worked out. For although Madison at the Constitutional Convention had "invented a sovereign people" in order to assure the primacy of the national government over the states, no mechanisms existed, other than the politics of deference to elites, to assure that the people's voice would be heard. And what exactly did it mean that the people were sovereign? The sovereignty of the people, historian Edmund Morgan argues, "like representation itself, is a fiction that cannot survive too close examination or too literal application." He explains that "it requires that we believe not only in the existence of something we call people, but also in the capacity of that something to make decisions and to act apart from the elected representatives of particular localities."[11] Thus, the people's role in the new government was an ambiguous and potentially troublesome one. What kind of oversight role could or would the people exercise? Would the people possess power, as some advocated, "only on the days of their elections" and in between times relinquish it to "their rulers" or would they be more involved?[12] What would happen in the event the people's voice speaking through representatives were divided? Could opposition to government policies and actions be expressed and, if so, how? What would be the test of loyalty to the country?

Certainly there was little in the way of useful precedent to aid Americans in understanding the concept of a national legitimate opposition in the 1790s. In the colonies prior to 1776, internal political conflict had taken place within a political consensus of loyalty to the English Crown. And England's example after the Revolution was not useful either, for, although the role of party had been discussed throughout the eighteenth century and even earlier by political commentators, the nature and character of political opposition in Great

Britain was fundamentally different from that which eventually developed in the United States. By the end of the eighteenth century and through the early part of the nineteenth century in England, it was said: "If a man is in opposition he opposes the Ministers and government not the King personally." And although an opposition was necessary "to maintain the full confidence and submission of the nation" to Parliament's decisions, the English were quick to point out that there was no "less loyalty among the members of the opposition" than among the members of the government.[13] In England, in other words, the monarchy—at least after 1714—was a symbol of unity and of sovereignty; it was the institution that bound together political opponents in a mutually acknowledged loyalty to country. But although the Colonial Americans and the English could legitimize opposition through loyalty to the king, there was no comparable institution in the United States symbolizing the unity and sovereignty of the country and providing consensual boundaries within which opposition might be expressed or party competition occur. Americans of the 1790s could not make that crucial distinction between a party, which might temporarily hold the power of office, and the government itself. This was critical. For, as one scholar has pointed out, this distinction is fundamental to the operation of representative government "because embedded in the idea of democratic government is the concept that the party is a conveyer of the people's will through the institutions of government, but is not [itself] the repository of state power."[14]

Thus, when conflict over government policies broke out and opposition to the new government developed in the 1790s under the aegis of the Republicans, what did *not* happen was perhaps more extraordinary than what actually did. Given the almost hysterical fear that was rampant, it is remarkable that the considerable civil unrest, including secession threats and insurrections, were not used by Federalist and Republican extremists to foment greater violence and even civil war.

III

Although most Americans in 1789 were not too sanguine about the new government's chances of success and the events of the 1790s made the prospects seem even gloomier, scholars have dealt with the period as if the fate of the Constitution and the union were never in doubt. They have overemphasized the *continuity* of institutions from the colonial to the national period and have minimized the *dissonance*.

"America was born with a government, with political institutions and practices imported from the seventeenth-century," one study concludes; therefore, Americans "never had to worry about creating a government."[15]

Because historians have minimized the anxiety most Americans felt at the outset about the tenuousness and fragility of the union and the Constitution, they have not fully understood the political developments of the 1790s—particularly the modes and stages of opposition that developed in the decade.

This misunderstanding has flowed from and been closely interlinked with a Whiggish perspective that regards history as simply prologue to the present and, thus, does not fully appreciate the unique character of the past with its endless variety of possible outcomes. English historian Herbert Butterfield critiques Whig history of the sort applicable to much of the historical treatment of the 1790s as imposing "a certain form upon the whole historical story . . . to produce a scheme of general history that is bound to converge beautifully upon the present."[16] There "is a clear risk of Whiggish teleological distortion," another historian, Lawrence Stone, observes, "if the main question uppermost in the mind of the historian is how we got from there to here." Thus, Stone instructs the scholar to "keep firmly in mind that the people in the past are different from ourselves" and "that at all times there were alternative possibilities open, which might have occurred but in fact did not."[17] Historian Lee Benson also takes such alternative possibilities seriously. In his discussion of the causes of the American Civil War, he asks: "How could the Civil War have been prevented, or its occurrence made less likely, by groups that wanted to prevent it, but who adopted policies that failed to achieve that goal?" In answer, he warns against dismissing such a "contrary-to-fact conditional question on the ground that it is an 'iffy' question." Benson claims that "in real life, that is precisely the type of question men must answer, consciously or otherwise, when they choose one course of action rather than another."[18]

Thus, when historians approach the study of history—events such as Jefferson's election in 1800 or the beginning of the Civil War in 1861—without a sensitivity to the alternatives that the historical actors saw themselves as confronting, they impose a deterministic logic upon events that sees these experiences as moving inexorably toward developments that are known to have taken place subsequently. Besides doing violence to the integrity of a historical moment, this approach distracts scholars from taking the people they study as seriously as they should and blinds them from appreciating the subtleties, shadings, and distinctions of the past.[19]

It is a Whiggish perspective, then, that has prompted a number of historians to misread the history of the United States by assuming that American political party development has been linear and that the modern two-party system can trace its origins to the 1790s.[20] This view misconstrues the two-party system as having been consensual, relatively stable, and undramatic in its evolution and as having remained relatively unchanged since its inception.[21]

The traditional view of politics in the 1790s, then, minimizes the intensity of the conflict throughout the decade and instead emphasizes the basic agreement among Americans on such fundamental points as commitment to the Constitution, the union, and republicanism. Richard Hofstadter has made, perhaps, the classic statement of this position. He writes, "The fierceness of the political struggles has often been misleading; for the range of vision embraced by the primary contestants in the major parties has always been bounded by the horizons of property and enterprise. However much at odds on specific issues, the major political traditions have shared a belief in the rights of property, the philosophy of economic individualism, the value of competition; they have accepted the economic virtues of capitalist culture as necessary qualities of man."[22]

While still holding to the belief that Americans shared a "general republican consensus," Hofstadter comes closer to the truth in a later work when he notes that, despite this consensus, the idea of a loyal opposition had not been established by the 1790s. Politically conscious Americans, he says, "were acutely aware of being involved in a political experiment in republicanism that was attended by difficulties of the most acute kind and that might face many hidden and unpredictable pitfalls." This tenuousness, this fragility of union and of republicanism, moreover, Hofstadter maintains, led to a "sincere" fear on the part of Republicans that "many of their leading opponents favored monarchy and would scheme for its restoration, perhaps in some thinly disguised form under a 'consolidated' state."[23]

But although Hofstadter admits that the Republican fears were "sincere," he still does not take them seriously enough. The Revolution, he argues, marked the beginning of an irresistible tide of American opinion "against monarchy and all its attendant institutions and practices, and any party that could be successfully saddled with secret monarchical preferences would carry a fatal burden." So, if the Federalists "believed in monarchy and in restricting popular government, then, no matter how properly they may have at first come into their power, the use they intended to make of it violated the general republican consensus upon which the Constitution had been based, and thus represented a betrayal of the common understanding from the outset."[24]

Contained within the work of Hofstadter and others is a paradox that has remained unresolved. These historians have argued that both the Republicans and Federalists were *sincere* in their fears of the basic untrustworthiness of one another. Yet, they have also maintained that most Americans, including Federalists and Republicans, subscribed to a basic consensus of political ideas and that this consensus explains the negligible amount of violence in reconciling conflict in the 1790s.

But a contradiction remains: if the participants in the 1790s were *sincere*—and there is little question that they were—how could there have been a consensus and how could it have played a role in ameliorating the conflict? The only valid explanation is a different one: that Americans in the 1790s may have shared a basic consensus but they *failed to recognize* that they *shared* a consensus. And this failure was a major factor in shaping the nature of the political divisions of the 1790s and in influencing the means and institutions that were adopted to resolve what were often perceived as irreconcilable differences. Thus, while it is obvious to us in the twentieth century that eighteenth-century Americans shared a broad allegiance to the Constitution and republicanism, this was far from clear to our ancestors. Unquestionably many believed that others did not share that attachment.

IV

Since the Constitution was flawed in its ability to deal with the challenges and divisiveness of the 1790s, and the classical republican quest for a "general good" paradoxically led to greater polarization and suspicion, Americans had to grope desperately for solutions outside the established governmental structure. Their efforts almost inevitably involved steps to improve or enhance the representativeness of the citizenry.

In the end, two proto-parties—Republican and Federalist—developed almost in spite of themselves. But the participants themselves did not view the birth of these extralegal organizations as a salutary development. On the contrary, the formation of political organizations of any sort was the furthest thing from the minds of public men at the time the Constitution was ratified.[25] Indeed, parties were reviled and feared as disintegrative institutions that represented a corrupting self-interest. Most Americans would have agreed with Lord Bolingbroke who wrote that a "party is a political evil and faction is the worst of all parties."[26] Jefferson himself probably spoke for the great majority of his countrymen in 1789 when he asserted that if he "could not go to heaven but with a party" he would choose not to go there at all.[27]

When two proto-parties did arise, the participants never saw them as alternating in office and sharing in power. Nor did they see these proto-parties as alleviating violence and brokering conflict. In fact, both Republicans and Federalists looked forward to some climactic battle, during which each hoped that the enemy would be vanquished and driven from the field. The Federalists considered themselves to be the government and their opponents to be illegitimate and seditious. The opposition Republicans, appalled by the apparent self-interested and self-serving nature of the Federalists, regarded themselves as forming a temporary organization that would only be needed until the truly republican citizenry of the country could drive out the Federalists and become self-sustaining in their defense of republicanism and the Constitution.

Although political conduct during the 1790s might bear some resemblance to present-day party activity, it would be a fallacy to conclude that political parties meant the *same* thing to Americans in the eighteenth century as they have to later generations. Partisan rhetoric and the nature of political disputes had their own eighteenth-century character and must be understood within the historical context. The use of the names *Federalist* and *Republican,* for instance, should not be taken to mean that two political parties had been formed. Instead, as they were used in the 1790s, these designations were generic terms of advocacy, public labels that signaled endorsement of certain principles.

The Federalists appropriated the name of those who had successfully urged ratification of the Constitution, thus wrapping themselves in the patriotic cloak of defenders of the new frame of government. By claiming the Federalist name, they attempted to discredit others by implying that any who challenged them had opposed ratification in 1787 and 1788 and were now traitorously opposing the Constitution and the federal government.

The use of the label *republican* or *Republican* began almost as a defensive tactic. By using a name that they saw as professing loyalty to the principles of the American Revolution and Constitution and embracing a republican form of government, the Republicans hoped to indicate opposition to certain policies and actions of the government and yet at the same time defend themselves against charges of disloyalty.

Republicanism, then, was initially embraced as a set of political principles. Later, it was raised as a banner for what became a proto-party, a proto-party that only hesitantly, haltingly, and reluctantly was formed to defend those principles from what adherents perceived to be hostile and politically incompatible forces. This Virginia-led proto-party was not seen by the participants as a vehicle for reconciling differences but rather as a means of organizing and mobilizing public opinion to form a national consensus and political hegemony based upon a particular ideological perspective. The Republicans believed that they and they alone were the interpreters and translators of the wishes of a fictive sovereign people.[28] But so did the Federalists. Under such circumstances, there could be little tolerance of opposition, for each proto-party was dedicated to the ultimate destruction of its political enemies, who were enemies of the people. The Republicans often referred to their Federalist opponents as "Tories," believing them to be not a loyal though rival political group but individuals who hoped to subvert the Constitution and reestablish a special relationship with Great Britain. This special relationship, the Republicans believed, would, in effect, revoke the American Revolution and reshape American institutions along British lines. For their part, the Federalists just as sincerely believed that the Republicans had an unnatural and seditious sympathy toward France and were selfish localists whose loyalties to their individual states were greater than their loyalty to the union. Federalists equated support for Federalism with loyalty to the government and Constitution. There was no place for opposition.

V

In the 1790s, political development went through three distinct stages, each characterized by certain political assumptions, beliefs, and strategies. The first stage lasted from 1789 to 1792, the second from 1792 to 1798, and the third from 1798 to 1801.

The first stage began with enthusiastic support for George Washington as charismatic leader and a near unanimous hostility to parties. The expectation was that a group of elites, who had had considerable experience dealing with one another in previous national bodies, would be able to resolve disagreements in a gentlemanly and trusting way and, even more importantly, would, in line with civic humanist ideas, be able to discern and legislate for the general good. Thus, an invisible bond of trust and mutual respect served to unite those independent gentlemen who were elected to the First Congress. And although they knew disagreements would by no means be uncommon, they expected that these could be handled and accommodated within the boundaries of an elitist, deferential political system.

By the end of the first stage, however, there were grave forebodings that government under the Constitution was not working out as planned. The Founders' faith in the problem-solving ability of a gentlemanly elite in the national legislature seemed to many to have been unwarranted. Public men were failing to play the detached, selfless role that had been expected of them. Congress, rather than being an arena of calm and objective deliberation, had become a theater of intrigue and passion.

In attempting to address the new nation's domestic and foreign problems, the Washington administration had taken controversial positions that had proved divisive. Many had become frightened and, thus, disenchanted with the administration and its policies. Slowly these critics reluctantly formed into a loosely organized, but increasingly hostile, sectionally based opposition whose objective was to challenge what were perceived as unrepublican policies. These men, however, did not see the Constitution itself as defective. Instead, they considered an alarming number of the men who had been elected to serve under it as misguided, even corrupt.

The second stage of political development, from 1792 to 1798, was characterized by the deepening and broadening of the country's political and sectional divisions. As the gentlemanly elites failed to agree on either policy or the nature and extent of federal power itself, the shifting and very personal factionalism found in the first stage of political development reshaped itself into two loosely defined groups of elites. Two extra-Congressional proto-parties—the Federalists as the defenders of the administration and the Republicans as its antagonists—slowly and haltingly developed as vehicles to conduct energy in the politically charged environment.

Aggravating and intensifying the volatility of the situation was the fact that followers of each proto-party believed that their vision exclusively embraced the national public good. The intolerance bred by such attitudes forced the leaders of the proto-parties to cast desperately around for new modes or approaches to vanquish their protagonists. As a consequence, they seized upon a strategy of taking their sectionally based and increasingly divisive disagreements outside of Congress, and of appealing to the people in an effort to shape and mobilize public opinion around their respective conceptions of the public good. Leaders sought to tap, organize, and channel the ultimate source of political strength in a republic—the people—in order to legitimize their own interpretation of the public good. The conception that the people would possess power "only on the days of their elections," had proved unworkable in a republican society torn by conflict and without any institutional symbol of common loyalty.

The uncompromising division between the proto-parties and their appeals to the people had an unintended ripple effect. By politicizing the electorate, the elites aroused a critical public spirit that both nourished and contributed to political ferment. For the most part, this political awakening, which created a suspicion of and challenge to authority, was channeled into more democratic, non-elitist, and even potentially destructive forms of opposition. Societies, similar to the revolutionary Committees of Correspondence, were formed to mobilize and educate public opinion in an effort to shape and influence government action. Conventions and public meetings were held to air grievances. Petitions were circulated. Insurrections were mounted. All of these actions represented a willingness to use extralegal, even disruptive and violent, means to achieve particular objectives.

The third and final stage of political development, from 1798 to 1801, was the most critical. As the country became dangerously polarized, the Federalists, in 1798 with the passage of the Alien and Sedition Laws, used the full power of the government in an effort to destroy their opponents, whom they saw as subversive. The Republicans, forced to battle for their very survival, were compelled to change their strategy radically. Prior to 1798 they had optimistically believed that the people would repudiate leaders who supported antirepublican measures hostile to the general good of society. By 1798, however, the Federalists' electoral successes and their hold on the federal government seemed to belie that belief. Therefore, the Republicans shifted their focus of attention from the national to the state level. And by emphasizing a more overtly, self-consciously sectional, political enclave strategy, they left the clear implication that state secession and the breakup of the union might follow if the federal government refused to modify its policies and actions to make them more acceptable to opponents, especially Southerners.

This third stage culminated in 1801 with an unprecedented and almost unrivaled constitutional crisis. As a challenge to the union and the Constitution, it stands second only to the Civil War. The newness of the nation, the fragility of its institutions, and the depth of the hostility and suspicion all contributed to the creation of a volatile situation in which the union's continued existence became highly problematic. At two separate times during this three-year period, the country stood at the brink of civil war. The first crisis arose in response to Federalist preparations for war with France and measures to repress internal dissent through the raising of an army and the passage of the Alien and Sedition Acts. The second and even more dangerous crisis came in the winter of 1800–1801 with the deadlocked presidential election between Jefferson and Aaron Burr. As the Federalists sought to take advantage of the tie in order to retain power, the country skirted dangerously close to armed conflict.

VI

The Constitution in the 1790s did not and could not provide the institutional stability or consensus that would have allowed it to be "accepted on all sides as a starting point for further debates," as some historians have claimed.[29] Although virtually all public men hoped that the Constitution would survive as the frame of government, almost nobody would have dared to predict that it would be as successful as it has been and many were the prophecies of its demise. Actually, widespread public confidence that the Constitution would survive as the basis for government did not come until the nineteenth century after the document had withstood the political, sectional, and foreign policy threats of the first quarter century. This establishment and acceptance of constitutional "limits" for political discourse and conflict also coincided with the development of Republican hegemony after 1801. It was the Republicans and their vision of a national public good that served as the focus of national unity and consensus.[30]

The birth of the United States was not an easy one. It was not inevitable that after winning their independence the thirteen bickering colonies with their localist and sectional biases and suspicions would be able to establish an enduring union. In fact, it was remarkable. The ratification of the Constitution in 1788 was just an important first step, a step that continued rather than concluded the debate over such fundamental questions as the nature of the union, the extent of federal power, and the meaning of republicanism.

Looking back over two hundred years of success and prosperity, however, Americans in the twentieth century have tended to forget or at least discount the struggle that was required to forge their democratic institutions. Americans have remembered and celebrated the end result rather than the process itself. But this dynamic process with its inherently dangerous debate and conflict did not follow a well-mapped road into the future. Instead, many unmarked paths led in many directions, each with its own potential perils and hazards.

Perhaps most important for Americans living at the end of the twentieth century to understand is that democratic government is a precious commodity and not something that can be created easily or bequeathed from one generation to another. It requires constant attention, sacrifice, and struggle. Furthermore, the assumption that the success of the United States was more or less inevitable makes it difficult for Americans to understand and to sympathize with the battle for democracy by peoples around the globe.

I hope my book will contribute to a better understanding of the birth of our republic. Historians, as Charles Andrews reminds us, have an important obligation, for "a nation's attitude towards its own history is like a window into its own soul and the men and women of such a nation cannot be expected to meet the obligations of the present if they refuse to exhibit honesty, charity, openmindedness and a free and growing intelligence towards the past that makes them what they are."[31]

PART I

The Breakdown of Elite Consensus
1789–1792

1.

George Washington and the New Nation

We are in a wilderness without a single footstep to guide us.

JAMES MADISON

After bright sunshine had replaced early morning clouds on April 13, 1789, New Yorkers must have breathed a collective sigh of relief that the eagerly anticipated day would not be ruined by the bad weather that so frequently accompanied mid-Atlantic springs. Excitement had been building for some time as Americans flocked to the capital on that day to catch a glimpse of the new president or simply to be part of the festivities surrounding his installation as the first president of the United States. Every tavern, inn, and boarding house was filled to capacity, causing one observer to speculate that some visitors might be forced to sleep in tents.[1]

George Washington, the object of this attention bordering on adoration, was a reluctant participant, who reported that he felt like a "culprit . . . going to the place of his execution."[2] Nonetheless, his countrymen were profoundly grateful for his willingness to accept the burden of the presidency. And the outpouring of popular support, as well as the fanfare and elaborate ceremony that accompanied him on the trip from Mount Vernon to New York, illustrates the gratitude, and even relief, that Americans seemed to share. At almost every step of the way Washington was greeted by official delegations, military escorts, ringing bells, and cannon fire. Particularly lavish was the display near Trenton, New Jersey, where "a triumphal arch, twenty feet high, and supported by thirteen pillars, twined with evergreens and laurel," had been erected. Mothers with their daughters dressed all in white lined either side of the arch, on which the dates of the battle of Trenton had been written in gold entwined with flowers. Thirteen girls "wearing wreaths of flowers on their heads, and holding baskets of flowers in their hands" sang a welcoming ode.[3]

Congress had appointed its own welcoming committee and, when Washington reached the New Jersey shore opposite New York City, he was greeted by a specially constructed white barge manned by thirteen white-uniformed master pilots. On the voyage across the Hudson, the barge, reported one member of the party in a letter to his wife, was met by "boat after boat and sloop after sloop, gaily dressed in all their naval ornaments." One large sloop pulled alongside with "twenty gentlemen and ladies, who, with most excellent voices, sung an elegant ode, prepared for the purpose, to the tune of 'God save the King.'" As Washington's barge neared the New York shore, "tens of thousands" of people gathered to welcome him, prompting one observer to note that for nearly "half a mile, you could see little else along the shore, in the street, and on board every vessel, but heads standing as thick as ears of corn before a harvest."[4]

Beneath the cheering and extravagant display, however, lingered a profound unease about the future of the new republic. It was if the joyous rituals of celebration themselves could relieve the apprehension or exorcise the demons of doubt. Many feared that the new republic with its heterogeneous and scattered population would be unable to achieve unity and maintain its independence.

The Constitution could provide only the skeletal framework. It would be up to the president and Congress to give the new government direction, life, and vitality.[5] There were few precedents. "We are in a wilderness without a single footstep to guide us," wrote Madison, who had been elected to the House of Representatives. "Our successors will have an easier task, and by degree the way will become smooth, short and certain."[6]

The greatest single problem facing the new government was to establish its legitimacy as the national authority. The creation of a national government under the new Constitution was a profoundly revolutionary act in the same sense that social scientist Clifford Geertz observes in other new societies. The "formation of a sovereign civil state," according to Geertz, "stimulates sentiments of parochialism, communalism, racialism . . . because it introduces into society a valuable new prize over which to fight and a frightening new force with which to contend." Thus the new national government was seen as so threatening and as such a radical departure not because it represented the "shifting or transfer of a fixed quantity of power between groups" but because it created "a new and more efficient machine for the production of power itself."[7]

Many Americans were gravely concerned that the Antifederalists, who opposed the Constitution, would perpetuate and sharpen the divisions spawned by the battle over ratification and do everything in their power to cripple the fledgling government.

Because of the threat of British arms, the Revolution had served as a "great unifying force . . . under whose banner private, ethnic, sectional, and other differences were submerged."[8] By 1789, however, with the Peace of Paris already six years old, the sense of national purpose that the Revolution had temporarily given Americans was clearly waning, and the corrosive forces of sectional hostility and suspicion were in ascendance. Furthermore, the Revolution, by eroding the authority of the traditional political elite and destroying the central and legitimizing authority of the crown, had politicized large numbers of people and had whetted the public's appetite for greater popular participation in public affairs.[9]

The crisis-induced unity of the Revolution and the imperfect union of the Articles of Confederation had not resulted in an effective national authority. Because of American suspicions toward government in general, but particularly toward government beyond the local or state level, the Articles had not required the yielding of state sovereignty. Now, with the ratification of the Constitution, Americans were attempting to take a giant step in the long, complicated, and agonizing process of creating a national community.

Many Americans in 1789 feared that the country was too large and too diverse to develop and sustain a sense of national community. The United States was similar to those societies described by one social scientist where local loyalties "to the more primordial social and economic groupings—family, clan, village, tribe, religion, social class —compete with and often supersede loyalty to the broader institutions of public authority."[10] And it would be difficult for Americans to subordinate their local allegiances to their states, which had long histories of being separate entities with familiar traditions, institutions, habits, and relationships that had evolved through custom and usage, to a national authority.

For a society to be a community, scholars have noted, the power of each of the individual social groups that make up that society has to be channeled "through political institutions which temper, moderate, and redirect that power so as to render the dominance of one social force compatible with the community of the many." Thus, any society in which groups "see each other only as archenemies cannot form the basis of a community until those mutual perceptions change."[11] Yet it was exactly this kind of antagonistic perception that had provided the basis for the political turmoil during the ratification struggle.

Also for a political entity to be a community the various groups and individuals involved must have a relationship "to something apart from themselves . . . to some principle, tradition, myth, purpose, or code of behavior that the persons and groups have in common."[12] Eventually this role would be played by the Constitution. But in the 1790s the newness of the Constitution, the widespread sense of its fragility, and the bitter antagonism between the contending groups in American society prevented that document from providing limits to the political debate and serving as the consensual touchstone for the nation.

All of these factors, Washington and his followers were only too aware, would test the imagination and skill of the officers of the new federal government in their attempts to secure a "more perfect union." The challenge before them was momentous and the stakes high. The Constitution represented the last chance to create a united country and to avoid the establishment of a number of petty, constantly quibbling and bickering confederacies.

II

The American empire in 1789 extended from the Atlantic Ocean on the east to the Mississippi on the west, from the Great Lakes and Canada on the north to the Florida boundary on the south. The face of the country had not changed much even after almost two centuries of settlement. Pockets of civilization dotted the landscape but were, for the most part, huddled along the Atlantic seaboard. But if one could have had a bird's-eye view of the young republic in 1789, it would not have been these scattered towns and settlements that would have struck the eye, but rather their insignificance in the midst of the overpowering presence of nature, with its impenetrable forests and barriers of mountains and rivers.

Historian Henry Adams has pointed out that it was one thousand miles from New York to the Mississippi River and twelve hundred miles from the future capital, Washington D.C., to Natchez. These distances contrasted sharply to western Europe where scarcely any portion was more than "three hundred miles distant from some sea," a span that "was hardly more than an outskirt of the United States." Adams somberly concludes that no "civilized country had yet been required to deal with physical difficulties so serious, nor did experience warrant conviction that such difficulties could be overcome."[13] One French traveler of the era saw the "widely and thinly scattered" population and the "extent of territory" as "nothing but a prolific source of present weakness." He gloomily predicted "future disunion."[14]

Poor communication networks increased the isolation of the settlements in the vast nation. By the end of the eighteenth century, only a few post roads had been completed, furnishing crude and sometimes nearly impassable routes of transportation. A series of these roads extended north and south along the eastern seaboard from the District of Maine to Georgia. A letter sent this distance of more than 1,600 miles took three weeks to deliver. And to travel the 717 miles from Portland, Maine, to Richmond, Virginia, required a twelve-day trip by stagecoach.

A number of important east-west roads linked important settlements but also required days of travel. One extended inland to Canandaigua in western New York and required about a week's travel from Boston or New York City. Another connected Philadelphia with Wheeling, Virginia, a distance of 389 miles necessitating an expedition of some eight or nine days. From the East Coast the main southwest route to Kentucky and Tennessee ran through the Shenandoah Valley to Fort Chiswell, Virginia, and then west along the Wilderness Road through the Cumberland Gap. The hardy pioneer wishing to travel the 636 miles from Philadelphia to Knoxville needed three weeks.[15]

This geographic isolation led to a localist insularity that, in turn, bred deep-seated sectional suspicion and even estrangement. But although considerable diversity existed throughout the entire union, the Southern and New England dichotomy was perhaps the most pronounced, with each region having strikingly different public habits, attitudes, and institutions as well as conflicting views of republicanism. One Southerner, for example, avowed that "we see plainly that men who come from New England are different from us."[16]

In New England, the town was the key institution shaping social and political outlooks. Homogeneous, geographically compact, and imbued with a social and political dynamic working against dissent and promoting harmony, the New England town had an active population that played an important role in local government affairs. Historian Robert Gross points out in his study of Revolutionary Concord, Massachusetts, that for a citizen "to insist on a formal count of the yeas and nays or to demand a record of one's dissent in the minutes of a [town] meeting was to subvert that perfect unanimity of minds that adorned the ideal community."[17]

This closely knit community of the New England town—with its relative ease of communication and tradition of citizens meeting together to discuss and to decide on common problems—was perhaps the best example of the working out of the principles of actual representation, which included "the strict accountability of representatives to the local electorate" and meant, in fact, "the closest possible ties between [governmental] members and their particular constituents."[18] As federal politics of the 1790s evolved and seemed further removed from the control of local constituencies, some men in other states envied New Englanders for their town meetings and searched for institutions that might play a similar role.

The New Englanders' version of republicanism was bound up with the Northerners' piety and morality and their belief that the United States was a national organic community striving to build a "Christian Sparta." Government, to the New Englanders, should play a positive and active role in guiding the "nation toward economic as well as moral health." And Americans, they believed, had a moral obligation to live industrious, hard working, frugal lives resisting seduction or corruption by the pursuit of wealth.[19]

The overwhelmingly rural and isolated Southern society, with its plantation economy based on slave labor and its local elite-controlled institutions, contrasted sharply with New England. The primary instrument of local government in Virginia—and the situation in the rest of the Southern states was similar—was the county court, an institution that reflected a deferential, hierarchical society ruled by gentlemen. The county court had wide powers for it included legislative, executive, and judicial functions. Unlike Massachusetts, where the town called for the widespread and frequent participation of its members, the Southern county court was in many cases insulated from the people's will. In Virginia, for example, the judges were not elected but appointed for life terms by the governor, who generally accepted the recommendation of the continuing local justices in filling vacancies.[20]

White Southerners were repelled by the moralistic and nationalistic republicanism of New England. Defensive about the institution of slavery, Southerners took a libertarian view and recoiled in horror from the idea that government might be called upon to intervene "in the lives of individuals to regulate their behavior according to moral values."[21] But Southerners, like New Englanders, placed a high value on harmony and homogeneity. Jefferson, in his *Notes on Virginia* published in the early 1780s, pointed out the dangers and "inconveniences" that an influx of a large number of foreigners with their diversity of ideas and traditions might bring to Virginia. "It is for the happiness of those united in society to harmonize as much as possible in matters which they must of necessity transact together," Jefferson argued. In time, he warned, a large number of foreigners would "warp and bias" the legislature and "infuse into it their spirit . . . and render it a heterogeneous, incoherent, distracted mass."[22]

In the South, republicanism and slavery were inextricably linked. Slavery was a consensus-producing institution, Southerners believed, that could elevate white citizens of the republic to a level where they would be able to be autonomous, independent, and virtuous, qualities that were essential to preserving the republic.

"Two-fifths of Virginia's people," historian Edmund Morgan contends, "were as poor as it is possible to get; but they were all enslaved, and all worked productively for private masters, who were thereby strengthened in their independence and able to take the lead in resisting British tyranny." Slavery was also an important factor, according to Morgan, in assuring equality among white citizens, for the elite believed that they "could more safely preach equality in a slave society than in a free one . . . because Virginia's labor force was composed mainly of slaves, who had been isolated by race and removed from the political equation." This meant that "the remaining free laborers and tenant farmers were too few in number to constitute a serious threat to the superiority of the . . . [elite] who assured them of their equality." Therefore, small as well as larger farmers had a "common identity" for "both were equal in not being slaves."[23]

The geographic, social, and political isolation caused by poor communications and the vastness of the new republic had been a major factor in shaping the Antifederalists' opposition to the new Constitution. An increased centralization and consolidation of the national government, they had feared, would be the inevitable result of attempting to extend republican government over a large geographic area with a heterogeneous population.

One Massachusetts Antifederalist had contended that governing such an "extensive empire . . . upon republican principles" was impossible. "Such a government will degenerate to a despotism, unless it be made up of a confederacy of smaller states, each having the full powers of internal regulation," he wrote. The "large and consolidated empires" might "dazzle the eyes of a distant spectator with their splendor" but, examined more closely, they were "always found to be full of misery." The reason behind this amounted to no less than a principle of government: "In large states the same principles of legislation will not apply to all the parts." He noted, for example, that the "inhabitants of warmer climates are more dissolute in their manners, and less industrious, than in colder countries." Therefore, it was concluded, the "idea of an uncompounded republic, on an average one thousand miles in length, and eight hundred in breadth, and containing six millions of white inhabitants all reduced to the same standard of morals, of habits, and of laws, is in itself an absurdity, and contrary to the whole experience of mankind."[24]

Revolutionary War hero Sam Adams feared that a national legislature would never be able to enact equitable laws for the entire country because of regional incompatibilities. Indeed, Adams predicted an ultimate civil war between what he saw as the more democratic New England states and the South.[25]

III

Considering the geographic, economic, social, and cultural diversity of the United States in 1789, it is not surprising that there would be conflicting expectations about the future of the nation.[26] And even though republicanism was an ideology shared and even revered by most Americans, it was a republicanism, in the words of one historian, that "existed in several different modes, each of which contained a different center of gravity, a different national vision."[27] As republicans, Federalists and Antifederalists alike expected that their citizen-legislators would be virtuous and selfless and legislate for the public good. But for what public? The Antifederalists, because of the heterogeneity and size of the country, rejected the Federalists' proposition that civic harmony could or would prevail at the national level or that a consensus upon a national public good could be realized. Thus, although the Federalists believed in the value of a national legislature removed from corrupting localist interests at the state level, the Antifederalists, while differing among themselves, tended to be more democratic and populistic, fearing the aristocratic control and the likely corruption of a national legislature far removed from constituent oversight.[28]

Antifederalist Amos Singletary of Massachusetts, for example, believed that a stronger and more remote national government would inevitably increase the power of the aristocracy, warning: "These lawyers, and men of learning and moneyed men, that talk so finely, and gloss over matters so smoothly, to make us poor illiterate people swallow down the pill, expect to get into Congress themselves; they expect to be managers of this Constitution, and get all the power and all the money into their own hands, and then they will swallow all us little folks like the great *Leviathan*; yes, just as the whale swallowed up Jonah!"[29]

Closely related to this concern about aristocracy was the Antifederalist idea that the people's representatives should be frequently elected (preferably annually), rotated in office, and have close and democratic relationships with their constituents.[30] None of this would be possible under the new Constitution, it was believed. Not only would the representatives be geographically isolated from their constituents, but, because they might represent as many as thirty thousand people, they would also be aloof and unresponsive to individual needs.

"The legislature of a free country," a Pennsylvania Antifederalist had written, "should be so formed as to have a competent knowledge of its constituents, and enjoy their confidence." And for this to occur, "the representation ought to be fair, equal, and sufficiently numerous, to possess the same interests, feelings, opinions, and views, which the people themselves would possess, were they all assembled."[31] Furthermore, the representatives should be "so numerous as to prevent bribery and undue influence, and so responsible to the people, by frequent and fair elections, as to prevent their neglecting or sacrificing the views and interests of their constituents, to their own pursuits." Unfortunately, he had concluded, the new Congress proposed by the Constitution failed miserably to meet this test, for "the sense and views of 3 or 4 millions of people diffused over so extensive a territory comprising such various climates, products, habits, interests, and opinions, cannot be collected in so small a body."[32]

Melancton Smith, an Antifederalist leader in New York, put his finger on the central issue about representation under the new Constitution when he asked pointedly, "How was the will of the community to be expressed?"[33] This, of course, was the crucial question in the 1790s.

How a community was to be represented, what the nature of that representation was to be, and how the public good was to be determined and defined were all questions the Federalists believed they had successfully answered in a number of forums, but perhaps none so notable as the *Federalist Papers*. In rebutting the Antifederalist criticisms, James Madison, in *Federalist* 51, wrote that in an extended republic like the United States with its great variety of interests, "a coalition of a majority of the whole society could seldom take place upon any other principle, than those of justice and the general good." How did he expect this general good to be defined and acted upon? A selfless and virtuous elite in Congress, Madison insisted, would be able to divine the general good for the entire country. And unlike the Antifederalists, who emphasized the representative-as-agent role of the legislator and the *actual* nature of representation, Madison stressed the benefits of an elite, deferential, virtual representative system. Through the process of representation, he argued, the public views would be refined and enlarged as they were passed through "the medium of a chosen body of citizens, whose wisdom may best discern the true interest of their country, and whose patriotism and love of justice, will be least likely to sacrifice it to temporary or partial considerations." Madison concluded that "it may well happen, that the public voice, pronounced by the representatives of the people, will be more consonant to the public good, than if pronounced by the people themselves, convened for the purpose."[34]

Madison's emphasis upon Congress's ability to define "the true interest of the country" and to legislate for the "public good" revealed the continuing influence of classical republican ideas on the Founding Fathers. Although Gordon Wood and others have argued that the ratification of the Constitution represented a victory of liberal republicanism with its celebration of social diversity and individualism over classical republicanism, which emphasized the organic wholeness of society, this was not the case.[35] For although the Founders recognized the diversity of interests within society, they believed, according to Madison, that an unselfish and disinterested elite could ascertain and legislate for the public good. Ironically, the apparent failure of the elites to act in a selfless, civic-minded way did not cause Americans in the 1790s to turn their backs on classical republicanism with its emphasis upon virtue and unity. It only strengthened its appeal. And as the decade wore on, Americans sought desperately to realize the classical republican vision. But perceptions of the national public good were antithetical and uncompromising. And as adherents of differing perceptions attempted to capture a monopoly on public virtue and equate themselves and their success with the survival of the new nation, the country came close to being torn asunder.

IV

The first major issue of business facing leaders of the new government was neutralizing, isolating, or converting those Americans who had opposed the ratification of the Constitution. The most effective weapon in the Founders' arsenal was and continued to be George

Washington himself. In fact, despite the Antifederalists' strenuous opposition and deep apprehensions, the Constitution had been ratified, perhaps in large part due to the popular perception that Washington would consent to be the first president.[36] This reluctant decision made by the immensely popular Virginian was the most important factor in helping to legitimize the new government at its outset. Symbol of the nation's victorious battle for independence, Washington was a "charismatic leader"[37] seen by contemporaries as representing the virtue, strength, aspirations, and values of his country. "In the well-worn phrase of Henry Lee," one historian writes, the Virginia general was *"first in war, first in peace, and first in the hearts of his countrymen. . . .* He was the prime native hero, a necessary creation for a new country. . . . For America, he was originator and vindicator, both patron saint and defender of the faith . . . Charlemagne, Saint Joan and Napoleon Bonaparte telescoped into one person."[38]

Washington, it was felt, could be trusted with power because of his well-known commitment to republicanism and perhaps also because of his often expressed distaste for office and longing for retirement. Even Thomas Jefferson, who had misgivings about the failure of the Constitution to limit the re-eligibility of the president, hoped that the defect would "remain uncorrected as long as we can avail ourselves of the services of our great leader, whose talents and whose weight of character I consider as peculiarly necessary to get the government so under way as that it may afterwards be carried on by subordinate characters."[39]

In his inaugural, Washington, recognizing the immensity of the task of his new government, pleaded for unity, beseeching Congress to shed "local prejudices, or attachments," to hold "not separate views," and to avoid "party animosities" that might "misdirect the comprehensive and equal eye which ought to watch over this great assemblage of communities and interests." If the public men were governed by the "pure and immutable principles of private morality," Washington assured, then Congress, being *above* petty, personal, local, and sectional interests, would be able to forge a truly "National policy."[40]

But Madison and many of the other Founders recognized that Washington's popularity would not in itself be enough to overcome "local prejudices, or attachments." Thus, even before the new Congress assembled in New York in early March 1789, they were at work to finesse the Constitution's opponents. Their strategy was twofold: (1) to ensure that supporters of the Constitution were elected to Congress and (2) to preempt Antifederalist agitation over the omission of a bill of rights in the Constitution by quickly amending the document to include one. It was essential that the supporters of the Constitution, according to Madison, marshal their strength to "kill the opposition every where" and put an end "to this disaffection to the Govt."[41]

It is important at this point to understand that the Federalists and Antifederalists, political associations of Americans who supported and opposed the Constitution, were only loose coalitions of local groups that had banded together during the ratification struggle for one climatic battle. Even though these organizations were sometimes referred to as *parties,* they were not parties as parties have come to be defined in the nineteenth or twentieth centuries because participants did not see themselves as operating within some consensual framework but as having differences that were *fundamental* and *irreconcilable.* This was different from the situation in Great Britain, one Pennsylvania Antifederalist pointed out during the ratification campaign, where the ever-present violent parties and factions formed "not from a dislike to the fundamentals" of the constitutional settlement of the Glorious Revolution of 1688, "but on account of mal-administration: All parties glory in the constitution, and disagree only, when it is infringed, or violated." This was not the case in the United States, he warned, where he and his colleagues opposed "the fundamentals of the constitution itself." And he concluded with the dire prediction that no "Constitution that is not popular can possibly be established in America; or if for a short time it were established, we would have nothing but anarchy and civil war."[42] Thus, as far as this and many other Antifederalists were concerned, the Constitution would fail in its role as the basic law to legitimate government and to provide the institutional framework that structured and set boundaries on political disputes.

To Madison and his Federalist colleagues such sentiment had to be discredited and vitiated. Thus, the first election under the new Constitution was in large part an extension of the battle over ratification and was characterized by much the same bitterness.[43] In Virginia, Madison was denied a seat in the new United States Senate by an Antifederalist legislature, which elected two opponents of the Constitution instead. Even the seat Madison eventually won in the House was closely contested by James Monroe, who had been brought forward by those hostile to the Constitution to run a losing race against his old friend.[44] In the end, however, only a few Antifederalists won seats, and some of those who did, Madison confidently reported, could be expected to "be restrained by the federalism of the States from which they come."[45]

During the contest over the ratification of the Constitution, one of the Antifederalists' most persuasive and pervasive complaints was that the proposed document did not contain a bill of rights. This was essential to curb governmental power, the Antifederalists argued, mindful of their bitter experiences during the Revolutionary period when arbitrary British action had threatened certain basic rights.[46] Richard Henry Lee of Virginia, for instance, one of the most outspoken Antifederalists, denounced the Constitution as "most highly and dangerously oligarchic" for lacking "a bill of rights" to secure those "human rights," such as the "rights of conscience, the freedom of the press, and the trial by jury."[47]

Madison and other Federalists worried that the Antifederalists' complaints were a subterfuge for weakening and enfeebling the national government.[48] But in order to blunt the Antifederalist criticism, the Federalists encouraged delegates at state ratifying conventions to propose such constitutional amendments as they deemed beneficial to the new nation and send them to the First Congress.[49]

In all, some 210 amendments were submitted. After the duplications were removed, 80 remained. From these, Madison drew up the first 8 amendments. He himself added a ninth and tenth, which further defined the rights of the people and limited the power of the federal government. Congress in the fall of 1789 eventually submitted 12 amendments to the states for ratification. By December 1791, the states had accepted 10 of the 12 amendments and the Bill of Rights had become part of the Constitution.[50]

Madison hoped that the Bill of Rights would weaken and perhaps even destroy the Antifederalists as well as preempt any move in the country to subvert the federal government.[51] There had been disturbing signs: Legislatures in the important states of New York and Virginia had supported an abortive plan to call a new national convention to revive the whole question of governance. Madison and other supporters of the Constitution feared that such a convention would lead to chaos and division by reopening questions settled during the original convention.[52]

Despite the fears of Madison and other Founders, however, the high tide of antifederalism had crested in 1788 with the unsuccessful effort to defeat the ratification of the Constitution. Antifederalism was doomed because it ran counter to powerful public sentiment that the new government should be given a chance to prove itself. But this simple, profound truth was unknown to most of the political participants in the early 1790s as the spirit of antifederalism continued to haunt the public debates. The Antifederalist label itself quickly became a political epithet, implying disloyalty to the country, and it was used to discredit enemies. But as the ghost of antifederalism lingered on after the battle for ratification, it mingled with and helped shape an opposition to the new government. Despite Washington's hopes and the desires of most Americans for a "happily-ever-after" ending to the battle over ratification between the Federalists and Antifederalists, this was not to be.[53]

2.

Disappointed Expectations
The Failure of Elite Consensus

Conflicting interests "of the States . . . [had] given birth to combinations, parties, Intrigues, Jealousies . . . to such a degree to give serious alarm to the friends of the Government." —JOHN BROWN

The day the First Congress convened—March 4, 1789—was inauspicious. Despite the festive air in New York, punctuated by the pealing of bells and the firing of canons, only eight of the twenty-six senators and thirteen of the sixty-five members of the House of Representatives had made it to the new capital. And it would be almost a month before the houses would be able to muster quorums and begin to conduct business.[1]

Virginia had the largest delegation with twelve (ten members of the House and two senators), followed by Massachusetts and Pennsylvania, each with ten. With three apiece, Rhode Island and Delaware had the minimum number. The ages of the ninety-one representatives ranged from twenty-seven to sixty-eight years, with the average being about forty-six. Almost 44 percent were lawyers; 49 percent had had at least some college education and 40 percent some military service.

Members of the First Congress were seasoned state and local officials, but they had considerably less experience at the national level. Although 94 percent had seen duty in their state legislatures, only about half (54 percent) had served in the Continental or Confederation congresses. Fewer than a fourth (only 23 percent) had been in Philadelphia to help draft the Constitution.[2]

Virginia was the most powerful state in the newly formed union and therefore the most feared by her sister states. With almost 700,000 inhabitants in 1790, Virginia ranked first in population, being almost one-third larger in population than the second-ranked state, Pennsylvania, and almost twice the size of New York or Massachusetts.[3] Virginians dominated the new government. Not only was Washington a Virginian, but so were his choices for secretary of state and attorney general, Thomas Jefferson and Edmund Randolph, respectively. Henry

Knox of Massachusetts, Washington's old chief of artillery in Revolutionary days, was asked to continue on as secretary of war, a position he had held under the Articles of Confederation. And for the head of the Treasury Department, the president chose New Yorker Alexander Hamilton, his aide-de-camp during the Revolution. The vice president, John Adams, was, of course, from Massachusetts.

Jefferson, who had missed the Constitutional Convention and the debate over ratification because he had been out of country serving as minister to France, was initially reluctant to give up his French post for a cabinet assignment.[4] Madison, however, concerned about sectional suspicion and hostility and anxious that Virginia and the South be well represented in the cabinet, encouraged Jefferson to accept the president's invitation, arguing that it was "of infinite importance that you should not disappoint the public wish on this subject." Jefferson's appointment, Madison said, would reassure many Southerners and Westerners.[5] Jefferson's response was influenced by his earlier experiences in the public service. Although he had distinguished himself as the author of the Declaration of Independence and as a member of the Confederation Congress and state legislature, Jefferson recalled with abhorrence his unhappy tenure as the harshly criticized war governor of Virginia when British forces overran the state. Thus, Jefferson replied to Washington's overtures indecisively, protesting in a self-effacing way that he was unequal to the task and preferred to remain as minister to France. Doubtless remembering his unhappy years as governor, Jefferson noted in the letter that public "criticisms and censures" would surely accompany such a cabinet post. However, he ruefully concluded that "it is not for an individual to chuse his post" and it was Washington's duty to "marshal us as may best be for the public good."[6] The president responded that he felt some "delicacy and embarrassment" from the position Jefferson had placed him in and offered Jefferson the choice of remaining in France or becoming secretary of state. As to the latter option, Washington assured Jefferson that "no person . . . could better execute the Duties of it than yourself" and that the "duties will probably be not quite so arduous and complicated . . . as you . . . imagine."[7] Jefferson's final acceptance of the post ended a needlessly prolonged episode.

Hamilton had resisted his friends' earlier appeals to become a candidate for the United States Senate or for the governorship of New York. The Treasury Department, newly organized and administered by a single executive rather than by a committee, offered, he felt, a far greater opportunity to exercise creative leadership and to help ensure the establishment of a strong national government, an objective that had been near to his heart for some time.[8]

As a delegate from New York at the Constitutional Convention, Hamilton had confessed that his own model of government was the British system, which "was the best in the world." Hamilton maintained that an effective government needed the ability to exercise physical force if and when the need arose. His own scheme would have had the executive as well as the upper house serve for good behavior, with the executive having the power of absolute veto over all legislation. Finally, in order to ensure that the states were subordinate to and their laws in compliance with the federal authority, Hamilton would have had all state governors appointed by the national government.[9]

Nonetheless, although disappointed with the completed Constitution, Hamilton worked mightily to secure its ratification. At the end of his public career in 1802, he expressed his ironic ambivalence when he wrote a friend that "perhaps no man in the United States has sacrificed or done more for the present Constitution than myself; and contrary to all my anticipations of its fate, as you know from the very beginning, I am still laboring to prop the frail and worthless fabric."[10]

II

Madison, upon meeting his new colleagues in Congress for the first time, was delighted with what he perceived as a lack of sectional and state friction. He noted that a spirit of "moderation and liberality" existed that would, he hoped, "disappoint the wishes and predictions of many who have opposed the Constitution." Congressmen "from the same State, or the same part of the Union," he reported, "are as often separated on questions from each other, as they are united in opposition to other States." This apparent absence of sectional hostility, he rejoiced, was "a favorable symptom."[11]

By the end of the First Congress's term two years later in the spring of 1791, Madison's optimistic hopes had been dashed. Bitterness, rancor, and fear for the union had replaced the spirit of "moderation and liberality." And, indeed, by the end of Washington's first term in 1793, trust had eroded to the point that two loosely formed antagonistic coalitions had formed—one, the Federalists, in support of the Washington administration and the policies of Secretary of Treasury Hamilton, and the other, the Republicans, led by Madison and Jefferson, in opposition. Each was no more than a proto-party, a premodern, preparty institution different from the modern parties that would emerge in the nineteenth century.

Sectionalism, as it had been since the Revolution and as it would be throughout the antebellum period, was the main catalyst inciting political conflict. The Founders' expectations that the diversity of the country with its multiplicity of interests and divisions could be overcome by a selfless elite acting in the national public interest were to be profoundly disappointed and frustrated. Although public men from all sections of the country and differing political cultures defended republicanism as the most enlightened philosophy of government, as well as the most demanding and fragile system of government, they also disagreed most intensely on how best to define republicanism and the general good. Ironically, however, the failure of this classical republicanism to reflect the complex and heterogeneous reality of the period did not destroy its ideological potency. Instead, the failure acted as a stimulus in shaping the proto-parties' intolerant opinions of one another.

The most explosive issue to come before the First Congress was the question of government finance. It had the effect of pitting the Founders against one another, most notably alienating Madison from Hamilton, a fellow author of the *Federalist Papers*. Crucial policy questions concerning taxes and the payment of state and federal debt had to be answered, questions that were inflammatory not only because they seemed to affect the balance of power between the federal government and the states but because they were also closely intertwined with the differing visions Americans had of their future: one of a complex, commercialized society, the other of a simpler rural, agricultural society.

Secretary of Treasury Alexander Hamilton, the architect of the administration's financial program, outlined his proposals in a series of reports to Congress in 1790 and 1791. Hamilton, who was sometimes audacious and always disputatious, sketched his vision of an industrialized and commercialized America with the federal government acting as a positive and guiding force in shaping economic growth. Specifically, he called for the restructuring or funding of the national debt at par value, the assumption of the debts of individual states by the federal government, the passage of an excise tax on distilled liquors, the creation of a national bank, the establishment of a mint, and the encouragement of manufacturing through a system of tariffs.

Of all of these proposals, funding, assumption, and the national bank were the most controversial. For in defining how the debt was to be funded—who was to be paid and how much—and in establishing a national bank to implement these policies, Hamilton's program favored certain groups in society at the expense of others. States with large Revolutionary War debts, wealthy individuals, speculators in government debt, and the more commercial parts of society stood to benefit from Hamilton's plan at the expense of the more agricultural and rural states with little debt. Furthermore, Hamilton's proposals —especially assumption—had important policy implications regarding the power relationships between the federal government and the states. Under Hamilton's program, the federal government was to assume a more prominent role vis-à-vis the states.

The first stage of the financial program was launched in January 1790, when Hamilton issued his first Report on Public Credit, which called for funding the national debt and assuming state debts.[12] There was little disagreement that the government should pay its creditors, but how the creditors were to be paid stimulated an acrimonious debate because Hamilton insisted that in order for the nation to retain a good name with creditors, debt must be paid at par or face value.

Thus, Hamilton's plan did not discriminate between the original and current holders of public securities and flagrantly seemed to favor the speculators. Madison led the fight in the House to include discrimination as part of funding the debt. The Virginian argued that it would be wrong not to provide some compensation for the original holders of the debt, many of them Revolutionary War soldiers who had later sold the drastically devalued paper to speculators. Indeed, he said, it was reported that a large proportion of the securities were in the hands of a relatively few speculators in Philadelphia, New York, Boston, Baltimore, and Charleston who had anticipated Hamilton's report. Madison wrote Jefferson that security hunters had scoured the country and were "still exploring the interior and distant parts of the Union in order to take advantage of the ignorance of holders."[13]

Discrimination was ultimately voted down, 36 to 13, with 9 of the 13 votes in favor of discrimination coming from Virginians.[14] And in fact, during the congressional debate in the spring of 1790, Madison's intelligence brought reports of unyielding opposition from the Old Dominion, where Hamilton's scheme was seen as a threat to their sectional interests. "Lighthorse Harry" Lee wrote that the federal government "which we both admired so much will I fear prove ruinous in its operation to our native state,"[15] for the proposed funding system would encourage useless expenses and larger national debts and draw to the support of the government "a numerous class of the people from the strongest motive of human action, viz self interest." If such a system, he said, which was designed primarily for commercial nations with arbitrary governments, were adopted, economic ruin and debasement of the national character would inevitably be the result.[16]

Hamilton's policies raised the specter of sectional conflict, confirming for many Antifederalist Patrick Henry's earlier fears of what the government under the Constitution might bring: a "system which I have ever dreaded—subserviency of Southern to Northern Interests."[17]

Disunion, although considered dreadful, might be "a lesser evil than union on the present conditions," Lee wrote Madison a month later. "I had rather myself submit to all the hazards of war and risk the loss of every thing dear to me in life," Lee claimed, "than to live under the rule of an . . . insolent northern majority." Significantly, the only solution in Lee's eyes was to change the seat of government to "the territorial center" of the union and repudiate "gambling systems of finance."[18]

Although the funding component of Hamilton's financial plan evoked outrage, Hamilton's assumption proposal threatened to destroy the newly organized government. Assumption was an arrangement, theoretically at least, where after a final accounting of the state expenditures in the Revolutionary War, all states were to be fully compensated for their donations to the effort. Many doubted this promise of equity at a time of some future accounting, however.

The large Revolutionary debts of Massachusetts and South Carolina made them enthusiastic supporters of assumption, as was Connecticut. The states that had retired much of their debt, namely Maryland, Virginia, North Carolina, and Georgia, were strenuous in their opposition. Assumption was also opposed by those Americans who recognized that by assuming the responsibility for state debt the federal government would gain power at the expense of the states.[19]

The first test of Hamilton's proposal came on April 12, when the House of Representatives defeated assumption by the narrow margin of 32 to 29.[20] Hamilton was not to be deterred. By July, he and his supporters revived the plan and successfully pushed it and his funding proposal through Congress. The vote—34 to 27—followed sectional lines with representatives from the Northern states voting 24 in favor and 9 against. In the South, 18 cast negative votes, while 10 voted aye.[21]

What had happened in the intervening months to salvage the unpopular assumption scheme? The traditional explanation comes from Jefferson himself and involves a deal between Hamilton, Jefferson, and Madison. This so-called "Compromise of 1790" called for Southern support for assumption in return for Hamilton's endorsement of a Potomac site for the permanent national capital.[22] And although there are questions about whether the famous "deal" was ever actually consummated, there is no question that Jefferson *believed* that a bargain had been struck and that it had been necessary to preserve sectional harmony.[23] The struggle over the permanent site for the capital symbolized a basic sectional antagonism that had developed under the new government. Lee had mentioned the Potomac site to Madison as an important measure to save the union, and Madison himself a year earlier had expressed his preference for it as well as his doubts that it would be accepted. The eventual splitting off from the union of the Western areas was feared unless certain accommodations were made, including a favorable location of the seat of government.[24]

Jefferson, desirous of maintaining as much unity within the government as possible, feared secession and separation if the assumption plan were not agreed to. In his first letters indicating that an agreement had been reached, Jefferson wrote of the "mutual sacrifice of opinion and interest . . . [that has] become the duty of every one" in order to preserve "the peace and continuance of the union." Because, he said, "it is evident that if every one retains inflexibly his present opinion, there will be no bill passed at all for funding the public debts," and, if Congress should adjourn without passing the funding bill, that would be the "end of the government."[25]

Jefferson's conclusions were shared by others. For example, before the final vote on assumption, Congressman Elbridge Gerry from Massachusetts warned his colleagues against postponing the issue until the next Congress. If this were done, he admonished, "the Government will be in danger of a convulsion."[26]

Thus, in 1790, Jefferson and Madison were willing to go to some lengths to work with Hamilton to preserve national harmony. The assumption and funding plans, however, remained bitter pills for many to swallow. After reading Jefferson's reasons for compromise, James Monroe concluded that the more he reflected on the subject of funding, the more convinced he was of its "impolicy." The action, he said, would make the individual states less powerful because it would diminish "the necessity for State taxation" and thus "undoubtedly leave the national government more at liberty to exercise its powers and increase the subjects on which it will act." Furthermore, he doubted the seat of government in Philadelphia would ever be moved to the rural Potomac.[27]

Virginians, both Federalists and Antifederalists, united to denounce Hamilton's financial plan after its passage. Coming out of retirement, Patrick Henry led the state legislature in adopting resolutions condemning both funding and assumption as "repugnant to the Constitution" and "dangerous to the rights and subversive of the interests of the people."[28]

The debate on funding and assumption made Americans increasingly aware that, although most of their countrymen desired unity and wished to preserve the union and the Constitution, a clear consensus in national politics was to be a difficult goal indeed. The first stage of Hamilton's financial program had been accepted but at the high cost of aggravating not-always-latent sectional fears, antagonisms, and suspicions. The issues of assumption and the seat of government, one congressman lamented, had aroused the conflicting interests "of the States and given birth to combinations, parties, Intrigues, Jealousies . . . to such a degree to give serious alarm to the friends of the Government."[29]

III

The second phase of Hamilton's financial scheme was still to come. In December 1790, nearly a year after outlining the first phase, the secretary of treasury submitted to Congress both a request for an excise tax on distilled liquors to raise funds to pay the debt and his Report on a National Bank, the linchpin of his entire program. The excise tax raised little controversy, but the bank proposal further alarmed those who had opposed funding and assumption.[30] Most important it brought Madison and Jefferson into sharp conflict with Hamilton. Both Virginians, although they primarily opposed the bank on constitutional grounds, were also disturbed by what the establishment of the bank seemed to represent, namely Hamilton's growing power and ambition, the centralization of authority in the federal government, and the apparent tying of government financial policy to the interests of a relatively small group of wealthy citizens. In addition, the bank seemed to portend a troubling future where debt, economic dependence, and a corrupting commercialization would erode the very foundations of an agrarian, Southern-based, republicanism.

Madison attacked the bank proposal in Congress, arguing that several banks might be more advantageous than one and opposing adherence to the example of the national bank in England where "the genius of the Monarchy favored the concentration of wealth and influence at the metropolis." The major objection he raised, however, was a constitutional one: the bank proposal rested upon an unwarranted and unconstitutional assertion of congressional power.[31] A Georgia congressman condemned the bank as in the same mold as the "ecclesiastical corporations and perpetual monopolies of England and Scotland" that "drove our forefathers to this country." Furthermore, echoing a widely held view, he charged that the bank was "calculated to benefit a small part of the United States—the mercantile interest only; while the farmers, the yeomanry of the country, will derive no advantage from it."[32]

In the House of Representatives, voting on the Bank of the United States, although similar to the earlier vote on assumption, was even more starkly sectional. Representatives in the Northern states voted 33 to 1 in favor of the bank, whereas their Southern colleagues opposed the measure 19 to 6.[33]

Washington was undecided whether to sign or veto the bill, and his closest advisers gave him markedly contrasting opinions. Both Jefferson and Attorney General Randolph agreed with Madison's constitutional objections.[34] Hamilton brilliantly defended the bank's constitutionality. as well as the doctrine of implied powers. And in language used by Chief Justice John Marshall the next century, the secretary of treasury declared that if "the end be clearly comprehended within any of the specified powers, and if the measure have an obvious relation to that end, and is not forbidden by any particular provision of the constitution—it may safely be deemed to come within the compass of the national authority."[35]

Washington signed the bill. Hamilton's arguments and his own experience during the Revolution when the Bank of North America had provided timely funds for provisioning his hungry and beleaguered army apparently convinced him of the usefulness of banks.[36]

The creation of a national bank, however, added weight to a growing belief that the Hamiltonian financial system was the basis of a bold scheme to fundamentally transform, and even subvert, the Constitution. This was to be accomplished, critics believed, through the corrupt inducement of a group of influential men to support certain measures of public policy, not out of any sense of selflessness or interest in what the general welfare might require, but out of avarice and self-interest. And this callous, avaricious, and selfish behavior, many believed, would destroy republicanism, which required a virtuous, civic-mindedness in order to survive. Madison reported in dismay to Jefferson from New York that the subscribers for bank stock and public bonds were engaged in a speculative frenzy, scrambling "for . . . public plunder." The entire affair, he said, indicated who owned the public debt "and by whom the people of the U.S. are to be governed." Of all "the shameful circumstances of this business," he lamented, "it is among the greatest to see the members of the Legislature who were most active in . . . grasping its emoluments."[37]

Hamilton's financial program contained within it a vision of an America with a strong national government protecting and stimulating commerce and industry and fostering close ties between the government and men of affairs and influence. This vision of a commercialized society was an anathema to Thomas Jefferson as well as to many Americans.[38] Jefferson reflected his own values when he so eloquently praised the virtues of the independent yeoman as providing the foundation for a new republican empire.[39] "Those who labour in the earth are the chosen people of God," Jefferson rhapsodized, in "whose breasts he has made his peculiar deposit for substantial and genuine virtue." But while "the mass of cultivators" were virtually incorruptible, Jefferson warned that they must retain their independence for "dependence begets subservience and venality, suffocates the germ of virtue, and prepares fit tools for the designs of ambition."[40]

Independence, Jefferson and his fellow Virginians believed, was compromised by debt. This had been the hard lesson learned by an earlier dependence on British creditors and the resulting loss of economic freedom that a number of Virginia tobacco planters had suffered prior to the American Revolution. Debt, Virginia gentlemen believed, "compromised personal autonomy, and with it honor, integrity, and virtue."[41]

Jefferson's views were shaped, at least in part, by wheat's replacement of tobacco as a major crop in Virginia and the upper South in the last half of the eighteenth century,[42] an important agricultural and economic transformation that had great political significance. To Jefferson, wheat was infinitely preferable to tobacco because the latter symbolized the earlier experiences of debt and dependence on British merchants, whereas the former symbolized independence and self-reliance. "Besides clothing the earth with herbage, and preserving its fertility," Jefferson wrote, wheat "feeds the laborers plentifully, requires from them only a moderate toil, except in the season of harvest, raises great numbers of animals for food and service, and diffuses plenty and happiness among the whole."[43]

This republican vision became an enduring and powerful force in shaping American politics. To be successful, Jefferson and his supporters would insist, republicanism had to be built upon a foundation of personal independence, virtue, and autonomy. Only in such an environment could men be expected to come together and selflessly govern for the general good. Essentially agrarians, they celebrated agriculture as a livelihood, as well as a way of life, and were deeply suspicious of banks and the commercialization they represented. And this agrarian hostility toward commercialism was to remain a powerful political force well into the nineteenth century. Andrew Jackson's ringing veto of a bill to recharter the successor to Hamilton's bank would be but another manifestation of this basic conflict.

But it was more than conflicting visions in Congress and the Washington administration about the shape and definition of republicanism that disturbed the Virginians. The passage of Hamilton's financial program, with its perceived sectional bias, brought forcefully home to them a fuller understanding of the menace of the unprecedented transfer of power from the states and localities to the new federal government. Whereas, as historian Rhys Isaac has written about Virginia, the Revolution had put the state courthouses "on the stage of a great historical drama," the "creation of the Federal Union had the effect of dwarfing local centers in comparison with the new national governmental structures that now loomed over them."[44]

This shift in power and responsibility, as the Antifederalists had predicted, also called into question the ability of the national government to legislate for the "general good." For the "general good" of Virginia, it was concluded, was quite different than the "general good" of Massachusetts. Consequently, as the new national government for the first time became the "court of last resort" with the power to act on great national issues such as peace and war and the economy, its decisions became particularly threatening and divisive. As historian Paul Goodman explains, "Groups used to getting their way at home were unused to being thwarted in the new arena," and this "aroused suspicions that 'the general welfare' was being sacrificed to faction."[45] It was particularly easy for the Virginians, as residents of the largest and most powerful state, to conclude that these suspicions were so.

IV

The passage of Hamilton's financial program placed Jefferson and Madison in a dilemma. Deeply attached and grateful to Washington for what they considered his essential leadership role, desirous of unity in the administration as well as the country, and fearful of the alternatives to union, they were nevertheless appalled by Hamilton's aggressiveness and the implications of his policies, which they saw as endangering the future of republican government. Vice President John Adams's sometimes eccentric and sometimes questionable dedication to republican principles was an additional worry. Further complicating the situation was the continuing presence of the Antifederalists, who were perceived as biding their time, awaiting any federal miscue or failure that might offer an excuse to weaken the new government or to reopen constitutional questions.

Therefore, Madison and Jefferson came to see themselves both as protectors of the Constitution and the republican form of government and, although with considerable uneasiness and nervousness, as informal opponents of the federal administration, especially of Hamilton and his policies. As such, the two leaders and their loose and informal group of like-minded colleagues began to refer to themselves as "Whigs," or "Republicans," identifying themselves as guardians of Revolutionary liberty and sentinels against the executive encroachment upon that liberty that they saw as being the result of Hamilton's actions. However, these references to "Republican" or "Republican party," which became more frequent as the decade wore on, did not signal, as far as Madison, Jefferson, and their colleagues were concerned, the acceptance of a modern conception of political parties. Not at all. These reluctant partisans reviled parties for the factious divisiveness they represented. Failing to recognize their own partisanship, they instead saw themselves as Republicans upholding and defending the republican consensus that had been bequeathed to the country by the Revolution.

The Virginians and their friends, however, had to walk a political tightrope. They had to distinguish their opposition to Hamilton's policies from any appearance of being hostile to the Constitution or to the union. Failure to do so would result in their being publicly and disastrously identified as Antifederalists. In addition, they had to be wary of being categorized as Southern particularists and obscurantists whose opposition was primarily motivated by the promotion of Southern and Virginia interests.

The leadership of the emerging opposition was divided between Madison and Jefferson based upon their own talents and political positions. Madison, as a member of the House of Representatives, took a more public role as an essayist (albeit an anonymous one) and political strategist, while Jefferson, restrained by temperament and by his position as a member of the Washington administration, stayed more in the background, constantly consulting with Madison and his Virginia colleagues.

Hamilton's dream of the United States becoming a commercial and industrial empire, his desire for a stronger federal government, his seeming lack of enthusiasm for republicanism, and his attraction to British institutions and procedures deeply disturbed Madison and Jefferson. They were particularly alarmed by what they perceived as Hamilton's use of Walpolean methods of corruption. The secretary of treasury's financial program, for example, aroused opposition not only on the basis of what it did, but also because of what it symbolized: the emergence of English practices and institutions in the United States where they were not appropriate. The Revolution, they felt, should have signaled a disentanglement from the trappings of the British monarchy.[46]

But Hamilton's actions did not simply represent the Americanization of what had gone on earlier in England.[47] Unlike in Great Britain, where conflict took place within a well-established national framework of loyalty to the crown, in the United States what was at stake was the attempt to build a national community, a republican community, out of a welter of competing local interests. But the question, of course, was what kind of national community it was to be and would the new government be able to resolve fundamental conflict and to legitimize its authority.

V

An important early step in promoting a program of opposition to Hamilton and bringing it to public awareness was the establishment of a public forum to counteract the secretary of treasury's strong editorial support in the influential *United States Gazette*. Published by John Fenno in Philadelphia, where the seat of government had moved after its initial home in New York, the newspaper was considered by Jefferson as imbued with "pure Toryism" in that it disseminated "the doctrines of monarchy [and] aristocracy." Early in 1791, only three days after Washington had signed the controversial bank bill, Jefferson, Madison, and others contacted Philip Freneau, a poet and former sea captain, in an effort to persuade him to come to Philadelphia and establish a competing "whig vehicle of intelligence."[48] After Jefferson had offered Freneau the "clerkship for foreign languages" in the State Department to supplement his newspaper work and after an extended courtship, Freneau finally assented. And in late October 1791, the first issue of the new national "whig" newspaper, the *National Gazette*, appeared.[49]

Almost immediately the pages of the *National Gazette* were filled with essays condemning Hamilton and his policies. Madison was particularly active. In December 1791, he warned that Hamilton's programs were resulting in the dangerous "consolidation" of political power at the national level at the expense of the states. This, he feared, would lead to an unhealthy increase in executive power and to the federal government's ignoring public opinion. In order to counter this dangerous tendency, Madison urged, it was essential to maintain a creative tension between the different spheres of government. In addition to acting as a restraint upon federal power, the states were critically important for mobilizing and effectuating public opinion. Without them, public opinion would be too diffuse, inarticulate, and ineffective. Madison believed that the American people were sound republicans but, if the government were to be consolidated, their wishes and natural impulses could not and would not be reflected accurately. And if the federal government were to be guided by only "partial expressions of the public mind" and were to begin a "self directed course," it would be difficult, if not impossible, for a "consolidation" of the "interests and affections" of Americans or for an "Empire of reason, benevolence, and brotherly affection" to be created. In order to prevent a consolidation of power at the national level, Madison urged, the people would have to be reminded of their republican duty and their mutual affections would have to be reawakened in order to recapture a consensus of republican harmony.[50]

Jefferson, too, believed that it was essential "to preserve the line drawn by the federal constitution between the general and particular governments," but he was less worried by encroachments from the state governments. These would "tend to an excess of liberty which will correct itself . . . while those of the general government will tend toward monarchy, which will fortify itself . . . instead of working its own cure."[51]

The logic of Jefferson's argument led in dangerous directions. For if one believed that opposition to federal government policy or encroachment could best be mounted on the state level, this in turn might ultimately lead to a particularistic and destructive fragmentation of the union. This was a danger that Jefferson, Madison, and their Republican followers flirted with throughout the 1790s as they formulated strategies of opposition.

In other essays Madison extolled the importance of an actively engaged public opinion. He asserted that even the most perfectly constructed and most delicately balanced governments were vulnerable to being diverted from "their regular path" without enlightened public sentiment.[52] It is not clear, however, what Madison believed the exact relationship between the public, their representatives, and the government should be. Although he believed that the basic virtue of the American people had been a major factor in shaping the country's republican institutions and that future success would depend upon an enlightened and watchful citizenry, he did not at this point suggest ways public opinion could be organized, mobilized, or articulated, apparently regarding such opinion as a fixed entity that was supportive of republicanism but essentially inert. Nonetheless, he was convinced that public opinion could ultimately be counted upon to rally behind the incipient opposition to the Federalists.

Madison's emphasis upon the important role of public opinion in a republic modified an earlier position he had taken. In *Federalist* 49, for instance, Madison had warned *against* frequent appeals to the public over *constitutional* issues because "every appeal to the people would carry an implication of some defect in the government [and] recurrent appeals would, in great measure, deprive the government" of "veneration" and "stability." In sum, it was dangerous to disturb "the public tranquility by interesting too strongly the public passions" because constant or periodic appeals to the people over deeply divisive problems would mean that "*passions* . . . not the *reason* of the public" would "control and regulate the government."[53] Although Madison in *Federalist* 49 was specifically discussing *constitutional* rather than *legislative* issues, legislative issues in the 1790s ultimately turned on one's interpretation of the Constitution.

Other writers in the *National Gazette* echoed Madison, envisioning the United States as being at one of those great historical crossroads, one fork leading backward to Europe with its corruption and monarchy, the other continuing forward along a republican path. The notion of a virtuous but sleeping public that would momentarily awaken and return the country to its proper republican course was a strong and frequent theme. Republicanism, born of the Revolution, one essayist wrote, was "still dear to the hearts of Americans" and the public, although "seemingly indifferent or inattentive to the present progress of things," was "not insensible" and would be united in their opposition to "a common sense of danger." This united effort, however, would not be the action "of party or of faction, or of any individual" but rather in "the common interest of every citizen." "Let them remember," another essayist warned, "that altho' the republican jealousy of the people may sleep for a time, that it is not extinct, and when they begin to feel the pressure of oppressive and perpetual taxes . . . they may . . . overturn . . . the funding system, the cause of all these evils."[54] But neither Madison nor the other essayists in the *National Gazette* went on to explain, however, *how* this public opinion, if and when awakened, was to be articulated.

Madison attempted to put the emerging conflict over Hamilton's policies into historical perspective. In so doing, in an essay, "A Candid State of Parties," he revealed another shift in his thinking from the battle over ratification. In *Federalist* 10, he had predicted that any parties and factions arising from local conditions and circumstances would be thwarted by the pluralism of the union. "The influence of factious leaders may kindle a flame within their particular States," he had argued, "but will be unable to spread a general conflagration through the other States."[55] But by 1792, despite his continued faith in the constitutional balances within the system itself and his belief in the ultimate triumph of a public opinion loyal to republicanism, Madison was forced to recognize the emergence of two national parties, or more properly proto-parties, which represented widely polarized interests.[56] They were not manifestations of local or minor grievances but rather represented deeply divisive fundamental differences over the nature of the union, the Constitution, and republicanism itself.

This polarization had led, he believed, to the third party conflict since the birth of the republic, each of which, although temporary, had in its own way reflected deep and intractable divisions in American society. The first parties, he wrote, appeared during the Revolution, the Whigs espousing "the cause of independence" with the Tories adhering "to the British claims." The second major division was between the Federalists and Antifederalists during the struggle over the ratification of the Constitution. That division, however, Madison pointedly wanted to make clear, had *ended* with the adoption of the Constitution.

The third and current party division, according to Madison, had arisen as a result of the conduct of the new federal government and was likely "to be of some duration." One party was composed of those who "are more partial to the opulent than to the other classes of society; and having debauched themselves into a persuasion that mankind are incapable of governing themselves, it follows with them, of course, that government can be carried on only by the pageantry of rank, the influence of money and emoluments and the terror of military force." These men preferred the government to serve the few rather than the many and hoped that the administration of the government "be narrowed into fewer hands, and approximated to an hereditary form." Members of the other party were those who believed "that mankind are capable of governing themselves" and hated "hereditary power as an insult to the reason and an outrage to the rights of man." This party took offense "at every public measure that does not appeal to the understanding and to the general interest of the community" nor is "conducive to the preservation of republican government."

Although Madison deemed the antirepublicans to have fewer adherents, he feared that they might be able to use their wealth and standing to compensate for their lack of numbers. In addition, Madison worried that the opponents to republicanism would scheme to weaken their adversaries "by reviving exploded parties and taking advantage of all prejudices, local, political, and occupational, that may prevent or disturb a general coalition of sentiments." This mention of "exploded parties" revealed Madison's concern over the emerging Republican opposition being linked with the Antifederalists, a concern that Jefferson shared. The Republicans must make clear, he advised, that the only distinction between them and their opponents was one "between enemies and friends to republican government."

Madison admitted that the future was not certain, but, nonetheless, he did feel that one party or the other would "ultimately establish its ascendance."[57] In both of the two earlier party contests, the losing party had faded from the scene, discredited, leaving the victorious party standing as the expression of society's political consensus. There is no reason to believe that he thought the outcome of the 1790s would be any different.

Madison believed that parties arose during times of upheaval and dramatic change, such as the period of the Revolution, ratification of the Constitution, or the 1790s. Their purpose was to reflect diametrically opposing views in a society. Resolution of such a conflict would require the triumph of one view over the other through the finality of some kind of action such as the successful completion of the Revolution or the adoption of the Constitution. And although parties reflected basic differences on fundamental issues, they were temporary institutions and would disappear when a clear-cut public consensus was reached. The decisions for independence and ratification of the Constitution, for example, were made by the people in their role as the sovereign power. Once made, these decisions were expected to end the debate.

VI

The establishment of the *National Gazette* in the fall of 1791 and its hostile treatment of Hamilton and his policies quickly led to an open rupture between Jefferson and the secretary of treasury. Almost from the beginning of their service in the cabinet, Hamilton and Jefferson had had fundamental disagreements. But their relationship became increasingly antagonistic in the winter of 1791–92 and then burst forth into a blistering public feud the following summer, when Hamilton, using a pseudonym, attacked Jefferson in the press, following Jefferson's assault upon him in a letter to Washington.[58]

In the spring of 1792 Jefferson presented the president with a lengthy indictment of Hamilton's policies, though Hamilton was not mentioned by name, and in the summer Jefferson amplified and extended his criticism in a private conversation with Washington. The funding of the national debt and the assumption of the debts of the states, Jefferson charged, had created means for corrupting the legislature that would ultimately lead to the destruction of the union and republican government.[59]

Hamilton, outraged by the public attacks upon him in the pages of the *National Gazette* and by Jefferson's private criticism, responded vigorously and vociferously. In a letter to a colleague he insisted that the "real threat to republicanism came not from Madison and Jefferson's imagined group of monarchists and aristocrats, but rather from the disorder and anarchy that would result from the destruction or lessening of the influence of the national government." Whereas the Virginians regarded the state governments as the principle bastions of republicanism, Hamilton feared their strength because he saw this as a threat to the national government. Virginia was a special concern. "If," he argued, "the States were all the size of Connecticut, Maryland or New Jersey, I should decidedly regard the local Governments as both safe and useful." But since large and powerful states, such as Virginia, seemed to be lined up in opposition, Hamilton had "the most serious apprehensions that the Government of the U States will not be able to maintain itself against their influence."[60]

In a series of essays published during the last half of 1792 and under several different pseudonyms, Hamilton vented his fury. Beyond the obvious differences over policy between Jefferson and himself, Hamilton was enraged over what he regarded as Jefferson's self-serving hypocrisy and general untrustworthiness. Hamilton questioned the propriety of the connection between Freneau and Jefferson, maintaining that Jefferson's patronage, with government funds, of the most outspokenly critical newspaper in the country was both highly irregular and corrupt. In addition, Hamilton attacked his rival's alleged role, albeit a hidden and secret one, of organizing and leading an opposition to the government. Obviously hoping to induce Jefferson to step down from his post, Hamilton insisted that a cabinet member who could not support the policies of the administration should in good conscience resign. Any official refusing to do so, Hamilton indicated, only continued in office out of a lust for power, prestige, or money.[61]

The distressed Washington, hoping to discover whether any basis existed for Jefferson's fears, wrote Hamilton and asked him to respond to the charges, although Washington did not reveal Jefferson as their source.[62] In his reply Hamilton defended himself and his programs and made an unusually perceptive comment that exhibited considerable, albeit temporary, analytic detachment. It is hard to imagine Jefferson having the same kind of detachment. In his letter, Hamilton called "anticipations of the different parties" curious. "One side appears to believe," the New Yorker maintained, "that there is a serious plot to overturn the state Governments and substitute monarchy to the present republican government. The other side firmly believes that there is a serious plot to overturn the General Government and elevate the separate power of the states upon its ruins. Both sides may be equally wrong and their mutual jealousies may be materially causes of the appearances which mutually disturb them, and sharpen them against each other."[63]

Indeed, Hamilton was correct. The protagonists, in attempting to order and understand the events around them surveyed the political landscape as if looking through hideously distorting spectacles, seeing grotesque and tormenting shapes and figures that were products of intense and deeply felt fears.

Shortly after receiving Hamilton's reply, Washington appealed directly to the strong-willed warring secretaries in an effort to bring peace and harmony to his dissension-filled administration. Although threatened from without by avowed enemies, his administration had more to fear, Washington argued, from its internal cleavages. He urged "liberal allowances, mutual forbearances, and . . . yieldings on *all sides*." There would always be differences in political opinions and these differences might even be necessary, he said. However, he went on, it was to be regretted "that men of abilities, zealous patriots, having the same *general* objects in view . . . will not exercise more charity in deciding on the opinions and actions of one another." The intractability, the unwillingness to compromise and the lack of trust between the enemies would, Washington feared, lead to a destruction of the union.[64]

Thus, Washington considered the differences between Hamilton and Jefferson to be over *means* and not *ends* and only false distinctions. He saw the great mass of patriotic Americans as holding in common a credo that revered republicanism and supported the union. Any issue threatening either, therefore, was a false issue not representing any fundamental division. Unfounded suspicions, personal jealousies, and sectional hostilities all worked to obscure the basic harmony and political consensus of the American people.

In their responses to the president, both Hamilton and Jefferson, after vigorously justifying their criticisms of the other, promised to refrain from any activity that would jeopardize the harmony of the administration. Jefferson assured Washington that in the time left before his anticipated retirement he would remain above the battle and concentrate his energies on finishing his duties as secretary of state.[65] This was a promise he found difficult to keep as he continued to play a major behind-the-scenes role in leading and advising the opposition until he left office in December 1793.[66]

By late 1792 and early 1793, the first stage of American political development in the 1790s was drawing to a close. It had begun with public men naively anticipating that political and sectional conflict would be resolved institutionally by the checks and balances and federalism of the Constitution and by the dedication and goodwill of a selfless elite. It ended with the realization that fundamental differences seemed to divide that elite. Disappointed in their expectations that Congress, corrupted by a greedy selfishness, seemed to be unable to agree upon and legislate for the public good, the nascent Republicans began to take steps to defeat Hamilton and his policies. But their opposition was immediately challenged by supporters of the administration, who fervently believed that the opposition opposed not just the policies of the administration, but the Constitution and the union itself. Thus, in the next stage of political development, it would be deemed vital for the Republican elite to justify and validate their opposition by appealing to the people in the name of republicanism in order to gain through the electoral process the mantle of legitimacy.

PART II

The Polarization of the Elite
1792–1798

3.

The Election of 1792
Grappling with the Concept of Representation

Political life is enjoyed by the power which influences the Legislature. This influence is possessed by the 5000—and the 5,000,000 are only allowed once in two years, a kind of political spasm, and, after one day's mockery of importance, sink again into its lethargy. A nominal election of, and an irresistible *influence* over the Legislature, are things of *real* difference. The first is the *shadow*—the latter—the *substance,* of power.
—JOHN TAYLOR

The election of 1792 marked the beginning of the second stage of American political development. Jefferson and his Virginia colleagues went to great lengths to develop a rationale and vindication for their opposition that expressed both a continuing loyalty to the Constitution as well as an unswerving faith in the people's republicanism. In order to legitimize their opposition to the government, they discussed strategies to collect, and indeed to mold, the will of the people to show that the people, consigned to a more or less passive role, supported their position. One Virginian, John Taylor of Caroline County, Virginia, a close colleague of Jefferson and Madison, emphasized the importance of the state legislatures, which were refinements of the people's will but possessed information that was superior to what the people themselves or the federal government possessed.[1]

Additionally, the Virginia leadership continued to cultivate and cooperate with like-minded political elites across the country in Congress to thwart what they saw as antirepublican legislation and to defeat antirepublican candidates in national elections, like the contest for the vice presidency in 1792. Athough the opposition leaders shunned political parties, by their mobilizing and organizing activities they inexorably, although haltingly, created something akin to, yet distinct from, what would ultimately come to be described as a modern political party.

Other, more democratic members of the opposition, however, rejected this elite paternalism. They argued that the people must play a more active role in overseeing and evaluating their legislators' conduct of the public business. And it was this democratic critique that animated the formation of the popular Democratic-Republican societies that began to flourish in the next few years.

II

Although the escalating dispute between the two cabinet secretaries and the widening opposition to some of the administration's measures were sources of exasperation for the president, Washington seemed above criticism for the most part. As Jefferson wrote one of his correspondents, "The prudence of the President is an anchor of safety to us."[2]

From the outset Washington had been concerned about sectional antagonisms and suspicions of the federal government, and in the summer of 1791 he had toured "every part of the United States" in an effort to dispel them.[3] After his southern travels, Washington reported with satisfaction that "tranquility reigns among the [Southern] people, with that disposition towards the general government which is likely to preserve it."[4]

Nonetheless, despite the president's prestige and efforts, by the last year of his first term (1792), criticism of Washington personally began to surface. Although Washington was not specifically named, one essayist in the *National Gazette* even went so far as to warn against the public's transferring their loyalty and affection from the principles of the Revolution to the man who symbolized its success. The writer denounced "reverence [for] the supporter of a principle, instead of *the principle itself.*"[5]

These frustrations of public life made Washington yearn for a peaceful retirement to Mount Vernon, but he was reluctant to abandon his country in a time of need. Explaining his quandary to Jefferson, he said that although "the government had set out with a pretty good general goodwill . . . symptoms of dissatisfaction had lately shewn themselves far beyond that he could have expected" and he worried as to "what height" these dissatisfactions "might arise in case of too great a change in the administration."[6] After asking Madison's advice on a farewell address, Washington throughout the spring, summer, and fall of 1792 consulted his advisers about whether he should seek a second term.[7]

The president was especially embittered by the personal attacks upon him that stemmed, at least partly in his view, from an unfounded and almost hysterical fear of a supposed conspiracy to transform the republic into a monarchy. Echoing Hamilton, Washington pointedly told Jefferson that the "suspicions against a particular party" had been "carried . . . too far," and, while there might be "*desires*" to change the form of government, there were no "*designs*" to achieve that goal. On the contrary, Washington warned his secretary of state, Freneau's *National Gazette* had stirred up opposition to the government to the point where a breakup of the union and anarchy might result. And *this,* in turn, might "produce a resort to monarchical government."[8]

Jefferson and Madison as well as Hamilton urged Washington to stay on for a second term. "The confidence of the whole union is centered in you," Washington was told by Jefferson, who feared a real threat of violence and secession if the president were to step down. In Jefferson's view, the source of this crisis was a "corrupt squadron" of men who, nourished by recent financial measures adopted by the government, had corrupted a portion of the legislature in order to rid themselves of the "limitations imposed by the constitution." The "ultimate object" of this group, according to Jefferson, was "to prepare the way for a change, from the present republican form of government, to that of a monarchy, of which the English constitution is to be the model." Attempting to prevent this subversion was the "republican party," who wished "to preserve the government in its present form." The Republicans, Jefferson conceded, were sometimes "joined by the two, three, or half dozen anti-federalists, who, tho they dare not avow it, are still opposed to any general government: but being less so to a republican than a monarchical one, they naturally join those" viewed as "pursuing the lesser evil."

The "only hope of safety," Jefferson continued, lay in the 1792 elections, which Jefferson believed would send a majority of Republicans to Congress. However, if this did not happen, Jefferson said glumly, "it is not easy to conjecture . . . what means would be resorted to for correction of the evil." Jefferson wished that any solution would be "temperate and peaceable" but feared for the union since "the division of sentiment and interest happens unfortunately to be so geographical." Thus, the sectional split plus the awful uncertainty of not knowing what would happen if the electoral system failed to halt what he saw as the subversion of the republic made it imperative, in Jefferson's eyes, that Washington serve another term. The president was assured that the crisis would be resolved in one or two sessions of Congress, but until then Jefferson hoped that the president would "add one or two more to the many years . . . [he had] already sacrificed to the good of mankind."[9]

Madison, like Jefferson, urged Washington to serve a second term, warning the president of the serious liabilities associated with any possible presidential successor. Unlike any other potential candidate, he said, Washington transcended sectional hostilities. Madison pointed out that Jefferson, being from the South, was unpopular in the North, whereas Adams and Jay, who shared monarchical principles, were Northerners and unacceptable in the South and the West.[10] Washington, after hearing the gloomy forecasts of the prospects of a federal government without his leadership, bowed to the inevitable and delayed his retirement.

III

The importance of the elections of 1792 loomed large in the minds of the leaders of the opposition. Most crucial were the congressional contests: the opposition felt that the first two Congresses had not properly or accurately reflected the American people's republicanism. To Jefferson and others it was critical that the next Congress be made up of men of integrity who were imbued with unshakable republican principles. Then, Congress could assume the independent and balancing role in the federal government that the Founders had intended. It was also thought essential by some members of the opposition that Vice President John Adams be replaced with someone sounder in his commitment to republicanism.

During that election year, the pages of the *National Gazette* blossomed with essays defending the right to oppose measures of the government. Making a distinction between opposition to the government and opposition to the Constitution, authors stressed that critics could disapprove the policies of an administration and still be loyal to the country. As one essayist put it, "a man may . . . be a sincere friend to the government as laid down in the constitution, and an enemy to principles on which the government is carried into practice; as also . . . a man may be a decided enemy in his heart to the republican principles of the constitution, and a zealous friend" to all of the "measures and objects pursued by the government."[11]

A major concern of those defending the right of opposition was disassociating themselves from the discredited Antifederalists. The true division in the country, one essayist wrote, was the "*Treasury of the United States against the people*" not federalism versus antifederalism.[12]

For opponents of some governmental actions to be branded Anti-federalists, it was argued, meant that no distinction was being made "between a *base opposition to the constitution and government and* a virtuous opposition to unconstitutional or unwise measures." The effort by some supporters of the government to taint opposition leaders with antifederalism had stemmed from "the most insidious and malevolent motives" by those who simply failed or refused to recognize that "a devoted attachment to the constitution, is the true impulse of this [Republican] opposition."[13]

The opposition's vulnerability to charges of disloyalty was heightened by the choice of Governor George Clinton of New York to oppose Adams in 1792 for the vice presidency. Governor Clinton had been a leading opponent of ratification in his state, where the Antifederalists had almost carried the day, and his candidacy, which emerged from a general agreement among New York, Pennsylvania, and Virginia opposition leaders including Jefferson and Madison, did not draw immediate and unanimous endorsement from all opposition leaders.[14] In addition to his liability as a highly visible opponent to ratification, Clinton was further compromised by certain irregularities surrounding his gubernatorial reelection bid earlier in 1792.

Jefferson, despite his support, had serious doubts about Clinton's candidacy and worried that "the cause of republicanism" would suffer from it. To Jefferson it hardly seemed worth the risk in order "to draw over the antifederalists" who were numerically insignificant.[15] Monroe, a former Antifederalist himself, agreed that Clinton's reelection under a cloud of suspicion was "not flattering to him." Yet, he saw that the opposition had few alternatives to supporting the New York governor because, as he reminded Jefferson, Clinton was the cohesive force of "the republican party" in New York.[16]

The question of who would oppose Adams was further complicated later in the fall when an opposition leader from Philadelphia suggested that Aaron Burr, another New Yorker, would be a superior candidate to Clinton. The argument was that Burr could attract support in the "Middle and Eastern States" that would elude Clinton.[17] In response, Monroe and Madison drafted a reply to Burr's Northern supporters. Privately they were concerned that Burr at age thirty-six was too young and had not had the public service that would give "unequivocal proofs of what his principles really were." Furthermore, it was believed that this "injudicious and improper" effort to promote Burr at Clinton's expense might jeopardize "the more important interests of the union" as well as any hope of defeating Adams. The Virginians agreed, however, that their refusal to endorse the switch should be couched in such terms as to protect Burr's ego, laying it on his youth and assuring him and his supporters of their high esteem.[18] In the meantime, a meeting was held in Philadelphia between the Burr faction and other opposition leaders in which it was decided to drop Burr's candidacy in favor of Clinton's.[19] Despite the Virginians' efforts to spare the feelings of Burr and his supporters, however, there is little doubt that this episode colored future relations between the New Yorker and the Virginians. Indeed, the nagging suspicions that dated from this incident continued to fester over the next decade and partially explain why Burr was unwilling to make any move to end the deadlock between him and Jefferson as presidential candidates in 1801.

Clinton's previous association with the Antifederalists was used endlessly and to good effect by Adams's supporters, who saw the governor and his supporters as "antifederals, demagogues, democrats, mobocrats, non-contents, dis-contents, mal-contents, enemies to the government, hostile to the constitution, friends of anarchy, haters of good order, promoters of confusion, exciters of mobs, sowers of sedition." So, Clinton and his political friends spent a considerable part of the campaign on the defensive. No man "of common sense and common virtues in America," one Clinton enthusiast argued, could be said "to be *anti federal,* if by that term is meant a wish to destroy the existing government." The Clinton forces also attacked those backing Adams's reelection as partial to the Eastern states and "attached to a government of king, lords, and commons . . . governed more by party names and prejudices, than by a regard to the principles of the constitution."[20]

In the end, Clinton was not successful, losing to Adams by a vote of 77 to 50. The vote revealed a significant sectional division. Out of the 50 Clinton votes, 37 came from his unanimous support in three Southern states, Virginia, North Carolina, and Georgia. Of the remaining 13, 12 came from his home state of New York and 1 from Pennsylvania.[21]

Noble Cunningham in his study of the Jeffersonian Republicans in the 1790s concludes that the elections of 1792, particularly the opposition's interstate and cooperative effort to attempt to replace Adams as vice president, revealed "a significant sign of party development on the national level." And he finds, for example, the development of parties in New York and Pennsylvania to have been more advanced than in other states.[22]

Yet it is difficult to see advanced party development or systematic partisanship even in Pennsylvania and New York. In Pennsylvania, state nonpartisanship seemed to have prevailed among the two widely circulated state tickets: *"The Ticket which will be supported by the* Federal *Interest"* versus *"The Ticket which will be supported by the* Antifederal *Interest."* For example there were thirteen names on the two tickets and seven of them were on both.[23]

In New York, although voter turnout was double what it had been in 1790, partisanship was ill-defined and tended to revolve around the great political families that had dominated the state. As the leading historian of the state observes, the "Republican interest" included "a loose coalition of former anti-Federalists connected to Governor Clinton, a smaller group of former federalists grouped around the lower manor Livingstons headed by the Chancellor, and men of various stripes who followed Aaron Burr."[24]

Apathy seems to have characterized the situation in Massachusetts, at least before 1800. Politics in the Bay State, according to historian Ron Formisano, was characterized by uncontested, low-turnout, or noncompetitive elections, and by a refusal of approximately one-half of the towns in the state even to send representatives to the state legislature.[25]

Not so surprisingly, in Virginia, which was in the forefront of the opposition, Republicans crushed their opponents in 1792, winning sixteen out of nineteen congressional seats.[26] The older, elitist, highly personal, deferential politics, however, continued to rule. In one constituency, a militia force was mobilized in support of one candidate, Francis Preston, in an effort to terrorize and intimidate voters intending to vote for his opponent, Abram Trigg. Both Preston and Trigg were sons of two of the most prominent families in the region and both were ardent Republicans. Their conflict, therefore, was not ideological or partisan, but rather passionately personal and represented conduct not unusual in the South. According to one observer, it was common in the South for "a man of influence" to come "to the place of election at the head of two or three hundred of his friends; and to be sure they would not, if they could help it, suffer anybody on the other side to give a vote as long as they were there."[27]

American politics in 1792 was in an important stage of transformation from an elitist, deferential system to a more democratic one. But it was a transition, stimulated by the Revolution and encouraged by proto-party battles of the 1790s, that would continue well into the nineteenth century and would develop unevenly in the various states. To be sure an opposition group in Congress was increasingly becoming identified as Republican or representing the republican interest. And during Washington's second term, in the Third and Fourth Congresses, there would be increasing cohesion within the two contending proto-parties, Federalist and Republican, with the groups polarizing on almost seven of every ten roll call votes in the House of Representatives.[28]

It is not clear, however, how much the new political ferment influenced the immediate outcome of the elections for Congress in 1792. It is true that approximately a third or more members of the House of Representatives did not return for one reason or another to their seats when Congress convened in 1793.[29]

What is also apparent is that the results of this election were immensely satisfying to the opposition leaders. Jefferson concluded that the balloting "produced a decided majority in favor of the republican interest." Furthermore, he maintained, "the tide of this government [is] now at the fullest, and . . . it will, from the commencement of the next session of Congress, retire and subside into the true principles of the Constitution."[30] For a brief period of time, therefore, at the end of 1792 and into 1793, Jefferson and perhaps other opposition leaders felt that as soon as the new Congress—made up of men who were true republicans—convened in December of 1793, the great threat to the Constitution and to republican government would be over. The crisis had been a temporary one and the basic republicanism and good sense of the people had prevailed.

IV

The election of 1792 prompted a vigorous discussion, which continued for most of the decade, exploring the nature of representation and defining and justifying the role of a political opposition in the federal republic. Jefferson and other Virginia opposition leaders, who had despaired that the system of representation was not working because many congressmen were acting in an antirepublican way and thus betraying the trust of their constituents, began to conclude that what had been at the heart of the problem was the relationship between constituent and representative. How was the public to know and evaluate the credentials of a public man who held or sought elective office? And how was the public to make its will known to the officeholder? Jefferson and his colleagues began to move from a position that held that the people's basic republican virtue would rouse them to defeat self-interested, antirepublican legislators to one that held that elite leadership would need to play a more active role in soliciting and educating public opinion.

Essayist John Taylor published several revealing and suggestive pamphlets in 1793 and 1794, and these writings perhaps best reflect the thinking of the Virginia opposition. In fact Taylor's most substantial pamphlet, *An Enquiry into the Principles and Tendency of Certain Public Measures*, represented not only his own beliefs but also the views of a group of prominent opposition leaders and, as such, was a major effort to articulate and rationalize Republican disenchantment with the Washington administration. Before publication, the Taylor essay was read and approved by Madison, Monroe, and Jefferson, among others. And Madison, at least, was evidently given veto power over the text; Taylor left it to his colleague's judgment whether the draft ought to be committed "to the flames or the press." Since Taylor's only objective was the public good, he wrote Madison, he did not have "that kind of paternal sensibility" about the manuscript, "which sometimes attaches us even to deformity." Madison should feel free, he instructed, to "correct, censure or condemn, without supposing it possible that the burning a few sheets of paper will affect me."[31]

In response, Madison told Taylor that his pamphlet had been well received and that Jefferson was "quite in rapture with it and augers the best consequences from it if its appearance be well timed." Jefferson, however, was concerned that the pamphlet might arouse sectional antagonisms and advised that there should "be no indication of the quarter of the Union producing" the pamphlet. And with that in mind he recommended that a passage referring to slaves be struck, for fear of alienating Virginia readers. Publication was delayed, as Jefferson had suggested, until after Congress convened, apparently sometime in early 1794.[32]

In the series of political pamphlets Taylor argued that the Constitution had established a republican form of government "flowing from and depending on the people." And although the people retained the ultimate "right of legislation," they "periodically delegated" this "right" by electing representatives to exercise this function for them. This "right of election" was a substantive right and not merely a form, it was maintained, for "legitimate representation" implied "an *existing operative* principle" impelling representatives to work "for the good of the represented." Therefore, when elections became merely a form or sham and representatives no longer depended upon the people nor legislated "for the good of the governed," government was "converted into an usurpation."[33]

The representative function of Congress, Taylor maintained, picking up a theme from the Antifederalists, was complicated by the size of the republic and the great number of constituents represented by each member. This made it all but impossible for a legislator to be well known by the voter. Furthermore, he complained, it was "scarcely possible to communicate that regular and thorough information, of all transactions, from the seat of government to the extremities, so indispensably necessary to enable the constituent to judge with propriety of the conduct of his representative." And this, he feared, lessened the representative's sense of responsibility because he had little fear of being censured for his actions.[34]

Taylor continued by asserting that if the people's representatives faithfully and responsibly represented the "will of the nation," the laws enacted would naturally produce the "common good." However, in the United States in the early 1790s, Taylor lamented, this governmental process was becoming perverted. A "paper interest" had influenced "a majority of the legislature," thus destroying "the principle itself, from which alone the end is deducible." It was a paper system that could count as its constituents some 5,000 favored citizens, although the total population of the country was nearly 5 million, he claimed. Thus, he lamented, "only the one thousandth part of the nation retains in *reality* political existence." Since "political life is enjoyed by the power which influences the Legislature," he went on, "this influence is possessed by the 5000—and the 5,000,000 are only allowed once in two years, a kind of political spasm, and, after one day's mockery of importance, sink again into its lethargy. A nominal election of, and an irresistible *influence* over the Legislature, are things of *real* difference. The first is the *shadow*—the latter—the *substance,* of power."[35]

Hamilton's financial program, which had created the paper system, was not objected to so much for what it was as for how it affected American society. The funding, assumption, and bank schemes were seen as instruments that destroyed public virtue and replaced it with an insidious and corroding selfishness that, in turn, corrupted the people's servants as well as republicanism itself. This "poisonous fountain," as an essay in the *National Gazette* had referred to the financial program, had "inflamed and divided the citizens of states formerly united like a band of brothers."[36] Thus, the consensus, harmony, and brotherhood, which it was thought had once characterized the United States, had been lost, contaminated by old world institutions and practices incompatible with republicanism.

The creation of this paper system, according to Taylor, had had the effect of dividing the interests of American society into natural and artificial interests. The natural interest existed without the direct aid of law, such as "agriculture, commerce, manufactures and arts," whereas the artificial interest was "immediately created by law," such as "public debt, public officers, and private banks." This powerful artificial interest, whose growth had led to the "accumulation of great wealth in a few hands" and to the creation of a "political moneyed engine," was seen as the sinister consequence of Hamilton's financial plan. As part of the secretary of treasury's grand design, the national bank and the assumption by the federal government of all state debts incurred during the Revolution had caused a dangerous centralization of authority and had eroded the power of "the republican state assemblies by depriving them of . . . political importance." As a result, Taylor concluded, a "*money impulse*" and not the "public good" was influencing Congress and the Constitution was being subverted.[37]

The remedy, Taylor asserted, was a vigorous insistence upon the principle that the people were "the only genuine and legitimate fountain of power." But how, Taylor asked, could the people effectively wield this power? How could the judgment of the people be ascertained, and how might this judgment be effectively implemented?

He recommended, first, that the people should elect members of Congress who shared with them "a similarity of interests—of burthens —of benefits and of habits." The "unbiased" voice of the electorate acting upon "good information"—presumably supplied by Republican leaders—would "correct political abuses and invent new checks against their repetition," he said.[38]

Taylor's younger colleague James Monroe also emphasized the importance of educating or providing "good information" to the electorate. An "uninformed" electorate, Monroe suggested in a letter to Jefferson, could not always be trusted to elect the good, the wise, and those committed to republicanism to public office. Thus, Monroe advised that it was important that the traditional, elitist leadership begin to play a more active role in helping mold public opinion. Any temporizing by this group of leaders, he contended, was particularly hazardous in a society where "the principles of government" depended "on the great mass of the society" who were generally "uninformed" and whose opinions were shaped by "those whom they have been long accustomed to look up to as their leaders."[39] According to Taylor, the state legislatures had a crucial role to play. They were, he said, "the people themselves in a state of refinement" and possessed "superior information" about the issues as well as a more precise understanding of the will of the people since their members were normally elected annually and were thus more "frequently accountable to the people . . . and incapable of forming combinations for their private emolument, at the public expense." In addition, since the legislatures were responsible for electing the Senate, they could and should have a decisive impact upon the federal government by "constituting the Senate according to a republican standard."[40]

Taylor's recommendations were based on the conviction, widely held by those in the opposition, that conflicting beliefs and interests could and would normally be brokered out and resolved in due course through the constitutional system of checks and balances and that public-spirited and virtuous men, although they might disagree on various matters, would keep the advancement of the public interest as their overriding goal. The great danger now, however, came from men who were no longer interested in serving the public interest but were only selfishly pursuing their own private advancements.

Political parties, according to Taylor, were part of the problem and not part of the solution. He, like most of his eighteenth-century colleagues, abhorred the term *party*, which was then defined as a "division of a whole: a part or portion."[41] Parties then, according to Taylor, were the antithesis of that for which the Constitution had been established, which was to promote the "national good" by implementing policy for the mutual benefit of all citizens, not for a portion or part of the citizenry. "Truth is a thing, not of divisibility into conflicting parts, but of unity," he contended, "hence both sides cannot be right."[42]

But although a "party" was a "confederation of individuals for the private and exclusive benefit of themselves, and not for the public good," there were those, the Republicans, who opposed the selfish interests of "party." They, in Taylor's words, deserved the "appellation of 'a band of patriots,' [rather] than the epithet of 'a party,' [since] they are not contending for the benefit of a party, but of the whole community."[43]

Thus, Taylor believed that there was such a thing as a "public good" and that unselfish, virtuous, and uncorrupted representatives would be able to rise above the petty and parochial interests of party and govern in the interests of all the people. Taylor's argument, of course, mirrored the one Madison had made earlier in *Federalist* 10; Madison had contended that a republican form of government would "refine and enlarge the public views, by passing them through the medium of a chosen body of citizens, whose wisdom may best discern the true interest of their country." And the decisions of these elite representatives, Madison had continued, "will be more consonant to the public good than if pronounced by the people themselves, convened for the purpose."[44]

It was this ideal of a pure, uncorrupted legislature, made up of selfless legislators making law, that prompted Jefferson to confess that he would "always be ready to acquiesce under their [determinations] even if contrary to my own [opinions], for . . . I subscribe to the principle that the will of the majority honestly expressed should give law."[45]

But in a large republic like the United States with an untried and vulnerable national government and diverse political cultures, each to a varying degree still relying on the long-held and venerable practice of the "uninformed" citizenry deferring to their "betters" for political instruction, it would be hard, if not impossible, to determine accurately whether or not the "will of the majority" was being "honestly expressed" either by Congress or by a state legislature.

Jefferson, Madison, and Taylor's view of representation came out of their Virginia experience with its highly personal and deferential political relationships. Under this system, it was presumed that there would be a "similarity of interests" between the representative and his constituents even though they would be of different socioeconomic classes.[46] And the existence of slavery created a perceived, though not actual, rough equality among the white population.[47] Because of his standing in the community and his ability to transcend the crasser motives of self-interest and greed, the gentleman representative was expected to exercise an "unbiased judgment" to determine the public good. Furthermore, the homogeneity of the Virginia society[48] seemed to confirm certain shared assumptions about political unity and engendered some unrealistic expectations about how much national harmony could be expected under the Constitution.

Ironically, the solution to the political impasse that Taylor and others in the developing opposition offered involved mainly reaffirming their old beliefs about the nature of representation and how the federal system was supposed to work. They continued to have faith in the Constitution and the fundamental republicanism of the American people and to be confident that the electoral expression of this republicanism would keep the country free of officials who put self-interest above the public interest. Taylor stressed the importance of the election of representatives who shared a "similarity of interests" with their constituents and of the state governments playing a greater role in offsetting the federal government's power. Nonetheless he and others were also convinced that more active intervention by the leadership was needed to educate and instruct a virtuous, but uninformed, public. As the Virginia leaders and others groped for a means to legitimize and validate their positions, they were ultimately forced to adopt procedures and tactics "to collect the will of the people." Petition campaigns, memorials, open meetings were to become part of the process.

Thus, as the issues of the 1790s further divided American society and as most Americans rejected disunion or violence, an embryonic opposition proto-party, a political organization to measure and shape the public will and to serve as a link between representative and constituent, was formed almost in spite of itself. It is crucial to remember, however, that to John Taylor and his friends it was not a political proto-party that was being organized, but rather a "band of patriots" who had joined together to save the country from what was perceived to be the treachery of a few men who had managed to deceive a trusting public. The Republicans believed that truth was not divisible and were persuaded that they exclusively reflected the "true" will of the people.

But if this were true of the Republicans, it was at least as true of the Federalists. They too were convinced that their opponents were bent upon destroying the Constitution and subverting the federal government. The intensity of the political conflict, which arose from a clash between two camps—each believing it had a corner on the truth—did not allow for the development of what were to become conventional political parties. Instead, the supporters of the administration and the opposition organized not merely to win and hold power, but to save the country from ruination.

V

Both opposition leaders and followers agreed that there was a great disparity between how the new government was supposed to have worked and how it was actually working. The Virginia leadership had faith that the ship of state could and would be put on the proper course once the government had been purged of corrupted, antirepublicans and the uninformed, but staunchly republican, public had been educated and mobilized by the natural leaders of society. In contrast, however, anonymous newspaper writers who opposed government policies voiced a growing dissatisfaction with the elite leadership and urged the *people* to take a more active and prominent role in public affairs. Citizens, they averred, needed to be more vigilant and assertive. In addition they needed to assume more civic responsibility for the safety of the republic and to adopt a more critical role in exercising their suffrage in order to be able to judge and evaluate the performance of their elected representatives.

"ATTEND to your real prosperity, *now or never*, and be not indifferent to the measures of your government," voters were told in the *National Gazette* by one who styled himself "An Independent Federal Elector." He cautioned against "re-electing men who were in partnership with brokers in New York" and who had profited from the funding and assumption programs. Another letter writer to the *National Gazette* indignantly rejected any suggestion that "citizens ought not to meddle with matters, that relate to the federal government." He was not ready to admit, he vowed, "that the business of managing elections, and choosing our representatives, can be performed by any authority, but that of the people." Every man "ought to be a politician in a degree," another author urged. And as a politician he must "conceive it his duty to attend the annual or periodical election of his rulers and magistrates: to watch against the intrigues of designing men, and vote for men of pure democratic principles; men of knowledge and abilities; men of religion and virtue."[49]

In Philadelphia there was an acrimonious discussion over a Pennsylvania election law enacted in 1792 providing for members of Congress and federal electors to be elected on statewide tickets.[50] Among those who disputed the procedure of allowing a "congregation of men to frame a ticket" was "Sidney," who saw the law as designed to induce voters to quite willingly bargain away their most basic political rights. "We want no *Ticket Mongers*," Sidney exclaimed; "let every citizen exercise his own judgment, and we shall have a good representation —intrigue, favoritism, cabal and party will then be at rest."[51]

A Connecticut essayist, "Algernon Sidney," complained about voter turnouts—which were sometimes lower than 5 percent in elections for magistrates, he said—and about the lack of vigilance on the part of the people. It was up to the people "to watch and employ the checks left in their hands" because the "continuation of their liberty does not so much depend upon the existence of the right of election, as upon a vigilant and careful exercise of it." Voters, he admonished, must take care in exercising their suffrage to discover as much information about the candidates as possible, for the longer any office remains in the possession of one man, or one family, the more numerous will be his adherents ready to cover his faults, and exhibit only the fairest part of his character." Condemning the old deferential political system as a threat to free government in rhetoric that was later to become characteristic of the Jacksonian era, "Algernon Sidney" claimed that although in

> Connecticut the compensations given for public services are in no cases so great as to produce a dangerous accumulation of wealth in the hands of those who receive them . . . it is very obvious, that the long continuance of dignified and important offices in the same family, begets an influence more dangerous to a republican government than that which is derived from wealth. Aristocratic sentiments, and aristocratic manners are here generated, nursed and matured. A man born and educated with exalted ideas of his own greatness and that of his ancestors, will never consider his fellow men as his equals, or of partaking of the same rights.[52]

Thus, one manifestation of the political awakening in the aftermath of the election of 1792, at least in some parts of the country, was a democratic dissatisfaction with the traditional elitist leaders of society. As the Revolution earlier had begun to weaken deferential political relationships, so the ground swell of opposition to the federal government in the early 1790s further eroded and undercut public confidence in this traditional and venerable political practice.[53] As the Antifederalists' fears that the federal government was too far removed from public opinion to act responsively seemed to be being confirmed by the government's actions and policies, members of the opposition, the elites as well as the non-elites, felt that they had but one legitimate republican recourse: to appeal to the people, or as it was to be termed later, to "collect the will" of the people. And, as an increased emphasis was placed upon the need for some demonstration or definition of what the people's will was, public men were to lose some of the traditional independence of action that had been associated with a deferential political system. Rather than operating as largely autonomous and unconstrained legislators who would through their own wisdom and virtue define the general good, public officials were to have their actions more closely scrutinized, and they themselves were to come to be regarded as *instruments* through which the public will would be expressed and realized.

4.

The French Revolution and the Awakening of the Democratic Spirit

The liberty of the whole earth [depends] on the issue of the contest.
— THOMAS JEFFERSON

Expectations that the election of 1792, which was characterized by democratic stirrings among the American electorate, would usher in a new era of consensus on the national public good were to be dashed—even before the Third Congress met in December 1793. The increasing radicalization of the French Revolution early in 1793—with the execution of Louis XVI and the French declaration of war against Great Britain, Spain, and Holland—had the effect of deepening and sharpening the conflict between the defenders of the government, whose sympathies were with Great Britain, and the opposition, who felt an attachment to France. The debate over the Washington administration's reaction to the war and the controversial activities of Edmond Charles Genet, the new French Republic's minister to the United States, was shaped and informed by support for or opposition to the French Revolution. Thus, the events of 1793 intensified the already exaggerated and distorted views the Federalists and Republicans had of one another.

The crisis over Genet, the course the American government had taken since 1789 (especially with respect to Hamilton's financial programs), and the seeming failure of governmental institutions to balance and reconcile differences convinced many Americans both inside and outside government that greater collective or group efforts were necessary to set the new nation on its proper course. But this was manifested in different ways.

As the Republicans were discussing how to legitimize their opposition by bringing their case to the people, Democratic-Republican societies were springing up across the country at the grass roots and offering a more radical and democratic critique. At community gatherings these more popular groups expressed discontent with government policies and urged the public to educate themselves and take a more active role by keeping a critical eye on the government.

Although many members of these societies would later become loyal Republicans, Virginia leaders of the opposition in 1793 discreetly kept their distance. They agreed with many of the principles and objectives of the Democratic-Republican societies, but the belligerent egalitarianism and the radicalism of some of the clubs, no doubt, convinced Jefferson, Madison, and others that, although they shared a great deal, the clubs were a political liability in national politics. The formation of the clubs also had an impact on the Federalists. They too were energized to organize events to mobilize public support.

II

Despite Washington's best efforts to insulate and protect the United States from being buffeted by the conflict raging in Europe, he and his successors, down through Madison at least, were unsuccessful. Indeed, the American republic was almost inexorably drawn into the vortex of the European storm, and this mortally threatened its very existence. The major catalyst for international involvement in the 1790s was the special relationship that existed between France and the United States as a result of the 1778 alliance between the two countries. Although the alliance had not been without its American critics, many of whom were suspicious of French motives, most citizens remained grateful for the indispensable aid France had rendered her struggling ally during the American Revolution.[1] So, the news in 1789 of the revolution in France, at a time when Americans were in the process of setting up their own new government, evoked an outpouring of American sympathy and support. In part, it reflected gratitude for France's help during the American Revolution. But perhaps most significant was the fact that Americans embraced the French Revolution as a confirmation of their own revolution. In their minds both revolutions were intertwined, and a failure in France was thus seen as endangering American institutions.

Since the seventeenth century, the belief that America had a special mission in the course of history had gripped imaginations in the New World. The Massachusetts Bay Puritans had believed that the founding and development of their colony was the working out of God's grand design and that they had been charged with furthering a worldwide reformation by the force of their example of spiritual and institutional purity, and Americans of the Revolutionary period were equally convinced that their republican institutions would act as a guiding beacon for the oppressed peoples of the world. Many saw the new republic as "the primary agent in redemptive history," an agent, according to one minister, that would "wake up and encourage the dormant flame of liberty in all quarters of the earth . . . and thereby open and prepare . . . minds for the more easy reception of the truth and grace of the gospel."[2]

Thomas Paine had captured a secular version of this enthusiasm at the time of the American Revolution in his electrifying *Common Sense,* in which he had rhapsodized to his countrymen: "O ye that love mankind! Ye that dare oppose not only the tyranny but the tyrant, stand forth! Every spot of the old world is overrun with oppression. Freedom hath been hunted round the globe. Asia and Africa have long expelled her. Europe regards her like a stranger, and England hath given her warning to depart. O receive the fugitive, and prepare in time an asylum for mankind!"[3]

Just as the Massachusetts Bay Puritans more than a century earlier had looked for signs that others were being inspired by their example, Americans of the post-Revolutionary period awaited a signal that their revolution had not been a historical anomaly. The events in France after 1789—revolution and subsequent adoption of republican government—seemed to fulfill this expectation and confirm that the American mission was succeeding.[4] The events also affirmed an optimistic and progressive view of the historical process particularly dear to Jefferson and many of his friends. For them the American Revolution signaled the "commencement of a Golden Age" in which the forces of despotism and tyranny would be defeated by the powerful alliance of reason and liberty and republican governments established throughout the globe.[5] To them the apparent French repetition of the American experience of revolution and republicanism, with its emphasis upon individual liberty, representative government, and the sovereignty of the people seemed to prove that the institutions of both countries were in harmony with natural law and that France and the United States were in the vanguard of historical forces that were destined to sweep anachronistic and tyrannical forms from the earth.

"Liberty," one enthusiastic editor wrote, "will have another feather in her cap"[6] while one of Madison's correspondents predicted that the "Fate of human nature" had been involved in the French Revolution and that European despotism would now "scarcely survive the 18th century." Thus, Americans should rejoice because they had "made the Rent in the great Curtain that withheld the light from human nature" and by their exertions "let in the day . . . [so that] the Rights of Man became legible and intelligible to . . . [the] World."[7] As Madison himself put it, the enemies of French revolutionaries were the "enemies of human nature."[8]

One historian has labeled the American preoccupation with the French as "national narcissism," claiming that the French Revolution served "as a kind of reflecting pool" and as "long as the French seemed to verify and confirm the American Revolution in a liberal, reformist, and peaceful way, Americans happily discovered their own reflection." Although French violence and instability estranged some Americans, the "serious issue that drove Americans from the reflecting pool was not violence but the realization that France would not fashion its government in the American image and that French notions of popular sovereignty, equality, and national statism admitted few of the checks and balances or restraints of Anglo-American whiggism."[9] Indeed, Americans were to continue to be disappointed, for their concern did not end with Napoleon or the restoration of the monarchy but continued throughout the nineteenth century with Americans desperately seeking, in France's continued struggle to establish a republic, greater insight into the history and perhaps fate of their own republic.[10]

Thus the affinity Americans had for France and its revolution raised American anxieties. If there were a close correlation between the two revolutions and republican experiments, then a failure in one country could mortally endanger the other. The *General Advertiser*, edited by the irrepressible and undaunted Francophile Benjamin Franklin Bache, declared that "upon the establishment or overthrow of liberty in France probably will depend the permanency of the Republic in the new world."[11]

America, Madison wrote, had every reason to pray for the survival of France's republican institutions, "not only from a general attachment to the liberties of mankind, but from a peculiar regard for our own." Already French events had influenced American politics, he claimed. The "symptoms of disaffection" to Republican government exhibited by the support for some of Hamilton's schemes, he said, had "risen and subsided" in the United States in close correlation with the "prosperous and adverse accounts from the French revolution" and that "a miscarriage of it would threaten us with the most serious dangers to our present forms and principles of our governments."[12]

In a letter to France, Jefferson expressed similar, though more optimistic, sentiments. "We too," he observed, "have our aristocrats and monocrats, and as they float on the surface, they shew much, though they weigh little." He hoped that France would be able to establish and maintain a "firm government, friendly to liberty," for "if it does, the world will become inevitably free." Failure in France, Jefferson said, would result in an increase in the number of "apostles of English despotism" in the United States.[13]

An essayist in the *Boston Gazette and the County Journal* asserted that the triumph of France's revolution had "had a great Tendency to '*check*' the spirit of Aristocracy in America. If the Revolutions had not taken Place, the 'wellborn' among us would, before this Period, have endeavored to establish Orders of Nobility." Thus, as a New York editorialist put it, the "downfall of nobility in France has operated like an early frost toward killing the germ of it in America."[14]

In a rather remarkable letter, Jefferson reproved his old friend and protégé, William Short, for criticizing the course of the French Revolution. Jefferson had a tendency to engage in hyperbole and, at the time he wrote the letter, he was not fully aware of the violent turn the revolution had taken,[15] but Jefferson's letter to Short is spontaneous and immediate and captures the almost euphoric hopes and excitement Jefferson felt at the prospects of the revolution and the fears he had about the subversion of republicanism in America. "The liberty of the whole earth," Jefferson wrote Short, depended on the success of the French Revolution, "and was ever such a prize won with so little innocent blood?" Although Jefferson reported that he had lost some close friends to the terror, he said that rather than see the revolution fail, he "would have seen half the earth desolated." Were "there but an Adam and Eve left in every country, and left free, it would be better than as it now is," he said. Although most Americans were friendly to the French cause and were firm in their support of the Constitution and republicanism, Jefferson continued, a few looked "to England as the staff of their hope" and only supported the Constitution "as a stepping stone to monarchy." However, Jefferson concluded, the "successes of republicanism in France have given the coup de grace to their prospects."[16]

The violent turn the French Revolution took in the summer of 1792, the proclamation of the French Republic, the execution of Louis XVI, and the enlargement of the European war to include Great Britain as well as most of the continental powers dramatically intensified and aggravated the ideological polarity between the federal administration and the opposition. Not only did Jefferson, Madison, and their followers believe that the drama between revolution and reaction was being played out in the United States as well as in Europe, so also did their opponents.[17] While Jefferson and his allies saw their enemies as attempting to subvert the Constitution and republican government in order to negate the effects of the American Revolution itself, Hamilton and the friends of the government perceived their opponents as agents of radical revolution whose aim was to destroy the Constitution and republicanism and replace them with democratic instability and fanatical egalitarianism. "Our greatest danger is from the contagion of levelism" one Federalist wrote, for it "has set the world agog to be all equal to French barbers." The Federal measures, however, he assured, would only "gain strength from opposition" because those who objected to them were nothing but "a noisy set of discontented demagogues mak[ing] a rant." The bulwark of government support came, he said, from "the great body of men of property" who "move slowly, but move with sure success."[18]

The Federalists were alarmed by the sympathy many Americans held for the French despite the increasing violence. Indeed the initial brutality of that revolution did little to tarnish its appeal among many conservative New England and Middle Atlantic states clergy. The execution of the king and the beginning of the great European wars, one clergyman predicted, would lead to "the Tameing, the Moderation and Amelioration [of] all the European Governments." Another hailed the Revolution as a great victory over "Papal corruptions and tyrannies" and a "very important pillar of Popery" that had "impiously combined against the civil and religious liberties of the people." It was not until late 1794 and into 1795 that the clergy, influenced by "the rise of militant deism, the threat of social disorder, and the growing intensity of national political issues," retreated from their support of France and became militant, and for some, hysterical, Francophobes.[19]

In addition to aggravating the growing split between friends and critics of the administration, the radicalization of the French Revolution after 1792 made Americans more apprehensive of being drawn more deeply into European affairs. Few men of *any* persuasion would actually have favored United States participation in the great European War. Nonetheless, this was not obvious to either the opposition, who worried that the Anglophilism of Hamilton and other Federalists might lead to an alliance with England, or to the Federalists, who were suspicious that the pro-French sympathies of Jefferson and his followers might ultimately induce the country into fighting on the side of France as a result of some "indiscretion" Jefferson might make as secretary of state. The news of the violent execution of the king, the Federalists fervently hoped, would "check the passions of those who wish to embroil us in a desperate cause, and unhinge our government."[20]

III

The widening European war in the spring of 1793 made it necessary for the Washington administration to develop a policy to respond to the conflict, a process complicated by the alliance the United States had made with France during the American Revolution. Consequently, Washington solicited his advisers' opinions concerning the country's relations with the combatants, the advisability of diplomatically receiving a new French minister, and the French treaties.[21]

At an initial meeting with Washington, his advisers unanimously recommended that the president issue a proclamation of neutrality and that the French minister already en route to Philadelphia be received, making the United States the first to recognize the new republic. The unanimity of support for these actions, however, belied the public controversy they would ignite. Jefferson, although favoring a policy of neutrality, did, however, object to the use of the term *neutrality,* believing that the president was bound to preserve the United States' relationships with all nations in the same state until Congress met again. In deference to Jefferson's position, the term *neutrality* was not used and the actual declaration proclaimed only that the United States would "pursue a conduct friendly and impartial towards the belligerent powers."[22]

The decisions to issue a proclamation and to receive the new French minister, however, did not answer the troublesome question of what to do about the treaties. Hamilton argued that the agreements should be suspended because the United States had made them with the *deposed* French monarch and, therefore, was under no obligation to continue them.[23] Jefferson rejected Hamilton's contention, maintaining that the treaties were not between *governments* but between *nations*. Admitting that nations were freed from treaty obligations when those obligations became self-destructive, he insisted that any danger absolving the United States from its obligations had to be "great, inevitable and imminent."[24] Washington sided with Jefferson, and it was decided not to suspend the French treaties.

America's attempt to "pursue a conduct friendly and impartial towards the belligerent powers" was beset with difficulties from the outset. With the French treaties, the United States had accepted certain principles governing commerce on the high seas, namely that free ships made free goods and that neutrals had the right to carry non-contraband goods into ports of belligerents. These were principles to which Great Britain, as a strong naval power, had never agreed. To

insist upon adhering to them would provoke England, while to acquiesce to England would alienate France.

France complicated the situation by dropping all previous barriers
the country had imposed on trade between the French West Indies
and the United States, making American traders happy by allowing
them free access to previously restricted trade. England maintained,
however, that this new trade was not protected by the rights of neutrals
and invoked its Rule of 1756, stipulating that commerce prohibited in
time of peace was also prohibited in time of war. So in June 1793, the
British navy began to intercept American ships engaged in this lucra-
tive Caribbean trade. Reports of confiscated ships and cargoes and the
impressment of seamen began to circulate, causing American public
opinion to become profoundly anti-British. As the depredations continued, war with England seemed imminent.

A number of plans to retaliate against British actions were offered.
Jefferson, representing the country as secretary of state, issued a report
on commerce critical of British practices. It recommended the passage of discriminatory duties. And in the spring of 1794, bills were
introduced in Congress calling for an embargo on foreign shipping,
which would have hit England especially hard, and for the sequestration of British debts. Alarmed at the seemingly real prospect of war
with Great Britain, the Washington administration and its Federalist
allies managed to scuttle most of the proposed anti-British legislation
and, in an effort to avoid war, decided to send a special mission to
London.[25]

In the meantime, however, the president's neutrality proclamation
of April 1793 generated considerable opposition from at least some
Americans who, as one newspaper proclaimed, believed that the "cause
of France is the cause of man, and neutrality is desertion." These
critics were indignant with American refusal to support France and
asserted that the great mass of the people did not condone such a
policy. Those few who did support it, it was charged, were aristocratic
"*mushrooms* of the Funding Systems" who wished "to draw the cords
of connection as tight as possible between the corrupt monarchy of
Great Britain and the United States." If France required active armed
assistance, it was argued, the United States should eagerly respond
because "the American mind is indignant, and needs to be but roused
a little to go to war with England and assist France."[26]

These sentiments, however, represented only the extremist wing of
the opposition. Monroe, for example, although acknowledging the
fact that public opinion supported the French Revolution, believed

that the majority also favored neutrality.[27] Even Bache, that irrepressible French enthusiast, supported, at least temporarily, the president's proclamation in his *General Advertiser.* Bache's interpretation of neutrality, however, had a distinctive pro-French bias.[28]

Madison was more critical, calling the proclamation "a most unfortunate error" that wounded the national honor by appearing to disregard America's obligations to France and offended "popular feelings by a seeming indifference to the cause of liberty." President Washington, Madison concluded, appeared to have been captured by those upholding the "unpopular cause of Anglomany." Furthermore, Madison challenged the president's authority to issue such a declaration, suggesting that the "right to decide the question whether the duty and interest of the U.S. require war or peace . . . seems to be . . . the right vested in the Legislature."[29]

Jefferson, as the president's chief foreign policy adviser, was embarrassed and chagrined at the chorus of criticism aimed at the proclamation and spent several months privately trying to defend himself for his role in its issuance. Describing the proclamation as a pusillanimous document badly drafted by Attorney General Edmund Randolph, he told Madison that he had not seen it after it had been drafted, and, being busy, had only quickly read it "to see that it was not made a declaration of neutrality." Jefferson agreed with Madison, he said, about its unconstitutionality and had himself argued that the president did not have the authority to issue, by himself, a declaration of neutrality. But inasmuch as England and France were at war with one another and the United States at peace with both belligerents, Jefferson said, the government had an obligation to instruct its citizens of their duties and proper actions towards the warring powers. This was particularly necessary, Jefferson claimed, since some Americans "imagined . . . that they were free . . . to take sides with either party, and enrich themselves by depredations on the commerce of the other."[30]

In an effort to justify the proclamation and whip up public support for it, Hamilton wrote a series of newspaper essays under the name "Pacificus" in June and July 1793. He argued that a proclamation of neutrality, which despite Jefferson's protestations it was being styled, was a usual and proper action for a nation to take to stay out of war and that it was appropriate for the executive branch to issue such a declaration insomuch as it was the "organ of intercourse between the nation and foreign nations." Hamilton denied that the proclamation in effect abrogated the treaties between the United States and France. The Franco-American alliance was *defensive,* he reasoned, while

France's action to initiate the war against England was *offensive*. Further-more, the idea that the United States owed France a debt of gratitude for its aid during the American Revolution was not based upon a realistic view of relationships between nations, Hamilton argued. Self-interest, he maintained, was the first and primary motive in governing the conduct of one nation toward another.[31]

Jefferson and Madison's reaction to Hamilton's essays provides a key to the state of mind of the two most prominent leaders of the opposition at the time. Although Jefferson was pleased with the con-gressional elections and the makeup of the Third Congress that was to meet later in the year, his optimism was now becoming overshad-owed by gloomy forebodings. The president's proclamation, and espe-cially Hamilton's interpretation of it, were seen not only as an apology for the aggrandizement of executive power but also as a threat to peace in the United States. "For god's sake, my dear Sir," Jefferson exhorted Madison about Hamilton, "take up your pen, select the most striking heresies and cut him to pieces in the face of the public."[32]

Reluctantly Madison agreed to do verbal battle with his old protag-onist, and in late summer 1793, he published a series of essays under the name of "Helvidius." Rejecting Hamilton's interpretation, Madison insisted that declaring war, concluding peace, and forming alliances were the "highest acts of the sovereignty; of which the legislative power must at least be an integral and preeminent part." It was the natural and legitimate province of the executive to execute laws, and it was the legislature's role to make laws. Inasmuch as treaties were the same as laws and the executive department did not have the power to both make and execute laws, it did not have the power to make and execute treaties. Since the Constitution did not support such an enlarged view of executive power, Madison asked what model might Pacificus have used to come to such an interpretation? Madison suggested only one answer was possible: "The power of making treaties and the power of declaring war are *royal prerogatives* in the *British government,* and are accordingly treated as *executive prerogatives* by British *commentators.*"[33]

IV

The arrival and subsequent activities of the brilliant, headstrong, and indiscreet new French minister, Edmond Charles Genet or Citizen Genet,[34] did much to inflame mutual suspicions already aroused by the proclamation of neutrality. Instead of coming directly to Philadel-phia, the youthful Genet disembarked in Charleston, South Carolina, in early April 1793 and journeyed slowly overland to the capital where he received his official reception. As he traveled north, the Frenchman was warmly greeted and lionized by Americans anxious to show their sympathy and affection for France. One of Hamilton's correspondents, who worriedly reported on an early meeting with the enthusiastic and ambitious French minister, described him as a very affable and sociable person who he suspected planned "to laugh us into the war if he can."[35]

Genet's mission, because of his own shortcomings, was fatally flawed almost from the very beginning. According to one historian, Genet "was religiously wedded to the immediate sovereignty of the people" and rejected any "interferences with that sovereignty."[36] Indeed this ideological rigidity, along with his self-righteous certitude and his flagrant misreading of Americans' support for France were to be major considerations in prompting him to overplay his hand.

The French Girondist government had instructed their new envoy to ensure that the provisions of the Franco-American alliance were carried out as propitiously for French interests as possible, especially the articles favoring French shipping and commerce. In addition, Genet was to strengthen the commercial ties between the two countries by negotiating new treaties and to seek American assistance in the conquest of Spanish and British possessions in America. Even while in Charleston, he initiated part of the scheme by laying plans to raise and support an army of American frontiersmen to move against Spanish territory.[37]

By the time Genet arrived in Philadelphia in the middle of May 1793, Jefferson—fearful that American neutrality really meant only "a mere English neutrality"—had become increasingly critical of the president's proclamation of a month earlier, even though his viewpoint in the cabinet meetings had carried the day with respect to receiving Genet and to the refusal to suspend the French treaties. Understandably then, the secretary of state became almost euphoric after his first meeting with Genet, during which he was assured by the envoy that, although France had the right under the Treaty of Alliance to demand America's help in protecting the French West Indies, she did not desire it. "It is impossible for anything to be more affectionate, more magnanimous than the purpose of his mission," Jefferson naively wrote Madison. Genet had claimed, Jefferson went on, that his country's only wish was for the United States "to do nothing but what is for your own good, and we will do all in our power to promote it. Cherish your own peace and prosperity."[38]

While Jefferson was delighted by his first impressions of Genet and the apparent generous French position, he soon discovered that the Frenchman's understanding of American neutrality was strikingly different from his own and that of the Washington administration. It was an understanding that led Genet to interpret the provisions of the treaties between the two countries as offering him great opportunities, opportunities that he acted on using American ports as virtual French naval bases where seamen were recruited, privateers commissioned and armed, and captured prizes sold and outfitted as privateers.[39] Jefferson tried to put an end to what he saw as provocative violations of American neutrality by instructing Genet that it was "the *right* of every nation to prohibit acts of sovereignty from being exercised by any other within its limits; and the *duty* of a neutral nation to prohibit such as would injure one of the warring powers."[40]

Genet refused to be restrained. The culmination of his defiant disregard for American neutrality was his conduct in the *Little Sarah* affair. After leaving Philadelphia in the spring of 1793, the English merchantman, *Little Sarah,* was captured by the French and sent back to Philadelphia where it was renamed the *Petite Democrate* and equipped as a French privateer. Warned by Pennsylvania officials as well as by Jefferson to detain the ship until its status was determined, Genet flew into a rage, defied all demands to keep the ship in the harbor, and ordered the *Petite Democrate* to sea. Reportedly it became one of the most successful privateers operating off the American coast.[41]

Thus, by late June, Genet's highhanded and flagrant disregard for American neutrality had driven Jefferson to despair. Although Genet continued to be admired and celebrated by the public, Jefferson feared that the excesses of his conduct would eventually alienate Americans from the French cause and perhaps subvert the political prospects of the opposition since they were closely associated with the French. Particularly worrisome to Jefferson was Genet's arrogant threat that, if the government were to continue its attempt to curtail his activities, he would appeal over its head to the American people, who would, he assumed, support him and "disavow the acts of their government."[42] Jefferson knew, however, that if the French diplomat ever pushed the controversy to that point, he would be angrily repudiated by the American public and the cause of France would be seriously damaged.

Washington and his advisers urgently turned their attention to dealing with Genet and early in August 1793 unanimously agreed to request the French government to recall the diplomat. Jefferson was given the task of writing the letter. Although an assignment that re-

quired considerable delicacy, Jefferson produced a diplomatic master-
piece. Carefully distinguishing Genet's activities from those of his government, the secretary of state marshalled an impressive indictment
against the envoy's actions while continually emphasizing America's
friendship for France. Genet, himself, was not immediately told of the
request for his recall by the American government.[43]

During late summer and early fall, Washington and his cabinet
frequently discussed what course of action—above and beyond the
private request for Genet's recall—should be taken concerning Genet,
who would not be officially replaced until February 1794.[44] Those
discussions reveal a deep uneasiness on the part of Washington and
Hamilton, who believed that Genet's activities symbolized a growing
threat to the stability and safety of the republic. Genet himself, while
arrogant and disrespectful, could be dealt with, the two leaders agreed.
More threatening was the possibility that the radical contagion of the
French Revolution, with the increasing violence and disorder that Genet
symbolized, would infect the American body politic.

Reports, for example, had come from Boston that John Hancock
and Sam Adams, governor and lieutenant governor of Massachusetts,
respectively, were flagrantly violating American neutrality laws by openly
supporting the arming of French privateers.[45] Furthermore, Bache,
who had initially somewhat inconsistently favored a pro-French neutrality, had been provoked by the *Little Sarah* affair into a spirited
defense of Genet in the pages of his *General Advertiser*. As part of this
defense, Washington was attacked by an essayist for his de facto
nullification of the Franco-American treaty contrary to the wishes of
the American people and their elected representatives. The treaty, it
was argued, clearly gave the French the right to equip privateers and
condemn and sell prizes in the United States. Other essays played
upon guilt, claiming that America had shown ingratitude by not recip-
rocating for France's aid during the Revolution.[46]

The Genet affair and the neutrality proclamation brought Washington under increasing public attack. The president, once above criticism, was now being called a "tyrant" by some of his most vociferous
critics, and there were rumors that he was going to be chased out of
Philadelphia. Perhaps the most outrageous expression of anti-Washington sentiment was a poster entitled the "funeral of George Washington," which pictured the president "placed on a guillotine." "Veritas"
also wrote a particularly vitriolic essay charging that Washington,
"buoyed up by official importance" and misled by his refusal "to mix
occasionally with the people," had failed to understand or respond to

public opinion. "Let not the little buzz of the aristocratic few, and their contemptible minions, or speculators, tories, and British emissaries," it instructed the president, "be mistaken for the exalted and general voice of the American people." The "spirit of 1776 is again roused; and soon shall the mushroom lordlings of the day, the enemies of American as well as French liberty, be taught that American whigs of 1776, will not suffer French patriots of 1792, to be vilified with impunity, by the common enemies of both."[47]

Washington became extremely sensitive to and embittered by the criticism. During one meeting with his advisers, Jefferson reported that the disheartened president had lost control when confronted with one particularly abusive story. Furthermore, in a conversation with Jefferson, he had "expressed great apprehensions at the fermentation that seemed to be working in the mind of the public" and appeared to be uniting "many descriptions of persons, actuated by different causes." How it would all end, Washington had lamented, "he knew not." Regretting that he had not resigned the presidency, he told Jefferson that he would rather be dead than endure his present circumstances. For those who charged that he would be a king, he would only reply that he preferred retirement to his farm to being made "Emperor of the world."[48]

All of the president's advisers agreed upon the necessity of recalling Genet, but Hamilton also recommended that more drastic steps be taken. The very life and well-being of the government depended, he argued, upon firm and resolute action. Therefore, the secretary of treasury urged that the entire confidential relationship between Genet and the United States government be made public in order to discredit and undermine the minister's popular appeal. Failure to do this, Washington was told, might lead to an overthrow of his government by faction.[49]

Jefferson strenuously opposed any move to make a public appeal for support of the government against Genet's intrigues, fearing that the fortunes of the envoy and the opposition might be somewhat entwined in the public mind. However, Jefferson also discouraged any Republican enthusiasm for Genet. In a private conversation with Washington, however, Jefferson was less than candid in discussing his own involvement with the opposition. "Without knowing the views of what is called the republican party here," he told Washington, he could nonetheless assure the president that the Republicans "were firm in their disposition to support the government" and did not advocate fundamental constitutional change that "went to the frame of the government." Furthermore, Jefferson predicted, the Republicans would abandon Genet "the moment they knew the nature of his conduct."[50]

Although Jefferson did not mislead Washington about the Republicans' intent, he did blur his own role in shaping Republican strategy. A week before his meeting with Washington, the secretary of state had enjoined Madison against any Republican attachment to Genet. The "republican interest," Jefferson had warned, would be seriously crippled if those associated with it did not publicly disassociate themselves from the French diplomat, who would "sink the *republican* interest if they do not *abandon him*."[51]

V

After the cabinet discussions in the summer of 1793, Washington decided to delay making an official appeal to the people in order to discredit Genet publicly, but Hamilton and other Federalist leaders attempted to gain the same effect through essays they wrote for newspapers detailing Genet's dealings and through resolutions they advanced for adoption at public meetings. These resolutions urged support for the president and condemned Genet's attempts to appeal to the people over the heads of government leaders. Less than a month after the cabinet agreed to seek Genet's recall, Federalist-sponsored resolutions had been adopted by meetings in New York, New Jersey, Delaware, Virginia, and Maryland, with the August 17 assemblage in Richmond, Virginia, being the most galling to the opposition leadership since it challenged them in their own stronghold and was widely publicized in the rest of the country.[52] The campaign the Federalists mounted against Genet transformed the controversy from a confidential diplomatic episode to an acrimonious public controversy.[53] The goal, of course, was more ambitious than simply that of discrediting Genet. Hamilton and his friends sought to use the actions of the French minister to destroy or at least neutralize the growing opposition to the Washington administration.[54]

Jefferson, Madison, and Monroe watched uneasily as the Federalists castigated Genet's excesses to weaken public support and sympathy for France and, at the same time, for political opposition. To Madison, the effort signaled an endeavor "to produce . . . an animosity between America and France, as the hopeful source of the dissolution of their political and commercial union, of a consequent connection with G.B. [Great Britain] and under her auspices to a gradual approximation to her Form of Government."[55]

In response, Madison and Monroe decided to organize their own effort to determine "the real sense of the people" in some of the "important counties" in Virginia and set "on foot expressions of the public mind . . . under the auspices of respectable names." Madison was confident of the outcome, for he knew that the people were attached to the Constitution, the president, France, the Revolution, and an honorable peace and were opposed to monarchy and a political connection with Great Britain. If it were possible to determine "the genuine sense of the people" on all the points at issue, "the calamity," Madison felt, "would be greatly alleviated if not absolutely controlled." This, however, he saw as an impossible task, for the "Country is too much uninformed, and too inert to speak for itself; and the language of the towns which are generally directed by an adverse interest will insidiously inflame the evil." Therefore, he concluded, it was essential that, at the least, "the sentiments of the People" of Virginia be understood.[56]

The Virginia Republicans, fearful of appearing to support the increasingly controversial Genet, were compromised in their efforts from the beginning. Resolutions offered in the late summer and fall of 1793 by Madison and Monroe were equivocal and evasive and avoided mentioning the Frenchman; instead they praised Washington and neutrality and warned against offending France. John Taylor of Caroline, however, did author more radical resolutions condemning the neutrality proclamation as aiding those who "desire a closer union with Britain and desire to alter the government of the United States to a monarchy."[57]

The Virginia Republicans were confident that the "genuine sense of the people" supported them. But in order to determine what that "sense" was, the Virginians concluded that it was essential that the natural leaders of society help inform, shape, and organize the inarticulate public opinion at least in the Virginia countryside. They knew that the more compact towns, which were centers of commerce and communications as well as bastions of support for administration policies, were more easily organized by the Federalists and their sentiments more easily expressed and more widely disseminated than those of rural residents. It was important, therefore, that the expressions of opinion from the towns not be taken as representing the "genuine sense of the people."[58]

VI

The Virginia elite's analysis—based on a deferential view of politics and a belief that the people were basically a passive factor in politics—did not go far enough for some Americans. Their ideas were in dissonance with the non-elite, more popular opposition emerging at the time of the Genet controversy as manifested by the formation of a number of popular citizens' organizations. These Democratic-Republican societies were the political and philosophical heirs of the popularly based, direct-action Sons of Liberty and Committees of Correspondence, which had acted as enforcers of the Whig orthodoxy and as patriot committees of vigilance during the Revolution.[59]

Specifically, members of the Democratic-Republican societies were drawn together by three general complaints. According to them (1) the new government under the Constitution was unresponsive to its citizenry, (2) the deferential style of representation, as outlined by Madison in *Federalist* 10, was inadequate to represent the American people, and (3) some means, not yet provided for in the Constitution, was needed to collect, channel, and formulate the public good. As one proponent of the societies argued, "the security of the people against any unwarrantable stretch of power" in a republic should not be "confined to the check which a constitution affords" nor to the "periodical return of elections; but rests also on a jealous examination of all the proceedings of administration."[60] According to the historian of the societies, Eugene P. Link, thirty-five of the eventual forty-two clubs were organized during the years 1793 and 1794.[61]

Although the ideas of the citizens active in the Democratic-Republican societies mirrored much of what Jefferson, Madison, and Taylor were saying, the clubs were much more outspoken in their criticism. Members of the groups saw the euphoric expectations of the dawning of a new era accompanying independence as having been transformed into a nightmare of dashed hopes by the early 1790s because the principles, idealism, and public virtue of the Revolution had been corrupted by selfishness, speculation, intrigue, and a thirst for wealth and power. The "desire of affluence and the love of ease," one New York member wrote, "have rendered us supine and indolent, and have nearly banished from our minds the sentiment of public virtue, destroyed the ardor of liberty, and diminished our attachment to the sacred interests of our country."[62]

For club members the country's seeming drift toward a closer relationship with England and away from France and the perception that the Washington administration, like the British political system, had been corrupted by special interests added up to irrefutable evidence of the country's fall from grace.

The membership of the democratic clubs was as heterogeneous as the larger American society, including professional men, merchants, planters, printers, small farmers and mechanics. One study of club support in Philadelphia shows that almost 70 percent of the members were either "craftsmen" or "unidentified." Assuming that the "unidentified" were mainly from the "lower order," the overwhelming majority of the members of this particular society were probably from non-elite groups.[63] Nonetheless, the wealthy and famous were represented in the clubs too. For example, David Rittenhouse, inventor, scientist, and president of the American Philosophical Society, and Alexander J. Dallas, secretary to Governor Thomas Mifflin of Pennsylvania and later secretary of treasury under Madison, were both prominent members of the Philadelphia society.[64] And in New York, according to one historian, the club's "leading officers were merchants of wealth and some status, its lesser officers young lawyers, teachers, and craftsmen, while its rank and file were men of the 'middling' and 'lower sort.'"[65] Kentucky had three clubs with differing memberships and political objectives, according to a student of Kentucky history. The Lexington club, chaired by John Breckinridge, who was to become a leading Republican, attracted "townsmen of all [political] persuasions." The Scott County club was composed of "well-connected planters," whereas the Bourbon County group, which included "wealthy and educated Kentuckians politically allied with Jefferson," was led by "obscure figures of little property."[66]

A central question to critics of the course the government was taking in the early 1790s was: what could be done to recapture the democratic promise of the American Revolution? The answer, according to one essayist, was to establish a "league of the virtuous."[67] And the founders of the societies believed that their organizations, dedicated to vigilantly observing government actions, would act as such leagues. But, more importantly, the clubs were intended as instruments through which the general will of the people would have a greater influence upon the government. One early circular of a democratic society maintained that "in a republican government it is the duty incumbent on every citizen to afford his assistance, either by taking part in its immediate administration, or by his advice and watchfulness, that its principles may remain incorrupt." And organized clubs were essential since citizens were unable to follow the activities of the government by themselves and "individual exertion seldom produces a general effect."[68] As a proponent of the Democratic-Republican societies argued, some organization was needed to play a similar role as the town meeting, enabling an ordinary citizen to "know and judge . . . the conduct of the agent he has entrusted" and learn "whether he is faithfully served or basely betrayed."[69]

The societies vigorously defended the notion that the people had a right and duty to oversee and critique the operation of the government. The "different members of the government are nothing more than the agents of the people," the Newark society asserted belligerently, and elected representatives "have no right to prevent their employers [the people] from inspecting into their conduct."[70] For the people "to resign themselves to the agents and delegates appointed by them, without any kind of attention to their own liberty and safety," a Massachusetts society resolved, "is a doctrine calculated to undermine the foundation of freedom, and to erect on her ruins the fabric of despotism."[71]

Hamilton and those around him in the Washington administration, of course, both feared and abhorred the Democratic-Republican societies. One of Hamilton's correspondents referred to the groups as a "Jacobin Club" that held out "an idea to the People of America that there are such defects in our Government as to require an association to guard against them."[72] Rumors that members of the societies were meeting with French representatives and the news early in the summer of 1793 that Genet had been appointed president of a Philadelphia society, the "Society of the Friends to *Liberty* and *Equality*," led Hamilton to describe the situation as a "subject of alarm."[73] "The history of diplomatic enterprise," Hamilton asserted, "affords no parallel to this: We should in vain look for a precedent of a foreign minister, in the country of his mission, becoming the declared head, or even acknowledged member of a *political Association*."[74]

Jefferson, although careful to disassociate himself from the societies, did argue in cabinet discussions that Hamilton's view of the societies was a mistaken one and discouraged any direct administrative attack. It would only have the effect of strengthening the societies' appeal to some Americans, he said. For Washington to take any public stand against the societies would, in Jefferson's view, transform the president from being the "head of the nation" into a "head of party." Washington decided to put any idea of an appeal in abeyance.[75]

Historians have generally agreed that there was a relationship between the Democratic-Republican societies and the Republicans but have disagreed over its nature. Eugene Link maintains that although the societies laid the groundwork for what was to become the Republican party, their primary role was that of a "pressure group," focusing public attention upon enemy or friendly candidates for public office.[76] In New York and Pennsylvania the societies showed no formal or obvious ties with the Republicans, although their activities were primarily political and their sympathies overwhelmingly Republican. In New York City the democratic society actively participated in electioneering but on a sub rosa basis, marshalling support for certain candidates, publishing addresses to the people, and sponsoring town meetings and patriotic parades.[77]

In his study of the development of the Republican party, Cunningham also carefully distinguishes between the activities of the Republicans and the societies. Acknowledging their rather widespread political activity, Cunningham rightly insists that the societies did not function as a part of the Republican organization and that the control and direction of opposition policy, through a network of informal relations, was at all times in the hands of the Republican leadership.[78]

But what was the true nature of the Democratic-Republican societies? The term *pressure group*, which Link and other historians have used, does not adequately convey their important, albeit brief, role in the politics of the 1790s. As the spiritual and ideological heirs of the Revolutionary Sons of Liberty and Committees of Correspondence, members and supporters of the democratic societies of the 1790s shared with their forebears a sense of living in a time of change and the hope that they would be in the vanguard of that change.

However, in a study of New York, Edward Countryman characterizes the democratic societies of the 1790s as different from their Revolutionary predecessors. Committees of Correspondence and other local Revolutionary groups, he contends, were "the means by which people excluded under the old order entered fully into politics," exercising "power directly, and in ways fundamentally opposed to the politics of normal times." On the other hand, he points out, the Democratic-Republican societies "made no claims to power, acting instead as pressure groups." But the major distinction between the Revolutionary committees and the democratic societies of the 1790s, Countryman insists, was in the profoundly different political contexts of the two periods. Whereas pre-Revolutionary politics had "postulated a single public striving to achieve a single good," the era of the 1790s, he maintains, could best be characterized as "one in which American faced American in an unending struggle for maximum possible gain."[79]

Yet this pluralist and liberal vision of a multitude of "pressure groups" or competing interests that Countryman describes as vying with one another was *not* the vision that most Americans shared in the 1790s.[80] Most Americans of that era, despite *Federalist* 10, still embraced an older view of politics that held that there was a unitary, definable public good and common purpose that could be discerned and articulated by virtuous and selfless men. And as the Revolution had united men of goodwill to win independence, the struggle in the 1790s, it was believed, was to unite men to preserve republicanism and the Constitution and to implement the democratic promise of the American Revolution. In both cases it was the politics of the *absolute* that dominated, not the politics of interest brokerage. And, as such, there was little room for dissent. The Democratic-Republican societies were organized, then, at least in the minds of their founders, not to participate in the brokering of a myriad of legitimate interests within a pluralistic society but to preserve the legacy of the American Revolution.

VII

The bitterness and divisiveness of the Genet affair hastened Jefferson's retirement. Tired of the infighting as well as the personal criticism, Jefferson longed to return to Virginia as a private citizen. Originally intending to resign at the expiration of Washington's first term, Jefferson had agreed, reluctantly, to stay on temporarily at his post, and in the spring of 1793 Madison further requested that he not make his "final exit from public life till it will be marked with justifying circumstances which all good citizens will respect, and to which your friends can appeal." Without setting a firm date for his departure, Jefferson gave Madison an emphatic and emotional reply, noting that he had "fully and faithfully paid" his debt of service to his fellow citizens and that "no commitment of their interests in any enterprise by me requires that I should see them through it." He longed for private tranquility and happiness in the company of his family, neighbors, and books, he said. And in a rather moving paragraph clearly written at a moment of great frustration, Jefferson firmly admonished Madison to forever drop the subject:

What must be the principle of that calculation which should balance against these the circumstances of my present existence! Worn down with labours from morning to night, and day to day; knowing them as fruitless to others as they are vexatious to myself, committed singly in desperate and eternal contest against a host who are systematically undermining the public liberty and prosperity, even the rare hours of relaxation sacrificed to the society of persons in the same intentions, of whose hatred I am conscious even in those moments of conviviality when the heart wishes most to open itself to the effusions of friendship and confidence, cut off from my family and friends, my affairs abandoned to chaos and derangement, in short giving [up] everything I love, in exchange for everything I hate, and all this without a single gratification in possession or prospect, in present enjoyment or future wish. Indeed my dear friend . . . never let there be more between you and me, on this subject.[81]

It was in late July, at the height of the Genet affair that Jefferson informed Washington that he wished to retire in two months time. Again, however, he was persuaded to make one last postponement and to stay in office until the new Congress met in December 1793.[82]

Jefferson, if his correspondence is to be believed, left office with a deep and abiding loathing for public service. In part, perhaps, his words were the obligatory rhetoric in keeping with the style of the age. While gentlemen were expected to selflessly give themselves to public service, proper etiquette dictated a certain coy reluctance. But Jefferson did sincerely have both a love and hate for the political arena. While he was attracted by the idea of service to the republic and by the opportunity to influence the course of the country, he was repelled by their total claim on his time and energy and perhaps most importantly by the constant criticism a public figure had to endure. Jefferson's long-awaited retirement and adamant injunction against further service, however, were not to stand. In fewer than three years he was to be elected to the vice presidency.

VIII

Thus the issue of American-French relations in 1793 had the effect of more deeply politicizing the American public. The election of 1792 introduced a debate over the nature of opposition and the relationship between the representative and his constituents, but the events of 1793 broadened, deepened, and sharpened this debate. For the first time there was widespread public discussion of a national issue —Genet and the French Revolution—initiated not only by the political elites who, as supporters and opponents of the administration, attempted to bolster their positions by organizing public support, but also by the grass roots Democratic-Republican societies.

This debate and the flurry of political activity in the summer and fall of 1793 had the effect of permanently and irrevocably broadening the base of national politics in the United States. Those invisible but sturdy bonds of trust and mutual respect between independent gentlemen that provided the foundation for an elitist, deferential political system had been seriously eroded by the bitterness of internal disputes and the deepening crisis in America's foreign relations. And as the ruling elites became seemingly irreconcilably divided, they sought to tap, channel, and shape public opinion. In the final analysis, therefore, the answers had to come from that ultimate body where sovereignty in a republic resided—the people. From this point it was only a short, but unintentional, step to the development of mediating institutions to serve as links between the public and public officials on a more or less continuous basis.

But the original objective in developing proto-parties was not to democratize politics. Rather it was to make the older, deferential, elite-led style of politics work. In other words, the Republicans in their efforts to collect the will of the people and to organize a proto-party were, among other things, attempting to salvage the Constitution and the national government with its large constituencies that "would guarantee the election of the right kind of people" and prevent "representation as the means by which the local feelings and circumstances of ordinary people found expression in government."[83] Republican leaders therefore did not go to their constituencies with a localist bid for support, but rather with a set of principles endorsing republicanism, the union, and the Constitution. Politics should, the Republican leaders believed, revolve around a deferential, elite-led system. And once the government was cleansed of corruption and returned to the natural harmony of a classical republican system, it would be set upon its proper and self-sustaining course.

5.

Threats to the Union

Solitary opinions have little weight with men whose views are unfair; but
the voice of many strikes them with awe.
—PHILADELPHIA *GENERAL ADVERTISER*, DECEMBER 27, 1794

In 1794, at the height of the popu-
larity and strength of the Democratic-Republican societies, some Americans, especially in the West, were becoming so estranged from the new
government and frustrated at its apparent unresponsiveness that they
forsook the normal political and institutional means of addressing and
solving problems and engaged in provocative collective actions that
threatened the stability of the union. These extreme activities were
necessary, the dissidents assured themselves, in order to put pressure
on national officials to take their concerns seriously.

Western Pennsylvanians resorted to violence in their opposition to
the federal excise tax on whiskey, and Kentuckians—unhappy about
navigation rights on the Mississippi River—became involved in a variety of schemes that could have led to the West's splitting off from the
union, or war with Spain, or both. These extralegal responses to grievances focused suspicion on the Democratic-Republican societies as
fomenters of all the trouble and provoked widespread discussions about
the appropriateness of the groups' activities in mobilizing public opinion and even of their very existence.

The questions raised by the whiskey rebels, the Kentucky seces-
sionists, and members of the Democratic-Republican societies revived
many of the gloomy forebodings the Antifederalists had had about
representation in their campaign against the Constitution some five
years earlier. Specifically these questions were: how was the will of the
people to be determined, what was the proper role of an opposition in
a republic, and how were the rights of a minority to be protected?
Underlying much of the Antifederalist opposition, of course, had
been the concern that a truly national public interest would be inde-
finable in a large, heterogeneous republic like the United States.

The crisis put the Virginia-led Republican opposition even more on the defensive, for administration supporters considered all opposition to the government, whether violent or peaceful, to be of the same ilk and to be bordering on the seditious. Condemning the violence, the Republicans attempted to distinguish their elite-led, congressionally based opposition from the ferment in the West as well as from the grass roots activities of the Democratic-Republican societies. Although the Republican elite may have agreed with the beliefs and goals of many in the more popular efforts hostile to the federal administration, they knew it would be fatal to their own efforts to be identified too closely with them. Additionally, the Republicans' Virginia leadership felt a challenge from another direction. At least a few staunch Northern supporters of the Washington administration, they were informed, had become so discouraged with the sectionally based divisions in the country that they were privately discussing a plan to dissolve the union peacefully.

During the debate that surrounded the Whiskey Rebellion, Kentucky secession plans, and the Democratic-Republican societies, the function and scope of political opposition in a republican government were heatedly discussed. And although armed resistance to the will of the majority was denounced by most political leaders, there was an effort to define the legitimate limits of opposition in the United States and to explore suitable institutional means for expressing this opposition.[1]

II

To many western Pennsylvanians in the early years after the new government was established under the Constitution, the worries expressed by Antifederalists during the ratification campaign must have seemed prophetic. In 1791, as part of Secretary of Treasury Hamilton's financial program, Congress levied an excise tax on distilled liquor that so outraged these Pennsylvanians on the frontier that it was virtually unenforceable. Although the "hateful tax levied upon commodities," as it was called by one of its critics, was voted down when it was first introduced in 1790, it passed easily a year later, winning the "almost unanimous" support of "urban mercantile districts" and being opposed by "virtually all the men who could be considered representatives of frontier districts."[2] The Westerners maintained that a land tax would be more equitable since Eastern land with more improvements would then carry the greater tax burden. Moreover, a land tax would force speculators to sell their Western land holdings at reasonable prices, which, in turn, would spur development.[3]

Western opposition to the tax stemmed from several sources. In the background lurked a latent and widespread general hostility to excise laws, which were regarded as a particularly odious method of raising revenue.[4] In England they had been administered harshly and arbitrarily, so much so that their very enforcement seemed to endanger individual liberty; this example was not lost on the Americans. During the debate over the Constitution, one of the Antifederalists' major concerns was the danger of the virtual unlimited taxing power granted to the federal government. American Whigs during the Revolution and Antifederalists during the ratification struggle had agreed that only state and local authorities should levy internal taxes like excise taxes.[5]

More specifically, however, Westerners were convinced that the tax worked a peculiar economic hardship upon their section of the country. "Moderate use of spirits is essentially necessary in several branches of our agriculture," one Western petitioner claimed. For without an abundant source of whiskey, laborers would refuse to work. Thus, in the West whiskey was not sold primarily for cash but was instead used as a barter item. In addition, with the lack of roads and commercial markets, there simply was not enough cash coming into the West for residents to pay the tax.[6] Another objection was to the provision in the law that called for trying Pennsylvania tax offenders in Philadelphia. For a Westerner to appear in court meant a journey of three hundred miles and an absence from farm and home for a number of weeks.[7]

After the passage of the excise law, it quickly became apparent that the tax would be fiercely resisted. Almost immediately tax collectors were tarred, feathered, and terrorized with threats of greater physical abuse. Even citizens who were sympathetic with or merely only in favor of complying with the law were sometimes treated to coats of tar and feathers. In a few cases barns were burned and houses pulled down.[8]

At a public meeting in western Pennsylvania in August 1792, disgruntled participants labeled the tax "oppressive upon the poor," "most dangerous to the civil rights of freemen," and a threat to liberty. It was further resolved that it was the community's obligation "to persist in our remonstrances to Congress, and in every other legal measure that may *obstruct the operation of the Law,* until we are able to obtain its total repeal." To implement this opposition, committees of correspondence in the four western Pennsylvania counties were established.[9]

The apparent institutionalization of violence as a mode of opposing the tax and the government's inability to collect the excise, not just in Pennsylvania but in Kentucky and the Carolinas as well, convinced Hamilton that a strong federal response was needed, and he recommended to the president that "vigorous and decisive measures" be taken to convince the "well disposed part of the community" that the executive was not "wanting in decision and vigor." Hamilton found particularly offensive the language of the Westerners' resolutions, which vowed to "obstruct the operation of the Law." "This is attempted to be qualified by a pretense of doing it by 'every legal measure,'" he wrote fellow New Yorker John Jay, but this was "a contradiction in terms."[10]

Hamilton's recommendations for the use of force, however, were overruled and the Washington administration instead issued a proclamation in September 1792 merely denouncing resistance to the Whiskey tax.[11] Distributed throughout the nation by newspaper and broadside, the proclamation warned that the president would take necessary steps "to prevent . . . violent and unwarrantable proceedings" and citizens should "refrain and desist from all unlawful combinations . . . to obstruct the operations of the laws."[12] A nearly two-year period of relative calm and stalemate followed the president's proclamation.

However, this stalemate was abruptly broken when the government decided to enforce the excise more energetically in Pennsylvania, both Washington and Hamilton agreeing that while there was noncompliance and opposition in the Carolinas and Kentucky as well, it would be easier and less costly to exert federal power in western Pennsylvania than in remoter regions. Pennsylvania, they determined, should be made a test case for federal enforcement and once the insurgency was quelled there, other resistance would be intimidated into submission.[13]

In the summer of 1794 a federal marshal appeared in western Pennsylvania with writs ordering some sixty distillers into court. Committing a major tactical error and adding considerably to the already tense situation, the marshal served his writs in the company of the unpopular federal excise inspector for the region, General John Neville. After a series of rumors and threats, an armed mob broke into Neville's fortified home in July 1794. Forcing the federal troops guarding the house to surrender, insurgents ransacked and burned the property to the ground. Within several weeks the rebels had developed a more ambitious strategy, which included intercepting the federal mails and attacking Pittsburgh to seize the garrison's military equipment and ammunition.[14]

The threat of violence by the rebels against Pittsburgh and the apparent escalation of lawlessness convinced a number of more moderate Westerners that they should intervene to prevent large-scale disruption and bloodshed. At a climactic meeting at Braddock's Field in Pennsylvania, in August 1794, a delegation from nearby Pittsburgh met with the radicals and agreed to support the cause of resistance to the excise and to ostracize and banish certain local supporters of the tax in exchange for the radicals' pledge to abandon their plan to attack Pittsburgh.[15] Thus, Pittsburgh was spared and immediate violence prevented, but the rebels' resistance and refusal to obey federal law and pay the excise continued to menace the Washington administration and the authority of the new Constitution.

When the news of the armed attack upon General Neville's house reached Philadelphia, most members of the administration would have agreed with a correspondent from Pittsburgh who described the incident as the start of a "civil war." As a result the administration immediately requested that Pennsylvania Governor Thomas Mifflin mobilize the state militia.[16] But both Mifflin and his chief adviser, Pennsylvania Secretary of State Alexander Dallas, were hostile to the administration and were reluctant to activate state troops to suppress the dissidents. Dallas, responding in the name of the governor, argued that "the military power of the government ought not to be employed until its judiciary authority . . . has proved incompetent to enforce obedience or to punish infractions of the law."[17]

Although Washington then decided against the immediate use of troops, he did send a preliminary alert to the militia in four other states. In an attempt to settle the crisis peacefully, the president issued a proclamation ordering the rebels to disperse and establishing a federal commission to begin talks with the insurgents.[18] However, the commissioners' mission was not successful. After a number of meetings, the government's delegates concluded that although the extremists among the rebels were in the minority, they had a coercive power over the majority and that "the Authority of the Laws will not be *universally and perfectly* restored, without military Coercion."[19]

The columns of Bache's *General Advertiser* evinced mounting sympathy for the rebels, savagely pillorying the Washington administration throughout the affair. "Shall Pennsylvania be converted into a human slaughter house because the dignity of the United States will not admit of conciliatory measures?" the paper asked. "Shall torrents of blood be spilled to support an odious excise system?"[20]

The Washington administration saw the situation getting out of control and determined that the only safe course of action was to use force to reestablish law and order. Thus, the president gave the final orders to assemble a 15,000-man militia to suppress the insurrection, and troops from Virginia, Maryland, New Jersey, and Pennsylvania under the command of Virginia's Governor Henry Lee were dispatched into the western Pennsylvania counties. Joining the expeditionary force were the president, who stayed only briefly, and Hamilton, who remained with the army because "twas very important there should be no mistake in the management of the affair—and I *might* contribute to prevent one." Hamilton's enthusiasm for the coercive action was scarcely contained. The show of strength and will by the federal government, he believed, would ultimately mean "that the insurrection will do us a great deal of good and add to the solidity of every thing in this country."[21]

The secretary of treasury was not to be disappointed. With the army's advance into the West, the spirit of insurrection wilted and many of the more outspoken leaders fled into the Western interior. Westerners repented, gathering at meetings to promise "obedience to the existing laws" and to pledge support for "the civil authority and all officers in the lawful exercise of their respective duties." In the aftermath, most of the dissidents who were eventually brought to trial were acquitted because of lack of evidence. The two who were found guilty were finally pardoned.[22]

The use of violence, real and threatened, by the whiskey rebels, as members of an aggrieved minority protecting their interests, was part of a long and established practice or tradition in eighteenth-century America. According to historian Pauline Maier, there were numerous colonial uprisings in which "insurgents defended the urgent interests of their communities when lawful authorities failed to act." For example, she points to large-scale rural insurrections in the mid-eighteenth century in New Jersey as well as the Carolinas, where the objective was "to punish outlaws, secure land titles, or prevent the abuses of public officials only after efforts to work through established procedures failed, and the colonists became convinced that justice and security had to be imposed by the people directly." This intervention by the people to protect their interests, however, Maier categorizes as "*extra-institutional*" rather than "anti-institutional," since it provided society an instrument for action in the absence of law or as a result of the inability of government to cope with a particular problem.[23] The most recent historian of the Whiskey Rebellion, Thomas Slaughter, notes as well that the western Pennsylvania rebels were very much influenced by the events of the American Revolution and that there was a "degree of continuity from the Stamp Act crisis through and beyond the anti-excise disorders of the 1790s." For the new government to pass an odious excise tax forcefully reminded the whiskey rebels of revolutionary opposition to the hated Stamp Act and convinced them that their revolution had been betrayed.[24]

The Whiskey Rebellion and ensuing debate clearly had colonial antecedents. They were also tied to the American Revolution with its undermining of all constituted authority. But most important, the uprising was part of the American struggle to come to grips with republicanism and the nature of representative government. The ratification of the Constitution had not ended the debate. Americans in 1794, and afterwards, continued to hold different and conflicting notions.[25] The whiskey rebels, as well as other aggrieved minorities of the time, failed to understand that compromise was essential in order for representative government to work. As historian Edmund Morgan points out in his discussion of the development of the concept of representation in the Anglo-American world, the maintenance of a representative system "requires that different communities represented be able and willing most of the time and on most issues to perceive their own local interests as being involved in, if not identical with, the interests of the larger society."[26]

III

The Democratic-Republican societies were closely tied to the Pennsylvania unrest in the minds of Washington, Hamilton, and most of their supporters. And although they undoubtedly magnified the extent of the connection, they did so with some justification. Although virtually all the clubs, as well as most political leaders, denounced the violence in western Pennsylvania and there is no evidence the societies as institutions fomented the outbreak, it is true that some members of the Washington County society in western Pennsylvania did actively participate in the insurrection.[27] It is also clear that the rebels and members of the societies had a common purpose. Furthermore, by resorting to "extra-institutional" means, that is armed resistance to obnoxious laws, the whiskey rebels were raising very clearly for Americans of 1794 the questions of how and in what form opposition should be manifested against the established authority in a republic, what limitations should be placed upon this opposition as well as upon the constituted authority itself, and, even more fundamental, whether a national legislature like Congress could define and articulate the public good in a way that was generally acceptable to most Americans in all sections of the country? Moreover, the societies did agree with the Westerners' criticism of the excise.[28]

Unlike the rebels, however, the societies maintained that, since the Constitution "emanated from the people," it was essential that "unjust and oppressive laws, and bad measures" be remedied by constitutional means and "that every other appeal but to the constitution itself, except in cases of extremity," should be considered "improper and dangerous." "In a democracy," it was argued, "a majority ought in all cases to govern."[29] Majority rule, members of the clubs argued, was an inviolable principle at the heart of the American political system and somehow synonymous with the public good.

It is not clear from the club members' writings how exactly they saw the sentiments of the majority being determined, let alone implemented, under a Constitution that did not provide machinery to insure and implement majority rule and whose checks and balances between governmental branches, whose indirect election of senators and the president, and whose division of sovereignty between state and national governments all worked against any kind of simple majority rule. Did, for instance, a temporary majority in Congress represent the true voice of a sovereign people? And other than eschewing extraconstitutional action "except in cases of extremity," the societies were also rather vague on how a betrayed majority could gain redress under such a system of government and what constituted "cases of extremity." What they did seem to be saying was that the traditional deferential style of politics, where a gentlemanly elite shouldered the responsibility for formulating and defining the public good after being filtered "through a federal sieve into political leadership," was inadequate.[30]

Furthermore, the members of the clubs were resolutely convinced that there was within the country a widespread sharing or consensus on the principles on which the clubs had been founded. That is, members believed, as did Jefferson, that the American people were united in their support of republicanism even though they also believed that the people, at least on certain issues, had been betrayed by their representatives.

Some western Pennsylvania opponents of the whiskey rebels did, however, attempt to spell out when armed resistance to a constituted authority was justifiable. At a September 1794, meeting of Fayette County citizens led by Albert Gallatin, later a Republican leader in Congress and Jefferson's secretary of the treasury, and others, resolutions were drafted that declared "resistance by force against oppression" to be "lawful only when no legal and constitutional remedy is within the reach of the people, and when the evils arising from the oppression are excessive, when they far surpass those that must ensue from the resistance." As the resolutions noted, this is what gave moral legitimacy to both the French and American revolutions.

The situation in western Pennsylvania, however, was seen as different because that constituency was represented in the legislature and "every mode of redress" in a "republican form of government" was available. Therefore, under such circumstances, it was avowed, the "violence and resistance" was no more than the "attempt of a minority to overrule, and . . . to oppress the majority of the people of the United States."[31]

In the late fall of 1794, amid an outpouring of popular support for the administration's crushing of the rebels, Washington, obviously still deeply troubled by the Pennsylvania violence, reignited the controversy by publicly denouncing the Democratic-Republican societies for encouraging the whiskey rebels. In so doing, he extended and deepened the political dimensions of the conflict. In his annual address to Congress, the president condemned as hypocritical and self-serving the resolutions of the Democratic-Republican societies critical of the insurrection.[32] Privately, he was even more outspoken. "My mind is so perfectly convinced," he wrote, "that, if these self-created societies cannot be discountenanced, they will destroy the government of this country." For Washington, the great danger of the societies lay not so much in their "design" as in their "tendency," and he proclaimed that he would "be extremely sorry . . . if Mr. M[adiso]n *from any cause whatsoever* should get entangled with them, or their politics."[33]

Washington's public and private statements thus exhibited an inclination to connect indiscriminately the various modes of opposition to his administration. As such, the whiskey insurrectionists' armed rebellion was viewed as merely a violent manifestation of the equally "subversive" ideas of the Democratic-Republican societies. Even his fellow Virginian, James Madison, who had led the opposition in Congress to a number of administration proposals, did not escape suspicion. To the embattled chief executive, the whiskey rebels, the Democratic-Republican societies, as well as Madison and his Congressional allies, all by different means and degrees of intensity, seemed to be challenging the government's authority, weakening its ability to govern, and therefore, threatening the stability of the republic.

Washington's use of the term *self-created* offers an interesting insight into his views about the illegitimacy and danger of extraconstitutional organizations whether they be democratic societies or proto-parties. By criticizing "self-created" societies, Washington was condemning political organizations that purported to be representative but were outside the purview of the Constitution and beyond the intentions of the Founders. According to the president, such extralegal organizations, whose grass roots nature seemed to threaten the government's elite control, disrupted and endangered the traditional and trusting deferential relationship that should exist between legally constituted representatives and their constituents. Historian Robert Wiebe writes that "self-created" meant the same as "self-elected," which, clashing "with the gentry's underlying conception of order," was "a clear violation of republican principles." In other words, critics of the societies feared them because they seemed to be alien interlopers in the affairs of state traditionally reserved for the men of property and standing. Or using John Marshall's words, Wiebe describes the societies as "'detached clubs,' agencies that warred from the outside against the total structure of American society."[34]

Washington's denunciation of the "self-created societies" set off a vigorous debate within the House of Representatives. The president's supporters sponsored a resolution condemning the societies as "misrepresenting the conduct of the Government, and disturbing the operation of the laws, and . . . by deceiving and inflaming the ignorant and the weak" having undoubtedly "stimulated and urged the insurrection." Washington's critics, wary of clashing openly with the chief executive by defending the societies, took the timid and politically safe position that the House should ignore the societies because to condemn them would "raise them into much more importance than they possibly could have acquired if they had not been distinguished by a vote of censure from that House."[35]

One supporter of the motion to denounce the societies maintained that such organizations might have been needed in France, "where Despotism, impregnable to public opinion, had reigned" and "where [there is] no channel . . . of Representation with the great body of the nation." In the United States, however, the case was totally different, he argued, for there was an "immense body of public functionaries . . . elected immediately by the people, or by their electors, in a Constitutional mode," including "every description of Legislators, Councils, Governors, Courts, Jurors, and Sheriffs." Thus, he concluded, the "whole country is full of well-constituted organs of the People's will."[36]

But how responsive were these "public functionaries" to the popular will? One defender of the societies pointed out that certain sections of the country were the beneficiaries of more institutionalized forms of democratic expression, particularly New England with its town meetings, than others. But although town meetings might be "the proper vehicles for the communication of political ideas" and a means for facilitating the flow of information between voter and officeholder in the more densely settled districts of the country, in other regions, such as the South, such institutions were impractical "because the population was too thin and too widely scattered." Therefore, Americans in more rural areas needed institutions like the societies for they "had to make the best of it . . . and meet and deliberate, no matter where, whenever they found a convenient opportunity."[37]

The acerbic Fisher Ames, congressman from Massachusetts, attacked the notion that the Democratic-Republican societies had a legitimate role and vigorously defended the concept of deferential representation. In an impassioned speech on the floor of the House, he ridiculed the societies as vehicles for dispensing "political information," describing them instead as devoted to spreading "jealousies, suspicions and accusations of the Government" and fomenting "daring outrages against the social order and the authority of the laws." The societies, he charged, had "arrogantly pretended sometimes to be the people and sometimes the guardians, the champions of the people" and had professed "to feel more zeal for a popular Government, and to enforce more respect for Republican principles, than the *real* Representatives are admitted to entertain." Because their membership was quite small, Ames denied that the clubs represented anyone but themselves. Thus, any action they took in the name of the majority was plain and simple usurpation and any suggestion that they were more representative of the people than the lawfully elected representatives blasphemous. In the final analysis, Ames concluded, the societies would destroy republican government for the "continual contest of one organized body against another would produce the alternative extremes of anarchy and excessive rigor of Government."[38]

Neither the societies and their advocates nor the critics, such as Fisher Ames, believed that the public good could be discovered or furthered by the contentious bickering between various interests or factions within society. But the critics were especially worried that the societies, which usurped the representative function of the legislature, were symptomatic of a fatal factionalism that would rend the republic into a multitude of competing interests. The role of representation must, Ames and others believed, remain in the hands of a disinterested, patriotic elite whose independent judgment might best discover the true public interest.

For the most part those in the House who were opposed to denouncing the societies kept a low profile and avoided the more general arguments about the nature of representative government. Instead, the assertion that the societies were responsible for fomenting the insurrection was challenged for lack of evidence. Madison, however, though wary about publicly and directly challenging the president, did declare that Congress should not have entered into the discussion and maintained that the very nature of republican government required "that the censorial power is in the people over the Government, and not in the Government over the people." And since he had great confidence in the "good sense and patriotism of the people," no great harm would come from the societies' expression of opinion, since ultimately they would "stand or fall by the public opinion."[39]

Finally, after lengthy debate, the initial resolution condemning the societies was defeated, and a more moderate one passed. It defended public order and expressed concern "that any misrepresentations whatever, of the Government and its proceedings, either by individuals or combinations of men, should have been made."[40]

Privately the opposition leadership was outraged by Washington's denunciation of the societies. To Jefferson it was "one of the extraordinary acts of boldness of which we have seen so many from the faction of monocrats," while Madison called it "the greatest error of . . . [Washington's] political life." The latter was particularly infuriated by the attempt in Congress "to connect the democratic Societies with the odium of the insurrection" and to link opponents of the administration "in Congress with those Societies."[41]

Other than privately criticizing Washington's denunciation of the societies, however, Jefferson and Madison offered little comment on the societies' activities. Although the two Virginians clearly sympathized with much of the clubs' critique of the state of American politics in the 1790s and agreed that some means was necessary to "collect the will of the people," public criticism of the societies, which linked them and all opposition with the violence of the Whiskey Rebellion, dictated prudence, for it would have been politically disastrous for the Republicans to become too closely identified with the controversial groups.

The issues raised by the House also were discussed at length in public throughout the winter and spring of 1794–95. Essayists critically examined the nature of the representative system. And, in general, there was a growing awareness of and appreciation for, at least among those who were becoming increasingly unhappy with the Washington administration, the pressing need for some sort of institution that would mediate or intervene between the people and the government to translate and transmit the public will to the legislator and to report the legislator's actions to the public.

The "Watchman," an essayist in the *General Advertiser,* defended the role of the Democratic-Republican societies as communicators of political information. "Tell me, if you can, in what manner you communicate information to the mass of people, but by forming them into town meetings or societies?" Without such information the public will cannot be determined, he argued, and "government has no solid basis," for it "is not in the power, of one fourth of our citizens to obtain information, by ordinary means—but in a town meeting or society." On the other hand, with the help of these local institutions, "every man may, at a very trifling expense, know and judge of the conduct of the agent he has entrusted" and "soon find out . . . whether he is faithfully served or basely betrayed."[42]

Philadelphia's German Republican Society made perhaps the most eloquent and forceful statement in defense of their organization as such an institution. "All governments," it was argued, were "combinations against the people" and were "states of violence against individual liberty," and the American constitutional checks and balances were only "inventions to keep the people in subordination." Something was therefore "necessary . . . to keep up the equipoise, between the people and the government." The Philadelphia club specifically pointed to a need for town or township meetings or associations like Democratic societies.[43]

Thus, by the spring of 1795 there was a growing acceptance within the ranks of the opponents to the Washington administration that the deferential system of placing the government in the hands of the traditional elite was calculated to ignore the public's wishes and that extraconstitutional organizations or institutions were needed to express and reflect the public will.

The Democratic-Republican societies, however, were not able to survive the disapproval of their more moderate countrymen and turned out to be a short-lived phenomenon. By 1796 most of them had disappeared.[44] Washington's denunciation of the groups as "self-created," his linking of them with the Whiskey Rebellion, and the almost hysterical attack on them by supporters of the government drastically curtailed enthusiasm for the grass roots movement. In addition, the popular revulsion toward the violent course of the French

Revolution worked against the societies, who had been among France's most active defenders.

IV

In 1794, the same year as the Whiskey Rebellion, there were other threats to the union, particularly emanating from Kentucky. Residents there, desperate over their economic isolation and the resulting financial hardship, were alienated by the federal government's failure to open up, either by force or diplomacy, the Spanish-controlled Mississippi River so vital to Western commerce. It was an issue of paramount importance. Free navigation of the Mississippi meant more to these Westerners than simply opening up markets for their crops; it also meant that the lands they had purchased on speculation would become more valuable. Bolstering these motives of self-interest was a widespread belief that free access to the Mississippi was a natural geographic right of the United States.[45]

Also, the victories of the French Revolutionary armies and the resulting diplomatic maneuverings in 1793 pitting Spain in an alliance with England against France made the cause even more appealing. The popularity of France and the unpopularity of Spain meant that Westerners could combine principle and self-interest in any move against Spanish territory in Louisiana to open up the Mississippi for the free passage of American goods.[46]

The West had been rife with rumors of plots and conspiracies since the mid-1780s, when John Jay, the Confederation government's secretary of foreign affairs, had made an abortive attempt to work out a treaty with the Spanish minister Diego de Gardoqui. Indeed, Jay's draft treaty, which was never ratified by the Confederation Congress, was seen as betraying Western interests in favor of Eastern commerce and convinced many Westerners that a national government would be of little help in gaining the right to ship crops to market down the Mississippi. In exchange for certain Spanish trade concessions, Jay had agreed to waive the use of the Spanish part of the river for thirty years.[47]

In the next few years, fearful of a growing and aggressive American presence in the West that threatened their control of Louisiana and Florida, Spain had attempted to neutralize American pressure on their territories by secretly hiring General James Wilkinson, Kentucky merchant, arch conspirator, and former Revolutionary War general, to work toward separating the American West from the Confederation.

Since most Westerners were disaffected because of the Mississippi River issue, a number of them were sympathetic to Wilkinson's plan to foment a revolution in Kentucky, which until 1792 was still part of Virginia, and then establish a Mississippi Valley republic, independent and separate from the Eastern United States and friendly to Spain. The climax to this "Spanish Conspiracy" came in a Kentucky Convention in 1788, when Wilkinson along with a group of co-intriguers urged delegates to establish a separate state outside the new federal union, a proposal that was rejected primarily because many Kentuckians felt that the time was inappropriate for such action.[48]

Another conspiracy was equally bizarre. Prior to the arrival of Genet or the outbreak of war between Spain and France, an embittered Western Revolutionary War hero, George Rogers Clark, had offered his services to the French Republic against Spain. Feeling neglected by an ungrateful country that had failed to reward him appropriately for his victories in the West during the Revolution, Clark evidently hoped to cash in on his very considerable reputation. So, he promised the French that with his name alone he could raise 1,500 men, a number that he considered sufficient to "take the whole of Louisiana for France." In order to spare the United States government diplomatic embarrassment, the men in the expeditionary force would depend upon "the Justice and generosity" of the French for their compensation in land and would become French citizens.[49] Clark evidently counted on using the frontiersmen's hatred of Spain, sympathy for France, and greed for land as inducements to join the expeditionary force.

Clark's offer was taken up by the indomitable Genet when he arrived in 1793 with instructions from his government "to take every measure" necessary to "germinate the principles of liberty and independence in Louisiana and in the other American provinces bordering on the United States."[50] As a result, Clark received a commission as a major general in the Army of France and the title of commander-in-chief of the Independent and Revolutionary Legion of the Mississippi.

Federal government officials, aware of the French intrigues in the West, became increasingly alarmed in late 1793 and early 1794 that irate Kentuckians, spurred on by promises of French support, might take matters into their own hands and attack Spanish Louisiana. Any action of this sort, it was concluded, could lead to war with Spain and possibly also with Spain's ally, Great Britain.

Jefferson, in his last months as secretary of state in the summer of 1793, was visited by Genet and told privately and unofficially of the French plans to encourage discontent in Kentucky and mount an attack against the Spanish. In response, Jefferson correctly expressed reservations that "enticing officers and soldiers from Kentucky to go against Spain, was really putting a halter around their necks, for . . . they would assuredly be hung, if they commenced hostilities against a nation at peace with the U.S." But, on a more supportive note, Jefferson went on to say that, if the United States could be left out of the plans, he "did not care what insurrections should be excited in Louisiana."[51]

In March 1794 President Washington, obviously responding to the Kentucky ferment, issued a proclamation forbidding American citizens from enlisting under the flag of another nation with the intention of "invading and plundering the territories of a nation at peace with the United States." And to give the proclamation legal authority, Congress enacted the Neutrality Act of 1794.[52]

Although Clark's mission had the sympathies of many Western settlers, it suffered from the first from a lack of money. As a result of this, the recall of Genet, and the pressure of Washington's proclamation and the neutrality act, the scheme collapsed early in 1794, when Genet's replacement, Joseph Fauchet, renounced all support of it.[53]

Wilkinson's intrigues and the proposed, but abortive, Genet-Clark scheme were just two manifestations of Kentucky's alienation in the late 1780s and early 1790s. Threats of secession from the union and of provocative actions in defiance of the federal government were also promulgated by the Lexington-based Democratic-Republican Society,[54] which had been founded in the turbulent Kentucky atmosphere by people who were convinced that the federal government, if not hostile, was at least indifferent to their needs. The judge of the federal district court for Kentucky, Harry Innes, who attended a number of the society's meetings at the time, became so alarmed at the violent and abusive rhetoric that he began to avoid the sessions for fear they might lead to lawless acts that would be tried in his court. One incendiary essay appearing at about that time, apparently written by Kentuckian John Breckinridge, told his fellow Westerners that they must take matters into their own hands and that "Louisiana groaning under tyranny, is imploring you with uplifted hands."[55]

Breckinridge, who was later to become a Republican leader and Jefferson's attorney general, drafted a strongly worded remonstrance in late 1793. In the document that was adopted by the Kentucky society for presentation to Congress and the president, the Kentuckians demanded "the undisturbed Navigation of the river Mississippi" and threatened "that if the General Government will not procure it for us, we shall hold ourselves not answerable for any consequences that may result from our own procurement of it." Although defending their love of union, the petitioners warned that "patriotism, like every other thing, has its bounds" and attachments "to governments cease to be natural, when they cease to be mutual." For "to be subjected to all the burthens, and enjoy none of the benefits arising from government, is what we will never submit to."[56]

The federal government was thus put on notice that unless steps were taken to open up the Mississippi, Kentucky might move to withdraw from the union and confront Spain unilaterally. As a first step, the Kentucky Democratic-Republican Society called for the establishment of committees of correspondence to organize public sentiment and to send an American ship in "a peaceable manner . . . properly registered and cleared into the seas through the channel of the Mississippi." This would have the advantage of bringing the situation to a head, for if Spain allowed the vessel to pass, this would be an acknowledgement of American rights, but if the vessel were stopped, it would force the United States government to take action.[57]

The relationship between the Kentucky Democratic-Republican Society and Clark's abortive enterprise or other actions is not clear. It appears, however, that despite the radical rhetoric of the societies, they did little except give Clark and his followers moral support. Breckinridge's biographer does say that the Kentuckian *promised* financial aid to Clark, but it is not certain whether any donation was ever made. Actually the men in the Kentucky Democratic Societies found themselves in the happy position of being able to threaten political sedition and not have to commit it because the Clark expedition was a constant reminder to the federal government that these threats had some credibility.[58]

Although Washington's proclamation and Fauchet's renunciation of the Clark expedition reduced the explosiveness of the situation in Western America, a clear danger did remain. If the federal government were unable to open up the Mississippi through diplomacy, Kentucky might yet secede from the union or attack Spanish Louisiana. The Whiskey Rebellion in western Pennsylvania in the summer and fall of 1794 heightened apprehensions within the Washington administration that this might, in fact, occur.

This put pressure on the government to make every effort to negotiate with Spain to solve the Mississippi question. Edmund Randolph, Jefferson's successor as secretary of state, wrote Jefferson in August 1794 that the president regarded the Kentucky situation with such seriousness that he was sending a special envoy to Kentucky to inform the Westerners of the status of Spanish–United States negotiations. And the urgency of these negotiations was such that Washington spoke of calling Jefferson out of retirement and naming him special envoy to Madrid in an effort to assure that the talks with Spain were concluded successfully. Randolph painted a rather gloomy picture of the administration's predicament: "What if the Government of Kentucky should force us either to support them in their hostilities against Spain or disavow and renounce them?" Losing Kentucky from the union, Randolph asserted, was "too dreadful to contemplate, even if it should not attach itself to some other power."[59]

Constrained by what they considered a growing threat to their Louisiana Territory and disenchanted with their alliance with Great Britain, Spanish officials in the summer of 1794 indicated a willingness to reopen negotiations between the two countries. After some delays, Thomas Pinckney was dispatched the following year as special emissary to the Spanish court. In October 1795, a treaty between the two nations was signed at San Lorenzo giving the United States free navigation of the Mississippi and the right to deposit goods in Spanish New Orleans for three years.

Pinckney's Treaty, as it became known, was a diplomatic triumph for the United States, for Spain accepted the American interpretation of the southern boundary between the United States and Spanish Florida at the thirty-first parallel as well as the American doctrine of neutral rights. In addition, each side agreed to prohibit hostile Indian attacks from being launched from its territory upon the other nation.[60] As far as the domestic politics of the United States were concerned, however, the major accomplishment of the treaty was the opening of the Mississippi River to American commerce.

Although secession was discussed in various quarters later in the 1790s as a political instrument to be used by dissatisfied minorities, the federal government had overcome a major obstacle to the preservation of the union by settling the Mississippi question and thereby pacifying the West.

V

Threats of disunion in 1794, however, were not confined to dissatisfied Westerners. At the same time as the Western crisis, a potentially more dangerous threat of secession was being discussed in the back halls of Congress. In May, two Federalists, Rufus King of New

York and Oliver Ellsworth of Connecticut, proposed privately to John Taylor of Caroline that plans be made to end the union peacefully. King argued that it was "utterly impossible for the union to continue" since "the southern and eastern people thought quite differently." The New Yorker feared that since the Southern interest would ultimately prevail in national politics and since those in the Eastern section would never abandon their own principles and interests, it would be better that the union be dissolved amicably and with mutual consent rather than through violence.

A shocked Taylor replied that the differences between the two sections were not as great as imagined, that the union had to be sustained, and "that an effort ought to be made to unite the two parties which distracted the government." Taylor, who saw the public debt as the major cause of the sectional antagonism, proposed that the two sections work together in an effort to settle their differences. And to that end, Taylor suggested that the size of the army be reduced, a new and more equitable tax be levied to replace the excise, and a land office be opened in the northwest, with the revenues produced by those measures being used to pay off the debt.

King, in an evasive and pessimistic reply, repeated his contention that the differences were such irreconcilable ones that the only remedy was to dissolve the union. The debt, he stated, was only one of several factors that divided the sections, pointing specifically to Madison's opposition to the government, which he suspected, had "some deep and mischievous design."

Deeply impressed by this conversation, Taylor sent a memorandum about it to Madison, claiming that a "British interest . . . lurks at bottom" and deducing that the Eastern states once independent to chart their own course could unite with the British and together they "could operate powerfully . . . to bring the south to their terms."[61]

Madison, himself, was not nearly so impressed with the threat as Taylor and jotted at the bottom of the memorandum that the "language of K and E probably in terrorem." In other words, Madison concluded that the Northerners were not serious about the proposal and simply wanted to frighten the Southern congressmen in order to force Southern acquiescence on certain matters of policy. And in support of Madison's conclusion, there is no evidence that the King and Ellsworth proposal went beyond that initial cloakroom discussion with Taylor.

Nevertheless, the proposal does reflect the depth of sectional feeling as well as the growing division in the country between the supporters of the Washington administration and those in opposition. It also shows an increasing willingness to talk of disunion and secession and to use such discussions as a means to gain political ends. Talk after all is the first step toward action. Once radical and initially unthinkable threats become part of the commonplace political rhetoric, the distance between talk and action shrinks considerably and the possibility for action dramatically expands. Ironically the shocked Taylor would flirt with the idea of secession himself before the decade was over.

VI

The fifth year of federal union under the new Constitution, then, was one fraught with danger for the young republic. A number of crises provoked by Americans disillusioned with their government's capacity and inclination to serve its people—especially in the West —tested the resourcefulness of the Washington administration and severely eroded the president's earlier immense personal popularity. To those who felt ignored or betrayed by their government, the country seemed to be controlled by violently partisan officials with narrow and provincial interests, men who were unable to rise above petty factionalism and sectional self-interest to legislate in the interests of the national public good.

The Democratic-Republican societies saw the failure to define a public good as a failure of the representative system. What was needed, they argued, were societies, like the Revolutionary Committees of Correspondence, to vigorously scrutinize the activities of government and to work to formulate, collect, and articulate the public good. The desire for these societies to engage in mediating activities grew out of the assumption that the public good could only be formulated by a close working relationship between the government and the people, who in turn had to adopt a more dynamic and less passive role.

Some Americans were even more alienated. Believing their own interests to have been either disregarded or betrayed, they dallied dangerously with insurrection or secession. The Whiskey Rebellion and the Western and Eastern threats of secession or disunion were indicative of the more extreme forms. By opting to bypass the normal and legal political institutions and adopt other means, some violent and disruptive, to achieve their objectives, at least a few Americans had clearly concluded that there was no longer any basis for mutual action nor for the continuation of the political polity.

The more dramatic events of 1793 and 1794 put the Republican opposition to the Washington administration on the defensive. Although Jefferson and Madison sympathized with many of the objectives of the Democratic-Republican societies and with the plight of Western Americans, the opposition leadership had to navigate very carefully to avoid being associated in the public mind with seditious, disloyal, or violent behavior. The danger was, as Washington's private letter indicated, that all opposition to the government, violent and peaceful as well as extreme and moderate, would be linked together in the public mind. This was a danger that was to plague the opposition for the rest of the decade.

The Republicans' refusal to embrace the societies, however, stemmed from more than simply a failure of political nerve. The societies' localist, democratic, anti-elite message challenged deferential politics and with it the only process, Madison believed, through which a general good could be divined and the fragmentation of the country into provincial and selfish interests be prevented.[62]

6.

The Jay Treaty

Foreign war—internal disorganization (nefarious and detestable conspiracies), French influence—disunion of states, bribery etc. etc. have
been sounded in the public ear, until the public mind seems to be distracted. . . . [It is, if not a] reign of terror . . . [at least a] reign of alarm.
—WILLIAM BRANCH GILES

The increasing shrillness of the
Democratic-Republican societies, reports of Western intrigue, sedition, and rebellion, as well as the growing American sectional
identification and defensiveness—as tumultuous as all these were
—were all eclipsed in 1794 and 1795 by a foreign policy crisis between
the United States and Great Britain that threatened to plunge the two
nations back into war against each other and to rip the United States
apart. And the Washington administration's attempt to deal with the
emergency by negotiating the Jay Treaty with Great Britain heightened the already serious domestic suspicion and intolerance by pitting
English and French sympathizers against each other, thus provoking
a firestorm of protest and further politicizing the American electorate.

Washington's decision to send Chief Justice John Jay to Britain, the
resulting treaty, and the vote to implement the treaty in the House of
Representatives represented serious setbacks for the Republicans. Although they ostensibly controlled the House after the elections of
1792 and 1794—Jefferson described the election of 1792 as a victory
producing "a decided majority in favor of the republican interest"[1]
—the Republicans were nevertheless repeatedly frustrated in their
efforts to alter what they perceived as the administration's pro-British
policy. In response even the popular Washington was attacked openly
by opponents of the treaty, many of whom were incensed with how
the administration had shrewdly used executive power to circum-
vent the more popularly controlled House of Representatives in its
effort to solve the crisis by passing trade sanctions punishing Great
Britain for the insolent and degrading way it was treating its former
colony.

Most opponents of the Washington administration were convinced, and unhappily so, that the Jay Treaty constituted proof that a substantial number of Federalists were committed to bringing the United States into a closer relationship with Great Britain. And this relationship seemed to have implications extending far beyond diplomatic ties. For the Jay Treaty, as well as Hamilton's financial plan with its perceived use of executive corruption to destroy congressional independence, was seen as part of a sinister design to use British institutions and practices to subvert the republic.

The anti-British views of the opposition, particularly in the South, were intensified by the embarrassing pre–Revolutionary War debt planters still owed British merchants. After the 1783 Peace of Paris Treaty ending the Revolutionary War, British officials had frankly indicated that they would not comply with the terms of the treaty unless the debts were paid.[2] And to the Americans' chagrin, the threat had not been an idle one. The British had, for instance, stubbornly refused to withdraw from the Northwest territories. In addition, certain British commercial and maritime regulations were construed by Americans as blatant violations of their neutral rights.

Following the American Revolution, the United States sought to establish trade with European countries based upon commercial reciprocity. This policy, while it met with some success, was a failure insofar as relations with Great Britain were concerned. As a result, from the establishment of the new government under the Constitution down to Jay's Treaty, how the United States might best get the British to enter into a more equitable trading relationship was an ongoing divisive issue.[3]

Madison's attempt in the winter and spring of 1793–94, through a series of resolutions, to gain congressional approval of Jefferson's earlier plan to discriminate "between nations who favor our productions and navigation, and those who do not" and to penalize offenders brought to a climax the effort to force Great Britain to modify her trade regulations.[4]

As might have been expected, Hamilton and his colleagues in Congress bitterly opposed the resolutions, which proposed discriminatory duties on products and vessels of countries that did not have commercial treaties with the United States, Great Britain in particular. The growth of American power and wealth, Hamilton believed, was intimately connected with friendly British-American relations, and thus any policy threatening those relations was subversive to the best interests of the country. In addition, he and his associates were convinced that passage of such hostile measures might even provoke war with Britain.[5]

Debate over the resolutions took on an even greater intensity when news reached the United States that British men-of-war were capturing American vessels engaged in trade with the French West Indies, an intercourse that the British interpreted as a violation of their restrictive trade policy. Acting upon the Orders-in-Council of November 6, 1793, British commanders suddenly swept almost 250 American ships into their dragnet,[6] and the resulting reports of the mistreatment of American seamen by their English captors—coupled with the news of an inflammatory speech by the governor-general of Canada inciting the Indians against the Americans—provoked a wave of anti-British sentiment both in and outside the halls of Congress.[7]

A one-month embargo on all shipping was quickly passed by both houses. This was only a temporary measure, however, and applied to *all* foreign commerce rather than to that of Great Britain exclusively. In the meantime, more stringent propositions were introduced in the House providing for, among other things, the sequestration of debts owed Britain and the suspension of imports from Britain and Ireland until English spoilations were stopped and the treaty of 1783 fully executed.[8]

Despite considerable support, these harsher proposals—which marked the high tide of Republican influence on policy toward Britain—were never passed as they were foiled by the Washington administration's nomination of Jay to negotiate the differences between the two countries. This move took the issue out of Congress's hands and virtually destroyed any chance the legislative branch might have had to pass strong anti-British commercial regulations. It would be inappropriate, the Federalists persuasively argued, to take action against Great Britain now as it would compromise and jeopardize the chances for the mission's success.[9]

Madison complained to Jefferson that despite the unpopularity of Jay's appointment it had nonetheless had "the effect of impeding all legislative measures for extorting redress from G.B." A nonimportation bill that had been passed by a large majority in the House of Representatives, Madison wrote, "was so instantly . . . rejected in the Senate as an interference with the proposed mission that no further efforts of the same type have been seriously contemplated."[10] It was the overweening stature and prestige of Washington, the Virginian complained, that had devastated the Republicans. For his influence "on events, the use made of them, and the public confidence in the P[resident] are an overmatch for all the efforts Republicanism can make." As a result, Jefferson was told, the Republican party in the

"Senate is completely wrecked; and in the H. of Rep. [it is] in a much worse condition than at an earlier period of the Session."[11]

The news of Jay's appointment as special envoy to Britain charged the political atmosphere with emotion. One observer warned that Congress had become dangerously polarized "into two parties nearly equal," each subscribing to essentially different principles. And it was this kind of fundamental division, he warned, "which must have been the . . . cause of the Bloody war in europe."[12] In Kentucky an angry crowd constructed a likeness of Jay, the "Evil Genius," dressed it in "a courtly manner" and placed it "erect on the platform of the pillory." And in reference to Jay's earlier willingness in the 1780s to give up the rights of navigation on the Mississippi and the Westerners' fear of another betrayal, they wrote on one side of the pillory that "No man e'er reach'd the heights of vice at first" and on the other that "A second is not wanting." After guillotining the hapless dummy, a torch was applied, "which finding its way to a quantity of powder, which was lodged in his body, produced such an Explosion" that the effigy of Jay was entirely destroyed.[13]

At the same time Congress was debating whether commercial restrictions should be levied against Britain, Federalists, for a variety of reasons—in part in response to the growing war fever in the country—took up the question of America's military preparedness. They proposed to raise between fifteen and twenty thousand troops, to provide for the fortification of forts and harbors, and to establish a naval force. This attempt to improve the nation's defense had the most sinister implications for some members of the opposition, who feared that a stronger military force might be used against enemies of the administration. Virginia representatives in Congress were virtually unanimous in their opposition to a resolution authorizing the building of six frigates, which was passed over their objections.[14]

Monroe said that while at first he had believed that the new interest in military affairs was only a diversionary move, he had concluded that it had a more profound and unsavory objective. He was worried that the proposed army would through patronage have an important influence upon the government and, even more disturbing, that Hamilton and the Federalists might use the threat of war with Britain to suppress the Republican opposition militarily. For if there were to be a war, he reasoned, the "country will be in the hands of the enemy of the public liberty," and this would pose more danger "than any now menaced from Britain."[15]

II

Jay signed the treaty with Great Britain on November 19, 1794, but it did not arrive in the United States until March 1795, just a few days after Congress had adjourned. Although the treaty itself was to be kept secret, rumors concerning its provisions abounded. R. R. Livingston wrote to Madison that his informants had told him enough about the agreement for him to conclude that "Mr. Jay has sacrificed the essential interests of this country." And this and other hearsay about the treaty had convinced Madison that "Jay has been betrayed by his anxiety to couple us with England."[16]

The treaty that Jay negotiated and that Washington sent to the Senate divided the country like no other issue in the history of the young republic. Yet in looking at the terms of the settlement, it is difficult to see why it was so controversial. It was, to be sure, far from a diplomatic victory for the United States. It did extract from Great Britain a promise to comply with the 1783 peace treaty and evacuate troops from the northwest posts that Britain had stubbornly held onto since the Revolution. Furthermore, American ships were given limited trading rights with British possessions in the West and East Indies. Moreover, the British agreed to put the questions of the British debt, Canadian-American boundary disputes, and American spoilation claims to an arbitration commission. What the treaty failed to do, however, was win English acceptance of the United States' more liberal definition of neutral rights and to gain compensation for American slaveholders whose slaves had been carried off by the British during the Revolution. Perhaps the most that can be said in favor of the agreement was that it did prevent, or delay at least, war between the United States and Great Britain, and it did represent English reaffirmation of American sovereignty.[17]

But the bitter confrontation over the pact with Britain arose not so much over the terms, but over how people perceived the treaty and what it represented. To the critics, Jay had compromised the republic's independence by moving to a closer (some would say dependent) relationship with the former mother country and had scuttled the opportunity to use commercial sanctions to punish Great Britain's violations of American neutrality. In addition, American friends of France denounced the treaty because it seemed to betray the 1778 French-American treaties. The Federalists and their merchant allies, however, after some initial misgivings, welcomed the treaty as preserving the country's crucial trading relationship with Great Britain. Hamilton even went so far as to warn Washington that British trade was so indispensable to the United States, that without its resulting tariff duties the Treasury Department would be forced into "an absolute stoppage of payment—an event which would *cut up credit by the roots.*"[18]

Very soon after the Senate was convened to consider the treaty in June 1795, the proceedings themselves were called into question. Senate leaders, attempting to cloak the pact in secrecy, forbade senators from making the treaty or any discussion of it public, thus provoking widespread suspicion.

It was not long, however, before this confidentiality was compromised, at least by the Republicans. Within days of the opening of the debate, Senator Pierce Butler of South Carolina began sending Madison the document a page at a time to read and then to forward on to Jefferson. Although he was "severely threatened by the Senate" for his actions, Butler held the conviction that if the terms of the treaty were revealed it would be more difficult for its supporters to obtain passage. Eventually, Senator S. T. Mason from Virginia released a copy for public distribution, and it was published by Benjamin Franklin Bache in the Philadelphia *Aurora* but not before the treaty was voted on in the Senate on June 24, 1795. Later, Hamilton and Rufus King, among others, finally did convince Washington to make the official terms of the agreement public.[19]

Near the end of the vigorous debate, Republican Aaron Burr of New York attempted to force the renegotiation of the entire treaty. This effort was, however, outvoted by the same two-thirds margin—20 to 10—by which the agreement was eventually endorsed by the Senate. The vote was, for the most part, sectional, with only two Southern senators voting in favor of the treaty, while seven of the ten in opposition were from the South and West.[20]

After the Senate's favorable action on the treaty, attention focused on Washington, for it was not clear whether he would sign the controversial agreement, which, when he had first received it, he had found so distasteful that he had deferred some time before submitting it to the Senate.[21] In an effort to influence his decision, numerous meetings were held around the country to draft memorials and resolves. Some of these were closely connected with either the Federalists or the Republicans, who attempted to employ the same techniques for so-to-speak collecting the will of the people and validating their own views. Both proto-parties had first made popular appeals during the political storm raised by Genet two years earlier, but in 1795 they went at it more systematically, extensively, and feverishly.

And these campaigns to legitimize the respective positions had a catalytic effect in politicizing popular opinion. For as the public men organized themselves into two conflicting, bitterly competitive, and mutually intolerant conceptions of the national good, and as the people were asked to participate in public meetings and to support resolutions, they were, in effect, asked to take a more active political role by throwing their support to one side or another.

Popular sentiment seemed to run heavily against the treaty. One prominent South Carolinian even went so far as to recommend that the president should be asked to impeach its namesake.[22] Madison wrote that in Virginia "an Appeal to the Inhabitants" to support opposition to the treaty would enjoy almost unanimous backing in every "Town or county" with the exception perhaps of Alexandria. In Boston, Portsmouth, New York, and Philadelphia, Madison reported, there had been unanimous remonstrances against the treaty. In Charleston, copies of the treaty as well as an effigy of Jay had been burned.[23]

Washington received a number of petitions warning that a ratified treaty would mean a breakup of the union. The citizens of Clarke County, Kentucky, for instance, told him that if he signed the treaty "western America is gone forever—lost to the union." Resolutions making the same point were passed in North Carolina, and a Richmond, Virginia, newspaper declared that accepting the treaty would prompt a petition to the Virginia legislature "praying that the said state may recede from the Union, and be left under the government and protection of ONE HUNDRED THOUSAND FREE AND INDEPENDENT VIRGINIANS." Washington did not dismiss these threats lightly and worriedly wrote Randolph expressing his genuine concern over the possibility "of a separation of the Union into Northern & Southern."[24]

At a large meeting in New York, Hamilton, who had resigned his cabinet post early in 1795 to attend to his personal finances, attempted to argue in favor of the treaty but was drowned out by hisses and catcalls, the mood of the audience being so ugly and the sentiment so hostile to Hamilton that several stones were hurled at him, an incident that led one pro-Hamilton observer to quip that the New York "Jacobins were prudent to endeavor to knock Hamilton's brains to reduce him to an equality with themselves." Feelings were running so high that several days later Hamilton got so wrought up in an acrimonious debate over the treaty that he rashly challenged all of his tormentors to a fight.[25]

The Federalists attempted to counter the torrent of popular opposition to the treaty by enlisting merchants and others who had a vital stake in trade with Great Britain. Rufus King reported to one corre-spondent that although the "Friends of order" had been shouted down at a New York public meeting convened to discuss the treaty, the merchants of the city had called a meeting of the Chamber of Com-merce that had supported the treaty in a series of resolutions. In another letter King regretted that a Boston town meeting had set a precedent in creating a kind of popular "Fever" against the treaty. "Will not your merchants," King asked his Massachusetts correspon-dent, "take any step to counteract the Opinion that Boston has been unanimous in their Condemnation?" In response to King's sugges-tion, the Boston Chamber of Commerce did hold a meeting of forty "of the most respectable class" and "with only a single dissentient approbated the Treaty and reprobated the attempts everywhere made to excite discontent and tumult among the People." Efforts were also being made, it was reported, to "induce Salem and Newburyport to express favorable sentiments of the treaty."[26]

Seeking to discredit the public meetings in the larger Eastern cities that had condemned the treaty, the Federalists argued that these as-semblages only represented a small percentage of the American re-public. For the participants, therefore, to purport to speak for the public was both presumptuous and arrogant, they said. However, it was a different matter, they claimed, for the Federalists to solicit men of wealth and influence, the kind of men who were most likely to be members of chambers of commerce, for they represented a more truly objective and dispassionate view of the national interest.

The more populistic and democratic press defended the urban opponents to the treaty as representative of the republican spirit of the American people. The dispersion of "our brethren in the coun-try," one author reasoned, prevented those more rural citizens from a close and immediate scrutiny of government, and, thus, it was the duty of those in the cities to exercise that "important constitutional right of expressing an opinion on public men and measures." Citizens in towns and cities, it was implied, seemed to carry a special burden of citizen-ship, for more isolated Americans had to rely on these fellow citizens to give proper oversight to public issues and officials. And in response to the Federalist charge that the urban gatherings might have aroused a fatal factionalism, the opposition essayist contended that it had al-ways been the trick of the aristocratic faction "to preach up the doc-trine of *blind* confidence and *silent* submission," for, once the people were "lulled in the arms of political lethargy," liberty would become "an easy prey."[27]

Hamilton and Rufus King wrote some thirty-eight "Camillus" essays defending the treaty and condemning the public meetings that had, they charged, passed resolutions against the treaty without serious discussions of its provisions. These meetings were directed, almost without exception, Hamilton maintained, by "the uniform opposers of the government" and had resulted in the "sudden ebullition of passion, excited by the artifices of a party." Thus, the authors of the "Camillus" essays felt it was necessary to give some balance to the public discourse. Contrary to what was being said, they insisted, the treaty made "no improper concessions to Great Britain" and violated no American treaty. And, they ominously concluded, the probable result of a refusal to ratify it would be war.[28]

The Republican response in print did not carry nearly the weight that the Hamilton-King effort did. Robert R. Livingston, Brockholst Livingston, and Alexander J. Dallas all contributed a number of articles,[29] but they were no match for Hamilton, whom Jefferson described as "a colossus to the anti-republican party" and a "host within himself."[30] Madison prepared a long critique of the treaty that was apparently sent to a number of his correspondents but never published. His major objections to the agreement were its "insidious hostility" to France and its abandonment of the American position in regard to neutral rights.[31]

Although Washington had some deep misgivings about certain sections of the treaty, he was inclined to accept it and did eventually sign it. Increasingly sensitive to criticism leveled against him and his administration, Washington was favorably disposed toward the treaty, for it, even if flawed, was the result of his own administration's initiative. His immediate decision in the middle of August, however, was affected by a curious mixture of events. In the midst of his deliberations, the British captured some controversial documents belonging to the French minister to the United States, Joseph Fauchet, and turned them over to two Federalist members of Washington's cabinet, Timothy Pickering, the secretary of war, and Oliver Wolcott, Jr., Hamilton's successor as secretary of treasury. One dispatch, imperfectly translated by Pickering, included damaging information about Secretary of State Edmund Randolph, who Fauchet's letter seemed to indicate had divulged government secrets to the French minister and had appealed for money to use for political bribery. The letter played into the hands of the Federalist leadership for it compromised Randolph, who had been the voice of opposition to the Jay Treaty in Washington's cabinet. When confronted by the evidence in a cabinet meeting, Randolph denied any wrongdoing but resigned his post. In retrospect, historians have agreed that Randolph was the victim of, if not trumped-up charges, at least dubious charges and that Randolph was mainly guilty of being pro-French while his accusers were pro-British.[32]

The revelations regarding Randolph and his alleged intriguing with Fauchet infuriated Washington, who felt betrayed by a close personal friend, and the president signed the treaty even though Britain had, in the meantime, seized a number of American ships, apparently on the grounds that foodstuffs were now considered contraband, and even though Britain refused to give any assurances that these outrages against American shipping would be stopped. Washington already tended to view the escalating hostility toward his administration —as shown by personal attacks upon the president himself, the Whiskey insurrection, the growth of the Democratic-Republican societies, and the threat of Western secession—as indiscriminate attacks generated by his opponents. Thus the outpouring of public declarations against the treaty only intensified his beleaguerment and strengthened his resolve not to buckle under to misguided and dangerous popular pressure. The extent of his exasperation is shown by his decision not to send a response to many of the resolutions or addresses against the treaty that were sent to him because they were "too rude to merit one" or too imbued with "Ignorance and indecency."[33]

Even as early as July 29, before Washington had learned of the Fauchet dispatch, it was obvious that the president considered the welfare of his administration, the government, and the treaty to be closely allied. In a letter to Alexander Hamilton, Washington had written that "the cry against the Treaty is like that against a mad-dog; and every one, in a manner, seems engaged in running it down." The president reported that he had "seen with pleasure" the first publication of "Camillus" defending the treaty but warned that future numbers needed wider dissemination because "the opposition pieces . . . spread their poison in all directions; and Congress . . . [probably] will assemble with the unfavorable impressions of their constituents." The "difference of conduct between the friends, and foes of order, and good government," Washington concluded, was "striking." The foes of government, he lamented, were "always working, like bees, to distill their poison," while the supporters of the government neglected organizing the public and depended "*too much, and too long* upon the sense, and good dispositions of the people."[34]

Washington was voicing the same complaint Jefferson often made, that public opinion in its purest and unadulterated form, though loyal to republicanism and the Constitution, was capable of being misled by factious and designing men. Thus, Washington was expressing the need to organize and educate public opinion. The friends of order and good government must not in the future "neglect the means" of effecting a favorable public response, he said.

III

The signing of the treaty did not silence the public clamor. In fact, some of the agreement's more vociferous and radical opponents began calling for the president's impeachment. Republican leaders, as far as can be determined, had nothing to do with this extremist political appeal, but they *were* clearly upset by the summer's developments. Feeling that Jay had betrayed America's interests, the Republican opposition fumed that the treaty made by the president and a small group of senators would prevent or checkmate any future effort to use American trade sanctions against Great Britain to force a more generous commercial policy and compliance with the United States' interpretation of neutral rights.

The Federalists' ability to use the Senate, where they prevailed, and the presidency to frustrate the Republican majority in the House was disappointing and dispiriting to Jefferson. "A bolder party-stroke was never struck," Jefferson charged about the ratification, "for it certainly is an attempt of a party, which finds they have lost their majority in one branch of the Legislature, to make a law by the aid of the other branch and of the executive, under the color of a treaty, which shall bind up the hands of the adverse branch from ever restraining the commerce of their patron-nation."[35]

The Republicans' estrangement from Washington was illustrated by a February House vote of 50 to 38 to reject a motion to adjourn for half an hour to pay respects to the president on his birthday. A year earlier only 13 congressmen had voted against making the tribute.[36]

In the summer and fall the opposition *General Advertiser* was filled with essays not only denouncing the treaty and the president, but also defending and articulating the people's right to organize opposition to the government and analyzing the nature of representation in a republican government.

"Gracchus" warned that a "party animated by the most dangerous principles" had deluded Americans "by extolling the excellencies of the Federal Government, by proclaiming dangerous conspiracies against its existence, and by stigmatizing their own enemies, as foes of tranquility, of union and virtue." This cabal of men had dominated the Constitutional Convention and the various state conventions, appropriated the influential offices to themselves and castigated their opponents as anarchists. "According to their logic," "Gracchus" contended, "an enemy to the system of administration, or to the most contemptible secretary of one of the departments, is an enemy to the Federal Constitution." The time had come, it was concluded, when the people could no longer be deceived and pitted against one another by "absurd, and artificial distinctions," such as the Federalists' assertion that their opponents were Antifederalists or opponents of the Constitution.[37]

But if the people had been misled by artificial distinctions (such as Federalist versus Antifederalist) and false issues (such as order versus anarchy), who was to say what the *true* majority will was, how it was to be "collected," and how it was to be translated into government policy?

"Atticus" asked in the same newspaper whether the people's "right . . . to express disapprobation of an iniquitous law" would be questioned, since the people had had the right to establish independence from England and to establish the Constitution. And if the majority of the people decided that the Constitution were antirepublican and subversive to liberty, "who would dispute their right to make another?" Although some Federalists had denounced the town meetings and other assemblages of people that had criticized the federal government, "Atticus" asserted that these meetings were essential for collecting "the sense of the people" and were, therefore, "republican and proper."[38]

"Atticus," like the whiskey rebels, however, failed to distinguish between two functions of a republican people. On the one hand, the Revolution and the ratification of the Constitution were sovereign acts of people in their constituent, constitution-making role in which the people could and had challenged the legitimacy of constituted authorities. And if the people in that sovereign capacity were to decide that the Constitution needed to be replaced, it would be within their power to do so. But on the other hand, the people also had an electoral role. They were responsible for choosing representatives to be their spokesmen in various governmental bodies once any Constitution were accepted so that every issue did not force a fundamental questioning about the basic underlying consensus of the polity and the frame of government. Otherwise, as Madison had warned in *Federalist* 49, the result would be anarchy and chaos.[39] But this lack of a distinction on the part of "Atticus" between the people's constitution-making and electoral roles illustrates a fundamental confusion in the minds of many Americans in the 1790s. Fresh from revolutionary and constitution-making experiences, it was natural for them to think in terms of such fundamental conflict.

But what was the "republican and proper" means of collecting the will of the people? The American government was a representative government and the act of choosing representatives was by its very nature a mode for determining the public's will. Yet, there was a crucial division of opinion here. Some had the more elite view and argued that the representative body was "not bound by the opinion of the body constituent." Yet others claimed that if this position were true, it contradicted "a fundamental maxim of American politics . . . that the sovereign power resides in the people."[40] Also, certain electoral practices, such as attempts by elites to organize the electorate or to influence voters, were frowned upon by many, who saw them as subverting the traditional relationship between voter and officeholder. Such attempts to influence the "elemental freedom of choice made by the voter on the spot at the time of election" were seen as means of interfering with "the agreed will of the sovereign people," and thus as a corrupting and even conspiratorial act, according to one historian.[41]

It was in this context of self-righteous political ferment that there were calls to impeach George Washington, calls that no doubt embarrassed the moderate leadership of Jefferson and Madison who undoubtedly saw them as exposing the imprudence and even the recklessness of democratic politics. Washington's enormous popularity and the widespread trust he inspired had been invaluable to the new government. As a charismatic leader, he had personified the political virtue of the new republic and, as president, at least for a time, he had been thought to have transcended the petty, local squabbles that divided other Americans.

For some Americans the disillusionment with Washington paralleled their earlier discovery that the institutions of government established under the Constitution were not functioning faithfully and fairly without public supervision or interference. One essayist reported that until Jay's Treaty was signed he had believed that the "Federal Government would be administered according to the strict text of the Constitution, and the unadulterated principles of republicanism." And such was his confidence in Washington that he had presumed that he might spend the remainder of his life "under the tranquil shade of the tree of liberty." The president's signing of the treaty, however, had destroyed this expectation.[42] Citizens, he implied, had better take a more active role in the government.

Throughout the late summer and fall of 1795, numerous articles extremely critical of Washington, many calling for his impeachment, appeared in opposition newspapers. "Casca" in the *Petersburg Intelligencer* charged that members of the House of Representatives had either to "impeach or renounce their sacred duties" for it was up to those in that branch to save the Constitution and to rescue liberty. For too long, he warned in the Virginia newspaper, a "servile adoration of one man has . . . degraded them to a subordinate rank in the government." The president was attacked for failing to preserve liberty by sanctioning the funding system, assumption, and the bank; signing Jay's Treaty and thus forming a close union with despotic England; being hostile to France; and condemning the Democratic-Republican societies. In addition, he was charged with having conducted his administration "upon principles incompatible" with the spirit of republicanism "and on precedents derived from the corrupt government of England." "Casca" further indicted Washington for "his unconstitutional appointment" of Chief Justice Jay to deal with the British, his use of "military force against a few deluded citizens [in Pennsylvania], who reason would soon have brought back to their duty," and his insistence upon maintaining a "standing army under the absurd pretext of preventing a return of that spirit of insurrection."[43]

Few thought that the impeachment effort would be successful.[44] "Pittachus" was resigned to failure because the Senate, which would be expected to try the president if the House of Representatives voted to impeach, was his accomplice in the appointment of Jay and the ratification of the treaty; thus a "vote for condemnation . . . would implicate them as much as it would him." But the effort should be made, it was contended, for there were "important purposes to be gained by even a vote of impeachment." Among other things, "Pittachus" said, it would "be a solemn and awful lesson to future presidents" and "exact a scrupulous administration . . . of the Constitution." He continued that "lessons like these would not be useless, for when even *a Washington* would not be permitted to sport with our rights, and trifle with things sacred, we might calculate upon transmitting our inheritance to posterity, and insure a secure asylum to the persecuted patriots of the other hemisphere, who would not look here in vain for liberty."[45]

Impeachment, however, was an extreme and dangerous step with little chance of gaining wide support, and none of the Republican opposition leaders, as far as it is known, gave any encouragement to those who were urging it. When one South Carolinian, for instance, proposed that in order to impeach the president, the Senate would also have to be impeached by the House, Madison (who eventually received the letter) urged caution and asked the correspondent for a more sympathetic consideration of Washington, reminding him of the president's long and faithful service to the republic.[46]

Nonetheless, although the Jay Treaty had been ratified by the Senate and signed by the president, the Republicans had not yet resigned themselves to defeat and hoped to use the popular outcry to bolster their future efforts to bring down the hated pact with Great Britain.

IV

Nationally, it was to the House of Representatives that treaty opponents looked to redeem the country from the blunder the president and Senate had made in ratifying the Jay Treaty, and discussion of the treaty was the first order of business in the lower house when it convened in December 1795.

In the fall of 1795 and winter of 1795–96, however, the battle was also being waged in the various states, particularly in Virginia where Republicans on December 15 pushed through the state legislature four resolutions calling for amendments to the federal constitution designed not only to rally popular support against the treaty but also to prevent the possibility that such a pact could ever be ratified by the same process in the future. The first resolution was based on the argument that the treaty's commerce clauses usurped congressional power to regulate interstate and foreign commerce and that no treaty that infringed upon these powers should be ratified unless approved by the House. Other resolutions called for prohibiting federal judges —obviously directed against Jay—from accepting other appointments, for reducing a senator's term to three years, and for creating a special tribunal apart from the Senate to try impeachment cases.[47] This last resolution not only displayed hostility to the Senate but also served as an ominous reminder of the anti-Washington acrimony that had been generated by the treaty. These Virginia amendments were later sent to other states for their consideration, but for the most part, met a hostile reception.[48]

Buoyed by Virginia's passage of the antitreaty amendments, treaty opponents believed their campaign would also win support in the federal House of Representatives. Under the Constitution the House of Representatives had not been given a direct role in the treaty-making process. Nonetheless, Republican congressmen, resentful of

having been excluded from participating in a critical diplomatic decision, hoped the House could nonetheless block the Jay Treaty because
the House did have the power to withhold funds for its implementation, and, under the terms of the treaty, certain arbitration commissions, costing $90,000, were to be established to hammer out unre-
solved issues. Thus, although the House had no specific constitutional
role in making or ratifying treaties, it did have, the Republicans argued, a direct responsibility for the treaty's execution since it was the
originator of appropriations bills.

This opposition strategy to withhold funding for the treaty, however, was not without difficulties because the Republican leadership
knew that their antitreaty majority could be split by differences over
subsidiary issues. The reputation of Washington, who was still popular
with most, had to be detached from the question of the treaty, and the
diversity among the antitreaty forces over the constitutional aspects of
the question had to be overcome. William Branch Giles, Republican
leader from Virginia, warned Jefferson that a "great majority of the
house is opposed to the treaty" but some "will not resist the weight of
the President and the senate." These halfhearted supporters, Giles
explained, believed that disagreements among the various departments should be avoided, so that, while they agreed that "the treaty is
a bad thing," they also believed that the treaty was "the act of the
constituted authorities" and that "the house of Representatives can
exercise no discretion, but as to the most advisable means of effectuating it." Any vote in the lower house would ultimately depend a great
deal on the way the question was presented, Giles concluded.[49]

This rather "soft" antitreaty majority, Giles reported in a succeeding letter, was not the result "of the daily discovery of intrinsic merit"
of the treaty. Rather, he explained, it was a reaction to pressure by the
treaty supporters. "Foreign war—internal disorganization (nefarious
and detestable conspiracies), French influence—disunion of states,
bribery etc. etc.," Giles complained to Jefferson, "have been sounded
in the public ear, until the public mind seems to be distracted." It was,
he protested, if not a "reign of terror," at least a "reign of alarm."[50]

The sectional nature of the political division was particularly
threatening, according to Giles, who had reported to Jefferson earlier
that the "Eastern representation seems to act more in covert and concert, than at any former period." Even new members had been so
unduly influenced by "calumny and misrepresentations" that they
seemed "to nestle under the wings" of the older members. And the
Eastern congressmen in general appeared to avoid "all communica-

tion" with, in Giles's words, their "disorganizing" and factious "Southern brethren."[51]

Fisher Ames, the Massachusetts Federalist, was also deeply pessimistic about the rampant sectionalism and the future of the republic. "A crisis now exists, the most serious I ever witnessed," he wrote, predicting that if the country survived the crisis over the Jay Treaty the government would have a "lease" for four or five years but "not a freehold—certainly not a fee simple." Ames asked whether, "when the day of trial comes," the "Yankees" would allow the "genuine spirit of the Constitution" to become adulterated? "When a measure passes by the proper authorities," he warned, "shall it be stopped by force?" If "the mob, or the leaders of the mob in Congress, can stop the lawful acts of the President, and unmake a treaty," it would, he feared, create a situation where there "would either be no government, or . . . a government by usurpation and wrong."[52]

Washington recognized the advantages of *delay* and refused to send the treaty to Congress until the original copy with the formal British ratification had reached the United States. Thus, it was not until March 1 that he put the treaty before the House, and in so doing he did not immediately request the money to put it into effect. This placed opponents to the treaty in an awkward position, for until the president requested the appropriations, the opponents had nothing they could react against. In other words, there was no procedural mechanism that they could use to attack the treaty.

Its impatience growing, the more radical wing of the opposition decided to take action anyway, and Edward Livingston of New York introduced a resolution calling for the instructions, correspondence, and all other documents relating to the Jay Treaty to be furnished to the House. Madison was shocked by what he considered a precipitous action and wrote Jefferson that Livingston's "policy . . . is so questionable that he will probably let it sleep or withdraw it."[53] In response, Madison tried to amend Livingston's resolution to offer the president discretionary power to decide which papers to present, but his amendment was defeated by a combination of the supporters of the treaty along with the "warmer men on the other side." The more radical, unamended Livingston resolution was then carried by a vote of 62 to 37, with Madison voting with the "ayes."[54]

Washington refused to send the papers to the House, claiming that the treaty-making power of the government rested in the hands of the executive and the Senate exclusively and to grant the request would "establish a dangerous precedent." Furthermore, Washington declared that "the inspection of the papers asked for, can[not] be relative to any purpose under the cognizance of the House of Representatives, except that of an impeachment, which the resolution has not expressed."[55] The president's flat refusal, which Madison termed "improper and indelicate,"[56] to submit to the House the papers and correspondence surrounding the negotiation of the treaty forced a constitutional crisis.

The opposition *General Advertiser* denounced Washington, charging that he had "frowned the Democratic societies into annihilation" by condemning them as "self created." And in the controversy over the Jay Treaty, the president was "now committed against the Democratic branch of the legislature [House of Representatives]," contemptuously referred to by one Federalist as "those plebeians 'collected . . . from all the obscure corners of the Union.'"

Another essay maintained that when two departments of "constituted authority" were deadlocked, as the House and the president seemed to be, the maxim that had to be followed was: "*All power flows from the People.*" Therefore, the people were exhorted to make themselves "informed on perhaps the greatest national question, which has ever been discussed in our councils," so that they might "think without restraint, . . . speak without fear, . . . and write without alarm." Above all, they must discuss their views with their representatives so that the people's will might be determined and the deadlock broken.[57]

In a lengthy speech in the House, Madison reviewed the issue of the confrontation between Congress and the president and defended the prerogatives of the legislative branch. Particularly troublesome to the Virginian was Washington's refusal to submit information needed by the legislature and his contention that the "particular object" in requesting the information had to be spelled out. This Madison thought was at best inappropriate and at worst dangerous. Using the example of impeachment that was mentioned in Washington's message, Madison pointed out that it would be "improper to state [impeachment] . . . to be the object of information which might possibly lead to it, because it would involve the preposterous idea of first determining to impeach, and then inquiring whether an impeachment ought to take place."

And finally, Madison sought to quiet the fears of those who worried about the possible consequences if the House failed to implement the treaty. Most likely, he suggested, the president would just renegotiate the "offensive parts of the Treaty." And the idea of a war as a result of nonimplementation "was too visionary and incredible to be admitted into the question," for it was inconceivable to Madison that an already overtaxed and overextended England "would wantonly make war on a country which was the best market she had in the world for her manufactures."[58]

The Federalists pulled out all stops in their counterattack. Organizing petition campaigns to support the treaty and to destroy the tenuous antitreaty majority in the House, they raised the specter of war and threatened to tie the newly negotiated Algerian and vastly more popular Spanish treaties to the Jay Treaty. Any threat to the implementation of the Spanish treaty was particularly effective in that the agreement granted the United States the long-sought-after right to navigate the Mississippi River and the right to deposit American goods in New Orleans. Congressman Albert Gallatin, for example, complained that western Pennsylvanians, eager for a southwestern water outlet for their goods, had been frightened into signing petitions supporting the Jay Treaty by consciously planted rumors claiming that the British and Spanish treaties "must fall or stand together."[59]

Furthermore, Federalists, in their efforts to undermine opposition to the treaty, used the public call for Washington's impeachment in late 1795 and the president's reference to impeachment in his message to the House as an issue to mobilize Washington's still considerable popular support. Congressman Robert G. Harper, a South Carolina Federalist, charged that the Republicans' single objective in their opposition to the Jay Treaty was to prepare the people for the impeachment of George Washington. Another supporter of the treaty asserted that opponents planned to defeat the treaty as a preliminary step to changing "our government, and for that purpose . . . [making] Jefferson President, and Burr Vice President."[60]

Perhaps the most effective weapon the Federalists used were the petitions that streamed into the House supporting the treaty with Britain. These public expressions in favor of the treaty, one Federalist claimed, were "generally, if not universally signed by persons of wealth and property." But while this might give supporters of the treaty some solace, he said worriedly, it also pointed unerringly to a sobering reality: that the men of "wealth and property" were in the minority. Thus, the counter petitions opposing the treaty might command even more names. For there were "thousands of people . . . who have no [financial] interests in the country, and are even unknown."[61]

Although no study has been made of the men who signed the various petitions, the Federalists, despite their misgivings, seem to have been more effective organizers than their opponents. Moreover, it was, perhaps, easier to mobilize the men of "wealth and property" because they more clearly identified ratification of the treaty with their own self-interest. In a nine-day period at the end of April, the House received 104 petitions, 64 favoring the treaty and 40 opposing it. And those petitions contained 10,200 names in support of the treaty, and 7,200 in opposition.[62]

The sickly and cadaverous Fisher Ames, against his doctor's orders and wife's pleadings, rose to address the House in support of the treaty and gave such a powerful and moving speech that it led John Adams to remark that not a dry eye remained in the House except for those of "some of the jackasses who had occasioned the necessity of the oratory."[63] Ames sounded the alarm as to what might be expected if the treaty were rejected and was particularly graphic and colorful in describing the horrors of the Indian attacks that the British might incite against the Western settlers. "Wake from your false security," Ames exclaimed, hoping his voice would "reach every log-house beyond the mountains," for in "the day time, your path through the woods will be ambushed; the darkness of midnight will glitter with the blaze of your dwelling." And with horrifyingly violent and bloody images, he warned: "You are a father: the blood of your sons shall fatten your corn-field! You are a mother: the war-whoop shall wake the sleep of the cradle." By rejecting the treaty, he assured his fellow congressmen, "we light the savage fires—we bind the victims" and would be answerable "to the widows and orphans whom our decision will make; to the wretches that will be roasted at the stake; to our country; and I do not deem it too serious to say, to conscience and to God."[64]

The Federalists' exertions paid off, and by the end of April, Madison was complaining that the Republican majority had "melted by changes and absences, to 8 or 9 votes." The petition campaign, Washington's influence, the warnings about foreign and civil war, and Western fears that the Spanish treaty would be held hostage until the Jay Treaty were implemented were all powerful factors in reducing congressional opposition to the treaty. On April 29, the House, meeting as a Committee of the Whole, took a preliminary vote on authorizing funds to implement the treaty. After a tie vote of 49 to 49, Frederick Muhlenberg of Pennsylvania, the Republican who served as chairman of the Committee of the Whole, cast his vote in favor of the treaty. Muhlenberg's betrayal of the Republicans later cost him dearly both politically and physically. A few days after the tie-breaking vote he was stabbed by his brother-in-law, a staunch Republican who was incensed by Muhlenberg's desertion. Later, he failed in his bid to win reelection to the House.[65]

Before the final formal House vote, one opponent of the treaty moved to amend the resolution implementing the agreement to include critical language condemning the treaty as highly objectionable and calling for efforts to stop the spoilation of American commerce and impressment of American seamen. Madison hoped that this amendment would carry so as to make "the pill a bitter one to the Treaty party as well as less poisonous to the public interest." The amendment, however, by a vote of 49 to 50 failed to carry because, as Madison put it, a "few wrongheads" deserted the antitreaty forces. On the final roll call vote, April 30, 1796, implementation of the treaty was approved, 56 to 48.[66]

V

The struggle over the Jay Treaty marked another battle in the deep-seated and enduring sectional conflict that plagued the young republic. One historian in his study of voting patterns in the federal House of Representatives during the 1790s has noted, for example, that New Englanders and Southerners were conspicuously hostile and tended to vote by section in opposition to one another, whereas representatives from the Middle Atlantic states provided the critical balance of power. The "cohesion differences between New England and the South were great throughout the first six Congresses," he concludes, when "an average of more than three-fourths of New England's representatives voted against an average of nearly two-thirds of the South's delegates."[67]

This sectional antipathy was shown by the treaty vote in the House of Representatives where a total of 79.6 percent of those voting to support Jay's Treaty came from the New England or Middle Atlantic states, while 73.5 percent of those who opposed the treaty came from the Southern states. Only 7.4 percent of those favoring implementation were from south of the Potomac River. Furthermore, Southerners and New Englanders were both more solid in their opposition to or support for the treaty than representatives from other sections of the country. For example, eleven representatives who supported the Livingston resolution calling for the treaty papers from the president deserted the opposition on the final vote and threw their support behind implementation. Of these eleven, only two came from south of the Potomac, the rest being from Maryland, Pennsylvania, New York, and New Jersey.[68]

The mood of the opposition prior to the legislative session was buoyant. In the summer of 1795, Jefferson, for example, was obviously exceedingly optimistic when he claimed that the Federalists had been reduced to a weak minority in the House.[69] Giles was equally confident as late as December 1795, when he reported to Jefferson that a "great majority of the house is opposed to the treaty."[70] But as Jefferson, Madison, Giles, and other members of the opposition found out much to their dismay, the expected majority did not survive and their support melted away.

What had happened? The House was made up of independent gentlemen, many of whom wore any partisan attachment lightly. First and foremost they were representatives from Massachusetts, New York, Virginia, and other states and only secondarily and intermittently, depending on the issues, did they consider themselves Republicans or Federalists. Uneasy about challenging the Senate and the president's right to make a treaty, some of the members, particularly those without an intense ideological commitment, refused to reject implementation of the treaty. In addition, when the Fourth Congress met in December 1795 to consider the implementation of the Jay Treaty, only 63 percent of its members were incumbents who had served in the previous Congress.[71] This meant, among other things, that more than one-third were without the attachments and allegiances of returning members. Thus, although Madison, as the leader of the opposition in the House, knew there were members he could count on for support, there were others, presumably many of the newcomers, that had to be wooed during the course of the session.

During his efforts to mobilize and conserve the antitreaty block of votes in the House, Madison must have called to mind his earlier words in *Federalist* 50, where he had condemned sustained and regularized legislative polarization. When "the same names stand invariably contrasted on the opposite columns" in a legislature, he had written, "*passion*, not *reason*, must have presided over their decisions." For when "men exercise their reason coolly and freely on a variety of distinct questions, they inevitably fall into different opinions on some of them." However when "they are governed by a common passion, their opinions . . . will be the same."[72] Thus, as representatives voted with like-minded colleagues during the battle over the Jay Treaty as well as other issues in 1795–96, Madison might well have recollected his earlier words. But he would have denied, no doubt, that "*passion*, not *reason*" was motivating the Republicans, who, he would have vigorously maintained, were the last bastion of reason, detachment, and a selfless concern for the public interest.

Even though public men were increasingly calling themselves

"Republicans" or "Federalists," they would have been highly indignant at the conclusion of one historian who has argued that the Jay Treaty controversy marked "the beginning point for national party machinery."[73] There was no acceptance of the modern definition of party as an institution representing various interests within a pluralistic society. The crisis did, however, give added impetus to both proto-parties in Congress to carry their cases to the people in an effort to gain legitimacy for their respective and competing visions of the public good. And in so doing the opposition began to use the term *Republican* more frequently and in a more self-conscious, descriptive, and approving way to describe their views and supporters. The term *party*, however, retained much of the pejorative meaning given to it in the eighteenth century, even as it was also beginning to be used in a holistic way to describe those, who by their actions or principles, believed that they and they alone represented the national public interest.

To John Taylor and his Republican friends, theirs was not a political party but rather a "band of patriots" who had joined together *temporarily* to save the country from what they perceived to be the treachery of a few men who had managed to deceive a trusting public. Jefferson agreed with his Virginia colleague and argued that "where the principle of difference is as substantial and as strongly pronounced as between the republicans and the Monocrats of our country, I hold it as honorable to take a firm and decided part." Furthermore, he maintained, it was "immoral to pursue a middle line" when the country was divided "between the parties of Honest men, and Rogues."[74]

But the Federalists also saw the contrast between themselves and the Republicans in equally stark terms and were convinced that their opponents were bent upon subverting the Constitution and federal government.

Hence the intensity of the political conflict arising from a clash between groups who each believed they had a corner on the truth did not allow for the development of more conventional political parties. Instead, the Republicans and the Federalists organized despite their own protestations, to win and hold power, and to save the country from their opponents.

The struggle over the Jay Treaty in 1795–96 represented the further development in the process of politicization that had begun during and following the election of 1792. Opposition to the Washington administration had initially developed as a two-tiered system. Madison, Jefferson, and their like-minded colleagues in Congress had contested a number of the administration's foreign and domestic policy initiatives. At the same time while these political elites vied with each other in the halls of Congress and within the administration, non-elites began to organize and protest through Democratic-Republican societies and other organizations that reflected local, regional, or more democratic interests.

By 1795, however, as most Americans rejected disunion or violence as a means of solving seemingly intractable problems and as the Democratic-Republican societies were in decline, this two-tiered system of opposition had all but disappeared. And in its place, the Republican proto-party began to act as a clearinghouse of opposition and to take shape as a crude political organization to collect, measure, and mold the public will and to serve as a link between representative and constituent. Ironically, however, the Republican leaders still embraced a system of representation that emphasized deference rather than democracy even as their proto-party became the sanctuary for most of the more radical opposition to the government. Madison and his colleagues were wary of democratic politics with its emphasis upon the representative as agent of his constituents because they feared such politics would splinter the nation into a multitude of competing interests.

The Federalists were particularly fearful of an appeal to the public, for as Fisher Ames pointed out, this is what Genet had "threatened," and "Heaven knows" what this public "court of appeals will do." But he was sanguine that at present, at least, "the *vox populi* seems to be *vox rationis.*" A Virginia supporter of the treaty also worried about politicizing the people. Some congressmen, he maintained, were too solicitous "of the rights of the Citizens." He wished that "it would be left to the people to watch their own rights," for "they can all read and understand the Constitution." And if they learn that their rights have been infringed upon "they will soon all know it."[75]

VI

Thus, even though the leaders of the two proto-parties were increasingly polarized and agreement on a national public good seemed even more elusive and quixotic, neither Federalist nor Republican leaders abandoned their faith in a system of politics controlled by a selfless elite rising above petty and provincial interests.

Jefferson captured the essence of this political polarization in several letters written while he was in temporary retirement at Monticello during the struggle over the Jay Treaty. American politics, he asserted, was divided between Republicans and "Monocrats," or "Rogues," or "antirepublicans." The antirepublicans, according to the Virginian, consisted of old Tories and refugees, British merchants, "American merchants trading on British capital," speculators and stockholders in banks and public funds, federal government officers, office hunters and "Nervous persons." The other group, the "Republican part of our Union," was made up by the "entire body of landholders throughout the United States" and the "body of labourers." However, despite the fact that the antirepublicans were outnumbered 500 to 1, Jefferson wrote, they enjoyed strength disproportionate to their numbers because they lived in cities, controlled the newspapers, and "can act in a body readily and at all times." Those composing the "Agricultural interest," on the other hand, were "dispersed over a great extent of country" with "little means of intercommunication with each other." However, they were confident of their own strength and were "conscious that a single exertion of . . . [their] will at any time [could] crush the machinations against their government."[76] Thus, like a slumbering, benign giant, the republican interest, while having the latent strength to subdue any threat to republican government and the Constitution, had not yet flexed or used its political muscle. In addition, however, Jefferson seems to have been acknowledging the need for some effort to organize this hitherto untapped reservoir of republican sentiment.

Even allowing for some exaggeration, it is obvious that the political situation Jefferson perceived in the 1790s was one that would be unfamiliar to the public men of nineteenth- and twentieth-century America.[77] There was little sense or awareness of commonality or consensus underpinning the political conflicts Jefferson described. The former secretary of state saw political society as being divided between a small group of unvirtuous men and the overwhelming body of citizens who were virtuous—or between the "Honest men and Rogues." Jefferson, like Taylor, saw the Constitution and republicanism threatened by this smaller group of self-interested men who acted in concert as a party for the "private and exclusive benefit of themselves and not for the public good." To counteract this, then, the great body of disinterested men, the virtuous of the community, were obliged to organize to oppose these selfish interests. And as they did so, these virtuous citizens, in Taylor's terms, acted not as a party but as "a band of patriots." Furthermore, neither Jefferson nor Taylor indicated that they regarded their actions as part of an ongoing process. Rather, they saw themselves involved in either a single action or at best a short-term activity that would sweep the corrupt from power once and for all.

7.

The Election of 1796

The change of the Executive here has been wrought with a facility and a calm which has astonished even those of us who always augured well of the government and the general good sense of our citizens. The machine has worked without a creak.　　　　　　　　—WILLIAM SMITH

The presidential election of 1796, the first *real* contest for the presidency in American history, was to be one of the most unusual in American history. It was not until September of the year that the incumbent finally and publicly announced his intention not to stand for reelection and that supporters of the contenders felt they could properly begin to mount campaigns. There were no conventions and no formal caucuses. Instead, it was through a system of informal meetings among leaders of both proto-parties in the winter and spring preceding Washington's announcement that an understanding emerged concerning who the candidates should be if the president were to step down, as it was expected he would. One of them, who at numerous times had staunchly defended his earlier decision to retire from public life, never formally or even informally accepted the nomination, but his followers presumed he would accept, if elected. None of the candidates campaigned or as much as lifted a finger to win the election. Nonetheless, to those in both camps the election was seen as absolutely critical because two different political visions were being offered to the public, and what the outcome might mean for the future of the union and the Constitution few would hazard a guess. Finally, caught up in the fever of partisanship, both the Federalists and Republicans engaged in activities that led to the alienation of important factions within their proto-parties. In both cases the wounds would not be easy ones to heal.

By 1796, of course, Washington's standing among the American people had slipped from the near demigod status he had enjoyed in 1789. The Neutrality Proclamation and the Jay Treaty with their perceived pro-British bias, the Whiskey Rebellion and Washington's denunciation of "self-created" societies, and Hamilton's financial program had all taken their tolls. But, despite this, the president was still the dominant figure in American politics, and opposition leaders generally avoided confronting him directly. The defeat of the Republicans in the House of Representatives over the Jay Treaty, they knew, had been due in large part to Washington's prestige and influence.

The president had been talking about retirement for some time and, thus, most political leaders believed that he would not stand for a third term. Nonetheless, the *timing* of the announcement was of great concern to Washington. Regretting that he had failed to "publish his valedictory address the day after the Adjournment of Congress" in the spring of 1796, he wrote Hamilton for counsel concerning the "*next best time*" to make his decision known. Any delay in making the announcement, the president worried, might lead some to the conclusion that retirement had been forced upon him by an increasingly hostile public opinion.[1]

Hamilton advised Washington to defer revealing his intentions "as long as possible" and to "*hold the thing undecided to the last moment*" so that he would be free to change his mind if need be. Playing upon Washington's fears of leaving office under fire, Hamilton argued: "If a storm gathers, how can you retreat?" Assuring the president that any further delay would not tarnish his reputation, Hamilton specifically recommended the valedictory address be postponed until two months before the electors were to meet in early December. Politically this would be advantageous, Hamilton maintained, since the parties would only be able to mount conditional campaigns until the president had made his plans known because "serious opposition to you will I think hardly be *risked*."[2] This strategy was also one that suited Hamilton, who deeply regretted Washington's imminent retirement and was despondent over the choices for his successor. No doubt, the former secretary of treasury was hoping for some last-minute political storm that would keep the revered Washington in office.

Washington followed Hamilton's advice and did not publish his Farewell Address until September 19, 1796. The valediction itself, although it contained parts of an earlier 1792 version composed by Madison and Washington, was mainly the work of Hamilton and has been primarily remembered for its call for neutrality in foreign relations, cautioning against "permanent, inveterate antipathies against particular Nations and passionate attachments for others."[3] More important, however, Washington's message was *mainly* devoted to a plaintive warning against sectionalism and party factionalism and to an appeal for unity in domestic politics.[4] As such, the remarks give insight into the president's perception of political developments in the country in 1796: his disdain for extralegal means of expressing public opinion and his antipathy to party and faction (both of which, it is obvious, he connected with opposition and not with Federalist activities). "Government for the whole" was indispensable for the country's political health, Washington pleaded. Condemning destructive sectional alliances, he stressed that a strong union benefited each area economically and also provided each "greater security" by preventing "those broils and Wars" between the states "which so frequently afflict neighbouring countries."[5]

In an obvious reference to the Whiskey Rebellion and the Democratic-Republican societies, Washington also insisted that it was the duty of citizens to respect the authority of the government, comply with its laws, and acquiesce in its measures. While admitting that the people had the right to alter the Constitution, he pointed out that this had to be done by an "explicit and authentic act of the whole people." Any obstructions to the execution of the laws and combinations or associations organized to impede the "regular deliberation and action of the Constituted authorities" were destructive "of this fundamental principle and of fatal tendency." These associations created "faction" and, "in the place of the delegated will of the Nation," they imposed "the will of a party," which was "often a small but artful and enterprising minority of the Community." A government led by party, he cautioned, would only reflect the "ill concerted and incongruous projects of faction," in contrast to being "the organ of consistent and wholesome plans digested by common councils and modefied [sic] by mutual interests."[6]

In extreme cases elsewhere, the chief magistrate reminded solemnly, the "alternative domination of one faction over another, sharpened by the spirit of revenge natural to party dissention [sic]," had driven men seeking peace and security to accept a despotic form of government. The more immediate problems raised by the spirit of party, however, were its distraction of the public councils and enfeeblement of the public administration as well as its agitation of the "Community with ill founded jealousies and false alarms," occasionally leading to the fomenting of "riot and insurrection" and opening "the door to foreign influence and corruption."

Some would assert, Washington said, that parties were necessary in free countries as "useful checks upon the Administration of the Government" and a means of "keep[ing] alive the spirit of Liberty." Within some limits, the president admitted, this was probably true, particularly in countries with a monarchical form of government. However, in countries with popular or "elective" governments "it is a spirit not to be encouraged." Party spirit, if it were allowed to spread, was a "fire not to be quenched," Washington concluded, and it demanded "a uniform vigilance to prevent its bursting into a flame."[7]

Washington, in his Farewell Address, and Hamilton, as its chief author, agreed in principle with Taylor and Jefferson on the destructiveness of party spirit. All four embraced the civic humanist ideal of the virtuous, autonomous citizen interested not in private or personal gain but in promoting the general good of society.[8] They all discussed this general good as having substance and clear definition and as transcending petty political squabbles and the base self-interest of individuals, factions, or geographic subsections of the community. Their definitions of the public good, however, were not in consonance.

There is, of course, a temptation to label the elaborate and pained distinctions made by the men of the 1790s as hypocritical. Yet the Anglo-American cultural traditions, as well as the political experiences and beliefs of these early day public men, argue against such an assessment. These persons did firmly believe—and their experiences as local magistrates, legislators, justices of the peace confirmed it—that the interests of the entire community could be determined and acted upon. The deferential nature of eighteenth-century politics dictated this conclusion. The gentlemanly elite, responding to a long-held tradition of duty and sacrifice of one's private life for a public one, were convinced that through common deliberation and action the best interests of the entire community could be perceived and served.

In the election of 1796, therefore, people in both proto-parties earnestly believed that, as they vied for control of the executive branch, they represented the interests of the whole community whereas their opponents spoke only for a small, factious, artful, and selfish few. In part, the difficulty of seeing opponents in any kind of reasonable or recognizable frame of reference stemmed from the shift of the arena from the states to the national government. The federal government under the Constitution, after all, represented the first instrument since the Revolution that had been invested with considerable political power on the national level. Thus, defining the common interest of a community on the state level, as the Antifederalists had warned, was a quite different proposition than that of defining the common interest of a federal community. The latter task would call for the shedding of certain eighteenth-century ideas about the unity of a community, the development of political parties, and a general understanding that one's opponents could also be loyal to the Constitution and republicanism. This would not be accomplished in the eighteenth century.

II

Although Washington did not publicly announce his intention to retire until September, there was much speculation in the late winter and early spring of 1796 about his plans. In general, there seems to have been a general consensus among partisans on both sides that, if Washington decided against a third term, Vice President John Adams and former Secretary of State Thomas Jefferson would be the main contenders.

Adams confided to his wife Abigail at the beginning of 1796 that the "President will retire" and that, although it was "not a subject of conversation as yet," he was the "heir apparent." The legacy would not be uncontested, as Adams believed that Patrick Henry, Jefferson, Jay, and Hamilton all would have support to succeed Washington. But the vice president had been assured in private conversations, he said, that "the federalists had no thought of overleaping the succession," or bypassing him. And indeed in the spring of 1796 Adams did emerge as the Federalist candidate to succeed Washington.[9]

While ruminating about the possible succession if Washington were to step down, Adams, in mid-February, reluctantly concluded that either Jay or Jefferson might also be acceptable as president: "The government will go on as well as ever," for "Jefferson could not stir a step in any other system than that which is begun" and "Jay would not wish it."[10] Within two weeks, however, Adams reported on conversations that reflected considerable apprehension—apprehension that perhaps he now shared—over a Jefferson presidency. Abigail was told: "I hear frequent reflections which indicate that . . . although in good hands, he [Jefferson] might do very well; yet, in such hands as will hold him, he would endanger too much."[11]

Vice President Adams was the logical candidate to succeed Washington, and the emergence of Jefferson's candidacy poses somewhat of a mystery. Jefferson, although recognized for his leadership of the Republicans, had been in retirement since 1793. Indeed, his resolve to withdraw *permanently* from public life had been so strong that he, at the time he had forsaken the public arena, had rejected Madison's plea to delay his retirement by admonishing his friend to "never let there be more between you and me, on this subject."[12]

In some respects retirement seems to have agreed with Jefferson, at least into 1795. In the spring of 1794 he boasted that he had not "seen a Philadelphia paper since I left it . . . and I feel myself so thoroughly weaned from the interest I took in the proceedings there, while there, I have never had a wish to see one, and believe that I never shall take another newspaper of any sort. I find my mind totally absorbed in my rural occupations."[13] More than a year later he continued to profess his happiness with his detachment from things political. "I have laid up my Rocinante in his stall, before his unfitness for the road shall expose him faltering to the world," he wrote Mann Page. "I consider myself now but as a passenger," he continued, "leaving the world, and its government to those who are likely to live longer in it."[14]

The isolation Jefferson experienced during these years is illustrated by the fact that from the time he returned home from Philadelphia until his reentry into politics he did not travel more than seven miles from his home. Even visitors to Monticello were warned that farming would be the main focus of conversation and, if the topic of politics were raised, Jefferson would put that subject "on very short allowance," with "now and then a pious ejaculation for the French and Dutch republicans, returning with due dispatch to clover, potatoes, wheat, etc."[15]

During these years, while reaffirming his own withdrawal from public life, Jefferson on several occasions expressed the hope that Madison would be elected president, and in December of 1794 he exhorted his old friend not to leave public life. Confirming that he "would not give up . . . [his] own retirement for the empire of the universe" and apologizing for his selfishness, Jefferson, nonetheless, said he hoped that Madison would only consider retiring from the House of Representatives in order to assume "a more splendid and a more efficacious post."[16]

A few months later Jefferson returned to the subject of the presidency in another letter to Madison. Claiming that the subject of his own candidacy had been forced upon him by his enemies who were attempting to "poison the public mind as to . . . [his] motives," Jefferson concluded that his "own quiet required that . . . [he] face it and examine it." And after conducting a thorough self-examination, Jefferson said he had resolved "that every reason which had determined . . . [him] to retire" from Washington's cabinet "operated more strongly" on him even in retirement. "The question," he emphasized, "is forever closed with me," explaining that he was only waiting for an appropriate time to publicly withdraw his name from consideration. His "sole object," he insisted, "is to avail myself on the first opening ever given me from a friendly quarter (and I could not with decency do it before), of preventing any division or loss of votes, which might be fatal to the Southern interest."[17]

In this crucially significant letter, Jefferson seems to close the door on the possibility of his agreeing to be the Republican candidate for president in 1796, or at any other time for that matter. Even more revealing, however, is his characterization of the political conflict in *sectional* terms by his use of the word *Southern* to describe the Republican opposition. Jefferson's own sense of the sectional nature of the conflict, which would grow even stronger in the late 1790s, belies the ways historians have depicted the conflict of the 1790s in terms of conventional national party politics.

But the Republicans did not give up on the idea of Jefferson as a presidential candidate, and throughout 1796 avoided giving him an opportunity to protest or to withdraw his candidacy. In early February, Madison wrote Monroe that he was confident that Washington was going to retire and that Adams would be the candidate of the "British party." Jefferson, he said, would be the only candidate in opposition with any hope of success but he would have to be pushed to allow his name to be considered and might "mar the project and insure Adams's election by a peremptory and public protest." Even after the Farewell Address, Madison warily avoided Jefferson, writing Monroe that he had "not seen Jefferson and have thought it best to present him no opportunity of protesting to his friends against being embarked in the contest."[18]

In the end, despite Jefferson's private disavowal to Madison in 1795 of any ambition for public office whatsoever, and despite his earlier pronouncements on the subject, the Republicans brought forward Jefferson's name as their candidate for president in 1796, and he did not take that opportunity to take himself out of the race. Why he had apparently changed his mind during that year remains an intriguing question and one on which Jefferson's biographers differ. One argues unconvincingly that Jefferson's commitment to retirement was never sincere.[19] Malone, in his exhaustive and authoritative biography, claims that Jefferson was apparently virtually unaware of his candidacy, and once he became aware, "in a fatalistic mood, he silently acquiesced in a judgment which the leaders of his party regarded as inevitable."[20]

Neither of these explanations, however, fully explain Jefferson's reemergence as a public figure given his loathing of the criticism that inevitably accompanies a political career. A complex person who both hated public life and found it irresistible, Jefferson was essentially a private person with a low tolerance for disapproval, and he suffered the torment of the damned under the lash of public censure. Repeatedly stung throughout his career by criticism of his conduct while Revolutionary War governor of Virginia, for instance, Jefferson went to almost fanatical lengths to exonerate himself and to answer any and all charges by exhaustive searches for evidence in affidavits and testimony.[21]

Part of the explanation for Jefferson's change of heart, as one historian has noted, is that retirement was not as idyllic as Jefferson had anticipated. In a moving letter full of loving advice to his daughter in 1802, Jefferson counseled that "happiness requires that we should continue to mix with the world . . . and every person who retires from free communication with it is severely punished afterwards by the state of mind into which they get." This conclusion, he said, was drawn from his own retirement from "1793 to 1797 [when] I remained closely at home, saw none but those who came there, and at length became very sensible of the ill effect it had upon my own mind," rendering "me unfit for society" and leading "to an misanthropic state of mind."[22]

Thus, the alluring prospect of a pleasant and fulfilling retirement was for Jefferson, as for many people, sharply at odds with the reality. Personal illness, the burden of debt, and family problems combined, according to one historian, to transform the anticipated idyllic retirement with books, family, peace, and tranquility into an unhappy time during which he became increasingly private, withdrawn, and unhappy.[23] As poet John Keats observed: "Heard melodies are sweet, but those unheard are sweeter." So public life, despite the pain and torment, offered Jefferson the sociability, the power, the gratification of public acclaim as well as the patriotic satisfaction of sacrificing his private happiness for the greater public good.

At the end of 1796, while awaiting the verdict of the voters, Jefferson himself attempted to clarify why he was now willing to leave retirement. Although he would have "rejoice[d] at escaping," he could not have refused the nomination out of respect for and obligation to the public, he explained, even though no "man will ever bring out of that office the reputation which carries him into it." He lamented that "the honey moon would be as short in that case as in any other, and its moments of ecstasy would be ransomed by years of torment and hatred."[24]

Buffeted by mounting private and personal concerns as well as increasing anxiety over the state of the republic, Jefferson allowed himself once more to be lured into public life. The American people were sound in their loyalty to republicanism, he reasoned, but the ship of state had been set on a dangerous course by a small group of selfish and misguided men. A president with a sound commitment to republican principles was needed, and it was unlikely, as Jefferson and his Republican allies knew, that the helm would be entrusted to any other Republican than the former secretary of state.

III

The manner in which vice presidential nominees were selected was even more ill-defined and vague than that for determining candidates for the presidency. Complicating the selection process was the troublesome constitutional provision that called for the person with the greatest number of electoral votes, providing it was a majority, to be elected president and the person with the next highest number of votes to be elected vice president. This arrangement, of course, became so unworkable that it was modified in 1804 by the Twelfth Amendment, which separated the balloting for president and vice president.

According to one scholar, the original constitutional process for selecting a president and vice president had been based upon the assumption by the Founding Fathers that after Washington's presidency there would be a number of presidential candidates, thus preventing any from receiving a majority vote in the Electoral College. In effect, the Electoral College had been seen as a screening and nominating institution that would forward the names of the five candidates with the most votes to the House of Representatives for the final selection.[25] However in 1796, with the retirement of Washington and the rampant partisanship, presidential and vice presidential candidates were informally nominated by "government" (or Federalist) and "opposition" (or Republican) proto-parties rather than by the Electoral College. The objective of each of the proto-parties in the Electoral College, then, was to attempt to get the maximum number of votes for its presidential candidate, while holding back a few votes from their choice for the lesser post so as not to risk a tie. But since the election process, before the Twelfth Amendment, did not discriminate between presidential and vice-presidential votes, the stage had inadvertently been set for manipulation and intrigue.

After Jefferson had been selected as the opposition candidate for president in 1796, the Republicans in Congress met and attempted to reach a decision on their vice presidential selection. A Northerner, it was felt, was needed to make Jefferson's own candidacy more attractive to voters above the Mason-Dixon line. In the fall of 1795, Jefferson had been visited by Aaron Burr, United States senator from New York, but there is no evidence that any deals were struck, although the Federalists later attempted to make an issue out of it.[26] Nonetheless, the name of Burr along with the names of Pierce Butler of South Carolina, Robert Livingston of New York, and several others were considered, and, although the discussions were inconclusive, it does appear that Burr emerged as the most available candidate even though many remained suspicious of Burr, who they believed was "unsettled in his politics" and might even "go over to the other side." By fall, however, even though Burr had become the Republican choice, there were indications that a number of Republicans were having second thoughts about his candidacy much as some had had in 1792 when they backed another New Yorker, Governor George Clinton, as their candidate to oppose John Adams for the vice presidency, thus scotching Burr's bid for the post. In response, the Federalists were gleefully reporting that the Republicans would not support Burr and, in fact, would vote for "Jefferson and any other man," with the exception of Adams and his running mate, Thomas Pinckney of South Carolina.[27]

One letter written during the election campaign provides some evidence that the evaluation of Burr by some of his Republican colleagues—that he was "unsettled in his politics" and might "go over to the other side"—was a plausible one. Jonathan Dayton of New Jersey, a friend of Burr's, wrote fellow Federalist Theodore Sedgwick of Massachusetts in November suggesting a scheme whose objective was to have the Federalists throw their support to Burr for president. His argument was that, although Adams was the preferred candidate and Jefferson the least desirable, it was becoming obvious that Adams would not prevail. Therefore, Dayton asked rhetorically, "is it not desirable to have at the helm a man who is personally known to, as well as esteemed and respected by us both?" Rejecting the contention that Adams could not win, Sedgwick pointed out that Burr, even with "every vote in Massachusetts," would not have "the least chance of . . . election to either of the offices." In fact, Sedgwick believed that the New Yorker did not even have the confidence of the Republicans because "their veiws [sic] and his are . . . opposite."[28] Despite the fact that the proponent of the plan was a friend of Burr's, however, there is no proof that Burr knew of or instigated the plot.

The most dramatic intrigue of the election of 1796 was on the Federalist side and revolved around attempts to elect the supposed vice presidential choice, Thomas Pinckney, to the presidency over Adams himself. Earlier on, Hamilton and some of his colleagues had been unenthusiastic about Adams's candidacy, considering him a liability to the Federalist cause. Therefore, it was essential, they had believed, to have a strong candidate on the ticket with the independent-minded New Englander. So, in the spring of 1796, members of the Hamiltonian faction unsuccessfully sounded out Patrick Henry, Virginia Revolutionary hero, staunch Antifederalist turned Federalist. They then turned to Thomas Pinckney, the South Carolinian who had just concluded the popular Spanish treaty and would have "greater southern and western support than any other man." Hamilton immediately found the idea to his liking and wished "to be rid of P.H., that we may be at full liberty to take up Pinckney," who was now "our man."[29]

By the fall there seem to have been four distinct campaign strategies championed by various Federalists. One group held that the most important objective was the election of Adams as president and that this was worth any risks that had to be taken. A second feared that the election would be so tight that both Pinckney and Adams had to be supported equally, and any attempt to throw away votes from Pinckney to protect Adams might endanger "the whole federal interest." The fear of Jefferson winning either the presidency or the vice presidency provoked the third group into preferring Pinckney over Adams if this were what it would take to keep Jefferson out of office. Those in the fourth group simply distrusted Adams and supported Pinckney.[30] To some within this group, especially the Southern Federalists, it was not "Pinckney or Adams" but "Pinckney or Jefferson," thus indicating a sectional as well as personal animus against Adams. Robert G. Harper wrote a fellow Southern Federalist that Pinckney must be "assured" that the intention of bringing him forward was to make him president and that he will be supported with that view." Pinckney's position was an ideal one, for, although "eastern people" would not prefer him over Adams, they would "infinitely prefer him to Jefferson" while, on the other hand, Jefferson's supporters would favor Pinckney over Adams. Thus, he was virtually everyone's second choice. In a letter written the same day to Hamilton, Harper confidently predicted that Pinckney would secure "a vote from every elector in the three Southern states." Adams, Hamilton was told, stood a chance for victory if Pennsylvania goes Federalist, "but Pinckney you are sure of, if you support him North of the Delaware."[31]

Oliver Wolcott, Hamilton's successor as secretary of treasury and a person well-connected in New England Federalist circles, seems to have been unaware that there was a plot to elect Pinckney over Adams. Wolcott began to panic in the fall, however, when he saw the election going against the Federalists and urged his father, a Connecticut elector, to "support both [Pinckney and Adams] equally and leave the issue to Providence" because the "election of Mr. Jefferson, I consider as fatal to our independence." As president he would "innovate upon and fritter away the Constitution," Wolcott wrote, and as vice president he would even be more dangerous because "he would become the rallying point of faction and French influence" and, "without any responsibility, he would . . . divide, and undermine, and finally subvert the rival administration." The idea of exposing Adams's election to any risk was a painful one to Wolcott, for Adams's "long service, his talents, integrity and patriotism demand the proofs of confidence" that election to the presidency offered. Furthermore, it was "disagreeable to think of elevating a person to the Chief Magistracy who has been recently hackneyed and vulgarized as Mr. Pinckney must have been in Europe." But despite the regrets and risks, it was of "the utmost consequence to prevent the election of Mr. Jefferson as President or Vice President."[32] Later, Wolcott wrote Hamilton that, although there were "still hopes that Mr. Adams will be elected," they were slim and it was necessary that Pinckney "be supported as the next best thing which can be done. Pray write to your Eastern friends."[33]

It is doubtful that Hamilton needed Wolcott's urging, but, nonetheless, he sent off a number of letters to his New England associates exhorting them to support the two Federalist candidates equally for "there can be no doubt that the exclusion of Mr. Jefferson is far more important than any difference between Mr. Adams and Mr. Pinckney." In other words, Hamilton concluded that if the New England states gave each of the Federalist candidates equal support, Pinckney, because of his popularity in the South, would win the presidency. And if this strategy were followed, one of Hamilton's close confidants, Robert Troup, reported, "we [will] have Mr. Pinckney completely in our power."[34]

So, although Hamilton and his cohorts feared both Jefferson and Adams, the testy New Englander seemed almost as dangerous since his candidacy split the supporters of the government. Surely Troup's confident boast that Pinckney would be "completely in our power" says something about the Hamiltonian clique's fear of losing their influence if Adams, who evidently was *not* in their power, were to be elected.[35]

IV

The election of 1796 took place in the aftermath of the acrimonious debate over the Jay Treaty—not to mention the aftermath of the most violent phase of the French Revolution with its terror and anarchy, the Whiskey Rebellion, and the uproar surrounding the Democratic-Republican societies. So, it was in a highly charged atmosphere that Americans learned of Washington's plans to step down and of the possible candidates to replace him. The president's decision did, in the minds of most public men, put the federal government and the Constitution in a vulnerable position. For despite the increasing public criticism, Washington continued to symbolize national unity. No other American had his charismatic authority and certainly no one had the loyalty and trust of both Northerners and Southerners that he did. Thus, the strains of sectionalism, ever present since Independence, were bound to be aggravated by his leaving.

Some Federalists were convinced that Washington's retirement would mark a critical milestone in the nation's history. Shortly after the president's decision was made public, the ever-gloomy Fisher Ames predicted that the announcement would "serve as a signal, like dropping a hat, for the party racers to start, and I expect a great deal of noise, whipping, and spurring . . . but I hope public order will be saved."[36]

The splintering of the union into several smaller confederacies was one of Hamilton's "strongest apprehensions."[37] Thus in Washington's Farewell Address, the former secretary of treasury had stressed the importance of the "unity of government," which was "a main pillar in the edifice of your real independence, the support of your tranquillity at home, your peace abroad, of your safety, or your prosperity." Threatening this federal harmony, he had written, were sectional antagonisms inflamed by "designing men [who] may endeavor to excite a belief that there is a real difference of local interests and views" and to organize "parties by *geographical* discriminations—Northern and Southern, Atlantic and Western."[38]

To Hamilton and most of his Federalist colleagues, like Oliver Wolcott and his father, Jefferson's candidacy in 1796 was a blatantly sectional one and, if the Virginian were ever to be elected president, he would never "have the northern confidence." "Unless a radical change of opinion can be effected in the southern states," the senior Wolcott warned, "the existing [federal governmental] establishments will not last eighteen months." Opposition in Congress to the Washington administration had become so hostile, divisive, and destructive, he charged, that the "people must change their representatives, or change their government." The "hostile principles" of the supporters of Jefferson and Adams, he asserted, were as incompatible as "Light and darkness."[39]

In the election of 1796, therefore, the Federalists had little sense that they shared with the Republicans a basic commitment to the union and the Constitution. Instead, they saw their adversaries as infected with the rabid contagion of the violent French Revolution and the two proto-parties as being as different from one another, to use Wolcott's words, as "Light and darkness." The intensity of polarization as well as the high level of distrust and suspicion meant, at least as far as the Federalists were concerned, that the federal government could be successfully administered only if their opponents were prevented from assuming power.

During the fall of 1796 an incident involving Pierre Adet, Fauchet's successor as the French minister to the United States, seemed to corroborate Federalist suspicions about their opponents' loyalty. As a result of the ratification of the Jay Treaty, which the French viewed as a violation of the 1778 Alliance between France and the United States and as having poisoned relations and endangered the peace between the two countries, French leaders had become convinced that drastic steps were needed. Therefore, Adet was given permission to intervene in the approaching presidential election in an effort to produce a victory for Jefferson, who would almost certainly be more sympathetic to France. Thus, in a series of diplomatic notes sent to the Washington administration and subsequently released by Adet for publication in the opposition *Aurora*, the French minister announced France's suspension of diplomatic relations with the United States and implied that only the election of Jefferson might prevent war between the two countries.[40]

The French had been encouraged to make this dramatic move by the deluge of public criticism over the Jay Treaty and by the private and sometimes indiscreet remarks by Republican leaders. For instance, Jefferson had assured Adet a year earlier that France was not without friends in the United States. And Monroe, who was in Paris as the American minister in 1796 and was inappropriately mixing American domestic politics with his diplomatic chores, had implied in conversations with French officials that, if the Republicans were to win the presidential election, good relations would be restored between the countries.[41]

There is little evidence that Adet's interference won any votes for the Republicans.[42] On the contrary, it became the cause of acute embarrassment, and Madison deplored it as "working all the evil with which it is pregnant." Not only would Adet's scheme backfire, Madison warned, but it could create a "perpetual alienation of the two countries."[43]

The Adet notes did, however, strengthen the Federalists' conviction that the Republicans were little more than tools of the French and Jefferson an extreme and dangerous Francophile who would sacrifice his own country's interests to France's. One Federalist charged that Adet's activities on behalf of the Republicans were "sufficient proof of some defect of character which renders [Jefferson] unworthy of confidence." For no "virtuous and wise man would . . . expose his country to the dangers, and his character to the imputations which must issue from election under the unmasked interference of a foreign nation." According to Hamilton, the situation was one "as critical . . . as our government has been in."[44]

Like the Federalists, the Republicans in 1796 feared for the future of the union and the Constitution. And if Jefferson's attachment to France and democracy seemed menacing to the Federalists, Adams's known fondness for the British constitution and his pessimism about the future of republican government made him highly suspect in the eyes of the Republicans. An Adams administration, the Republicans reasoned, would continue and aggravate an already dangerous trend toward partisanship begun during Washington's presidency.

Writing in the spring of 1796 at the height of the Jay Treaty controversy to a neighbor who had returned to Europe, Jefferson spelled out his conclusions about the state of American politics and revealed a deep disappointment in Washington's behavior. American politics, he lamented, "has wonderfully changed since you left us," for in "place of that noble love of liberty, and republican government which carried us triumphantly thro' the war, an Anglican monarchical, and aristocratical party has sprung up," with the "avowed object" of emulating in substance and form "the British government." Although Jefferson saw most Americans, including "the whole landed interest" and the "mass of talents," as continuing "true to their republican principles," there were, he said, arrayed against these defenders of republicanism, "the Executive, the Judiciary, two out of three branches of the legislature, all the officers of the government, all who want to be officers, all timid men who prefer the calm of despotism to the boisterous sea of liberty, British merchants and Americans trading on British capital, speculators and holders in the banks and public funds." And in a passage that was to be later used by the Federalists against him, Jefferson expressed the strongest criticism that he is known to have made of Washington. "It would give you a fever," Jefferson wrote, obviously alluding to the president, "were I to name to you the apostates who have gone over to these heresies, men who were Samsons in the field and Solomons in the council, but who have had their heads shorn by the harlot England."[45]

This letter to Philip Mazzei, even with its hyperbole, gives an excellent insight into Jefferson's frame of mind in the months preceding the election of 1796. A familiar refrain was sounded: the Revolutionary spirit and commitment to republicanism was being corrupted and as a result, most of the institutions of government were in the hands of those who had been corrupted. However, Jefferson continued to be optimistic about the future, because "the main body of our citizens . . . remain true to their republican principles." And it was this faith in the ultimate republican soundness of the great mass of Americans that would allow Jefferson to act as a moderating influence within opposition circles during the difficult times that lay ahead.

The immediate test, however, the presidential election of 1796, was pivotal. For despite their growing disenchantment with Washington, most Republicans had faith that he did at least share their basic commitment to republicanism, the union, and the Constitution. Adams, they feared, did not, and this was to be the major issue in the campaign. As part of this the Republicans scrutinized Adams's *Defense of the Constitutions of Government of the United States of America,* published initially in 1786, and found it a "libel" on the various state constitutions and "a continued eulogium upon the British form of government."[46]

John Taylor of Caroline, who later was to enter into an extended dialogue with Adams over the nature of republican government, analyzed Adams's constitutional theories. Adams, Taylor found, preferred a constitution that balanced the "powers of the one, the *few,* and the *many*" as in the English system with its King, Lords, and Commons. This was unacceptable as far as Taylor was concerned because Adams's system, by giving certain rights and privileges to each *order* or *group* within society, "inevitably destroys" equality among citizens.[47]

In language and argument similar to Taylor's, "Sidney" in the *General Advertiser* accused Adams of desiring "different stations filled with men of different orders or ranks, of different qualifications, not of wisdom and virtue; but of birth and riches." Thus, it was alleged that Adams believed that a properly balanced government had to have the

power divided and "in the hands of different *orders* of men with different *prerogatives* and *privileges*."[48]

Adams's basic pessimism about the future of republican government also troubled Republican critics. Insisting that the vice and corruption in Europe prevented and would prevent the successful and
continuous functioning of a republican type of government there,
Adams had also concluded that republicanism would only last in the
United States while the country was relatively young. As the country
aged, Adams insisted, governmental institutions of the United States
would be forced to change dramatically for "no government could
long exist," or "no people could be happy, without an hereditary first
magistrate, and an hereditary senate, or a senate for life."[49] How could
a man with so many doubts about the very nature of republicanism,
his critics reasoned, be expected to fulfill his duties and to exercise his
power within the restraints of a frame of government that he felt was
so flawed?

V

It was not until the end of December that the results of the election
in the Electoral College were known and it could be announced that
Adams had been elected president with 71 electoral votes and Jefferson vice president with 68. The distribution of the candidates' support
vividly demonstrates their appeal to different sections of the country.
Jefferson did not receive a single electoral vote north of Pennsylvania,
the area in which Adams collected two-thirds of his total. In addition
to New England, Adams won New York, New Jersey, and Delaware
and a scattering of votes in Pennsylvania, Maryland, Virginia, and
North Carolina. Jefferson won the unanimous support of South Carolina, Georgia, Kentucky, and Tennessee plus 11 of 12 votes in North
Carolina, 20 out of 21 in Virginia, 14 out of 15 in Pennsylvania and 4
out of 10 in Maryland. Pinckney ran third with 59 votes. And despite
Hamilton's efforts to get Adams's supporters in New England to give
Pinckney equal support, the South Carolinian received only 21 out of
the 39 possible votes in that section. Burr ran a poor fourth with 30
electoral votes. Significantly, Jefferson's home state of Virginia, in a
display of distrust and suspicion that deeply offended and antago-
nized Burr, only gave the New Yorker one out of a possible 21 votes,
with the remainder scattered for a mixture of reasons among Pinckney,
Sam Adams, George Clinton, and Washington.[50]

The public response to the election of 1796 was as diverse as the union itself. In only half of the sixteen states—New Hampshire, Massachusetts, Pennsylvania, Maryland, Virginia, North Carolina, Georgia, and Kentucky—did the voters directly choose presidential electors either by general ticket statewide or by district within the state. And while public interest in the presidential contest was relatively high in these states, it was markedly less so in states where the electors were appointed by the legislatures.[51]

There was little contest in New England, it being Adams's home region. Jefferson's strong identification with Virginia and the South made it difficult for the Republicans to make an impact there. With the exception of Boston, the two proto-parties exhibited little evidence of the organizing associated with races elsewhere. For example, rather than two partisan candidates contending against one another for an office, there were large numbers of office seekers with few or no partisan distinctions among them. In New Hampshire twenty-six candidates contended for four seats in Congress, while in one Massachusetts district fourteen candidates vied for a single position. The Massachusetts political organizations, one historian has noted, were "particularly unstable," being only "loose collections of provincial interests . . . [that were] [h]ighly local, evolving from rivalries within the towns and cities, counties, and states."[52]

The Southern states showed almost the same kind of political solidarity for Jefferson. In addition to receiving the brunt of the sectional hostility to Adams and his Yankee background, the Southern Federalists suffered from being associated in the popular mind with the Jay Treaty and with the 1795 Yazoo land frauds in the Georgia legislature through which thirty-five million acres of land in the Yazoo River country of Alabama and Mississippi had been sold for a paltry $500,000 to several land companies that were closely connected to several Federalist legislators. The Republicans saw the land bonanza as a Federalist-inspired, unethical, get-rich-quick scheme for the benefit of a few investors at the expense of the general population. In Virginia, apparently, Adams was so unpopular that the Federalists' candidates for presidential electors did not even "dare to mention him by name."[53] And despite some promising organizational gains the Federalists had made earlier in the Old Dominion, one historian claims that after the election of 1796 they were either "disbanded or dormant."[54]

In the Middle Atlantic states, there was greater competition between the two proto-parties and more evidence of political organizing. Party tickets made their appearance in several states, but in Pennsylvania they were the most extensive and effective. John Beckley, clerk of the United States House of Representatives and an ardent Republican, masterminded the efforts of the Pennsylvania Jeffersonians to organize a ticket of electors and to politicize the electorate. In late October, up to eight thousand electoral tickets or handbills listing the Republican electors were sent from Philadelphia to all sections of the state. And in a remarkable display of straight ticket voting, the fifteen Republicans each won by approximately 650 votes in the city of Philadelphia and by about 1,430 votes in the county. The Federalists, who organized their own slate of fifteen electors, enjoyed the same kind of solidarity in Chester County.

Despite this level of activity, however, it was the state contests that evoked the most public interest. Turnout for the 1796 presidential election in Pennsylvania was only about 75 percent of the turnout for gubernatorial elections in the state from 1790 to 1796. This disparity of turnout between the presidential and gubernatorial elections is even more remarkable when it is considered that Thomas Mifflin ran virtually unopposed for governor in 1796 and the election drew almost 32,000 voters to the polls, in sharp contrast to the 24,487 voters Jefferson and Adams attracted.[55]

In New York, the Antifederalists had provided the organizational antecedent for the Republicans. And by 1797, as one historian notes, "there clearly was a Democratic-Republican movement in New York State which embraced not only the Republican party but the Republican societies and the Republican press as well." Unlike elsewhere, the Democratic-Republican societies had survived and flourished in New York City, and they had become particularly adept at "perfecting the techniques of direct democratic expression: the 'town meeting,' the patriotic parades and celebrations, the circulation of public petitions." Relying on newspapers, broadsides and pamphlets, campaigners had drawn "more and more people . . . [into] the political process: in making nominations, in campaigning, and in voting." Even so, seekers of political office often refused to identify themselves with political affiliations. And the gubernatorial elections were the least partisan. In 1795, for example, Chancellor Livingston and Burr attempted to get the nomination for governor from both Republican and Federalist "interests."[56]

But what does this activity across the country indicate about the development of political parties in the new nation? Most historians have argued that by the election of 1796 two national political parties had been established.[57] William Nisbet Chambers, among others, maintains that the "stability and close rivalry that Federalists and Republicans had finally achieved by the time of the election of 1796 revealed how far they had moved to establish themselves as national political parties, well ahead of modern parties in England or any European nation." The election, he contends, marked a kind of maturity as it was "the first full opportunity for the electorate in the new American republic to choose between two established, competing parties and their nominees."[58]

Noble Cunningham agrees and concludes that the election marked a milestone in the development of modern political parties. "The election of 1796," he argues, "was clearly a contest between Republicans and Federalists, and as each party sought to give victory to its candidate, party lines tightened, party spirit rose to new heights, and political parties became a more ineradicable part of American political life than ever before."[59] Robert Kelley, in a more recent study and in a similar vein, concludes that the "Jeffersonian Republican party took form in the mid-1790s and inaugurated a two-party rivalry which was not to subside until the 1820s."[60]

Yet, how valid is this interpretation that emphasizes the formation as early as 1796 of a national two-party system that "instituted an orderly means of settling differences without resorting to violence," as Paul Goodman argues?[61] Certainly there were some crude indicators that something similar to a national two-party system had developed in 1796. The electioneering, the organizing, the making of tickets, and the tendency to divide the electorate, at least in some states, between Republicans and Federalists all seem to bolster that conclusion.

Nonetheless, this is a conception and ordering of the events that would not have been recognized by the participants themselves, including one observer, who no doubt represented the views of the many Americans who saw the partisanship as an aberration. In a pamphlet he condemned the mode of the 1796 election as "very objectionable, and, if continued, seems in its tendency, not only calculated to foment and keep up heats and animosities amongst us, but in no long time . . . to overset our union, or split and shiver us into many different governments." By splitting "itself into two parties, through *predilection* for two citizens [Adams and Jefferson]," the United States had seemed to be "countennancing [sic] parties," and, by declaring whom they would vote for, the electors had violated the "*spirit and vitals* of the constitution." If the Founders' intention to use the Electoral College to nominate candidates for the House of Representatives' final selection had been followed, the pamphleteer declared, "sixteen candidates" instead of two would have been put forward. And a multi-candidate election would have helped curtail the "prevailing spirit of jealousy and party."[62]

In truth, the Federalist-Republican division was primarily a manifestation of sectional strife. And although both Federalists and Republicans had firmly held, though badly distorted, images of one another, it would be a mistake to view the election as a contest pitting two national political parties against one another. As Stephen G. Kurtz argues, "eighteenth-century political life was still predominantly local in both outlook and operation."[63] Sectional suspicion had imperiled the success of the Revolution, the work of the Confederation, and the ratification of the Constitution. Now it plagued the new nation under the Constitution.

And although the protagonists all professed to be *republicans*, their understanding of *republicanism* differed, reflecting the various sectional political cultures. The core of Federalism was centered around the moralistic republicanism of New England, which contrasted sharply with the libertarian republicanism of the Virginia Republicans, who rejected any call for government to regulate moral values.[64] Moreover, these sectional and cultural distinctions were amplified and underscored by a less clearly defined, but nonetheless important, commercial-agrarian division that had some relationship to the sectional division. The agrarian-minded Republicans based in the rural South were highly suspicious of strong government and commercial banking, while the more commercial-minded Federalists, centered in the more urban North, looked to a strong government to promote their economic and social objectives.[65]

As early as 1794 at least some New Englanders had been talking about their section's incompatibility with the South and suggesting that a peaceful breakup of the union should be discussed. In 1796 the question was also raised. For instance, "Pelham" questioned in the *Connecticut Courant* whether or not New England should leave the union to prevent being corrupted by French influence and whether or not "we have not already approached the era when . . . [the union] must be divided." The "moral and political habits of the citizens of the Southern states," he concluded, virtually guaranteed that the union would be of short duration.[66]

Few Southerners, at least by 1796, were discussing secession. But it is clear from their opposition to Adams that, while part of their suspicion of him was personal, another part was born of an almost irreconcilable Southern hostility to New England. Jefferson's use of the term *Southern* in a letter to Madison to characterize the Republican interest indicates that he viewed the political struggle between "Federalists" and "Republicans" as being primarily sectionally grounded.[67] Washington as a Southerner and national hero had commanded the respect of people in all sections and had transcended, for the most part, any sectional identity. John Adams, the second president of the United States, would have to prove to a suspicious South that he could rise above a parochial attachment to section.

VI

Despite the predictions of gloom and disaster by the Republicans and Federalists alike, the election results did not threaten the political order of the country. On the contrary, the choice of Jefferson and Adams to serve together in a national administration and the splitting of the Federalist ranks over the Hamiltonians' efforts to swing the election to Pinckney operated to bring the warring forces together. Thus, paradoxically, the election appears to have acted as a healing balm, at least temporarily, upon the most acute symptoms of political polarization. For the Republicans this meant that Adams and his supporters grew to be seen as a moderate bulwark against the more dangerous policies of Federalist extremists. And the Republicans' resulting conciliatory gestures, coupled with Adams's fury over the betrayal of the schemers in his own party, led him to be receptive to a more harmonious relationship with his erstwhile opponents.

Adams was an extremely proud man, and Hamilton's scheme to elect Pinckney—whom Adams referred to as "such an unknown being"—to the presidency had deeply embittered him.[68] "There have been maneuvers and combinations in this election that would surprise you," Adams wrote his wife. In the same letter he disparagingly alluded to Hamilton by maintaining that "There is an active spirit in the Union, who will fill it with his politics wherever he is," and he "must be attended to, and not suffered to do too much."[69] Hamilton himself was told by a correspondent that the "blind or devoted partisans of Mr. Adams, instead of being satisfied with his being elected, seem to be alarmed at the danger he was in of failing." And this danger, the writer said, was blamed on Hamilton's attempt to bring in the more pliable Pinckney over the more independent Adams. The Adams adherents had concluded, the correspondent related, that it was in the best "interest of the Country to have Mr. Jefferson for vice president rather than Pinckney" as Jefferson would "serve readily under Mr. Adams, and will be influenced by and coincide with him."[70]

Thus, during the election of 1796, the seeds of discord were being sown that would bear bitter fruit four years later as the split between the Hamilton and Adams factions would virtually destroy any hope that the Federalists might have had of perpetuating their hegemony in American politics.

In the short run, however, the rupture within the Federalist ranks seems to have been the most important force in bringing Republicans and the Adams Federalists together, at least temporarily. For, at the end of 1796 and in the beginning of 1797, there was a perceptible, although mutually suspicious, movement of both the Adams and Republican forces in the direction of forming an alliance and thus breaking down proto-party distinctions. This effort at cooperation was more in keeping with the Founders' expectations of national nonpartisanship as articulated in the *Federalist Papers*. And while this goal continued to be an elusive one, it remained the aspiration of the public men in the early republic.[71]

Adams appears to have been pleased by the remarks of William Branch Giles, a Virginia Republican, which he quoted in a letter to Abigail: "Giles says, 'the point is settled. The V.P. will be President. He is undoubtedly chosen. The old man will make a good President too. . . . But we shall have to *check* him a little now and then. That will be all.'" In explaining the Republican change in attitude to his wife, Adams concluded that the "southern gentlemen" probably preferred him over Pinckney "because Hamilton and Jay are said to be for Pinckney."[72]

Elbridge Gerry, a close Massachusetts friend of Adams, saw the possibility that an Adams-Jefferson administration might unite the country. In a letter to Adams, he expressed the hope that Adams would be as fortunate in his vice president as Washington had been in his, and should Jefferson "adopt a similar line of conduct toward you, it will ensure to him the Chair" when it was relinquished.[73]

Despite a furor caused in 1791 when Jefferson had inadvertently criticized the New Englander publicly, Adams himself was optimistic about the future of their relationship, for the two had labored "together in high friendship" since the Continental Congress in 1776.[74] Relying on Jefferson's "ancient friendship, his good sense and general good disposition," Adams said he expected his vice president would maintain at least a decorum of conduct toward him, "if not as cordial and uniform a support" as he had given to Washington, "which is and shall be, the pride and boast of my life."[75]

Other Federalists reported on the mood of harmony. "The democrats are besetting Mr. Adams with attention," Chauncey Goodrich wrote. "Since his election has become ascertained, the scurrility in Bache's paper has ceased, and it is said the democrats are recommending to him conciliation of parties."[76]

Even Hamilton, although skeptical, remarked on the equanimity. In writing to Rufus King, he observed sarcastically, "Our Jacobins say they are well pleased and that the *Lion* and the *Lamb* are to lie down together." They have concluded that Jefferson "is not half so ill a man as we have been accustommed [*sic*] to think him." As a result of this new found (and ill-founded in Hamilton's eyes) confidence in Jefferson, the Adams supporters, Hamilton wrote, were predicting "a united and a vigorous administration."[77]

The Federalists were correct in their assessment of the conciliatory Republican frame of mind. Even before the results of the balloting were known, Madison warned Jefferson that the House of Representatives might be called upon to decide the election. If the contest went to the House, Jefferson responded, it would be his "duty and inclination . . . to relieve the embarrassment." He, therefore, authorized Madison "to solicit on my behalf that Mr. Adams may be preferred" since he had always been Jefferson's "senior, from the commencement of my public life, and the expression of the public will being equal, this circumstance ought to give him the preference."[78]

Madison, knowing that Jefferson had been a reluctant candidate from the first and fearing that his friend might now balk at serving as vice president, wrote Jefferson that he understood the objections that might be raised to his assuming the vice presidency, among them "the irksomeness of being at the head of a body whose sentiments are at present so little in unison with your own." But, Madison argued, it would be "essential" for Jefferson to accept the post for he might "have a valuable effect" on the foreign policy of the Adams administration. Furthermore, it was "certain that . . . [Adams's] censures of our paper system and the intrigues at New York for setting P [Pinckney] above him, have fixed an enmity with the British faction," and, therefore, would set the stage for greater cooperation between the president and his vice president. On a more personal level, Madison felt that Adams would be gratified by Jefferson's acceptance of a subordinate role.[79]

Jefferson responded that he had no objections to being in "a secondary position to Mr. Adams" and that the only reason that he had allowed his name to stand for the presidency in the first place "was to put our vessel on her republican tack before she should be thrown too much to leeward of her true principles." The next four years would be critical ones, he said, and perhaps Adams could "be induced to administer the government on its true principles and to relinquish his bias to an English constitution." Above all, Jefferson cautioned Madison, Adams was "the only sure barrier against Hamilton's getting in."[80]

The expectations of a new national accord under an Adams-Jefferson administration were not confined to private correspondence. The Philadelphia *General Advertiser,* the chief Republican organ, which had unmercifully condemned Adams during the fall of 1796, was eloquently optimistic. Adams was compared to Washington, and it was predicted that the new president would be successful where the old had not been in soothing "the irritated public mind" and harmonizing "the different parties" because "ADAMS and JEFFERSON, lately rivals, and competitors for the most distinguished station which a free people can confer, appear in the amiable light of friends. . . . Surely this harmony presages the most happy consequences to our country." The installation of the new administration, then, was perceived as signaling an abatement of "THE VIOLENCE OF PARTY" with "the air of our political hemisphere . . . not so keen and piercing as formerly."[81]

Shortly after the Adams administration took over, the South Carolina Federalist William Smith, deeply impressed by the atmosphere of goodwill, related to Rufus King that the "change of the Executive here has been wrought with a facility and a calm which has astonished even those of us who always augured well of the government and the general good sense of our citizens. The machine has worked without a creak."[82]

Thus, in the winter and early spring, 1796–97, there was a definite, although temporary, ebb in the proto-party passion that had been whipped to a fever pitch a year earlier by the Jay Treaty controversy and sustained in intensity through the election of 1796. Although there had been and continued to be a perception of wide political differences among the public men, moderates on both sides felt a profound sense of relief in late 1796—the raging party spirit that had threatened to destroy the country had apparently been dampened, and the main threat to the country's stability, the Hamiltonian Federalists, had been discredited and isolated. The new administration of Adams and Jefferson held great promise. It was a partnership, many Americans felt, that had been formed during the American Revolution and held the prospect that politics might be restored to that pre-proto-party level where selflessness, harmony, and common purpose would, as had been envisioned by the Founders, dictate the actions of men of affairs.

8.

The War Crisis and the Alien and Sedition Acts

This [Sedition Bill] and its supporters suppose that whoever dislikes the measures of the Administration and of a temporary majority in congress, and shall, either by speaking or writing, express his disapprobation and his want of confidence in men now in power, is seditious, is an enemy, not of Administration, but of the Constitution, and is liable to punishment.
—ALBERT GALLATIN

The apparent harmony and spirit of reconciliation that marked the period following the 1796 presidential election were short lived. Almost immediately after his inaugural, Adams was plunged into a diplomatic crisis and quasi-naval war with France that lasted virtually his entire term of office and dashed the hopes that an Adams-Jefferson administration would rise above partisanship and provide a high-minded, selfless government of gentlemen as the Founders had intended. The Republicans found themselves on the defensive as they struggled to legitimize their criticism of Adams's handling of the emergency at a time of trial for the new nation. Although sympathetic to France in its great war with Britain, the Republican leadership condemned both English and French depredations on American shipping and called for a policy of strict neutrality in the war between the European powers. In the final analysis, however, they feared that Britain posed a greater threat to America's independence than France, and that Adams's policy, if not checked, might lead to war with the country's old ally and a virtual alliance between the United States and its former mother country.[1]

The public hysteria and anger accompanying the diplomatic and naval crisis with France raised proto-party passions to new heights and put the Republicans at peril, threatening, in fact, their very existence. Their failure in the congressional elections of 1796 to hang on to the slight majority that they had held earlier in the House of Representatives,[2] coupled with the Federalists' control of the executive and judiciary, increasingly frustrated the leaders of the opposition in their efforts to shape and influence federal policy and, perhaps more important, to prevent the Federalists from passing the repressive Alien and Sedition Laws and measures to strengthen the country militarily.

The crisis began within a month after Adams took office with the shocking news that the French Directory had insultingly refused to receive Thomas Pinckney's brother, Charles Cotesworth Pinckney, the American envoy who had been sent to Paris by Washington to replace James Monroe. And in March, to make matters worse, the Directory decreed—in direct violation of the Franco-American commercial treaty of 1778—that France would no longer adhere to the principle that free ships made free goods and, henceforth, would consider all neutral vessels carrying British goods as liable for seizure. In addition, it was declared that any Americans captured while serving on enemy ships would be dealt with as pirates.[3]

The crisis with France was not a total surprise for it had been building since the fall of 1796 when Adet had expressed France's ire over the Jay Treaty. Only the timing, extent, and exact nature of France's reaction had been unknown. Thus, even before the news of Pinckney's rejection reached the United States, rumors and plans had been afloat about sending a special new American diplomatic mission to France to iron out the differences between the two countries.

In fact, Adams had already concluded that for domestic political reasons, as well as for making any new mission acceptable to the French, new diplomatic initiatives should include Republicans and be representative of all sections of the United States. At the time of the inauguration the new president had told Jefferson that he wished the Virginian were free to accept a mission to France but supposed that his constitutional duties as vice president would not allow him to undertake such an assignment. Therefore, Adams had said, it was his intention to nominate his close friend, Elbridge Gerry (later Republican governor of Massachusetts) and Madison to join Pinckney in Europe. And the president had asked Jefferson to sound out Madison concerning his availability.[4]

A number of prominent Federalists had come to the same conclusion as Adams, including Henry Knox, the former secretary of war, and Hamilton. It was Hamilton's view that the addition of one of the well-known Republicans would undermine their criticism of Federalist foreign policy and "disarm them of the Argument that all has not been done which might have been done towards preserving peace."[5]

Adams's inherited cabinet, however, was unsympathetic to a new mission to France and adamantly opposed to Madison's being selected for it. Oliver Wolcott, Jr., the secretary of treasury, warned the president of the cabinet's disapproval and cautioned him that, if he persisted in his plan to send Madison, "we are willing to resign."[6] Wolcott, a disciple of Hamilton's who always kept his predecessor thoroughly briefed about the inside deliberations of the Adams administration, disagreed with his mentor only reluctantly. But Madison's appointment, Wolcott argued in a letter to his predecessor, "would deliver the country, bound hand and foot, to French influence."[7]

The cabinet's opposition apparently carried the day, and at the end of May 1797, Adams nominated Pinckney and two Federalists, Francis Dana of Massachusetts and John Marshall of Virginia, as envoys. Dana refused the nomination on account of ill health in his family, and Elbridge Gerry, whose name had earlier been rejected by the cabinet, was nominated. The Senate confirmed the three men in June.[8]

Although it was not known in Federalist circles at the time, the debate over Madison's candidacy for the peace commission, was wasted effort because Madison had no interest in the post.[9] Nonetheless, as it was to turn out, the rejection of Madison for the appointment was significant even so—because it signaled the virtual end of cooperation between Adams and Jefferson and pointed up the rather substantial barriers to a bipartisan administration of national unity headed by the two leaders.

Looking back, Jefferson saw the discussions over the French mission as a turning point in his relationship with Adams; he particularly recalled one conversation with Adams following a dinner hosted by Washington. Walking home with the newly elected president, Jefferson had told him of Madison's refusal. As Jefferson recalled later, Adams replied "that, on consultation, some objections to that nomination had been raised which he had not contemplated; and was going on with excuses which evidently embarrassed him, when we came to Fifth street, where our road separated." After that, Jefferson said, Adams had never mentioned the subject again "or ever consulted me as to any measures of government." The Virginian concluded from Adams's behavior that, while initially the president had "forgot party sentiment" and had intended "to steer impartially between the parties," the cabinet had diverted him from this course and he had "returned to his former party views."[10]

Jefferson's version of the events was confirmed by Adams, who years later recalled that following the initial discussion of a Madison mission Jefferson and he had "parted as good friends as we had always lived; but we consulted very little afterwards." This was due, he said, to the "Party violence" which "soon rendered . . . [cooperation between the two] impracticable, or at least useless, and this party violence was excited by Hamilton more than any other man."[11]

What is not known, however, is just how much Jefferson had wanted to be or expected to be consulted or how much Adams had ever planned to consult him. In the early days of the republic there were few if any precedents, and it was not clear just what the vice president's role should be. During the Washington administration, Adams himself had played an insignificant part in the formation of policy, only participating in cabinet discussions two or three times during the two terms.[12] And Jefferson, soon after taking up his new office, decided that his constitutional duties as the presiding officer of the Senate made him a member of the legislature and that he was thus prevented from taking a role in the executive branch.[13] Nonetheless, above and beyond the constitutional scruples Jefferson might have had against participating as a member of the Adams administration, it is doubtful whether Adams or his Federalist colleagues would ever have accepted Jefferson as a working partner. The party rancor was too deep and divisive.

Of course, the estrangement between Adams and his vice president was not an unhappy development for the Hamiltonian wing of the Federalists, who, already uneasy about an Adams presidency, had become even more alarmed over the prospect of a partnership between Adams and Jefferson.[14] In fact, Jefferson sensed that the Federalists had been working toward such a goal. In a letter to Gerry, Jefferson acknowledged that he knew that efforts would be made to produce a schism between himself and the president and that these "machinations will proceed from the Hamiltons by whom he is surrounded, and who are only a little less hostile to him than to me."[15]

These Federalists had little confidence in Adams's abilities and were deeply pessimistic about the future of the republic. One expressed grave misgivings about an Adams's presidency claiming that he had always considered "Mr. Adams a man of great vanity . . . capricious, of a very moderate share of prudence, and of far less real abilities than he believes he possesses." And because of the lack of leadership, he gloomily forecast a civil war: "We shall divide under the names of Federalist and Democrat, and war as we did under those of Whig and Tory, with the same acrimony."[16]

Another Federalist predicted the breakup of the union because the sections were "so different in manners, in opinion, and in activity and exertion." The Northern states were clearly superior and had for "a number of years . . . [carried] the Southern on their backs." Disunion, however, was not the worst alternative, for he feared that American states or sections would once again become attached to European powers. If the choice was between dissolving the union or becoming colonies of France, then he was "for a Separation." But if states or sections were forced to become colonies and "we are, in the Northern States, to be Colonies to France or England, I choose the latter."[17]

II

In addition to laying plans for sending a new commission to France, Adams called for a special meeting of Congress to deal with the crisis brought on by France's haughty behavior to Pinckney. In his speech to the session, which was convened in May of 1797, the president condemned France's violation of the long accepted "right" of nations to exchange ministers and their refusal to receive Pinckney until the United States had "acceded to their demands without discussion." France's action, Adams charged, treated the United States neither as an ally, friend, or sovereign state. Therefore, "France and the world" had to be convinced "that we are not a degraded people, humiliated under a colonial spirit of fear and sense of inferiority, fitted to be the miserable instruments of foreign influence." In addition to urging new efforts at negotiation, the president outlined plans to strengthen the nation's defense. He called for the "establishment of a permanent system of naval defense" and for Congress to consider strengthening "the regular artillery and cavalry" and to form "a provisional army."[18]

Apparently having little confidence that Adams would take the strong steps necessary to meet the French threat, Hamilton busied himself preparing a long memorandum on what course of action the government ought to take. And in June, William Loughton Smith, South Carolina congressman and a close ally of Hamilton's, introduced into the House of Representatives a series of resolutions that closely followed Hamilton's suggestions. Among other things, the resolutions called for levying new taxes, improving fortifications at ports and harbors, completing three frigates that had been authorized earlier, increasing the size of the naval force, and raising a Provisional Army.[19]

After a great deal of discussion and strenuous opposition from the Republicans, Congress did pass some watered-down defense measures, authorizing an increase in the size of the navy, the improvement of harbor fortifications, and the equipping of an eighty-thousand-man militia force. Taxes were not immediately raised, although a tax on salt and stamps was to be levied later and the borrowing of $800,000 was authorized.[20]

The Republicans were aghast at what they saw as the militaristic character of the president's speech and the Federalists' behavior in Congress. Adams and the Federalists, they were convinced, were dom-

inated by warhawks who had deliberately overblown the seriousness of
the crisis to pave the way for war with France. Virginian William Branch
Giles, Republican leader in the House, confessed that he had been
mistaken in his earlier belief that Adams was worthy of confidence,
and Madison was told by a dismayed correspondent that all his apprehensions had been "verified by the President's warlike speech."[21]

Jefferson believed that the calling of Congress had been an "experiment of the new administration to see how far and on what lines"
Adams "could count" on support. Adams, he was certain, had been
advised to pursue a policy that would lead to war, but, seeing that
sentiment in Congress would not support more extreme measures, he
and his advisers had backed off, at least for the time being. But Jefferson was still worried about the anti-French uproar, and even Adams's
decision to send new envoys to France did not persuade the vice president that the administration was bent upon a policy of peace.[22]

The president's speech and the debates in Congress, not to mention the pressures of the foreign crisis itself, so intensified political
antagonisms that by late June Jefferson reported that "passions are too
high at present, to be cooled in our day." In the past, he said, when
differences were sharply drawn, "gentlemen of different politics would
then speak to each other, and separate the business of the Senate from
that of society." But, he went on, "it is not so now," and "men who have
been intimate all their lives, cross the streets to avoid meeting, and turn
their heads another way, lest they should be obliged to touch their hats."[23]

While the Republicans felt that they had prevented Adams and the
Federalists from taking more drastic action during the congressional
session, they recognized that it was of vital importance that they now
gird themselves for future trials and lay the groundwork for an effective strategy of opposition.

It was with this in mind that Jefferson in June of 1797 renewed
contact with his former running mate, Aaron Burr, who was still sting-
ing from the lack of support the Virginia Republicans had given him
the previous year. Jefferson wrote Burr that he was convinced that the
president's intention in the spring had been war and that the calling of
the special session had been "an experiment on the temper of the
nation to see if it was in union." Furthermore Jefferson related, the
promise of negotiation did not impress him, given the temper and
mood of the Adams administration.

Jefferson had hoped, he told Burr, that when Washington retired
"the natural feeling of the people towards liberty would restore the
equilibrium between the Executive and Legislative departments, which

had been destroyed by the superior weight and effect" of the first president's popular appeal. Unfortunately, Jefferson asserted, the crisis with France had produced "an effect which supplies that of the Washington popularity." Thus Jefferson saw the country as at a critical point where its "future character" and "future fortune" were in the balance, particularly "if war is made on us by France" and if Louisiana were to become a French colony. What especially concerned Jefferson was that what he viewed as the contrived anti-French hysteria would "at length effect what force could not, and . . . we shall, in the end, be driven back to the land from which we launched 20 years ago."[24]

Sectionalism, as Jefferson saw it, was at the heart of the political confrontation. When, he asked, would the people of the Eastern states, "who are unquestionably republicans," discover that "they have been duped into the support of [war preparation] measures calculated to sap the very foundations of republicanism." But, more important, can "the middle, Southern and Western states hold on till they awake?"[25]

Burr was receptive to Jefferson's call to buckle on the armor, replying that the "moment requires free communication among those who adhere to the principles of our revolution." And in light of the gravity of the situation, Burr called for a private meeting with his former running mate within the week.[26] To this end a meeting was held in Philadelphia between Monroe, who had recently returned from France, and Burr, Gallatin, and Jefferson.[27]

III

In the summer of 1797 Jefferson was also involved in preparing a defense against an action by the federal judiciary that seemed ominous to the Republicans. In the spring a federal grand jury in Richmond had served a presentment to Samuel J. Cabell, the Republican representative from Jefferson's section of Virginia. Foreshadowing the Federalist congressional attack against the opposition the following summer with the Sedition Law, the presentment had charged that Cabell in his circular letters to constituents attacking the Adams administration had "at a time of real public danger" disseminated "unfounded calumnies against the happy government of the United States." The purpose of Cabell's letters, it had been charged, had been "to separate the people . . . [from the federal government] and to increase or produce a foreign influence, ruinous to the peace, happiness, and independence of these United States."[28]

The presentment alarmed Jefferson, who saw it as an attempt to use the Federalist-controlled federal courts to intimidate the opposition and stifle their criticism of the government. And in response to this threat, Jefferson began to develop a strategy of *state* interposition to protect certain inherent rights and to thwart *federal* usurpation. A risky strategy of opposition that flirted with disunion and possible civil war, it would be at the core of the Kentucky and Virginia resolutions the following year.

In discussing with Madison and Monroe his plan to submit to the Virginia legislature a petition urging the impeachment of the grand jurors involved in the Cabell presentment, Jefferson dismissed Monroe's suggestion that the proper appeal would be to Congress rather than to the Virginia legislature. He asserted that that would only increase the dominance of the federal government, which Jefferson referred to as a "foreign jurisdiction." It was a time when the "system of the General government" was becoming too powerful through its efforts to "seize all doubtful ground," and it was, Monroe was told, "of immense consequence that the States retain as complete authority as possible over their own citizens."[29]

Therefore, in an effort to attack and to expose the explicit and implicit dangers of the grand jury's action, Jefferson submitted an anonymous petition to the Virginia House of Delegates, where a resolution was passed affirming its essential principles but not recommending any action.[30] Arguing that the grand jury's action violated the people's right to be represented by legislators "free from the cognizance or coercion of the co-ordinate branches, Judiciary and Executive," Jefferson's petition called for the impeachment of the grand jurors, who had endangered the "safety of the State" and the constitutional rights of its citizens. For the judiciary to impose itself this way between the representative and his constituents, the petition argued, meant that any communication between the two could henceforth be inhibited by the judicial officials and "the representative [put] into jeopardy of criminal prosecution . . . if his communications, public or private, do not exactly square with their ideas of fact or right, or with their designs of wrong." This would, in effect, Jefferson's petition charged, subjugate the legislative branch to the judiciary and, thus, unconstitutionally aggrandize the power of the federal judiciary, whose jurisdiction was expressly limited by the Constitution.[31]

Although the case against Cabell was never brought to trial, the episode illustrates how far relations between the Federalists and Republicans had deteriorated by the summer of 1797. The same forces, the opposition felt, that had united to pass the Jay Treaty continued to dominate the federal government, and, as long as the threat of war with France remained, they would continue in control. As is shown by the Cabell petition, Jefferson was beginning to view the *states* as a last bastion of defense against powerful Federalist adversaries who he believed to be subverting the Constitution and marshaling the resources of the federal government to destroy opposition. His reference to the federal government as a "foreign jurisdiction" well indicates just how alarmed he had become.

IV

The future course of politics in the United States was highly dependent upon the outcome of the negotiations by the three American commissioners who had been appointed to go to France. French seizures of American neutral shipping were continuing, and a full-scale war between France and the United States hung in the balance. By October 1797, Napoleon's victories had made France the unquestioned master of Western Europe, and it seemed only a matter of time before England would be invaded by her neighbor across the channel. Thus, France was in an exceedingly strong bargaining position.

As a result Marshall, Pinckney, and Gerry found when they arrived in October 1797 that the French were not only hostile, but contemptuous. Napoleon's conquests, the Jay Treaty (which was interpreted as a betrayal of the Franco-American Alliance of 1778), and what was considered an unduly antagonistic speech by President Adams in May 1797 had all put the French Directory in an unconciliatory mood. Talleyrand, the minister of foreign relations, refused even to deal with the American envoys officially. Instead, most of the talks were conducted between the Americans and four unofficial French representatives, later dubbed W, X, Y, and Z by President Adams. After demanding an apology for the purported insulting portions of Adams's speech, Talleyrand's agents also attempted to extort from the United States a loan to France and a bribe of approximately $250,000 for French officials. And, if these demands were not met, it was strongly intimated, war between the two countries would be the result.

Marshall and Pinckney took the position that little could be gained from these unofficial, and in their eyes unacceptable, discussions, while Gerry urged that the talks be continued. The envoys did remain in Paris but with little result. Talleyrand exploited the differences between Gerry and his two Federalist colleagues, and soon the three Americans were scarcely on speaking terms. Threatened with expulsion from France in the early spring of 1798, Marshall and Pinckney asked for their passports and returned to the United States. Gerry, however, stayed in France in an effort to break the deadlock in the negotiations, but he also failed to reach an accommodation with the French. When he finally returned to the United States in the fall, he was excoriated by the Federalists for what they considered almost treasonable behavior.[32]

Although the commissioners' early dispatches recounting the insults of the French and the frustrations of their mission did not reach the United States until March 4, 1798, few Americans had been optimistic about the chances for reconciliation between the two countries from the start. Anticipating the worst, President Adams in January asked his department heads about contingency plans. In the event of a diplomatic breakdown, the president asked, should he recommend to Congress an immediate declaration of war? What policy should the United States pursue with other European countries, particularly Great Britain? Would it be prudent "to connect ourselves with Britain," even though it might "impede us in embracing the first favorable moment or opportunity to make a separate peace?" Becoming an ally of Great Britain further concerned Adams in light of the internal political unrest there and what he saw as Britain's vulnerability to social revolution, which might, in time, lead to the establishment of "a wild democracy," which might, in turn, revive and extend "that delirium in America."[33]

Albert Gallatin, the Pennsylvania Republican, reported to his wife from Congress long before the XYZ dispatches reached the United States that "our situation grows critical," and it would "require great firmness to prevent this Country being involved in a war." Even though members of the opposition would be "branded with the usual epithets of Jacobins and tools of foreign influence," he wrote, they must have "fortitude enough to despise the calumnies of the war faction and to do our duty notwithstanding the spirit of our administration and by the haughtiness of France."[34]

When the discouraging news from the peace mission arrived in early March, it was not greeted with uniform dismay. Some Federalists saw political advantage in the diplomatic stalemate. Senator Theodore Sedgwick from Massachusetts rejoiced that "it will afford a glorious opportunity to destroy faction." And, after Pickering leaked the dispatches detailing the XYZ affair to Hamilton, the former secretary of treasury told the secretary of state that he was "delighted with their contents."[35] Jefferson himself, although believing that the "first impressions" of the news from France would strengthen those who desired war," said he believed that "their ultimate effect on the public mind will not be favorable to the war party." Always the optimist although sometimes a naive one, he had "considerable expectations . . . of changes in the Eastern delegations favorable to the whig interest."[36]

In response to the breakdown of the Paris negotiations, Adams again queried his cabinet, asking whether he should recommend "an immediate declaration of war" as well as whether he should convey to Congress the entire account of France's insulting behavior, which was certain to be inflammatory.[37] In reply Secretary of State Timothy Pickering urged that war be declared immediately and details of the negotiations released. Adams himself first took this extreme position as well, as is shown in an early draft of his March 19, 1798, message to Congress. Upon reflection, however, he softened his stance, recognizing that making the dispatches public might endanger the envoys. And, although the accounts of France's contemptuous behavior would no doubt be greeted with strong anti-French sentiment in Congress, it was unlikely, Adams surmised, that it would sway enough votes to support a declaration of war.[38]

Adams's message to Congress on March 19, then, reflected his more measured second thoughts. The dispatches, he told legislators, had caused him to give up hope that an accommodation with France could be arrived at "compatible with the safety, honor, or the essential interests of the nation." Therefore, in order to prepare for any eventuality, Adams urged that prompt attention be given to his earlier recommendations for strengthening the nation's defenses by providing for the manufacture of arms and munitions and the raising of revenue. In addition, he announced that he was lifting the prohibition against the arming of the nation's merchant fleet.[39]

And, hoping to rally public support for vigorous government measures, Hamilton wrote a series of vitriolic essays for the New York Commercial Advertiser, challenging the patriotism of the opposition, whom he saw as standing in the way of appropriate action. The Republicans, he charged, had made "unremitting efforts to justify or excuse the despots of France, to vilify and discredit our own government, of course to destroy its necessary vigor, and to distract the opinions and to dampen the zeal of our citizens," and worse, "to divert their affections from their own to a foreign country."[40]

Jefferson saw events moving quickly in the direction of bloodshed. Even though Adams had not called for a declaration of war in his "almost insane message," as Jefferson termed it, the vice president felt that it would only be a matter of time before the president would do so. Therefore, in order to stop the momentum of the Federalists and gain time for passions to cool and the opposition to mobilize, Jefferson recommended that the "Whigs" in Congress call for an adjournment to allow them to "consult their constituents." This strategy would provide an opportunity for "every member to call for the sense of his district by petition or instruction" and would demonstrate to "the people with which side of the House their safety as well as their rights rest, by showing them which is for war and which for peace."[41]

The vice president's use of the term *Whig* is noteworthy for increasingly in 1798 members of the opposition saw themselves as the Whigs of 1798, who, following in the footsteps of their 1776 predecessors, were the guardians of the principles of the American Revolution against modern day Tories. Jefferson attempted to explain his understanding of the terms when he wrote a presumed Federalist acquaintance that it was well known "that two political Sects have arisen within the U.S." One was called "federalists, sometimes aristocrats or monocrats, and sometimes tories, after the corresponding sect in the English Government," the other "republicans, whigs, jacobins, disorganizers." And in a phrase that would be used again in his famous first inaugural, Jefferson continued that "both parties claim to be federalists and republicans, and I believe with truth as to the great mass of them." Thus, the terms *Republican* and *Federalist,* Jefferson complained, failed to characterize accurately the political division in the country. It was only the older terms *Whigs* and *Tories,* he insisted, "which alone characterize the distinguishing principles of the two Sects."[42]

But if the country were divided into "Whigs" and "Tories," as Jefferson apparently believed, then there could be little hope for accommodation. For more than a decade following the Revolution and Independence, the so-called Tories seemed now to be rejecting the principles as well as the conclusions of that revolution.

The war fever continued to build in the spring of 1798. Congress, controlled by the Federalists, was in no mood to follow Jefferson's suggestion to adjourn and return home to collect the will of the people. Some Republicans, oblivious to the negative political repercussions, joined with Federalists in calling for the XYZ dispatches from President Adams, who was only too willing to oblige.[43] Then, after failing to temper the anti-French feeling aroused by the dispatches with a proposed resolution stating that it was inexpedient to go to war with France, the Republicans in Congress simply had to ride out the storm. All that "advocates of peace can now attempt," Jefferson wrote Madison, "is to prevent war measures *externally,* consenting to every rational measure of *internal* defence and preparation."[44] Still, Jefferson believed that time was on the Republicans' side and that it was possible that Gerry, by remaining in France, would be able to conclude a treaty and prevent war between the two countries.[45]

Rumors, the product of the war hysteria, spread through the capital. Adams received three letters revealing alleged plots to burn Philadelphia, and considerable preparations were made to thwart the would-be arsonists. The threats engendered so much fear that "many weak people," Jefferson wrote Madison, "packed their most valuable movables to be ready for transportation." Fortunately, the fears were groundless and the assigned day for the conflagration passed without incident.

But passions continued to be hot and tempers short. In early May there was a riot in Philadelphia between young men who evinced sympathy for England by wearing the black cockade and those who purportedly sported the tricolored French cockade although it was later explained that the supposed tricolor was in reality the blue and red cockade of the American Revolution. "A fray ensued," Jefferson explained, "the light horse were called in, and the city was so filled with confusion from about 6 to 10 o'clock last night that it was dangerous going out."[46]

Anti-French resolutions came pouring into Congress from an outraged citizenry, and patriotic demonstrations and outbursts became commonplace. Abigail Adams attended the first performance of the nation's new national anthem, "Hail Columbia," in a Philadelphia theater. The packed audience, she related, sang the song six times "and the last time, the whole Audience broke forth in the chorus whilst the thunder of their Hands was incessant, and at the close they rose, gave 3 Huzzas, that you might have heard a mile."[47] Adams, an unlikely public hero, now became the popular symbol of America's defiance of France.

Adding to all the excitement was John Marshall's ceremonial return from France, which underscored the diplomatic impasse with France and emphasized the gravity of the situation. "The secretary of state and many carriages, with all the city cavalry, went to Frankford to meet him," Jefferson reported to Madison. And once Marshall reached Philadelphia, "the bells rung till late in the night, and immense crowds were collected to see and make part of the show, which was circuitously paraded through the streets before he was set down at the city tavern."[48]

As a result of the publication of the XYZ dispatches with their incendiary revelations of France's insolent behavior, sympathizers of France and leaders of the opposition were viewed by some as little more than public enemies. The extent to which opposition leaders felt harassed and besieged is shown by Jefferson's admonition—in virtually every letter he wrote at the time—for the recipient to check the wax seal to determine whether or not the communication had been intercepted by political enemies. In line with this he was reluctant to deal with controversial political subjects in mail that traveled by regular post.[49]

In June 1798, some of the more fanatical Federalists construed as a treasonable conspiracy a trip by Dr. George Logan, a Philadelphia Quaker and Republican sympathizer, who sailed for Europe in an attempt to settle the dispute between France and the United States by personal diplomacy. He unwisely, according to Jefferson, "made a mystery" of his trip, and this "was seized by the war hawks" and "given out as a secret mission from the Jacobins here to solicit an army from France, [and] instruct them as to their landing etc."[50] The rabidly Federalist *Porcupine's Gazette* impassionedly warned: "Watch Philadelphians, or the fire is in your houses and the *couteau at your throats.* . . . Take care; or, when your blood runs down the gutters, don't say you were not forewarned of the danger."[51] The discussion of Logan's trip was going on at the same time Bache, editor of the opposition *Aurora,* was being attacked for publishing a letter from Talleyrand to the American commissioners before the president had even notified Congress of the communication. The Federalists charged that this proved the existence of a "traitorous correspondence" between the American Jacobins and the French Directory. Robert Goodloe Harper, the South Carolina Federalist, claimed that he was collecting evidence and would soon be able to divulge the entire plot.[52]

V

Emboldened by this wave of antirepublican feeling, the Federalists moved to consolidate their strength and destroy their political opposition in June and July of 1798 by proposing and passing the Alien and Sedition Laws. As the Federalist minister to Great Britain, Rufus King, was told by a correspondent, the "Spirit of the People is roused" and "ripe for the Support of the most decisive Measures of the Government." And this "spirit of patriotism" could be used, Hamilton suggested, to crush the Republicans so that "there will shortly be *national unanimity.*" And if the Republican "leaders of Faction" continued their opposition to the government, he said, the public would revile them much like "the *Tories* of our Revolution."[53]

The three repressive anti-alien acts, including the Act Concerning Aliens, the Naturalization Act, and the Alien Enemies Act, reflected the increasing Federalist concern about the growing number of immigrants coming into the United States. Not only did what were considered dangerous political ideas circulate among these new residents, but also the vast majority of them seemed to support the Republican opposition. The legislation, then, established a registration and surveillance system for foreign nationals in the United States and gave the president extensive powers over them, including the power to deport any whom he considered dangerous to the country's peace and security.[54] These measures, which Jefferson deemed as "worthy of the 8th or 9th century," had "so alarmed the French who are among us," he said, "that they are going off," and a "ship, chartered by themselves for this purpose, will sail within about a fortnight for France, with as many as she can carry."[55]

The Sedition Law, however, was even more ominous and threatening to the Republicans because of its potential to stifle internal dissent. It provided for the punishment of any persons who "unlawfully combine or conspire together, with intent to oppose any measure or measures of the government of the United States . . . or to impede the operation of any law of the United States, or to intimidate . . . any person holding a place or office in or under the government of the United States." The law further prohibited "any false, scandalous and malicious writing or writings against the government . . . or either house of the Congress of the United States; or the President . . . with intent to defame . . . or to bring them . . . into contempt or disrepute; or to excite against them . . . the hatred of the good people of the United States." Infractions could be punished by fines of up to $5,000 and imprisonment for up to five years.[56]

Hamilton had urged that his fellow Federalists use caution in shaping the Alien and Sedition Acts, having been concerned that his colleagues might push too far and cause a reaction that could have considerable political liabilities. "Let us not be cruel or violent," he had warned Timothy Pickering. Also upon reading an earlier and more radical version of the Sedition Act, Hamilton had exhorted his successor, Oliver Wolcott, that the act might "endanger civil War." "Let us not establish a tyranny," he had written, for "energy is a very different thing from violence," and "if we make no false steps we shall be essentially united; but if we push things to an extreme we shall give to faction *body* and solidarity."[57]

The debate within Congress over the measures was acrimonious and accusatory. Federalist Robert Goodloe Harper of South Carolina, one of the most outspoken and zealous supporters of the laws, noted that the same persons who had been against the military measures were now opposing the proposed Alien laws and charged that they did so from the fear that the laws would put "a hook into the nose of persons who are leagued with the enemies of this country." The "zeal shown in this House, and in other places, against this bill," he charged, was evidence of "the deadly hatred of certain people toward . . . [the United States]." Furthermore, Harper saw the efforts of the Republican opposition as treasonable in that the goal was "to completely stop the wheels of Government, and to lay it prostrate at the feet of its external and internal foes."[58]

Although a number of Federalists outdid themselves in conjuring up sinister images of seditious conspiracies, a giant of a man, "Long John" Allen, a six-foot-five-inch, 230-pound Federalist representative from Connecticut, was probably the most passionately and creatively vituperative and paranoid. Accusing Republican newspapers as well as congressmen of treasonable plotting against the government, Allen defended the Sedition Law as essential to the country's well-being. If there ever "was a nation which required a law of this kind," he said, it was the United States. He challenged his colleagues to look at certain newspapers and "ask themselves whether an unwarrantable and dangerous combination does not exist to overturn and ruin the Government by publishing the most shameless falsehoods against the Representatives of the people." These falsehoods and seditious statements, Allen said, included claims that Federalist representatives were "hostile to free Governments and genuine liberty, and of course to the welfare of this country" and should "therefore . . . be displaced" by the people "rais[ing] an *insurrection* against the Government."[59] Allen's apparent equating of Republican efforts to defeat the Federalists at the polls with "an *insurrection* against the Government" reflected a view of the opposition shared by most Federalists.

The Republicans, of course, opposed the Federalist-backed measures. For them there were disquieting parallels between their own government and that of Great Britain in that both governments seemed willing to use almost any means, no matter how arbitrary, to solidify and retain power. For example, in the same year the William Pitt government, fearing a French invasion, suspended habeas corpus and moved against radical clubs in Britain. And indeed, some of the Federalists' arguments during the debate over the Alien and Sedition Laws admitted an admiration for the stringent policies governing internal security in England. Harper maintained that both countries faced similar situations in that their external enemy relied upon "an internal support," which he referred to as being made up of "domestic traitors."[60]

Albert Gallatin was one of the major Republican spokesmen against the Sedition Act. He charged that advocates of the bill had failed to show evidence of any criminal conspiracies or seditious intent. "This bill and its supporters suppose in fact," he concluded, "that whoever dislikes the measures of Administration and of a temporary majority in congress, and shall, either by speaking or writing, express his disapprobation and his want of confidence in men now in power, is seditious, is an enemy, not of Administration, but of the Constitution, and is liable to punishment." Thus, the Sedition bill was no more than a blatant power grab by the Federalists, who hoped to use it to "perpetuate their authority and preserve their present places."[61]

Gallatin's distinction between opposition to the administration and opposition to the Constitution was one that most Americans of both proto-parties of the late eighteenth and early nineteenth centuries were not able to make. The political crisis, coupled with the lack of a tradition of a "loyal opposition," had created a climate of opinion inhospitable to political dissent. Congressman "Long John" Allen, for example, had been so outraged by Gallatin's remarks that he accused the Pennsylvanian of promoting "that spirit which, by preaching up the rights of man, had produced the Western insurrection [Whiskey Rebellion]."[62]

The debate was not confined to Congress. President Adams responded to a large number of petitions from citizens around the country with a series of addresses, some quite inflammatory in their depiction of the dangers posed by the country's external as well as internal foes. He told the citizens in and around Baltimore that while republics were often divided in opinion, these divisions were normally harmless "except when foreign nations interfere, and by their arts and agents excite and foment them into parties and factions." This kind of insidious interference, he said, however, "must be resisted and exterminated" or it would result "in our total destruction as a republican government and independent power."[63]

The Republicans thought that Adams's vehement addresses, which Madison said contained some of "the most abominable and degrading [language] that could fall from the lips of the first magistrate of an independent people,"[64] and the scathing attacks being made upon the opposition within Congress and in the Federalist newspapers were just a prelude to war with France, which was being called for by many Federalists. James Lloyd, for instance, author of the Senate version of the Sedition Bill, looked upon a declaration of war as vital to the success of the Federalist program. "I fear that Congress will close the Session" without a declaration of war, he wrote Washington, "which I look upon as necessary to enable us to lay our hands on traitors."[65]

Other Federalists, however, were less enthusiastic. Although Theodore Sedgwick thought that "a wise policy required a declaration of war," he explained to Rufus King, several Federalists were unwilling to go along, fearing that "it would tend to discredit them among their constituents" and that the "opposition would endeavor to create, in the popular estimation, a new denomination of parties—those of peace and war."[66]

The Republicans had expected the declaration of war to coincide with the anniversary of independence, but they later reported to Jefferson that a Federalist caucus had not been able to agree on the timing. The Federalists *were* able, however, to pass the Sedition Act through the Senate on July 4, and a colorful account of the proceedings was given to Jefferson. "The drums, Trumpets and other martial music which surrounded us, drown'd the voices of those who spoke on the question," Jefferson was told, and the "military parade so attracted the attention of the majority that much the greater part of them stood with their bodies out of the windows and could not be kept to order." Finally in the uproar and confusion the bill was passed.[67]

The martial spirit was widespread elsewhere and not just on the Fourth of July. "Our city resembles a camp rather than a commercial port," one of Rufus King's correspondents wrote from New York. "Volunteer companies of horse and infantry are raising; and meetings of the old officers of the army and navy—and of the citizens, in the different wards have been had to concert measures for the defence of our port."[68]

VI

Despite the building militancy and the desire of a number of Federalists for an immediate declaration of war, it was not forthcoming. Adams, it may be recalled, initially favored asking Congress for war in March but, having had second thoughts, later decided against it. Nonetheless, while the Federalists did not get their declaration, they did push through Congress a host of measures aimed at fighting a war. In the period between the receiving of the XYZ dispatches and the adjournment of Congress in July 1798, the Federalist majority—in addition to passing the Alien and Sedition Acts—established a Navy Department, increased the size of the navy, and authorized it "to seize, take, and bring into port" French ships suspected of lurking near the Eastern seaboard with the intent of taking American prizes. They also bolstered and enlarged the regular army (now New Army) by authorizing the president to raise an additional force of twelve regiments of infantry (700 men each) and six troops of light dragoons. In addition a Provisional Army that could be called into being "in the event of a declaration of war against the United States" or a foreign invasion was approved.[69] Finally, in the waning days of the session, the French-American treaties were abrogated.

While the Provisional Army was only a paper army, Federalist leaders, particularly Hamilton, organized the New Army with much energy and enthusiasm. Washington was made commander-in-chief of the force, and Hamilton, after considerable maneuvering, was given second-in-command over the vigorous objections of rival candidate Henry Knox, Washington's former secretary of war, who denounced the former secretary of treasury as a "man of insatiable ambition."[70] Adams also strenuously resisted giving the post to Hamilton over his Massachusetts colleague Knox. Knox was trustworthy and loyal, as far as Adams was concerned, while Hamilton's personal ambition and intrigues in the 1796 election continued to rankle the president. Ultimately, however, the pressures of an unrelenting cabinet sympathetic to and indeed controlled by Hamilton, the threat of Washington's refusal to serve without Hamilton, and the near-fatal illness of his beloved Abigail all combined to force Adams to acquiesce in Hamilton's appointment.[71] Adding to Adams's reluctance to make the appointment and Hamilton's eagerness for the post was the presumption that Washington's role as commander-in-chief would be merely symbolic, and the main business of leading the army would fall upon the former secretary of treasury's willing shoulders.

Once the appointment was made, one of the first major objectives of Hamilton and his colleagues was to guarantee that the proposed army was politically reliable—a primary consideration if the force were to be used to crush the domestic opposition. Therefore, it was critical that the background of each candidate for officer's rank be screened. Elaborate lists of prospective officers were prepared and circulated to prominent Federalists for comment. As part of this process, Washington warned Secretary of War James McHenry about "brawlers against Government measures" who "are very desirous of obtaining Commissions." He feared that their presence might "divide

and contaminate the Army," and by their "artful and seditious dis-
courses" they might at "a critical moment bring on confusion."[72]

The importance of the army's political and military reliability also
was emphasized by Hamilton, who warned of the "possibility of domestic disorders." His experience during the Whiskey Rebellion had
convinced him that the "efficacy of Militia for suppressing such disorders is not too much to be relied upon," and he had "trembled every
moment lest a great part of the Militia should take it into their heads
to return home rather than go forward."[73] Yet, the search for politically
orthodox officers for the New Army was conducted with so much zeal
that even Hamilton complained that "the objection against antifederalism has been carried so far as to exclude several characters
proposed by us." He told McHenry that while he and his colleagues
"were very attentive to the importance of appointing friends of the
Governt. to Military stations," the standards should be relaxed when it
came "to the inferior grades."[74] Appointments to higher grades, however, required the strictest scrutiny, and Hamilton and his colleagues
vetoed the president's plan to appoint Aaron Burr and Frederick Au-
gustus Muhlenberg to the post of brigadier general.[75]

VII

During the second stage of political development in the 1790s, and
prior to July 1798, even during the controversy over the Alien and
Sedition Laws themselves, the Republican opposition, for the most
part, was based upon the optimistic assumption that the great mass of
Americans believed in a republican form of government and were
loyal to the Constitution. Therefore, it was thought, those leaders who
persisted in "unrepublican actions" and pushed constitutionally questionable measures hostile to the general good of society would ultimately be rejected. Jefferson and other Republican leaders, as they
organized an opposition of clusters of like-minded representatives in
Congress, constantly reassured one another that it would only be a
matter of time before an aroused citizenry would act decisively to
secure republicanism and the Constitution. However, efforts to educate and mobilize the electorate in the elections of 1792 and 1796 and
to oppose Jay's Treaty had all ended in frustration, as the Federalists
not only continued to hold power but appeared to be solidifying it.

Following the failure of the mission to France, in an effort to mobilize support against Federalist policy and to gain time and legitimacy,
both Jefferson and Madison had agreed that Congress should adjourn

and its members return home "to collect the will of the people." With the breakdown of the negotiations, it was believed that the consequences of the alternatives were so momentous for the future of the country that the public had to be consulted. Madison saw the practical value in such a course of action, pointing out that it would fix in the public mind which members were for peace and which for war.[76]

All Republican leaders seemed to believe, at least prior to the passage of the Alien and Sedition Laws, that the Federalists' excessive policies would eventually lead to their political demise.[77] But it was Monroe, out of government since his recall from France and under attack from the Federalists for what they believed to have been his naive, incompetent, and even disloyal diplomatic service, who pushed this position to the extreme. Let the Federalists hang themselves, Monroe argued in an almost comical excess of rhetoric, for the "further they plunge the sooner will the people recover the use of their intellects." He urged that the Federalists be allowed to "fight on, plunge our country inevitably in a war with France, intimidate and traduce the republican party and promote civil discord at home as they are doing." This was not, he concluded, "the way to merit or preserve the esteem of the good people of this country." These Federalist excesses, Monroe believed, would convince the people in the Eastern states that more was "at issue than a mere controversy between northern and southern members." Therefore, it was important that Southern Republicans keep a low profile, for the more they criticized representatives from the Eastern states, the more the public perceived the debate as a sectional question rather than one of principle.[78]

Monroe's sentiment that the Republicans should remain as inconspicuous as possible and that the Federalist excesses should be allowed to run their course seems to have been shared, although not to the same extreme, by many opposition members in the weeks prior to the passage of the Alien and Sedition Laws. Although it is not certain this was the motive, for one reason or another a number of Republican congressmen left for home during this critical congressional session. As early as April 19, Jefferson reported to Madison that "Giles, Clopton and Cabell are gone." And by early June, one Federalist gleefully noted that while "Gallatin continues to clog the wheels of government . . . he has not sufficient strength to stop its motion." Giles, he reported, had "gone home with a broken heart and ruined constitution," and "Edward Livingston has been home for several weeks and I see no symptoms of his return."[79]

Despite Madison's assurance that the "only hope is that . . . violence by defeating itself may save the Country," Jefferson, possibly because he was witnessing the war buildup first hand in Philadelphia during the early summer of 1798, constantly complained about the departure of Republican members. He speculated that, had they stayed, the more odious aspects of the Federalist program might have been defeated or at least mitigated.[80] But whatever the motive might have been for the Republicans' withdrawal from Congress, it did make it easier for the Federalists to enact their program. Madison called it deplorable that "a standing army should be let in upon us by the absence of a few sound votes" but added that it "may . . . all be for the best."[81]

With the "Tories," as Jefferson called them, or Federalists firmly in control of the government, as they were in 1798, it was to be a major challenge to the vice president and his Republican colleagues to maintain a legitimate opposition in the face of pressure to equate dissent with sedition. The passage of the Alien and Sedition Laws, coupled with the growing war delirium, threatened their very survival. For if opposition to measures of the federal government and criticism of federal officers could be punished as seditious and even treasonable, how might an opposition continue to oppose and act as an agent for registering dissent?

Thus, the political crisis of 1798—the enactment of the Alien and Sedition Acts as well as the military measures—forced the Republicans to rethink their strategy of opposition. A year earlier during the Cabell controversy, Jefferson's petition to the Virginia legislature, which reflected a loss of faith in the federal government, had been a harbinger of a future states' rights strategy. Now, in reaction to the Federalists' repressive program and their apparent willingness, indeed eagerness, to use the authority of the government to crush their opponents, Republican leaders increasingly turned to the idea that the states would have to become sanctuaries for opposition and republicanism.

PART III

The Crisis of Union
1798–1801

9.

The Kentucky and Virginia Resolutions
Making a Refuge for the Oppressed

Unless the people are instructed and combined, by something they can
understand, nothing can save us from an anglo-monarchic-aristocratic-
military government.　　　　　　　—JOHN TAYLOR OF CAROLINE

T he years 1798 and 1799 were
ones that put the Virginia leaders of the Republican opposition to the
supreme test. For although Jefferson and his colleagues continued to
believe that they would ultimately prevail, their erstwhile optimism
was being tempered by the grim reality of a succession of defeats.
Their exertions, they had to acknowledge, had failed to build an effective interstate coalition to electorally wrest national power from the
Federalists. So, feeling under siege and politically isolated after the
passage of the Alien and Sedition Laws, the Virginia Republicans began
to regroup and debate among themselves about their role as a political
opposition and the course they should be taking. Although there was
little tradition or precedent in Western European history justifying
organized opposition to a government during times of national crisis,
the Republicans hoped that a policy of opposition could be developed
that would, on the one hand, check Federalist excesses, yet still preserve the union and Constitution.

What came out of the Republican deliberations was a radical change
in Republican strategy, a change that represents the beginning of the
third stage of political development in the 1790s, a stage marked by
mounting sectional militancy. Instead of focusing their attention on
the *national* level, particularly on Congress, the Republicans began to
stress the exercise of political power at the *state* level. And in so doing
they left the clear implication that state secession and the breakup of
the union might follow if the federal government refused to modify its
policies and actions to make them more acceptable to the opposition,
especially the Southerners. Significantly, this Republican advocacy of a
states' rights philosophy, which was frightening to many potential sympathizers and supporters, particularly in the Northern states, laid the

ideological groundwork for more than a century of Southern particularism in the United States.

This new defensive enclave strategy developed by Virginia Republicans in the wake of the passage of the Alien and Sedition Acts embraced constitutional as well as military preparedness dimensions. The Kentucky and Virginia resolutions, the constitutional and ideological rationale of the opposition, pitted the power of the states against that of the federal government and constituted a last-ditch effort to defend republicanism against an increasingly powerful, aggressive, and successful adversary. And although some historians have denied it, there are a number of indications that the Virginians were also arming for a possible military showdown by quietly building up their state's defenses in the event the political conflict were to turn violent and its citizens were to need defending.

Considering the intensity and apparent intractability of the differences between the state and the federal government, it did not require too great a stretch of imagination for the Virginians to be concerned that the newly organized and invigorated federal army might be used to coerce Virginia into obedience. And, in fact, this is exactly what was on Hamilton's mind in the winter of 1799 as is demonstrated by his letter to a Federalist colleague in which he advocated that once a sound military force was raised it should "be drawn towards Virginia . . . and then let measures be taken to act upon the laws and put Virginia to the Test of resistance."[1]

The extent of Southern alienation is shown by John Taylor of Caroline's call in the spring of 1798, even before the Federalists had passed their legislative program, for an opposition strategy that would protect liberty and Southern interests, which in his mind were closely intertwined. In March he seemed despondent. Unless certain changes were made, he wrote Monroe, "the southern states must lose their capital and commerce—and . . . America is destined to war—standing armies—and oppressive taxation."[2] A couple of months later Taylor wrote Jefferson pessimistically that secession must be considered as a possible opposition strategy, and "it was not unwise now to estimate the separate mass of Virginia and North Carolina, with a view to their separate existence."[3] While Jefferson himself had referred to the federal government as a "foreign jurisdiction" during the controversy over the Cabell presentment a year earlier,[4] he, nonetheless, was startled by Taylor's radicalism.

Later in the year Jefferson too would embrace more radical action as a strategy of opposition, but in June he was not ready to do so.

Then, still holding on to the hope that Republicans in Congress might temper the excesses of Federalist repression in the weeks prior to the final passage of the Alien and Sedition Laws, Jefferson feared any talk of disunion would not only jeopardize Republican support outside of the South but also would endanger the union itself.

Jefferson responded to his more radical Virginia colleague with a long thoughtful letter urging moderation and patience. While admitting that "we are completely under the saddle of Massachusetts and Connecticut, and that they ride us very hard, cruelly insulting our feelings," Jefferson assured Taylor that the "reign of witches" would pass and the people would restore "their government to its true principles." The popularity of Washington and "the cunning of Hamilton" were the original causes for placing the government into "anti-republican hands" or turning "the republicans chosen by the people into anti-republicans." But, he repeated, this was "not the natural state," and he predicted that the prospect of war, tax increases, and the Federalists' attack upon the principles of the Constitution would cause a popular reaction.

"In every free and deliberating society," Jefferson went on, "there must, from the nature of man, be opposite parties, and violent dissensions and discords; and one of these . . . must prevail over the other for a longer or shorter time." And perhaps "this party division is necessary to induce each to watch and relate to the people the proceedings of the other." But, he warned Taylor, "if on a temporary superiority of one party, the other is to resort to a scission of the Union, no federal government can ever exist." Furthermore, Jefferson doubted whether the problem would be solved by secession from a union with the New England states. Will "our nature be changed," he asked Taylor, and "are we not men still to the south of that, and with all the passions of men?" Even a simple union between Virginia and North Carolina, Jefferson feared, might not survive the inevitable conflict.

Therefore, Jefferson concluded, "an association of men who will not quarrel with one another is a thing which never yet existed, from the greatest confederacy of nations down to a town meeting or a vestry," and, since "we must have somebody to quarrel with, I had rather keep our New England associates for that purpose, than to see our bickerings transferred to others." Significantly, however, Jefferson expected that the New Englanders "will ever be the minority" and that they, "marked like the Jews with such a perversity of character," will "constitute, from that circumstance, the natural division of our parties."[5]

Historians have pointed to Jefferson's letter to Taylor as evidence that Jefferson had accepted or was accepting a modern conception of permanent political parties, alternating in power and balancing one another.[6] This interpretation, however, misreads Jefferson's intent and the nature of the political conflict of the 1790s. Far from envisioning a future where parties alternated in power within a mutually perceived consensual framework of political principles, Jefferson believed instead that the main perpetrators of antirepublicanism, the New Englanders, would "ever be the minority." In other words, the New England–based Federalists' accession to national power was not "natural" and had only come about through Hamilton's intrigues and Washington's popularity. Thus, the Republicans, Jefferson implied, could soon look forward to the day when their overwhelming public support would assure a more-or-less permanent Republican hegemony.

To understand Jefferson's words, it must also be remembered that he was writing *prior* to the passage of the Alien and Sedition Acts and undoubtedly wanted to minimize the differences between the two proto-parties as a means of heading off any precipitous action by the more radical Republicans. At this point Jefferson was still an optimist. It was only a matter of time, he believed, before the great mass of people, who were both federalists (as supporters of the Constitution) and republicans (as supporters of republican government), would repudiate those who stood for alien principles.[7]

Responding at the end of June to Jefferson's plea for patience and moderation, Taylor first protested to the vice president that all he had ever desired in his earlier letter was the "perfection, and not the scission of the union," but, significantly, he warned nonetheless that if persons or principles were threatened some measures would be needed for self-defense.[8]

More important for an understanding of Jefferson's thinking, however, was Taylor's critique of the vice president's analysis of the causes and consequences of "party spirit." Declaring Jefferson's analysis contradictory, Taylor gently reproved and corrected his old friend. Both Jefferson and Taylor began with the assumption that "party spirit" was the direct consequence of the antirepublican Federalist hegemony. Indeed Federalist dominance had been possible only through party intrigue, according to the two Virginians. However, Taylor argued that Jefferson contradicted himself when he maintained that it was "not the natural state" for the government to be in the hands of the antirepublicans and, yet, at the same time, claimed that party spirit and divisiveness would naturally spring up among citizens holding different views. How could Jefferson conclude, Taylor asked, that if the present state of Federalist hegemony were unnatural, "party spirit would still be natural?" Taylor believed the "unnatural" Federalist success depended on the "unnatural" party activities of the Federalists, and he vehemently denied what he thought Jefferson seemed to be implying—that "parties, sufficiently malignant to destroy the public good," were "naturally the issue of every popular government." For proof he cited the experience of "Connecticut, which has [for] about two centuries enjoyed a compleat unanimity under a government, the most democratic of any representative form which ever existed."[9]

Jefferson, Taylor conceded, was correct in his view that "individuals have robbed liberty of its ascendancy, so as to be able to convert the resources of the nation to the purpose of buying and supporting a party." But Taylor denied that the remedy involved "depriving individuals of this ascendancy, and restoring it . . . to other individuals." For instance, he said, a Southern dominance of the federal government would be as "detestable" as a Northern one.[10] Similarly, in an earlier letter, Taylor expounded on his belief that "government" was not just the officeholders, but rather the principles "upon which it is constituted." Therefore, the opposition was "not entirely right in directing . . . [their] efforts towards a change of men, rather than a change of principles." Taylor explained that a change of men in public office only would bring temporary relief for it would "be . . . like the lucid intervals of a madman" (however, even this would have its merits, as "a little sunshine is better than none").[11] Indeed, to Taylor, then, the only solution was to restore the ascendancy "to liberty."[12]

Tactically Taylor opposed allowing the antirepublicanism of the times "to run through its natural course," which a number of Republicans had apparently decided to allow it to do, as he feared any delay in addressing the problem would make the situation worse. For, if "the mass of our citizens are now republican," he asked, "will submission to anti-republican measures, increase that mass?"[13]

Despite his pessimism, then, Taylor saw the evils of party and antirepublicanism as not without a cure. In addition to calling for two somewhat conventional solutions—the extension of suffrage and "rotation in office"—he made two innovative proposals: a "new mode of abrogating law" and a means for giving states (or state conventions) the power and right to interpret the Constitution. What Taylor was suggesting by a "new mode of abrogating law" was that laws should no longer be enacted in perpetuity but should have to be renewed periodically. Legislatures, then, would be compelled to agree to *continue* a law just as they had had to agree to *pass* it in the beginning. For, according to Taylor, a "concurrence in favor of existence ought to be the same with that necessary for creation."[14] Jefferson, himself, had made a somewhat similar argument almost a decade earlier in his famous "the earth belongs to the living" letter to Madison advocating that "every constitution . . . and every law, naturally expires at the end of nineteen years." Because of the imperfections of representative institutions, he had argued, "a law of limited duration is much more manageable than one which needs a repeal."[15]

Taylor's final remedy would have given state governments the "right . . . to expound" or interpret the Constitution. And if this were "insufficient, the people in state conventions, are incontrovertibly the contracting parties, and . . . may proceed by orderly steps to attain the object."[16] Taylor's belief in the importance of the role of the states in "expound[ing] the constitution," which he shared with other members of the opposition, was to be the ideological foundation of the Virginia and Kentucky resolutions written later that year.

The views of John Page, a lifelong friend and political supporter of Jefferson's and Republican congressman from Virginia from 1789–97, offer further insight into Republican thinking in the early summer of 1798. Writing the vice president in June 1798, he depicted party conflict as between the virtuous and the corrupt, reasoning that in all countries there had been a division between a "pure patriotic Party" and those who, corrupted by a narrowly partisan and selfish "party spirit," conspired against the "Liberty and true Interests of the people." A "patriotic Party" of the "truly virtuous," therefore, was "necessary in a free State to preserve its Freedom" and to frustrate "the wicked designs of the Enemies of the Doctrine of Equality and the Rights of Man."[17]

It is clear, then, that Jefferson, Taylor, and Page, influenced by the civic humanist tradition, were not thinking about parties in any modern sense. The antirepublican party or Federalists, according to them, represented only a "part" or factious and selfish few of society and survived by artifice and manipulation. The Federalist party, therefore, was the antithesis of the general good and of the civic humanist vision, which held that a republic could only persist "as a partnership in virtue among all citizens" who "could be equally and immediately participant in the pursuit of the universal good."[18] The main difference between Jefferson and Taylor was that Taylor believed that "party spirit" could be eradicated, while Jefferson believed that the Federalists or a similar antirepublican party might continue to menace the republic but, significantly, would "ever be the minority."

In line with this, the Republicans saw their task as organizing the "truly virtuous" into a band of redeemers whose aim it was to recapture the essence of the civic humanist ideal. Their ultimate victory not only would signal a triumph over the foes of freedom, republicanism, and the Constitution, but also would represent the reinstatement of public virtue and the renewal of the quest for the "universal good" as primary objectives in the republic.

The endeavor to awaken the virtuous public to their responsibilities as autonomous citizens of a republic had been frustrated, Page implied in his letter to Jefferson, by the "Abolition of the Republican and Democratic Societies," which had led to the "rapid Propagation of anglo-monarchical" and "aristocratical Principles among us." For had the societies "boldly done their Duty . . . the People would have learned their Rights, and understood their Interests . . . ."[19]

Nonetheless, the people, in the view of Page and his fellow Republicans, while now inert, were the sovereign force in the republic and only waiting to be aroused from their lethargy, educated, and mobilized to perform their rights and duties as citizens. The Democratic-Republican societies had once taken a leadership role in energizing the public, at least according to Page, but with their demise the job was now the responsibility of the Republican elite.

II

Jefferson's initial optimism and moderation in 1798 were sharply challenged in June and July by the final passage of the Alien and Sedition Laws, the accompanying anti-French hysteria, and the growing Federalist appetite for repression of political dissent. The cumulative effect of these events was to push the Virginian in a more radical direction and convince him that, with the national government firmly in the hands of the Federalists, the situation was critical and a radical change in opposition strategy was needed to protect the right of dissent and check what he considered to be the Federalists' unlawful and dangerous usurpation of power. Departing from the hitherto ineffective, nationally based, congressionally oriented strategy, he and other Republicans began to believe that republicanism could best be defended at the state and local levels.

In a grim effort to save the union and republicanism and to preserve liberty, Republicans, especially in Virginia, resolved to strengthen the states as bastions of safety from illegal and repressive federal actions. Years later Jefferson would recall that the "leading republicans in Congress," who "found themselves of no use there," decided "to retire from that field, take a stand in their state legislatures, and endeavor there to arrest" the progress of Federalist domination.[20]

The centerpiece of this new Republican state enclave defense of 1798–99 was the doctrine of state interposition, which was most militantly reflected in Jefferson's draft of the Kentucky Resolutions charging that the Alien and Sedition Laws were an unconstitutional assertion of federal power and calling for state nullification of usurpatious federal laws.

Unquestionably, the strategy that emerged in the late summer of 1798 was a tactic of last resort. As Jefferson and others knew only too well, this strategy reflected a disillusionment with government under the Constitution and raised the very real possibility of a fragmentation of the union. Nonetheless, it was not a strategy without antecedents. A year earlier, for instance, when a grand jury of a federal court had issued a presentment to Congressman Cabell of Virginia for letters to his constituents criticizing the government, Jefferson had urged the state legislature to intervene. And Taylor in his letter to Jefferson in late June had discussed the value of having states interpret the Constitution.[21]

Letters written by the Republicans in the summer and fall of 1798 clearly show the thinking that emphasized using the power of the more virtuous, more republican state governments to confront the corrupting hold the Federalists had on the federal government. For instance, one Republican wrote Monroe that he and Burr were going to Albany to meet with Republicans in the New York legislature, for it was "highly important, at this moment and will be more so every day, to pay particular attention to the State Legislatures, and to get into them men of respectability" for "if any good can be expected it must be through their means."[22] And Jefferson assured one of his correspondents that if he chose Virginia as his place of asylum, he would not find the "delusion" that had produced the Alien and Sedition Laws. Virginians, the vice president wrote, were "sufficiently on their guard" and the "laws of the land, administered by upright judges, would protect you from any exercise of power unauthorized by the Constitution of the United States."[23]

In another letter Jefferson expressed his shock at witnessing how far the "delusion" of the people had been carried and concluded that there was "no length to which it may not be pushed by a party in possession of the revenues and the legal authorities of the US" and "no event . . . however atrocious, which may not be expected." Therefore, Jefferson "contemplated every event which the Maratists of the day can perpetrate," and he was "prepared to meet every one in such a way, as shall not be derogatory either to the public liberty or my own personal honor."[24]

Such was Jefferson's mood in August 1798 when he wrote the resolutions labeling the Alien and Sedition Laws unconstitutional and calling on the states to declare them null and void. In his draft of the resolves that eventually came to be known as the Kentucky Resolutions, Jefferson argued that the general government was the product of a "compact" among the states and that it had been established under the Constitution for "special purposes" and had "certain definite powers," while each state reserved to itself "the residuary mass of rights to their own self-government." Therefore, whenever the general government assumed "undelegated powers, its acts are unauthoritative, void, and of no force." And, as in all compacts "among powers having no common judge, each party has an equal right to judge for itself" the "infractions" as well as "the mode and measure of redress." The federal government, he insisted, was not competent to be the "final judge of the extent of the powers delegated to itself." For instance, Congress, not being a party to the compact, was "merely" its "creature."

Jefferson drew a significant distinction between actions involving the abuse of *delegated powers* and the usurpation of *undelegated powers* by the federal government. In the first instance, "a change by the people" of those in power "would be the constitutional remedy." But "where powers are assumed which have not been delegated, a nullification of the act is the rightful remedy."[25]

After building a general case for each state's right to judge whether the federal government had assumed unauthorized power, Jefferson declared that the Alien and Sedition Laws did, in fact, represent such an unconstitutional aggrandizement of power. Thus, he urged the states to join "in declaring these acts void, and of no force" and to take precautions to insure that "neither these acts, nor any others of the General Government not plainly and intentionally authorized by the Constitution, shall be exercised within their respective territories." In order for the states to take steps to implement his proposal curtailing the federal government's right to exercise certain powers within state jurisdictions, Jefferson called for the establishment of a "committee of conference and correspondence . . . to communicate the . . . resolutions to the Legislatures of the several states" and to reassure those in other states that supporters of the resolutions were loyal to the union and "sincerely anxious for its preservation."

Jefferson's draft of the resolutions represented a radical presentation of the emerging political enclave defense strategy. Furthermore, his call for the establishment of a committee of correspondence, an extralegal institution dating from the days of Whig opposition to Great Britain during the American Revolution, as a device to bypass the Federalist-controlled federal government indicates just how dangerous Jefferson believed the political situation had become.

How far Jefferson was willing to push was not completely spelled out, but it is obvious that at a minimum he supported state nullification of federal law, and, as a last resort, secession.[26] Nonetheless, he ardently wanted to keep all options open. In sending a copy of his resolutions to Madison, Jefferson explained that "we should distinctly affirm all the important principles they contain, so as to hold to that ground in the future, and leave the matter in such a train as that we may not be committed absolutely to push the matter to extremities, and yet may be free to push as far as events will render prudent."[27] Jefferson echoed these sentiments in a letter to John Taylor, warning against doing anything "which should commit us further" but nonetheless recommending keeping any and all possibilities open for taking action "to shape . . . future measures or no measures by the events which may happen." But Jefferson emphasized again that it was the state governments that had to be relied upon to preserve liberty for they were the "very *best in the world*, without exception or comparison," while "our general government has, in the rapid course of 9 or 10 years, become more arbitrary, and has swallowed more of the public liberty than even that of England."[28]

Jefferson originally intended that his resolutions be introduced in North Carolina, but a change in the political climate there made that impractical. His agent for bringing forward the resolutions, Wilson Cary Nicholas, a Virginia Republican and member of the Virginia legislature, apparently on his own gave the resolutions to John Breckinridge to introduce in Kentucky, where numerous public meetings had been held throughout the state condemning the Alien and Sedition Acts. Breckinridge was sworn to secrecy about Jefferson's involvement; the vice president wanted to keep his own name out of the controversy for two reasons. First, he was a member of the government and his participation might have been seen as inappropriate and, second, his name was already linked in the Federalist mind with every rumored plot against the government and Jefferson believed that if he were to be publicly associated with the resolutions it would automatically heighten Federalist resistance.[29]

Breckinridge introduced Jefferson's resolutions in the Kentucky legislature but not until after he had made some significant modifications. Whereas Jefferson had specifically meant to bypass Congress, claiming that Congress was a mere "creature" of the compact and, thus, subsidiary to the states, Breckinridge, in an effort to bring the resolutions into harmony with the many resolves of Kentucky counties, directed that efforts be made to address Congress for the repeal of the Alien and Sedition Acts. More important, Breckinridge deleted the passages declaring that Kentucky and the other states had the right to nullify usurpatious federal laws.[30] Thus, the more radical intent of Jefferson's initial draft was tempered by Breckinridge, who rejected nullification and chose an appeal to Congress rather than the solicitation of state action. These amended resolutions were passed virtually unanimously by the Kentucky legislature.[31]

III

The Republicans' next goal was to introduce resolutions similar to the Kentucky Resolutions in Virginia, and Madison agreed to prepare a draft of the proposed resolutions for consideration. But by the late fall of 1798, Jefferson had become concerned that some members of the opposition in both Kentucky and Virginia, including Madison, were too solicitous of Northern opinion and too hesitant to make a strong and principled stand against the Federalists' unconstitutional use of power. When a copy of Madison's draft of the Virginia Resolutions was shown to Jefferson prior to its introduction in the Virginia legislature, the vice president responded by urging that more radical language be used. Instead of inviting other states "to cooperate in the annulment" of the Alien and Sedition Acts, Jefferson insisted that these states be invited "to concur with this commonwealth in declaring, as it does hereby declare, that the said acts are, and were *ab initio*, null, void and of no force, or effect."[32] In other words, Jefferson insisted, Virginia should first unilaterally decide that the laws were null and void and simply ask her sister states to agree, rather than following Madison's milder course of consulting other states.

The Madison draft of the Virginia Resolutions with Jefferson's more radical revisions incorporated into it was introduced in the Virginia legislature by Taylor. Immediately the Federalists challenged the Republicans' sincerity. Not only did the Federalists recall to mind that the Republicans had been responsible for a Virginia Sedition Act in 1792 that punished slanderous and libelous assertions, but they also pointed to a letter by Jefferson in which he had argued that "in preventing the abridgment of the freedom of the press, punishment for uttering falsehoods, ought not to be inhibited."[33]

Despite the Federalist accusations, however, the Virginia Republicans were not, in their own eyes, being hypocritical. Since they sincerely believed they were the defenders of republicanism, they saw the powers of government in *their* hands being used to further noble goals, whereas power in the hands of the Federalists, who represented factious interests, was being used to undermine the general good. Politics in the early republic, particularly at the national level during this time of international crisis, was the politics of the absolute and not the politics of interest brokerage. Unlike later in the nineteenth and twentieth centuries, public men in the 1790s did not have the comfort of looking back over the successful history of union and republicanism under the Constitution. And, without that perspective, political differences became magnified and crises assumed union-threatening proportions.

In the debates over the Virginia Resolutions, the Federalists continued to probe for Republican weaknesses, with one Federalist defending the Alien Enemies Act as a protection against outside agitators who might stir up slave discontent. Using white Virginians' fear of slaves in an effort to bolster their own image as the friends of order, the Federalists depicted the Republicans as the witting or unwitting proponents of disorder. One Federalist legislator graphically described a lurid scene, suggesting that such could result in the absence of the Federalist legislation. "The inexorable and blood-thirsty negro would be careless of the father's groans," he said, while "wives and daughters . . . with naked bosoms, outstretched hands and dishevelled hair" were torn away "to gratify the brutal passion of a ruthless negro, who would the next moment murder the object of his lust."[34] Indeed the fear of slave insurrections and sexual violence, which were to be raised to new heights by the news of Gabriel's Plot in the summer of 1800, amplified the Virginians' sense of danger and vulnerability.[35]

After two weeks of debate, Taylor, bowing to pressure, amended the resolutions to restore Madison's original, more moderate, wording that called upon the other states to join Virginia in declaring "that the acts . . . are unconstitutional."[36] With the deletion of Jefferson's more radical language endorsing state nullification, the resolutions passed, 100 to 63.[37]

From the beginning, Madison had been uneasy about the more radical action advocated by Jefferson and Taylor. His draft of the

Virginia Resolutions reflected his moderation as well as his doubts about the doctrines expressed in Jefferson's original draft of the Kentucky resolves.[38] At the end of 1798, he reported to Jefferson his fear that in their "zeal," the more radical Virginia Republicans in the legislature may have forgotten "some considerations which ought to temper their proceedings." Furthermore, he was concerned that Jefferson may not have "considered thoroughly the distinction between the power of the *State* and that of the *Legislature,* on questions relating to the federal pact." For if the state "is clearly the ultimate Judge of infractions, it does not follow that the . . . [legislature] is the legitimate organ" since a convention and not the legislature "was the organ by which the compact was made."[39]

Taylor, however, was disappointed with the watering down of the resolutions, writing Jefferson that it had been his hope "to declare the unconstitutional laws of Congress void," thus creating an impasse that would have forced a confrontation between "the State and general government." The resulting deadlock would then have forced the submission of the issue to "the people in convention as the only referee." In Taylor's view a convention had the advantage of representing the people's sovereign voice and, as such, of having virtually unlimited authority to alter, amend, or dissolve the former relationships between the governors and the governed. Thus, calling a convention, Taylor concluded, was an essential strategy of last resort for the people in a "popular republic" to protect their republican institutions because it represented a means of appealing to the people over the head of government and of mobilizing public grievances when normal channels were perceived as having failed to give relief. However, Jefferson's reluctance to support Taylor's more radical venture and to push "on at present to this ultimate effort" forced Taylor to drop his scheme.[40]

The Virginia legislature, however, did not limit its attack on the Federalists to the Virginia Resolutions. In addition, the Virginia Republicans introduced and passed an "Address to the People," written by Madison, which catalogued the dangers of the Federalist system.[41] After being warned about "lover[s] of monarchy" who would corrupt the country "by distributing emolument among devoted partisans" and delude "the people with professions of republicanism," the people were told that the preservation of the Constitution rested upon the willingness of the state legislatures to meet their obligation in maintaining "the line of partition" between the state and federal spheres of power. "The acquiescence of the states under infractions of the federal compact," it was declared, would either result in a "consolidation," by reducing "the state Governments into impotence and contempt," or provoke "a revolution, by a repetition of these infractions until the people are roused to appear in the majesty of their strength." The people, the Virginia Republicans contended, had a "momentous question" before them: would they continue to accept a construction of the Constitution "which defies every restraint and overwhelms the best hopes of Republicanism?"[42]

IV

Reaction to the Virginia and Kentucky resolutions from the other states was either overwhelmingly critical or deafening in its silence. State after state north of the Potomac denounced the doctrines set forth in them. The House of Delegates in Maryland condemned Kentucky's action as "highly *improper*" and maintained that, in regard to both Kentucky and Virginia, "No State government by a Legislative act is competent to declare an act of the Federal Government unconstitutional and void." This was a theme adopted by many of the legislatures in responding to the resolutions, although some, like Massachusetts, also included a specific defense of the constitutionality of the Alien and Sedition Laws.[43]

Defense of the resolutions even by the Northern Republicans was mild and hesitant. Afraid of being cast as disunionists, they supported Virginia's and Kentucky's opposition to the Alien and Sedition Laws but opposed the idea that state legislatures could rule on the constitutionality of a federal law. One New York Republican did offer an unsuccessful resolution in his legislature stating "that in cases of dangerous encroachments and innovations on the rights and sovereignty of the State Legislatures, it would become . . . [the states'] bounded duty to mark and proclaim such innovations." But, since he was impressed with the "necessity of preserving harmony between the national and state governments at the present eventful period," the legislator said he did not think "it expedient or proper to adopt the resolutions of the States of Virginia and Kentucky."[44]

While the states south of the Potomac did not join the chorus of denunciation, they did remain tellingly silent. To many Southern Republicans outside of Virginia and Kentucky, the resolutions of those two states had passed beyond the point of political acceptability and, although these Southern Republicans virtually all probably agreed with the *end* sought, the repeal of the Alien and Sedition Laws, they feared that the *method* employed would lead to political disaster.[45]

From the outset Republican leaders were concerned about the general public reaction to the Kentucky and Virginia resolutions and worried that their radicalism might be counterproductive and cause the Republicans to be branded disunionists. This certainly was in Madison's mind when he objected to Jefferson's more extreme language in the original draft of the Kentucky Resolutions.

In an expression of this concern, George Nicholas, brother of Virginia's Wilson Cary Nicholas and a Republican from Kentucky, felt constrained to publish a pamphlet early in 1799 denying that his state had plans to leave the union. In this pamphlet Nicholas argued that Kentuckians would obey laws that were constitutional but impolitic but would ignore laws that were both unconstitutional and impolitic. Nonetheless, he added, "we contemplate no means of opposition, even to these unconstitutional acts, but an appeal to the *real laws* of our country."[46]

Although Jefferson was one of those urging a more radical and forthright position in opposition to the Federalists, he was aware, as he told Madison in January 1799, that the South must follow a course of "firmness . . . but a passive firmness" because "anything rash or threatening might check the favorable dispositions of these middle States, and rally them again around the measures which are ruining us."[47] Thus, he believed it was critical that the Southern-based opposition not do anything reckless that might imperil support from Pennsylvania and New York. And in February 1799, at the time of the Pennsylvania Fries Rebellion against a federal tax,[48] Jefferson became concerned about the possible violent outcome of opposition activities and the possible "fatal" political consequences. "Anything like force would check the progress of the public opinion and rally . . . [the public] round the government," he said, as this was not "the kind of opposition the American people . . . [would] tolerate." On the other hand, Jefferson maintained with his usual optimism, "keep away all show of force," and the people will eliminate "the evil propensities of the government, by the constitutional means of election and petition." Therefore, he concluded, "if we can keep quiet . . . the tide now turning will take a stead[y] and proper direction."[49]

Nevertheless, John Taylor of Caroline, writing his friends in the early months of 1799, saw few portents that the "tide" was turning or that the South would be able to avoid being subjugated to Northern domination. He told Jefferson that "I see nothing to change . . . [my] opinions," repeating some of the language he used a year earlier to Monroe, "namely—that the southern states must lose their capital and commerce—and that America is destined to war—standing armies—and oppressive taxation, by which the power of the few here, [as] in other countries, will be matured into an irresistible scourge of human happiness."[50]

Taylor was disillusioned by the Constitution's system of checks and balances, claiming that "constitutional prohibitions" and "paper restrictions upon great power" were "ineffectual." By following the example of England and "checking power by power," he said, the United States not only had adopted a highly defective device for restricting power but had also surrendered public control over the government. The "only security for liberty," Taylor concluded, was a form of government that retained in the people's hands "as much political strength as may be consistent with good order and social happiness."[51]

Quite critical of what he recognized as a temporizing spirit within the Republican camp, Taylor was disappointed in the lack of support for nullifying the Alien and Sedition Laws at the time the Virginia Resolutions were considered. The "republican cause," he wrote, was "daily declining on account of its fashionable maxim of moderation in its efforts, and waiting . . . for the public mind." And this "inert mode of proceeding," he predicted, meant that the "public mind" would instead be "cultivated, deceived, solicited and corrupted, by strenuous efforts" of the Federalists.

In order to prevent this, Taylor urged the Republicans to instruct and organize the people "by something that they can understand," otherwise, "nothing can save us from an anglo-monarchic-aristocratic-military government."[52] Furthermore, Taylor advised his colleagues to be single-minded about opposing the Federalists and to avoid any distraction that would weaken their efforts. For instance, the Virginian admonished a correspondent to avoid or postpone any controversy in Kentucky over a plan for the gradual emancipation of the slaves for "so many angry passions will be roused by the question of emancipation, as that the danger of your own subjugation will be lost sight of."[53] Taylor also disputed Jefferson's hope that a "tax-gatherer" would be "the doctor which will cure the disease" by reminding his friend that "this doctor is now under the protection of an army and navy" and "may safely administer what doses he pleases."[54] Thus, although Taylor and Jefferson disagreed on the prognosis of the political pathology, they did agree that it was essential for Virginia and Kentucky to be maintained as bulwarks of republicanism. They undoubtedly shared the view of one Kentuckian, who reported that his state, in addition to Virginia, could be regarded "as the ultimate refuge of those in the

Atlantic States who will not submit to the oppression and Tyranny which must be the results of federal measures."[55]

V

The reaction to the Alien and Sedition Acts in the form of the Kentucky and Virginia resolutions was dramatic and controversial. But even more dramatic and controversial were Republican calls for Virginia to prepare itself militarily for any prospective provocation by the Federalists or the Federalist-controlled federal government. This extreme response was a reflection of the fear of violence that was on the minds of both Federalists and Republicans in the latter months of 1798 and throughout 1799. It was a time of countless rumors, not only about the hoarding of arms by Republicans,[56] but also about Federalist plots to use the newly strengthened army led by Alexander Hamilton to destroy domestic opposition.

A sensational letter by John Nicholas, member of a rather prominent Virginia Republican family, was published in the spring of 1799 and appeared to substantiate the reports that had been circulating in the country. In the letter, Nicholas repudiated the Republicans and charged that the Virginia legislature was storing arms in Richmond as part of a plan of rebellion. The Republicans denied the startling charges and disavowed Nicholas. In fact, Wilson Cary Nicholas was so upset by what he regarded as his brother's traitorous behavior that he urged him to change his name so as not to disgrace his family further.[57] Nonetheless, considerable credence was given Nicholas's declaration, especially since the Virginia legislature of 1798–99 that passed the Virginia Resolutions also reorganized the militia, purchased additional arms, provided funds to build an armory in Richmond, and increased taxes by 25 percent.

Charges similar to Nicholas's were repeated by others. A North Carolina Federalist wrote that a friend had lately returned from Virginia and reported that the Virginians "were determined upon the overthrow of the General Government and if no other measure would effect it, that they would risk it upon the chance of war." Some, he went on, "talked of 'seceding from the Union,' while others boldly asserted the policy and practicability of 'severing the Union.'"[58] Similar reports were given to Hamilton, who was told by a Virginian that the building of a penitentiary in his state had been halted so that the money could be used for "the purchase of Arms." And a Massachusetts Federalist warned that the Old Dominion was making "its militia as formidable as possible" and supplying "its arsenals and magazines."[59]

It appears that there was some basis for these charges that the Virginia Republicans were preparing for a violent confrontation with the federal government. Without doubt there was an interest in military preparedness, but it is also probable that some actual steps were taken to arm the state against possible federal action.

Almost twenty years later John Randolph, a Virginia Republican leader, admitted on the floor of Congress that Virginia had prepared for the possibility of armed conflict. However, eventually, he recalled, the Federalists' "mad career of ambition and usurpation" had been defeated at the polls in the election of 1800. If that had not happened, he explained, Virginia "might have been compelled to resist at the hazard of civil war, for there was no longer any cause for concealing the fact, that the grand armory at Richmond was built to enable the State of Virginia to resist, by force, the encroachments of the then Administration upon her indisputable rights."[60]

In addition, in 1827 William Branch Giles, Virginia governor from 1827 to 1830 and member of the Virginia General Assembly in 1798,[61] recollected the "successful" defensive measures taken in 1798–99 by the Virginia legislature, some involving the arming of the state:

Virginia was . . . threatened for daring to assert her rights—for daring to resist the Alien and Sedition laws. Her representatives on the floor were threatened with arms—with incarceration. Did they then meanly, and timidly yield to these alarms. No sir! They determined again to regain their rights or perish in their attempt. They went earnestly and systematically to work. The first measure they then adopted was to pass a law to protect them in freedom of debate; requiring the State Judges, in the event of any member being imprisoned for words used in debate, to issue a writ of habeas corpus; and to replace the incarcerated member in his place on this floor. They then determined to arm the militia, and to make provision to purchase 5,000 stands of arms. Then it was sir, that the foundation for the regular supply of arms to the militia was laid in the establishment of your armory. To defray the expenses of these measures, they raised the whole taxes of the state twenty-five per cent, with the single scrape of the pen. Backed by these measures, they entered a solemn protest against the offensive laws. . . . Did they eventuate in war, in disunion? No sir. They saved the Union —they saved the union. These measures regained our liberties; and once more, we were free. These measures well deserved success; and they were successful.[62]

How convincing are these accounts by Randolph, Giles, and other Republicans and Federalists? Some other members of the same 1798–99 Virginia legislative session, for example, denied that Virginia intended to use the arms in their opposition to the federal government. And it has been argued that the defensive measures (the tax increase, reorganization of the militia, construction of the armory, and purchase of arms) were not immediate responses to the crisis of 1798–99 but had been discussed in the legislature for a number of years prior to the passage of the Alien and Sedition Laws.[63]

Nonetheless, there is considerable evidence that the Virginians did, in fact, intend to defend themselves by force of arms if necessary. The mere fact that the purchase of arms, the building of an armory, and so forth had been *discussed* prior to 1798 does not eliminate any relationship between the Alien and Sedition Acts and the *passage* of those defense measures. The Virginia legislature earlier had been notoriously negligent in providing arms and men when the Indians had posed a real physical threat. So, even though these defense measures had been discussed earlier, it is unlikely they would have passed had not the passage of the Alien and Sedition Laws as well as other hostile acts by a Federalist-dominated federal government raised an unprecedented challenge and threat to Virginia sovereignty and the safety of Virginia institutions. The Virginians' defensive measures were a natural response to this perceived menace. Moreover, the votes on defense spending prior to 1798 had been nonpartisan. However, during the 1798–99 session defense measures were suddenly passed and by votes that followed fairly strict proto-party lines.[64]

Finally, in addition to John Nicholas and the Federalists who were warning their colleagues of Virginia's action, one Republican at the time did confess publicly that "the object of the last Virginia legislature in increasing taxes upon the people to twenty five per cent is to purchase arms to put in the hands of the people of this state for the purpose of enabling them to oppose the government of the United States."[65]

It seems clear, then, that the Virginia Republican leadership were steeling themselves and preparing for any eventuality in 1798–99. The defense measures of the Virginia legislature were, to be sure, precautionary steps in the event that the federal government were to try to force its will upon the state. But they were steps not inconsistent with the level of apprehension among Virginia Republicans, which had been raised by the passage of the Alien and Sedition Laws (under which Republican editors were now being persecuted and the extraordinary energy and expense that were being devoted to expanding the army, which, for all practical purposes, had Alexander Hamilton at its head. And the fears were not without foundation as letters between Hamilton and his colleagues indicate.

However, for their enclave strategy of pulling their wagons in a circle to work as a tactic to resist what they believed to be a Federalist usurpation of power, Virginia and Kentucky had to avoid any provocative acts that might give the federal government the excuse to move against them or might alienate potential allies in other states. The concept of union appeared to have widespread popular support nationwide. Thus, it was imperative that Kentucky and Virginia walk a tightrope between appearing firm but not irresponsible, resolute and determined but not strident and hostile. Leaders had to enunciate the states' principles in such a way that it would be recognized that they were serious enough to take that last desperate step and secede from the union if the abridgment of their rights continued but also that they would not jeopardize the union by inflammatory, radical, and precipitous actions.

VI

Since the doctrines of nullification and states' rights came to be used in the nineteenth and twentieth centuries to defend slavery and racial discrimination and thus became discredited in the eyes of most contemporary Americans, many scholars have unconsciously attempted to disassociate the demigods of the early republic from the latter-day demagogues of the Old and New South. Thus, the state particularism of John C. Calhoun, Edmund Ruffin, Robert Barnwell Rhett, Henry Flood Bird, and George Wallace as well as others has been seen as outside the tradition and something distinctly different from Jefferson's and Madison's intent in the Kentucky and Virginia resolutions. And it is true that the Jeffersonians were interested in using state interposition to defend personal liberty while the doctrine was subsequently used to defend slavery and racist practices.[66]

But it is also true that Jefferson, Madison, and Taylor clearly had in mind that they were defending their section of the country and its institutions from an oppressive federal government controlled by a section hostile to it. Thus, although the distancing of Jefferson and his allies from later Southern states' rightists has considerable validity, it has been pushed too far and has tended to distort the nature of the politics of the 1790s. One twentieth-century editor of a historical journal, for example, enthusiastically proclaims that the doctrines of the Kentucky and Virginian resolutions "provided the unifying element in the great North-South intersectional alliance" and were the basis for making "the Virginians the outstanding national leaders of American liberalism."[67] It is this emphasis on the "national" and "liberal" aspects of Madison and Jefferson and their resolutions that has hindered many historians from appreciating the strongly sectional character of Jeffersonian Republicanism and from recognizing the real potential for violence in the 1790s.

10.

1799
Virginia versus the Hamiltonian Federalists and the Fears of Armed Conflict

> Once a sound military force is raised it should "be drawn towards Virginia . . . and then let measures be taken to act upon the laws and put Virginia to the Test of resistance." —ALEXANDER HAMILTON

The year 1799 was one of peril for the new republic. As the Republicans had been shocked and enraged by the Alien and Sedition Acts as well as the measures to build up the nation's national defenses, so the Federalists were shocked and enraged by the Kentucky and Virginia resolutions and rumors that Virginia was stockpiling arms. These internal challenges coupled with continuing French depredations against American shipping heightened the Federalists' sense that theirs was a country under siege.

In fact, many Federalists were convinced that they were facing a subversive and seditious internal enemy made up of Virginia and her Southern allies—an enemy that, having mounted political opposition to the government within Congress and the public press, was now threatening to reject the constitutionality of federally enacted laws, thus undermining the Constitution and the union. Even more horrifying was the suspicion that Virginia and France might be working together. It did not take much to envision an armed insurrection, reinforced by French bayonets, against federal authority.

Vivid recollections of the Whiskey Rebellion lurked in the minds of the public men in 1799, and rumors of the storing of arms and preparations for the use of arms as a strategy of opposition magnified and strengthened this memory and made the use of violence to solve political problems seem possible and perhaps even inevitable.[1] Hamilton, for instance, was warned by a Virginian to "take care of yourself" since the Republicans in his state wanted "Nothing short of DISUNION, and the heads of JOHN ADAMS, and ALEXANDER HAMILTON, and some few others." By suspending the building of the state penitentiary in order to use the money for "the purchase of Arms," the Virginians were preparing for violent confrontation, Hamilton was told.[2]

The Federalists were equally alarmed by the Kentucky and Virginia resolutions and what they signified. Theodore Sedgwick, the Massachusetts Federalist, considered them "little short of a declaration of war," and Pickering reported the rumor that Giles, the Virginia Republican leader, had "said expressly that he desired that the Union of the States might be severed."[3]

The situation, however, was to appear even graver to the Federalists with the outbreak of Fries Rebellion in eastern Pennsylvania and President Adams's decision to reopen negotiations with France. So, to Hamilton and his colleagues it seemed to be the time to discuss bold, even extreme, new steps to meet these late 1798 and early 1799 provocations. And while the more radical measures were only discussed, the Federalists did throw themselves into the electoral process, with the express objective of challenging the Virginia Republicans in their home territory during the elections of 1799 and using the provisions of the Sedition Act to try to destroy their political opponents. It was a strategy that met with considerable success and provoked the disheartened Republican leaders to redouble their efforts to create citadels of refuge in Kentucky and Virginia. And by the end of 1799 there was evidence that both Virginia Federalists and Republicans were making some preparations for an unlikely but much feared armed confrontation.

Early in 1799, however, the Federalists' attention was diverted from the South to the heavily German areas of Bucks and Northampton counties in eastern Pennsylvania where residents went on a rampage to protest what they considered a hostile and alien intrusion into their lives. The immediate cause of Fries Rebellion, as it has been styled after its leader John Fries, was congressional approval in 1798 of an act providing for a direct tax to be assessed by federal agents on lands, houses, and slaves. In order to facilitate the collection of the tax, each state was divided into districts with federally appointed assessors assigned to report on the sizes of houses, the types of building materials used, and the number and dimensions of all windows.[4]

The plan outraged a number of Pennsylvanians, who banded together under Fries's leadership to damn the house tax, the Alien and Sedition Acts, the Constitution, Congress, the president, "and all the friends to government, because they were all tories."[5] Furthermore, the insurgents physically and verbally abused and threatened the assessors and also mobilized the local militia to release prisoners who were being held for violating the law.

Although there was no apparent direct relationship between the Republicans' passage of the Kentucky and Virginia resolutions and this outbreak of local resistance to federal authority, the Federalists viewed both actions as part of a general conspiracy against the federal government. For instance, Oliver Wolcott, the secretary of treasury, reported to the president that the rebellion had been caused by "misrepresentations of the measures of government, in seditious pamphlets and newspapers, and in letters from popular characters." By "various artifices," he claimed, these letters and publications had "rendered exceedingly odious" all "the acts for increasing the revenue, the army and navy, and for restraining seditious foreigners."[6]

Hamilton worriedly advised Secretary of War James McHenry against responding with "inadequate force" and thus "magnifying a riot into an insurrection." When the "Government appears in arms," he cautioned, "it ought to appear like a *Hercules*, and inspire respect by the display of strength."[7] Hamilton's fears were groundless, for when the regular army forces reinforced by militia arrived at the troubled area, they found that all traces of the rebellion had vanished. Fries and two others were arrested, tried, and found guilty of treason. But after lengthy legal proceedings, which included two trials and convictions for treason, Fries and his companions were pardoned by President Adams much against the Federalists' wishes.[8]

The Republicans, for their part, disassociated themselves from the insurgents, condemning the violence. They did, however, criticize the government for what they considered an overreaction and an uncalled-for display and use of federal force.[9] Concerned about the reception the Kentucky and Virginia resolutions were facing in the various states, the Republicans felt somewhat vulnerable in the popular mind to Federalists' charges of sedition and disunion. Thus, in order to create as favorable a climate as possible for their resolutions, they no doubt were anxious to maintain some distance between their own constitutional challenges to the government and the violence of the Pennsylvania rebels.

II

The next challenge to the Federalists came from within their own ranks—from the president himself. However it was probably not altogether unexpected. Many Federalists, including Hamilton, had for some time been concerned about Adams's political reliability. The abortive efforts in 1796 to scuttle the New Englander's bid for the presidency were largely triggered by the fear that the testy, fiery, and independent-minded leader would steer a course contrary to the best interests of the Federalists' political future. Nevertheless, Adams's cabinet and the rest of his party were startled early in 1799 when he announced his decision to reopen negotiations with France.

As early as the fall of 1798 the president had begun to soften his earlier stated opposition to negotiating with France. In October, William Vans Murray, the American minister at the Hague, had reported to Adams that the French feared an Anglo-American alliance and that solutions to French attacks upon American shipping could be arrived at short of war. John Quincy Adams; Gerry, who had finally returned to the United States from France; and George Logan, the Pennsylvania Quaker and self-appointed peace emissary; also had all reported peace overtures by the French.[10]

Then in early February 1799, Adams's view of French-American relations was further influenced by crucial dispatches from Murray, relating that the French appeared to be eager for reconciliation, as well as by a letter from Washington, indicating that he supported any movement toward an honorable peace with France. The letter was important, for it seemed to mean that, in the event of a showdown with the pro-war Federalists, Adams could count on Washington's neutrality, if not open support.[11]

The increasing friction between Adams and other Federalists about expanding and equipping the army further impelled Adams toward reopening formal negotiations with France as did Adams's belief that Hamilton and his supporters were usurping his power as commander-in-chief. Sedgwick, who was pushing for speedier action in organizing the army, was alarmed at what he perceived as Adams's antagonism toward the army and its proponents. In a confidential letter to Hamilton, Sedgwick described an extraordinary meeting he had had with the president, in which Adams had told him that he was not worried about Virginia and its challenge to federal authority. It was "weakness to apprehend anything from them," Adams had declared, "but if you must have an army I will give it to you, but remember it will make the government more unpopular than all their acts." The public, he had told Sedgwick, had "submitted with more patience than any people ever did to the burden of taxes," which had been "*liberally laid on,* but their patience will not last." Getting increasingly exercised, Adams had charged that the proposal to elevate the rank of the commander-in-chief of the army was part of a plot "to appoint him general over the President" and to subordinate the civilian to the military authority.[12] Adams's fears were not entirely unjustified: when he gave his address to

Congress in December 1798 and was joined on the speaker's platform by Generals Washington, Hamilton, and Pinckney, the ominous symbolism was readily apparent.[13]

Despite the pressure of pro-war militants in his party, by mid-February Adams had made up his mind to reopen negotiations with France. To implement this, he nominated William Vans Murray as minister plenipotentiary to France. Stunned by the president's action, the Hamiltonian Federalists vowed to scuttle Adams's plans. "Had the foulest heart and ablest head in the world, been permitted to select the most embarrassing and ruinous measure, perhaps it would have been precisely the one, which has been adopted," Sedgwick declared. Pickering assured Hamilton that the deed was "wholly *his* [Adams's] *own act,* without any participation or communication with any of us."[14]

Sedgwick and a Senate committee met with Adams in an effort to persuade him that, if he insisted upon reopening negotiations with France, he should at least send a commission rather than one man. It was obvious that the commission idea sprang from the hope that it might be used to blunt the peace efforts as well as reflect the Hamiltonian Federalists' lack of confidence in Murray, who although a Federalist had been the liaison between Adams and Talleyrand. Adams refused to back down, threatening to resign. But when faced with Murray's rejection by a Federalist caucus, he agreed to a commission. The commission, however, was not immediately dispatched to France.[15]

Despite the apparent compromise in late February over the mission to France, for the remainder of the year—indeed for the remainder of his administration—the Hamiltonian Federalists were in a virtual state of rebellion against Adams. In fact, almost immediately after the compromise was reached, Adams left the seat of government at Philadelphia and retired in isolation to Quincy for some eight months. Historian Peter Shaw has called this episode "the turning point" of Adams's presidency, a presidency marked by "a few grand gestures" without "an administrative program." Thus, although Adams's decision to reopen negotiations was a statesmanlike gesture of "selflessness" and exhibited a patriotic concern for country above politics, it also indicated a leader who always "lacked the instinct for the required follow-up."[16]

After Adams's retirement to Quincy, the anti-Adams Federalists denounced what they saw as their betrayal by the president and schemed to rid themselves of him. Robert Troup complained bitterly to Rufus King that Adams was governing "by fits and starts—without the advice of his friends around him—nay without even consulting them."[17] And George Cabot told King that Adams was practicing the "pitiful politics of Gerry," which had "been reprobated by 9/10ths of the good Federalists and by a good majority of the people."[18] In other words, Adams's perceived moderation and even nonpartisanship, like Gerry's, was viewed as inimical to the welfare of Federalism, and Federalism was seen as synonymous with the welfare of the country. Relations had so deteriorated between Adams and his critics by the late spring and early summer that Hamilton urged the cabinet to step in and assume more responsibility since Adams was so flagrantly neglecting his duties. At the same time, Washington was being encouraged to come out of retirement and seek a third term.[19]

In September 1799, when Adams finally did rejoin the government in Trenton, New Jersey, where it had retreated to avoid the yellow fever epidemic in Philadelphia, his cabinet and Hamilton beseeched him to continue to delay the envoys' departure for France. As part of this appeal, Hamilton and Adams had an extraordinary meeting in which the former secretary of treasury addressed the president, as Adams recalled, "in a Style the most peremptory and even Swaggering." Adams, however, saw himself as retaining his "good humor" and even pitying "the little man" who spoke with such "a degree of heat and effervescence" and with so little knowledge of France and Great Britain. "Never in my life," Adams remembered, "did I hear a man talk more like a fool." Faced with Hamilton's attempted coercion and the cabinet's effort to delay or cancel the envoys' mission, Adams ordered them to leave for France immediately.[20] This left the Federalist opposition to Adams in despair. The president had betrayed the cause and the defeat of Federalism seemed inevitable and would bring with it "a temporary reign of *American Jacobinism*."[21]

III

In 1799 the anti-Adams Federalists considered a number of strategies to overcome the dangers they saw facing the country. As before, they believed that a strong military force was necessary to deter both internal and external enemies. But, in addition, there was an increasing interest in using the military and the popular patriotic sentiment that military preparedness had evoked to achieve policy goals. In foreign affairs it was proposed that war with France or a United States strike against Spanish territories in the Southwest and South America would awaken latent nationalist pride and rally most dissidents around the flag in support of the government. Internally, a number of suggestions were made to weaken the sectional nature of the opposition. In addition to increasing the jurisdiction of federal judges to neutralize localist bias against the federal government, Hamilton proposed breaking up the larger states and redrawing the geographical boundaries. This project, the most nationalistic and most radical of any of Hamilton's proposals, would have virtually assured the breakup of the union and possibly caused a civil war had there been an attempt to implement it. It was clear that Hamilton as well as the Republicans regarded the states as the last bulwark of opposition defense.

Hamilton did not wait long to propose strong action to counter the threat posed by the Kentucky and Virginia resolutions. In a letter to Sedgwick, Hamilton called for a "special Committee" to consider the hostile actions of the two states.[22] Outlining its conclusions in advance, Hamilton wrote that the committee would affirm the "constitutionality and expediency" of the Alien and Sedition Laws and charge that "the doctrines advanced by Virginia and Kentucky . . . [would] destroy the Constitution of the United States." In addition, the report would disclose "the full evidence . . . of a regular conspiracy to overturn the government" as well as the Southerners' intent to encourage France "to decline accommodation and proceed in hostility." Care must be taken, however, "to distinguish the people of Virginia from the legislature" and to express "strong confidence in the good sense and patriotism of the people."

While the public would be digesting the proposed report's indictment of the actions of Virginia and Kentucky, Hamilton, who had earlier stressed the importance of a strong army to deal with the "possibility of domestic disorders," recommended that every effort be made to continue to strengthen the regular army forces. And once a sound military force was raised it should "be drawn towards Virginia . . . and then let measures be taken to act upon the laws and put Virginia to the Test of resistance." A regular army was essential because Hamilton doubted that the militia forces would be up to the task of subduing such a *"refractory* and powerful *state."*[23]

But in addition to playing a substantial role in intimidating internal opposition, the army, in the minds of some Federalists, was also seen as becoming an important instrument in an expanded and more aggressive United States foreign policy. Not only would a larger army protect the country from bellicose French designs, but it might also be used in a grandiose scheme to link up with British naval strength and liberate Latin America from Spain, thus keeping Latin America out of French hands. This plan, initially put forward by a Venezuelan patriot,

Sebastian Francisco de Miranda, began when Miranda approached King in London early in 1798 and suggested that the United States furnish a ground force of fifty thousand troops for the project.[24]

It did not take long for Hamilton, Rufus King, and other Federalists to endorse the venture with enthusiasm, with the former secretary of treasury writing to King that he was "glad" that the United States was "to furnish the whole land force necessary." And the command of the force, Hamilton assumed, "would very naturally fall upon me —and I hope I should disappoint no favourable anticipation."[25] Despite or perhaps because of Hamilton's eagerness, Adams was cool to the idea. A disappointed but determined King beseeched Hamilton: "For God's sake, attend to the very interesting subject. . . . Providence seems to have prepared the way. . . . Our children will reproach us if we neglect our duty."[26]

As long as war remained undeclared between the United States and France, Hamilton recognized that there would be less opportunity for the kind of bold stroke envisioned in the Miranda scheme and more opportunity for the president to drag his feet. Early in 1799, therefore, he proposed declaring war on France if negotiations for a peaceful settlement had not begun by August 1, 1799. At the same time he warned of French designs on Spanish-held Florida and Louisiana and urged that the United States acquire these territories on the grounds they were "essential to the permanency of the Union." This preemptive strike by the United States, Hamilton explained in a letter, would nicely complement Miranda's plan "to detach South America from Spain which is the only Channel, though [sic] which the riches of *Mexico* and *Peru* are conveyed to France."[27]

But while Hamilton dreamed of the glory that might accompany a joint British-American expedition against France in Latin America, his more immediate concern continued to be Virginia and her Southern allies. And in the fall of 1799 he wrote a remarkable letter in which he expressed his antagonism toward the Southern Republicans and then outlined various schemes to weaken them. Despite the "disastrous and disgusting scenes of the French Revolution," which should have made Americans wary of social and political disorder, Hamilton told Federalist Jonathan Dayton of New Jersey, "sentiments [in the United States] dangerous to social happiness have not been diminished." Political opposition to the government had "acquired more system" and had become "bolder in the avowal of its designs, less solicitous than it was to discriminate between the Constitution and the administration, and more open and more enterprising in its projects."

The Kentucky and Virginia resolutions, he charged, were no less than "an attempt to change the government."[28]

Hamilton's effort to justify the government's position toward its political opposition provides insight into the way the government and its friends perceived their opponents in late 1799. According to Hamilton, the opposition, which no longer discriminated between "the Constitution and the administration," threatened through their resolutions to change the nature of the federal government, the union, and the Constitution. In looking at the situation, of course, he conveniently ignored the fact that, from the beginning, the Federalists had equated support for the government with support for the Constitution and had tended to discredit all opposition by questioning their loyalty to both.

Virginia's action to approve the so-called seditious resolutions was made even more ominous in Hamilton's eyes by the state's reported preparations to support its position by force. Hamilton warned that the Virginia dissidents were "preparing considerable arsenals and magazines" as well as improving the state of readiness of the state's militia. "Vigorous measures of counteraction" had to be adopted, he concluded, for it had become obvious that the opposition had resolved to make the union's "existence a question of force." It was imperative, therefore, that the government and its supporters act quickly while they controlled "all the constitutional powers" for it would be "unpardonable" if they did not "exert them to surround the Constitution with more ramparts and to disconcert the schemes of its enemies."

Perhaps the most extraordinary part of Hamilton's letter to Dayton, however, were his proposals. In addition to calling for "augmenting the means and consolidating the strength of the government," which included raising more revenue and increasing the naval and military strength of the country," Hamilton suggested taking steps to "extend the influence and promote the popularity of the government." Among these were strengthening the hand of the federal judiciary by subdividing each state into districts and by appointing federal justices of the peace to avoid obstruction by local judges in some states. He also recommended the improvement of roads, which "would be a measure universally popular," and the passage of a constitutional amendment empowering Congress to construct canals across several jurisdictions.

Furthermore, Hamilton recommended the passage of additional laws that would restrain and punish "incendiary and seditious practices" since it was necessary to "preserve confidence in the officers of the general government, by preserving their reputation from malicious and unfounded slanders." Apparently, Hamilton felt that the Sedition Law of 1798 was not adequate and additional protection from popular criticism was needed for the federal government and its officers.

Most radical among Hamilton's proposals, however, was his scheme to amend the Constitution in order to subdivide "the great states," which, he was convinced, would be the most effective way of crippling Virginia's power. He felt this action was "indispensable [to the] security of the general government, and with it of the Union." He argued that "Great States will often be supposed to machinate against it, and in certain situations will be able to do it with decisive effect." Therefore, the "subdivision of such States ought to be a cardinal point in the federal policy, and small States are doubtless best adapted to the purposes of local regulation and to the preservation of the republican spirit." Hamilton, however, acknowledged that such a plan might be inexpedient and even "dangerous to propose, at this time."[29]

Hamilton was surely right that any attempt to implement such a radical scheme was "dangerous" and most likely would have led to a breakup of the union and to armed conflict between the federal government and at least some of the Southern states. In a real sense it might be said that Hamilton's proposed treatment was worse than the disease and might well have killed the patient. The plan for subdividing the large states was obviously aimed at Virginia, the center and headquarters of the opposition, with the objective of protecting the union by reducing sectional conflict. Both sides recognized that the major political cleavages seemed to be hardening along sectional lines. And sectional division, as Madison had noted earlier in the decade, was the most menacing since it posed the greatest threat to the union. But whereas the Republicans regarded sectional opposition by Virginia and its allies to Federalist policies as a reluctant strategy of last resort to preserve liberty, the Federalists viewed the same activities as nothing short of seditious.

IV

Hamilton and his Federalist allies discussed a number of radical actions, military, legislative, and constitutional, that they *might* theoretically take, but they were also very successful in the legal and electoral strategies they *actually* employed. In addition to a relentless attack on the Republican press, they made a major electoral effort to weaken their Virginia protagonists by attempting to build support for the government in the center of opposition, Virginia and the South.

The Federalists believed that the opposition press represented a seditious threat to their continuance in power, and, therefore, to the stability of the government and the Constitution.[30] Among others, Republican editors of the New York *Time Piece,* the Boston *Independent Chronicle,* the Bennington *Vermont Gazette,* the New London, Connecticut, *Bee,* the upstate New York *Mount Pleasant Register,* the New York *Argus,* and the Philadelphia *Aurora* were prosecuted under the Sedition Law, which made it a crime to print material critical of government leaders.[31]

Deciding to test Virginia's opposition to the law as pronounced in the Virginia Resolutions, Federalist Supreme Court Justice Samuel Chase, during a tour of the Southern circuit of the court, began criminal proceedings against Thomas Callender, one of the most vitriolic of the Republican publicists. To escape prosecution at the time the Sedition Act was passed, Callender fled from Philadelphia, where he had been living, and took refuge in Virginia. Once in Virginia he renewed his attacks upon Adams and the Federalists, and in late 1799 he published *The Prospect before Us,* a scathingly critical attack on Adams, whom he called a "hoary headed incendiary." Tried in federal court in Richmond before the highly partisan Justice Chase, Callender was convicted, sentenced to serve nine months in jail, and fined $200. Although Virginia Republicans did not attempt to interfere with the prosecution, both Jefferson and John Taylor of Caroline raised money for Callender's defense, and Jefferson believed that the editor "should be substantially defended" either by state counsel "or private contributions."[32]

Perhaps the most significant Federalist prosecution under the Sedition Law, however, was the trial of William Duane, editor of the Philadelphia *Aurora,* one of the largest papers in terms of circulation and the most outspoken in its criticism of the Federalists.[33]

The successor to Benjamin Franklin Bache, who had been beaten twice by "Federalist hoodlums"[34] and had died during the yellow fever epidemic in 1798, Duane had been born in New York prior to the Revolution, had gone to Ireland with his mother before the onset of the war and, after a controversial career as a newspaper critic of the British government, had returned to America in 1796. Because of his long absence from the United States, his Irish ancestry, and his vigorous denunciation of the Federalist-sponsored Alien Friends Act, Duane immediately became a target of Federalist suspicion and abuse. After a scrape with authorities early in 1799 over his attempt to circulate petitions calling for the repeal of the act, Duane further enraged the Federalists in the summer of 1799 by charging that through corruption and intrigue England was influencing the operation of the American government.[35]

Immediately afterward Secretary of State Pickering warned the president about the *Aurora,* charging that it contained "an uninterrupted stream of slander on the American government" and that its editor was a dangerous alien, who, as a captain of a company of volunteers, would "oppose the authority of the government; and in case of war and invasion by the French," would join them.[36] Adams, who had a short fuse when it came to criticism directed against himself, as much of it had been, raged: "Is there anything evil in the regions of actuality or possibility, that the Aurora has not suggested of me?" If the prosecutor, he wrote Pickering, did "not think this paper libelous," he was "not fit for his office." The "matchless effrontery of this Duane merits the execution of the alien law," the president raved, and he was "very willing to try its strength upon him."[37] Duane was hauled before a court, but the proceedings dragged on without resolution and the Federalists despaired of ever being able to jail him.[38]

Then a Senate bill, which was no less than an attempt to assure continued Federalist control of the government, brought Duane's troubles with the authorities to a head. James Ross, Federalist senator from Pennsylvania, introduced the remarkable bill, which would have set aside the constitutional provisions for counting electoral votes in presidential elections. The bill, which was eventually defeated in the House of Representatives, would have given a committee made up of six members from each house plus the chief justice of the Supreme Court the power to decide which votes to count and which ones to disallow. No appeal of their judgment was to be allowed. And since the Federalists controlled both houses of Congress as well as the Supreme Court, the committee would have been virtually "an adjunct of the Federalist party."[39]

Free on bail and waiting for the resumption of his trial, Duane angered and defied the Federalists by obtaining a copy of the bill, condemning it, and permitting its unauthorized publication in the *Aurora.* The Republican leadership, along with Duane, were horrified at the boldness of the Federalists in what appeared to be an attempt to steal the election by bypassing procedures established by the Constitution. In a letter to Jefferson, Madison worried about "how far the choice of the Ex. may be drawn out of the Constitutional hands, and

subjected to the management of the Legislature." This was particularly dangerous, Madison believed, since Adams might "be bribed
into the usurpations [of the bill] by so shaping them as to favor his
re-election."[40]

Responding with a vengeance-seeking vigor, the Federalist-controlled Senate charged the intrepid Duane with a "high breach of
privileges" for his unauthorized publication of the Ross bill. Duane,
recognizing the tenseness of the moment, warned his readers "not to
be led by mistaken zeal to say or do anything discreditable to the
republican cause." When he realized that the Senate planned to act as
judge and jury in their case against him, however, Duane went into
hiding until Congress adjourned in order to escape almost certain
conviction and jailing.[41]

Some Republicans, however, were not unmindful of the propa-
ganda value of Duane's case and were not pleased with his decision to
flee. Monroe argued that Duane should "have met the censure and
judgment of the Senate." As it was, the Virginian maintained, the
Senate had established "the principle" and avoided the "odium of his
prosecution," and Duane will suffer "all they can inflict with out exciting publick sensibility in his favor."[42] In other words, Monroe complained, an opportunity had been lost for the creation of a Republican
martyr.

Despite the tenseness and the potential danger of the political
division, many Republicans, such as Monroe, recognized the possible
political value of the Federalists' excesses. Yet two possible negative
outcomes persisted. First, through repressive actions under the Alien
and Sedition Laws and the proposed Ross Bill, the Federalists might
be successful in their efforts to destroy the opposition or to prevent the
Republicans from taking power even though they might win a popular
mandate. Second, frustrated members of the opposition might by
their own excessive reaction to Federalist provocation, in Duane's words,
"be led by mistaken zeal" to do something that might discredit "the
republican cause." This might alienate potential supporters in Northern and Middle Atlantic states.

V

The Federalist election strategy in 1799, which stood a better
though far from certain chance of success, was to get popular Southern public men, such as Washington, John Marshall, and Patrick Henry,
to come forward under the Federalist banner in areas of opposition

hegemony. Electoral success in the South, it was believed, would shatter the notion of the opposition's invincibility in Virginia, ameliorate antigovernment sentiment in the South, and provide the Federalists and silent supporters of the government with a means to legitimize and sustain their cause.

During the early years of union, Washington had commanded such enormous respect and trust from all sections of the country that his presidency had done much to mitigate the deep, underlying sectional animosities and suspicions. With Washington's retirement, however, a powerful force for union had been lost. But Hamilton hoped that the former president's "influence . . . [could] be brought in direct action" to counter the "Opposition-Faction" that was assuming "so much a Geographical complexion."[43] And Washington, increasingly bitter and angry toward the opposition, willingly cooperated with Hamilton to do what he could to build Federalist strength. In addition to recruiting loyal Federalists to officer the recently authorized New Army, he succeeded in persuading the Revolutionary hero, Patrick Henry, to run for a seat in the Virginia General Assembly. It would be the converted Federalist's last race, however, for he died only months after his successful election.[44]

John Marshall, whose popularity had dramatically increased after his return from the failed mission to France, was promoted by the Federalists for a seat in the House of Representatives, which he won. Sedgwick, convinced that Marshall would "give a tone to the federal politics South of the Susquehanna," claimed that there had never "been an instance where the commencement of a political career was so important as is that of General Marshall." He was not only "highly and deservedly respected by the friends of the Government from the South," but "we can do nothing without him."[45]

The Federalists regarded the April 1799 elections in Virginia as the key to their efforts to thwart the development of a sectionally based opposition. In addition to putting popular names such as Marshall and Henry in the field beneath their standard, the Federalists increased the scope and intensity of their political activity, which included the establishment of a newspaper, the *Virginia Federalist*, in Richmond. It was "not sufficient that we content ourselves with victory," one Federalist wrote, "it must be followed up until every germ of faction be destroyed."[46]

Political fears and animosities fueled rising tensions within the state leading to the formation of political mobs as well as other manifestations of a bitterly divided society. And to prepare for any eventuality, including violence, Federalists in Richmond and Petersburg organized private militia forces.[47]

The Republicans also looked to the elections in the spring of 1799 as an important opportunity to mobilize Virginians in defense of republicanism and to elect key Republican leaders to positions of authority and responsibility. Anticipating a possible violent confrontation between Virginia and its allies and the Federalist-controlled federal government, Taylor, for example, urged that Monroe be pushed for the governorship of Virginia. He stressed the "immense importance" of having a "decided character at the head of one government" for "the influence it will have upon public opinion." The governor, Taylor reminded Jefferson, wielded substantial powers, including "the important one of commanding the militia." Thus it was essential that this power be in the hands of the right person. The Republicans, Taylor warned, had "been too inattentive to the consequences of having a tory first magistrate and military commander of the state."[48]

Madison, who had led the battle against the Jay Treaty in the House of Representatives and had retired from Congress in 1797, was also being urged to become politically active again and run for a seat in the state legislature. Virginia, Taylor wrote Madison, was "the hope of republicans throughout the union," and, if the Federalists were successful in electing the popular Patrick Henry to the legislature, he might be able to remove "her resistance to monarchical measures." If this were to happen, "the whole body will be dispirited and fall a sudden and easy prey to the enemies of liberty." "If you will not save yourself or your friend," Taylor implored him, "save your country," for the "public sentiment of Virginia" was in a "crisis" and "at the next assembly it will take a permanent form which will fix the fate of America."[49]

In a petition to Madison, several supporters also argued that his services in the state legislature were urgently needed. They maintained that it was essential that "the powerful agency of *wise* and *firm* State measures" contain "the general government within the just limits of the Constitution."[50] Jefferson added his encouragement for Madison to serve at the state level.[51]

The Republicans did have some success in the spring of 1799 in electing a number of their leaders to positions of responsibility and power in the state government. Madison was elected to the Virginia legislature and was congratulated by Jefferson, who reminded him that "much good may be done by a proper direction of the local force."[52]

The Republican accomplishment was a limited one, however, for the Federalists had scored an important electoral triumph in doubling their strength in Virginia's contingent in the United States House of Representatives. The Federalist victory, which increased the number of Federalist congressmen from 4 to 8 out of a total of 19 or 20,[53] and apparently modestly increased the number of the friends of the government in the heavily Republican General Assembly,[54] startled and unsettled the Republicans, who were particularly dismayed by the success of Federalism in the very citadel of opposition.

Outside of Virginia in other Southern states, the Federalists also triumphed. They won 5 out of 10 congressional seats in North Carolina, 5 out of 6 in South Carolina, as well as both seats in Georgia. And nationally, in elections that ran through the fall, winter, and spring of 1798 and 1799, the Federalists increased their margin in the House of Representatives from a 64 to 53 split in the Fifth Congress to a 63 to 43 division in the Sixth Congress.[55]

VI

Following the elections, the Virginians and Kentuckians sought to deal with the disappointing reception the Virginia and Kentucky resolutions had received. Jefferson had repeatedly asserted that time was on the Republicans' side and that public revulsion against a standing army and taxes to support it would finally open the eyes of a sincere but naive public.

But the pressure had to be maintained. And in August 1799, Jefferson proposed to Madison that "the principles already advanced by Virginia and Kentucky" should not "be yielded in silence." Therefore additional resolutions should be adopted that would respond to criticisms of the original resolutions. For Jefferson continued to be "confident that the good sense of the American people and their attachment to those very rights which we are now vindicating will, before it shall be too late, rally with us round the true principles of our federal compact." The new resolutions, according to Jefferson, should affirm the "rights" of the states to protect themselves from "palpable violations of the constitutional compact by the Federal government" but express "in affectionate and conciliatory language our warm attachment to union with our sister-states, and to the instrument and principles by which we are united." And in language reminiscent of the Declaration of Independence, Jefferson suggested that the resolutions declare that Virginians and Kentuckians were "not at all disposed to make every measure of error or wrong a cause of scission" and, in fact, "willing to sacrifice to . . . [union] every thing except those rights of self government the securing of which was the object of that compact." Indeed Virginians and Kentuckians should make it clear, Jefferson urged, that they were willing "to wait with patience till those passions and delusions shall have passed over which the federal government have artfully and successfully excited to cover its own abuses and to conceal its designs."[56]

However, Jefferson ominously added a final warning that was to be his most extreme statement on the possibility of the ultimate disruption of the union. If Virginians and Kentuckians were to be disappointed in their expectations, Jefferson threatened, they would "sever . . . [themselves] from that union we so much value, rather than give up the rights of self government which we have reserved, and in which alone we see liberty, safety and happiness."[57]

Madison, however, convinced Jefferson to moderate his language and by the time Jefferson wrote another Republican leader a couple of weeks later he had revised the last sentence to read: "we should never think of separation but for repeated and enormous violations, so these, when they occur, will be cause enough themselves."[58]

Following Jefferson's advice, both Kentucky and Virginia drafted resolutions in 1799 and 1800 answering the criticisms of their earlier resolutions and renewing their attack on the Alien and Sedition Laws. Kentucky, while it affirmed its "attachment to the Union," also warned that "a nullification of those acts by the States [was considered] to be the rightful remedy."[59] The Virginia Report of 1800, authored by Madison, denounced the Federalists' centralizing tendencies and defended certain basic rights that were guaranteed by the Bill of Rights. In addition Madison pointed out that a stable union could be endangered by an excess of state or federal power with the latter transforming "the republican system of the United States to a monarchy," while the former would create a state of chaos worse than had existed under the Articles of Confederation. Denying that the Virginia Resolutions had promoted disunion, the Report argued that the sole purpose of the resolutions had been to articulate an opinion "unaccompanied with any other effect than what they may produce . . . by exciting reflection."[60]

VII

By the beginning of the election year 1800, then, the Republicans in Kentucky and Virginia had restated their objections to the Alien and Sedition Laws and had attempted to meet and to answer the criticisms expressed by their sister states. It was recognized that the success or failure of the new diplomatic mission to France, at last departed, would be a critical factor in the approaching election. But Madison questioned whether Adams and his envoys were sincerely committed to peace with France and warned that "the possibility of failure in the diplomatic experiment will present the most specious obstacle to an immediate discharge of the army."[61]

Jefferson, like Madison, was concerned about the army and argued that "the disbanding of the army on principles of economy and safety" should be a major objective. In addition there should be "a sincere cultivation of the Union," but there should continue to be "protestations against violations of the true principles of our constitution" in order to "prevent precedent and acquiescence from being pleaded." And to prevent "any pretext for keeping up the army," there should be "nothing . . . said or done which shall look or lead to force." Finally, Jefferson advised exploiting the developing rift in the Federalist ranks. If "the monarchical party" were "really split into pure Monocrats & Anglo-monocrats, we should leave to them alone to manage all those points of difference" and do "nothing which may hoop them together."[62]

Indeed Jefferson's strategy was a good one. A lowered profile by the Republicans and the reduction of international tensions made it difficult if not impossible for the Hamilton and Adams's factions to "hoop" themselves together to battle the Republicans. And the bitter internecine warfare among the Federalists was to be a major factor in shaping the political events of the next year.

11.

The Election of 1800

There is scarcely a possibility that we shall escape a *Civil War*. Murder,
robbery, rape, adultery, and incest will all be openly taught and practiced,
the air will be rent with the cries of distress, the soil will be soaked with
blood, and the nation black with crimes.
— A CONNECTICUT FEDERALIST ON THE POSSIBILITY OF A
JEFFERSON VICTORY IN 1800

The election of 1800—even after more than 200 years of American history—stands as one of the country's two most critical presidential elections, second only to the election of 1860 that polarized the nation, sent Abraham Lincoln to the presidency, and led to Americans choosing sides and fighting a bloody civil war. The elections were in many ways similar. Both occurred during times of extreme sectional hostility and suspicion. Both were characterized by an acutely divided polity. And both were surrounded by rumors of violence and the dismemberment of the union. The major difference, of course, was that Lincoln's election *did* result in the breakup of the union and a civil war, while, although Jefferson's election *could* have shattered the union, it did not.

But the fact that the dismemberment of the union and civil war did not occur in 1800 should not obscure the fact that the public men in 1800 did not know that the election process would eventually arrive at a peaceful outcome. Indeed, there were disturbing signs that this would not be the case. On the one hand, Virginians and their Southern allies felt under siege. The Alien and Sedition Laws, they believed, were clearly efforts by the Federalist-controlled government to destroy the Republican opposition, just as the newly expanded army was seen as a means of overcoming particularly intransigent resistance. On the other hand, the Kentucky and Virginia resolutions, coupled with the alleged stockpiling of arms and other defensive measures by Virginia, had convinced the Federalists that the Virginia Republicans were at the forefront of a movement to defy the government.

Most Republicans would have agreed with Elbridge Gerry that the election was no less than a contest pitting the forces of republicanism against "a party extended throughout the union, both active and powerful [and] . . . utterly devoted to a monarchical system."[1] And, thus, they saw a Republican victory, in the words of Monroe, as vital to "secure to us forever those liberties that were acquired by our revolution; which ought never to have been put in danger."[2]

But if the Republicans deeply distrusted their opponents, so did their adversaries. To some Federalists, a victory of the Republicans, with their affinity for France and its revolution, would mean the triumph of Jacobinism and anarchy over order. One Connecticut Federalist outdid himself in forecasting how grim the results of a Republican victory would be. "There is scarcely a possibility that we shall escape a *Civil War*," he bewailed. "Murder, robbery, rape, adultery, and incest will all be openly taught and practiced, the air will be rent with the cries of distress, the soil will be soaked with blood, and the nation black with crimes."[3]

As the presidential election approached, neither the Federalists nor the Republicans could confidently assume victory. The Republicans were anything but overconfident. The congressional elections the previous year, for example, had been relatively successful for the Federalists, especially in the Southern states of Virginia, North Carolina, South Carolina, and Georgia, where the Federalists had won ten formerly Republican seats.[4] Although the Federalists appeared to be at the crest of their wave of power, however, they were split by a bitter internecine dispute that would only worsen as the months were to go by.

While no one could predict the outcome of the election with any assurance, what *was* clear to everyone in 1800 was that the election had a devastatingly negative potential that could be played out in such scenarios as the breakup of the union along the North-South fault lines of American politics or possibly even civil war.

II

The presidential election of 1800 was similar to the election four years earlier in that the same set of presidential candidates faced each other. But there was a major difference. The election of 1800 was the first one the country faced without Washington, who died late in 1799. The enormously popular leader had served, even in retirement, as a source of great strength and comfort for the Federalists and for his country, and, as a Virginian, he had served to mitigate Republican influence at the center of opposition strength.

But there were other dissimilarities between 1796 and 1800. In

1796, for example, Jefferson had, after the years of political inactivity following his retirement, been a reluctant candidate, so much so that his friends had even worried that he might not serve if elected. In 1800, however, not only was it a foregone conclusion that Jefferson would be the Republican candidate, he had also become the active leader of the Republicans since his election to the vice presidency.

Republican political strategy had changed in the four years as well. In 1798 the Federalist-sponsored Alien and Sedition Laws had moved the country into the third stage of political development in the 1790s, a stage in which the Republicans emphasized a more overtly self-conscious sectional political enclave strategy. This strategy included calls for nullifying federal law and considered secession as a desperate step of last resort. And although the Southern-led Republicans in 1800, like 1796, continued to reach out for support from other sections in order to win the presidency, the opposition had become an increasingly Southern and Virginia phenomenon.

Thus, in 1800, as opposed to 1796, the Republican mood was profoundly different. Prior to 1798 the Republicans had been optimistic that leaders who supported unconstitutional measures hostile to the general good of society would be repudiated by the people. However, after 1798 they were less confident about their ultimate national success, for the Federalists had increased their strength while the Republicans had seemingly become more isolated and beleaguered. The Federalist buildup of the army, the prosecution of Republican editors, and the attempted elimination of other forms of dissent had confirmed the Republicans' worst fears. Prior to 1798, the Republicans had only speculated what their opponents might do given sufficient political power. After 1798 their gloomy speculations had become a terrible reality. So, sobered by the ferocity of their opponents' intolerance, the Virginia-led opposition believed that the election of 1800 might well be the last opportunity to save the Constitution and the union.

Therefore, while the election of 1796 had been the first truly contested presidential election in American history and reflected considerable mutual proto-party intolerance, fear, and distrust, the political divisions in 1800 were of a different magnitude. The XYZ affair, the undeclared naval war with France, the Alien and Sedition Laws, the defense buildup, and the Virginia and Kentucky resolutions all had created an unprecedented political crisis in the new republic that had seen a number of crises during the course of its troubled twelve-year history. One English observer, impressed by the gravity of the political situation, wrote in the spring of 1800 that the "whole system of the

American Government seems to me to be tottering to its foundations, and so far from being able to enforce upon the country good faith towards foreign powers, I much doubt their power of maintaining internal tranquility."[5]

While Jefferson's nomination as the Republican presidential candidate was unquestioned in 1800, Adams's Federalist nomination was not. In fact, as the year 1799 ended, the Federalists faced a real quandary regarding their presidential choice. Adams's decision to reopen negotiations with France had irrevocably split the supporters of the government at the very time when unity was needed to deal with Virginia's challenge to national authority. Never having had the enthusiastic support of the Hamiltonian faction of the party, Adams further alienated that group by apparently disregarding, on a number of occasions, the advice of his cabinet members, who, for the most part, were getting their cues from Hamilton. The president was condescendingly regarded by that group as vain, vindictive, unreliable, and quixotic.

Hamilton outlined the dilemma of the anti-Adams faction in a letter to Rufus King early in 1800. Shall the Federalists "risk a serious schism by an attempt to change" presidential candidates, Hamilton asked, or should "they annihilate themselves and hazard their cause by continuing to uphold those who suspect and hate them?" The urgency of the situation, Hamilton said, was underscored by the threat posed by Virginia where the "spirit of faction" was "more violent than ever." The Virginians, Hamilton warned, "possessed completely all the powers of the local government," but, in addition, were "resolved to possess those of the national, by the most dangerous combinations." And, "if they cannot effect this," he cautioned ominously, they would "resort to the employment of physical force."[6]

Despite Hamilton's concerns, Adams was renominated. In December, 1799, a group of Federalist leaders met and, after considerable disagreement, supported Adams for reelection.[7] And in May, the Federalist delegation in Congress agreed to "support, *bona fide*, Mr. Adams and General [C. C.] Pinckney," the latter a South Carolinian and brother of Thomas Pinckney, Adams's running mate in 1796. Remembering only too well Hamilton's scheme to have Thomas Pinckney elected over him as president in 1796, Adams was angered by the caucus agreement, which failed to designate him as the presidential candidate and C. C. Pinckney as the vice presidential candidate.

The Hamiltonian Federalists were also dismayed with the ticket, obviously for different reasons, but were resigned to it. Although deeply concerned about Adams's decision to reopen negotiations with France and his resulting estrangement from "those whom . . . [Adams] theretofore [had] deemed his best friends," Sedgwick concluded that the division of the Federalists into pro- and anti-Adams wings was an "evil" of an "alarming nature," and, despite the reservations about the president, urged that the caucus agreement "be executed" or "otherwise we cannot escape the fangs of Jefferson."[8]

While the Federalists were squabbling among themselves over Adams's nomination, the Republicans were articulating their political ideas and attempting to broaden their base of support by reaching out to sympathizers in solidly Federalist areas. Jefferson and the Virginia Republicans recognized that they had to gain the support of states outside the South and West in order to win the election. Thus, in an effort to weaken the Federalist hold on New England, Jefferson cultivated, among others, Gideon Granger, a Republican leader in Connecticut, and Elbridge Gerry of Massachusetts.

In a letter to Granger, Jefferson stressed the importance of New England to the country and his hope that the "delusion" created by the Federalists was waning there. "Should the whole body of New England continue in opposition" to certain principles including "freedom of religion, freedom of the press, trial by jury and to economical government," he said, the future of the federal government and the union itself would be imperiled because the government could "never be harmonious and solid, while so respectable a portion of its citizens support principles which go directly to a change of the federal constitution, to sink the state governments, consolidate them into one, and to monarchize that." The United States, as he was to reiterate many times, echoing an Antifederalist theme, was "too large to have all its affairs directed by a single government."[9]

In his letter to Granger and another letter to Gerry, Jefferson enunciated and developed his political principles. Concerned that the federal government was usurping the share of power the Constitution gave to the states and to Congress, he argued that the Republicans would reestablish a proper balance and also protect those freedoms guaranteed by the Bill of Rights—of religion, press, and trial by jury—while they would oppose "paper systems, war, and all connection, other than commerce, with any foreign nation." In addition, Jefferson condemned "all violations of the constitution to silence by force and not by reason the complaints or criticisms, just or unjust, of our citizens against the conduct of their agents."

"I am for a government rigorously frugal and simple," Jefferson maintained, "applying all the possible savings of the public revenue to the discharge of the national debt; and not for a multiplication of officers and salaries merely to make partisans, and for increasing, by every device the public debt, on the principle of it's [*sic*] being a public blessing." And with Hamilton's exertions to build an army fresh in his mind, Jefferson cautioned that the militia should be the primary force to provide for the national defense and that the navy's main mission should be to protect the coast and harbors. This kind of shrunken defense establishment would, Jefferson believed, lead to a reduction in taxes and render it impossible to be used to "overawe the public sentiment." And he added that although he supported the French Revolution and hoped that a free and orderly republic would emerge, he was not insensitive to "the atrocious depredations . . . [the French] have committed on our commerce," for the "first object of my heart is my own country."[10]

Although heavily criticized by the Federalists for his role in the XYZ affair, Gerry did still have a reputation for being the voice of moderation and compromise in New England. And the unusual course he adopted during the election of 1800 has interesting things to say about perceptions of partisanship in 1800. After the election of 1796, Gerry was one of the many who had enthusiastic hopes that the administration of Adams and Jefferson would be a major step toward the elimination of partisanship and the establishment of a national government based upon harmony and consensus. But, unlike most others, he stubbornly continued to be optimistic even after an Adams-Jefferson administration of national harmony had failed to materialize. So, in 1800, he ran, unsuccessfully as it was to turn out, on a state ticket for governor of Massachusetts as a Republican who supported Adams for the presidency and Jefferson for the vice presidency. Their reelection, he urged, would "unite their parties, both of which are true friends to this country." And while the two men might differ on some matters, it was "the antirevolutionists united with the war faction" who "have aimed with too much success, to inflame the two parties . . . to excite them, if possible to hostilities."[11]

Gerry, according to historian Ronald Formisano, was a man of "the Revolutionary Center" whose career showed "the continuance of a nonparty and antiparty ethos."[12] Gerry's antipartyism, however, was not peculiar to him. Even the most rabid partisans, Republicans and Federalists, were also likely to subscribe to antipartyism, even as late as 1800 and beyond. They would argue that it was their opponents who had organized a "party" that was fatally dividing the country. Their own efforts, Republican or Federalist, were seen as seeking to unite the country in support of the union and Constitution.

By 1800, the term *party* itself had at least two connotations. When people referred to their opponents as constituting a "party," they meant their opponents were involved in a self-interested and power-hungry cabal that hoped to capture the government and exercise power so as to further sectional interests or their own grasping selfishness. On the other hand, when "party" was used in reference to one's own supporters, it usually described a loose collection of virtuous public men, a "band of patriots," who aspired to power only to serve and advance the common good. While this might appear to be egregiously cynical or hypocritical, it was a position sincerely and genuinely held by most public men in the early republic. As one historian has put it, "partisanship does not necessarily imply the acceptance of parties themselves."[13]

Later, after his election to the governorship in 1810, Gerry looked back at the American Revolution and emphasized that political unity had been the key to its success. "Had a party spirit then prevailed, it would have been fatal," he argued, maintaining that a "'house divided against itself cannot stand.'" He urged that true patriots must "relinquish a party system, and the practices of misrepresenting, and unjustly reprobating . . . [their] political opponents."[14]

Ironically, Gerry, a sincere believer in the virtues of consensus over partisanship, has had his name attached to a practice of political manipulation, gerrymandering, that involves the redistricting of constituencies strictly along partisan lines. While Formisano argues that the gerrymandering and the intense partisanship of Gerry's second term as governor "signaled the end of Gerry's centerism," it would appear that, considering the perception of partisanship in the early republic, Gerry's earlier and later behavior were not inconsistent. Fervently and without hypocrisy, Gerry believed throughout his career that the survival of the republic depended upon eradicating divisive partisanship. So, when confronted with what he considered a virulent party spirit, he saw it as his job to take extraordinary steps, *nonpartisan* steps in his eyes, to combat the evil. In other words, Gerry and most other public men of the late eighteenth and early nineteenth centuries were convinced that they were *not* acting in a narrowly partisan way, as their opponents were, but rather that they represented the interests of the collective public good.[15]

Although Jefferson did maintain an active correspondence with his New England friends and others, he avoided any other direct role in the campaign, as was the norm for his day. Vigorous campaigning by presidential candidates was rare until the late nineteenth century.[16] For example, Jefferson explained to Monroe that he was going to avoid Richmond during his trip home from Philadelphia in the spring of 1800 because of his "hatred of ceremony." And, although Jefferson recognized the value of "occasions for the flame of public opinion to break out from time to time" to rally support and knew that the Federalists used such means, he rejected participating in such events himself. The Republicans, he argued, should rely "solely on the slow but sure progress of good sense and attachment to republicanism." The "pomp and fulsome attentions by our citizens to their functionaries," Jefferson lamented, was "degrading [to] the citizen in his own eye, exulting [to] his functionary, and creat[es] a distance between the two which does not tend to aid the morals of either."[17]

III

An early and critical turning point in the presidential election of 1800 was the Republican victory in the New York legislative election in May. The New York contest was particularly important since the newly elected legislature, dominated by Republicans, would select the state's twelve electors. Furthermore, the importance of the state to the Republican victory virtually sealed the selection of a New Yorker as the vice presidential candidate, especially that of Burr, who had distinguished himself in the state campaign as a political strategist and organizer. One observer noted that Burr had held "open house for nearly two months, and Committees were kept in session day and night during that whole time at his house. Refreshments were always on the table and mattresses for temporary repose in the rooms. Reports were hourly received from sub-committees, and in short, no means left unemployed."[18]

Burr had concluded that the balance of power in the state rested in New York City and vicinity. Consequently, he had directed that a list of every voter in that area be prepared and that they all be solicited door to door by canvassers. Burr's masterstroke, however, was his persuasion of a number of prominent New Yorkers to be Republican candidates for the Assembly. Whereas the Federalists had nominated a number of political unknowns for the seats, Burr had put together a Republican ticket of luminaries headed by George Clinton, who had served six terms as governor of the state. As a result the Republicans carried all thirteen of the seats in the New York City area, thus capturing a majority in the Assembly and assuring New York's electoral vote for

Jefferson. The Republican victory marked a stunning turnaround in New York politics. A year earlier the Federalists had carried New York City and the surrounding county by 900 votes, but in 1800 the thirteen Republicans won with an average majority of 250 votes. One Republican leader was so struck by the achievement that he attributed it to "the Intervention of a Supreme Power and our friend Burr the agent."[19]

In the days following the state election, negotiations were undertaken to choose Jefferson's running mate. Burr's selection was not automatic although he had assuredly strengthened his hand with his masterful electioneering victory. One of Madison's correspondents had earlier recommended George Clinton on the grounds that "he would be more acceptable to New York and New Jersey than anyone else,"[20] while Albert Gallatin, Republican congressional leader from Pennsylvania, was advised that Burr was "the most eligible" of the several candidates.[21]

Immediately after the New York election, Gallatin, who was apparently acting as liaison between the New Yorkers and the Virginians, wrote his father-in-law, James Nicholson of New York, asking him to sound out both Clinton and Burr.[22] After completing his assignment, Nicholson informed Gallatin that Clinton would only consent most reluctantly to be a candidate and then only if it be understood that he would resign after the election. Burr, on the other hand, Gallatin was told, became most "agitated" when the subject was broached, claiming that he had been "ill used by Virginia and North Carolina" in the last election and that he preferred the certainty of being elected governor of New York to the uncertainty of becoming vice president. However, after a short conversation with two colleagues who urged him to accept a national nomination, Burr agreed—"if assurances can be given that the Southern States will act fairly." Armed with this information, Gallatin met with other Republican congressmen and they "unanimously agreed to support Burr for Vice President."[23]

News of the New York election was greeted by the Federalists as portending disaster for them. Hamilton, however, saw a way of possibly circumventing a Republican victory in the Empire State and wrote to the New York governor, Federalist John Jay, asking him to take swift and drastic action to prevent the selection of electors pledged to Jefferson. The New York legislature, still controlled by Federalists until the newly elected legislators were installed, should be called into immediate session, Hamilton advised, to change the mode of electing the state's presidential electors. Instead of continuing the practice of having the legislature choose the electors, the Federalists, while still in power, should adopt a new district election system that would "insure a Majority of votes in the U States for Federal Candidates." This was imperative because otherwise some of the Republicans or Antifederalists, Jay was told, would "overthrow . . . the Government by stripping it of its due energies" while others would bring about a "Revolution after the manner of Bonaparte." The legislature must be warned, Hamilton pleaded, "that without their interposition the executive authority of the General Government would be transferred to hands hostile to the system heretofore pursued with so much success," and this would be "dangerous to the peace, happiness and order of the Country."[24]

Jay refused to go along with Hamilton's daring suggestion. The Federalists themselves had formulated the procedure by which the state legislature chose presidential electors, and they could ill afford the odium that would follow any attempt to change the rules once the game had been played.[25]

IV

The New York election had the effect of setting in motion a series of events that aggravated the hostilities already rampant among the Federalists. Adams took the loss in New York as a personal blow, and this caused him to become deeply pessimistic about his chances for reelection. In that frame of mind, then, he decided to make some long overdue changes in his cabinet and summarily fired Pickering and McHenry.

Upon receiving his letter from Adams offering him an opportunity to resign, Pickering haughtily refused, explaining that he had "contemplated a continuance in office until the 4th of March next; when, if Mr. Jefferson were elected President, (an event which, in your conversation with me last week, you considered as certain,) I expected to go out, of course." Adams, after receiving Pickering's defiant reply, immediately dismissed the contemptuous and arrogant secretary of state, who had long been a thorn in his side. Surely one of Adams's most basic mistakes was to retain for so long the disloyal cabinet member whom Abigail Adams aptly described as a man "whose manners are forbidding, whose temper is sour and whose resentments are implacable" but "who nevertheless would like to dictate every measure."[26]

McHenry, whose disloyalty was only exceeded by his incompetence, was berated at some length in a personal interview with Adams before being asked to step down, the chastened secretary of war believing that the New York elections and the Federalist congressional caucus that had pledged support to Adams and Pinckney "without giving a preference" had triggered Adams's explosion.[27] According to McHenry's recollection of the meeting, Hamilton was the object of much of Adams's wrath, with the president claiming that the former secretary of treasury had cost him the New York election. Hamilton was "an intrigant," McHenry remembered Adams as having furiously charged, "the greatest intrigant in the World—a man devoid of every moral principle—a Bastard, and as much a foreigner as Gallatin." On the other hand, Adams described Jefferson as an "infinitely better" and "wiser" man, adding that, if Jefferson were to become president, he "would rather be Vice President under him, or even Minister Resident at the Hague, than indebted to such a being as Hamilton for the Presidency."[28]

Adams's frenzied eruption against Hamilton coupled with his firing of the two cabinet members immediately set off rumors in some circles that Adams was attempting to form a coalition with Jefferson, and the heads of McHenry and Pickering were being presented "as peace offerings." McHenry, for example, was requested by Hamilton to forward any information that might "shew the probability of Coalitions with Mr. Jefferson."[29]

In early June, a Federalist paper in Trenton, New Jersey, gave public voice to the rumors. It charged that Adams's "conduct, at this crisis, is evidently the result of a political arrangement with Mr. Jefferson." Knowing that his own reelection was doubtful, the paper maintained, Adams had schemed with Jefferson "to produce a *common interest,* which shall place them again in the seats of magistracy, and produce a neutralization of the two great contending parties." For his part, Adams had "put down the *oligarchy* of the present councils" by getting rid of the two most overtly partisan members of his administration, while Jefferson presumably had promised to support the measures of the Adams administration and to proscribe "the ambitious and disorganizing views of the *Demagogues* and *Democrats*" among his supporters.[30] This view, while it had no substance, was to have special appeal to Americans of the 1790s. Regarding the deep divisions between Republicans and Federalists as unnatural and unhealthy for the body politic, they yearned for a coming together, a consensus of views, an agreement among the public men on what the public good was and how it could be achieved.

Neither the Republicans nor the Federalists, however, took the rumors seriously in the long run. The Republican *Aurora* in Philadelphia denounced the Trenton paper's story as so farfetched that it was "impossible to conceive that any two men of common sense would ever form such a project." And even though Hamilton would probably have been prepared to believe almost anything about Adams, whom he considered "more mad than I ever thought him and I shall soon be led to say as wicked as he is mad," the former secretary of treasury also came to the conclusion that the only basis for any such plot was "mere conjecture."[31]

The energies of the Federalists in the summer and fall of 1800 were mainly spent in vituperative attacks upon one another rather than upon their Republican opponents. After the Federalist caucus had proposed Adams and Pinckney as the two candidates, Hamilton wasted no time in making his own anti-Adams position clear. Even though Jefferson might be elected, Hamilton wrote Sedgwick, he could never again take the responsibility of supporting Adams's election. "If we must have an *enemy* at the head of the Government," Hamilton declared, "let it be one whom we can oppose and for whom we are not responsible, who will not involve our party in the disgrace of his foolish and bad measures." Under either Adams or Jefferson "the government will sink," and the "party in the hands of whose chief it shall sink will sink with it and the advantage will all be on the side of his adversaries."[32]

This view was by no means exclusively held by Hamilton. To a number of prominent Federalists, salvation would come with Pinckney's election. Fisher Ames pointed out that "the object is to keep an *anti* out, and get a federal President in; and that the only way to do it, is, by voting for General Pinckney, at the risk . . . of excluding Mr. A."[33] For George Cabot, Pinckney would unite "*the true men* . . . under the banner of the Constitution."[34]

To most of the anti-Adams Federalists, the president's unpardonable sin had been to embark upon a course that seemed bound to destroy that system of harmonious and inextricable relationships between men, principles, and institutions that made up the Federalist party. Under Washington's leadership, Adams's critics contended, the Federalists had been venerated as a party of virtue dedicated to the protection and preservation of the principles of the American Revolution, the Constitution, and the union. But Adams's egocentric and erratic behavior had endangered all of this.

Adams, Ames maintained, had "fancied parties could not do without him"; and it was this "extravagant opinion of himself, this ignorance of parties and characters, this pride . . . this caprice . . . that forbids him ever to have a sober reflected system." When "a man is lost with his party," he "is irretrievably lost," claimed Ames, who believed the country now to be torn between three not two parties. One, the dreaded "Jacobins," was composed of "Men, who from mere want or folly abhor restraint," while the second, his own, was the rallying point of "those who from principle, habit, or property" would impose restraint. The third was made up of the followers of Adams, "whose caprices and weaknesses have been . . . often blindly used to weaken our party and to animate the other."[35]

Wolcott was dismayed that the president's "revolutionary, violent, and vindictive" temper of mind, his "passions and selfishness," and his "pride and interest" had weakened the government in the people's eyes and destroyed "the principles by which alone a mild government under any form can be sustained." Thus, while Adams had been "elected by a joint effort of the federal party, under an expectation that he would maintain their system," and while his administration was once "as secure as that of Gen. Washington," Wolcott said, Adams had betrayed the trust and "subverted the power and influence of the federalists," thereby proving "himself unfit to be their head." Since he was "incapable of adhering to any political system, . . . the characters of individuals and the interests of the federal party cannot be safely committed to his disposal."[36]

Neither Adams nor Jefferson measured up well with Wolcott. Both would "refuse to consult and pursue the advice of able and virtuous men," Wolcott charged, obviously fearful that he and his friends, whom he naturally saw as having the best interests of the country at heart, would be driven from the councils of government. And while "Mr. Jefferson's influence would be too feeble to controul [sic] the factions of our country and preserve internal peace," another Adams administration would only bring "repetitions of those acts of violence, which have almost subverted the government by rendering it contemptible in the eyes of both parties." Both men were liable, as well, to involve the country in a war and violate the public faith by the destruction of credit. Even though Jefferson would probably be elected, Wolcott concluded, the Federalists had to remain attached to their principles, for if "these are not abandoned we shall remain a party" and "in a short time regain our influence." If, however, "we resort to temporary expedients, and permit the opinion to prevail that the two parties are equally influenced by personal and sinister motives, and that neither are in fact directed by system and principles, we may soon bid adieu to the constitution, and to the hope of maintaining internal peace or free government in our country."[37]

Here Wolcott, like his adversaries and most public men of the day, argued that a party of principle, the embodiment of the general will, was synonymous with the protection and survival of the Constitution. There was little or no sense of sharing power on an alternating basis, but, on the contrary, Wolcott felt that any Republican victory would be only an aberration because only the principles symbolized by the Federalists guaranteed the future security and prosperity of the union.

John Adams, like Wolcott, subscribed to the idea of a nonpartisan party of principle. But Adams believed that it was he and his supporters who embraced a generic nonpartisanship that was "founded in principle and system." To Adams it was his factious opponents who were narrowly rooted "in private interests and passions." An "honest party will never exclude talents, and virtues, and qualities eminently useful to the public, merely on account of a difference in opinion," he asserted, while a "factious man will exclude every man alike, saint or sinner, who will not be a blind, passive tool."[38] Therefore, the Hamiltonian Federalists, were, according to Adams, mere members of faction, while he and his supporters, more latitudinarian and less restrictive, belonged to a Bolingbroke-like party of patriots dedicated to the general good.

The campaign against Adams within his own party got underway in earnest when Hamilton, under the guise of a military inspection trip, spent the better part of June campaigning against the president in New England. The supposed military reasons for Hamilton's travels did not fool Abigail Adams, who insisted that he was scheming to replace Adams with Pinckney at the head of the Federalist ticket. Since Hamilton knew "that he cannot Sway" her husband "or carry such measures as he wishes," she said, he was conniving "to make a stalking Horse of the president" in order to "bring in a military man" to the presidency. Claiming that Pinckney "may or may not be a good Man," she said she would therefore rather give her "vote for mr. Jefferson."[39]

Adams's supporters warned the anti-Adams conspirators against betraying the president. Massachusetts Senator Samuel Dexter advised Sedgwick that Adams was the most popular man in the United States and the "best qualified to perform the duties of the President." And any attempt by the Federalists to "displace him" would "crumble the federal party to atoms."[40]

Even as Hamilton labored, it appeared that his scheme to replace Adams with Pinckney as president would fail and the Federalist party in which he had invested so much time and energy would end up on the verge of destruction. And to add a crushing blow, Hamilton's most recent enthusiasm and love, the New Army, was ordered dismantled in the spring of 1800, Adams and the Federalists in Congress having decided that the army was a political liability and that there was enough evidence from France that negotiations were going smoothly to make it unnecessary.[41]

These setbacks on top of a long and festering hatred of Adams, climaxed by Adams's denunciations of Hamilton, finally goaded Hamilton into a frenzied retaliation. And in September, he drafted a lengthy indictment of the president. In his attack, which was published the following month in pamphlet form and—much to the delight of the Republicans—widely circulated, Hamilton charged that Adams did "not possess the talents adapted to the *administration* of government, and that there are great and intrinsic defects in his character, which unfit him for the office of chief magistrate." Adams's "disgusting egotism . . . distempered jealousy, and . . . ungovernable indiscretion of temper," Hamilton said, had contributed to his making a number of serious errors while president. By "his ill humors and jealousies," Hamilton charged, "he has already divided and distracted the supporters of the government" and "has furnished deadly weapons to its enemies by unfounded accusations." Most serious, according to Hamilton, was Adams's undermining of "the ground which was gained for the government by his predecessor," for a "new government, constructed on free principles, is always weak, and must stand in need of the props of a firm and good administration, till time shall have rendered its authority venerable, and fortified it by habits of obedience." Thus, Hamilton concluded, there was a real danger that the government "might totter, if not fall, under . . . [Adams's] future auspices."[42]

Hamilton's attack on Adams intensified the enmity among the Federalists and led Noah Webster, Connecticut Federalist and lexicographer, to denounce Hamilton publicly, charging that the New Yorker was destroying the party.[43] Indeed, Hamilton's pamphlet was regarded by many Federalists and Republicans as excessive to the extreme, even to the point that some felt that Hamilton's hatred of Adams was no longer rational. Even a Republican newspaper, the *New London Bee,* in the solidly Federalist state of Connecticut, complained that the pamphlet contained "the most gross and libellous charges against Mr. Adams that have ever yet to be published."[44]

V

While the Federalists were battling and struggling for their very existence, the Virginia Republicans were confronted by their worst nightmare. In the summer of 1800 a slave insurrection was attempted in Virginia that sent a tremor of terror throughout the state and seemed to offer a dangerous challenge to the Republicans at the moment of their greatest political vulnerability. At the same time it offered the Federalists an opportunity to charge that the insurrection had been incited by the Republicans' own rhetoric of opposition and liberty and their apparent acceptance of French revolutionary ideas.

A slave named Gabriel from the Richmond area had planned and organized the Virginia uprising over a period of months. Armed with homemade weapons, he and other slaves had conspired to march on the state capital, capture arms, massacre the white citizens, and incite a mass revolt. About a "150 slaves, 'mulattoes,' and 'some [lower-class] whites'" rendezvoused outside of Richmond, as it was explained to Jefferson. But their plan was thwarted by two slaves who betrayed them by alerting the authorities and by a torrential rainstorm that washed out a bridge and made the roads into Richmond impassable on the night of the planned revolt.[45]

News of the failed intrigue, however, terrorized an already nervous Southern white population, deeply fearful of the contagion of slave unrest. Vivid in their memories were reports of the violent West Indian slave revolts earlier in the decade, graphic and horrifying stories of which had been circulated by white refugees as they arrived in American ports.

In 1793, for instance, Jefferson had been convinced "that all the West India Islands will remain in the hands of the people of colour, & a total expulsion of the whites sooner or later will take place" and had warned about the probability of racial strife spreading to the United States. "It is high time," he said, "we should foresee the bloody scenes which our children certainly, and possibly ourselves (south of [the] Potomac [River]), [will] have to wade through, & try to avert them."[46] Later, in 1797, after the massacre in Santo Domingo, Jefferson had written again about the likelihood of racial violence erupting in the United States, gloomily predicting that "if something is not done, and soon done, we shall be the murderers of our own children . . . ; the revolutionary storm, now sweeping the globe, will be upon us."[47] To Jefferson and others like him, the black revolution in Santo Domingo seemed to hang like a sword of Damocles over the South, threatening at any time to incite a racial blood bath.

The Federalists immediately moved to make political capital out of what came to be called Gabriel's Conspiracy, both tying the event to Republican ideas and trying to convince Southerners that the Federalists, with their interest in social order, would make them safer than would the Republicans. The Federalist Philadelphia *Gazette of the United States* asserted that the insurrection "*appears to be organized on the true French plan*" and should convince every Southerner to vote for General Pinckney whose "military skill and approved bravery . . . must be peculiarly valuable to his countrymen at this moment."[48] And a Virginia Federalist charged that "this dreadful conspiracy originates with some vile French Jacobins, aided and abetted by some of our own profligate and abandoned democrats." The doctrines of "Liberty and equality have brought the evil upon us . . . [and it] cannot fail of producing either a general insurrection, or a general emancipation."[49]

Federalist William Vans Murray, the United States minister to Batavia, wrote John Quincy Adams that there were "motives sufficiently obvious, independent of Jacobinism, to account for an insurrection of the slaves; but I doubt not that the eternal clamor about liberty in Virginia and South Carolina both, has matured the event which has happened." But there were "good things in most species of adversity," Murray said. He recalled all the talk a year or so earlier about "a separation from the Union . . . by some of the leaders of the opposition in Virginia" and the fear that they had "some plan on foot" as evidenced by the replenishment of the state arsenal from Europe and the state's "rigid collection of extra taxes." Now, Murray reasoned, the threat of slave insurrection would temper any desire on the part of Virginia Republicans to secede from the union.[50]

The Federalists, then, both privately and publicly, argued that it was the Virginia Republicans' own rhetoric of protest and liberty that had stimulated slave unrest and had culminated in attempted insurrection and thus believed the conspiracy would have a salutary effect in Virginia, causing the Republicans to soft-pedal their opposition and reconsider any idea of secession. To defeat any future full-fledged slave revolt, Virginians would need, the Federalists reckoned, the military resources and support of the federal government.

Indeed the Federalists were not too far off base in their charges, according to one historian. Gabriel's Conspiracy did introduce a volatile mix of revolutionary ideas and black resentment into a highly charged political environment that was intensely polarized. And making the situation even more incendiary was some evidence that two Frenchmen had been involved in the affair. It was evidence that

Governor Monroe, sensitive to the Republicans' political vulnerability, deemed so provocative that he took steps to suppress it.[51]

The Republicans were not without charges of their own. The Adams administration was attacked for concluding a trade agreement in collaboration with Great Britain with the black revolutionary Toussaint L'Ouverture of Santo Domingo, as well as extending naval support to him in his battle against his French-backed rival.[52] This policy, Southerners believed, was provocative and risky since it conferred a certain legitimacy upon the revolutionary government of Toussaint. Living at the mercy of their own large slave populations, Southern whites were extremely sensitive to any federal action that might increase their vulnerability. And this fear, of course, was to be a major theme throughout the history of the antebellum South.

VI

The 1800 election of presidential electors, which took place in the states on various days from May to December, was not a popular outpouring of democratic sentiment. In fact, it would be difficult to conclude with any precision what the election indicated about popular sentiment in the country.[53] Most citizens were only indirectly involved. For example, in ten of the sixteen states—New Hampshire, Vermont, Massachusetts, Connecticut, New York, New Jersey, Pennsylvania, Delaware, South Carolina, and Georgia—the state legislatures chose the electors. Rhode Island and Virginia voters selected the electors by general ticket, while the electorate in Maryland, North Carolina, and Kentucky voted by districts. Tennesseans used a combination of the district and legislature methods.[54]

Despite the Federalists' internal wrangling, the Republicans were not claiming victory before the election. The 1796 election had been close, 71 to 68 electoral votes, with Adams receiving 62 of his 71 ballots (or 87 percent) from Northeastern and Middle Atlantic states, while Jefferson received 54 of his 68 (or 79 percent) from the South. The 1800 election promised to continue this sharp sectional division.

The Federalists were considered safe in Delaware and the New England states of New Hampshire, Vermont, Connecticut, and Massachusetts. There was concern in the Federalist ranks, needless as it turned out, about the reliability of Rhode Island. Four years earlier Adams had received some support in Maryland, Virginia, and North Carolina, and in 1800 the Federalists, particularly with South Carolinian Charles Cotesworth Pinckney on the ticket, expected to make greater inroads in the South, the center of Republican strength. As a Maryland Republican warned, "Gen. Pinckney may divide the Southern States, and if supported generally to the Eastward . . . he may be a dangerous rival." North Carolina had for several years been a source of worry to the Republicans; in the spring of 1800, Jefferson judged it to be in a "most dangerous state." South Carolina, because of Pinckney being a native son, was also seen as unreliable by the Republicans.[55]

Jefferson had virtually swept the South in 1796, receiving all the votes in the section with the exception of 1 each in North Carolina and Virginia and 7 in Maryland. And in 1800 it was conceded that Virginia, Kentucky, Tennessee, and Georgia were safe Republican states. But even if Jefferson won all of the 62 possible Southern and Western electoral votes, he would still need 8 additional votes to get a bare majority of 70 electoral votes out of a total of 138. Thus, retaining Southern support and winning the Middle Atlantic states was essential for a Republican victory. Republicans in Congress from New York, New Jersey, and Pennsylvania were predicting victory in their respective states. The situation in Pennsylvania, however, was clouded by the inability of the Federalist-dominated Senate to agree with the Republican-controlled House of Representatives on an electoral law. The legislature adjourned in January 1800 without taking action, thus making it a distinct possibility that Pennsylvania might not even participate in the presidential election.

Many saw the New York state elections in May 1800 as an important early test of proto-party strength. Jefferson had predicted in March that "if Pennsylvania votes, then either Jersey or New York giving a republican vote decides the election." But if "Pennsylvania does not vote, then New York determines the election."[56]

Thus, the New York victory of the Republicans contributed substantially to the demoralization and disintegration of the Federalists and led to considerable optimism among the Republicans. "The republic is safe," one enthusiast reported to Madison when the results of the election became known. Another enraptured Republican went so far as to report that he had even heard an arch Federalist from that bedrock of Federalism, Connecticut, lament that something had to be done immediately "to arrest the present current of opinion" or the Federalists "should be entirely ousted from power" in his state.[57]

Nonetheless, Connecticut and the other New England states cast their votes solidly for the Adams-Pinckney ticket, as they had in 1796. However, partisanship in the section was often ambiguous. Gerry, as has been mentioned, ran unsuccessfully for governor of Massachusetts as a Republican, but supported Adams for the presidency. And, while Connecticut Republicans actively circulated party tickets to voters, party names there as well as elsewhere in the section were often a source of confusion. In Rhode Island, the Republicans referred to themselves as Republican-Federalists, while in New Jersey, the Federalists went by the name Federalist-Republican. It was no wonder that one Connecticut farmer complained that he wished that "we might reject the words, *federal, anti-federal, democrat, aristocrat, jacobin,* etc., and go back to our old language Whig and Tory."[58]

New York and Pennsylvania, as Jefferson had stated, were critical. In 1796, Adams had taken all of New York's 12 votes, while Jefferson had received 14 of the 15 Pennsylvania ballots. But after the Republicans' stunning capture of New York's 12 electoral votes, Pennsylvania remained the biggest question mark. For a time it appeared that Pennsylvania might not cast any electoral votes because of the legislative deadlock, but early in December a compromise was worked out. And in this compromise between the Federalist Senate and Republican House of Representatives, 8 electoral votes were given to both Jefferson and Burr, while 7 each were cast for Adams and Pinckney.[59]

In New Jersey and Delaware, the Federalists swept the election, as they had in 1796. New Jersey was particularly disappointing to the Republicans for they had made strong efforts there while the Federalists, confident of their strength, had not duplicated the organizations they had built in some other states but rather had resorted to holding some county meetings and appointing committees to draft campaign appeals.[60]

In 1796 Maryland had split its vote, 7 to 4, in Adams's favor. Four years later it again divided the tally, with Adams and Jefferson each receiving 5 votes. There was a vigorous and active campaign in the state, perhaps owing to the fact that the electors were chosen by the people themselves, voting in districts, rather than by state legislators. According to historian Noble Cunningham, the style and technique of campaigning was extremely "advanced," with election meetings being held around the state to take advantage of any large crowds, whether they be assembled for a horse race or a church meeting. One critical observer noted that the "candidates, on both sides, are now travelling through their districts, soliciting the favor of the individuals . . . and men of the first consideration condescend to collect dissolute and ignorant mobs of hundreds of individuals, to whom they make long speeches in the open air."[61] The dismissed secretary of war, James

McHenry, in a fit of peevishness and resentment toward his former boss, had determined that the Maryland Federalists should "make little or no exertions for the federal candidate; not from any indifference to the good old cause, but from a kind of conviction that our labour would be lost" because of the "utter unfitness of one of the federal candidates to fill the office of President."[62] McHenry, however, misread the political signs in assuming that his Maryland colleagues shared his anger, for, despite his predictions, Adams still managed to win one-half of the state's vote.

From Virginia south, including the states of Virginia, North Carolina, South Carolina, Georgia, Tennessee, and Kentucky, it was a virtual sweep for the Republicans, with the exception of an 8-to-4 split in North Carolina in favor of the Republicans and a very closely contested race in South Carolina. The Virginia Republicans, after their setback in the 1799 state elections, had taken nothing for granted, as is shown in a letter by one of Jefferson's correspondents describing the elaborate campaign organization that had been put in place there. In addition to a central committee of five in Richmond to coordinate the state campaign, there was a committee of the same number established in each county "to communicate useful information to the people relative to the election." These committees were to "repel every effort which may be made to injure either the ticket in general or to remove any prejudice which may be attempted to be raised against any person on that ticket." The Republicans also profited from Monroe's having been elected governor in 1799, for in that office he could "form a center around which our interest can rally."[63] The Federalists had difficulty in finding political notables to act as electors, and they became so desperate that they ultimately had to present their slate to the public as "The American Republican Ticket."[64]

By the end of November, Adams and Jefferson stood tied with 65 votes apiece with only South Carolina's 8 votes outstanding.[65] Jefferson, recognizing the tenseness of the moment, reported that "the issue of the election hangs on S. Carolina."[66] The anti-Adams Federalists had hoped that South Carolina would play a key role in their plans to push native son C. C. Pinckney into the top spot ahead of Adams. "The only chance of a federal President" being elected, Pickering had maintained, would be through the support of Pinckney's candidacy. The former secretary of state reasoned that if both North and South Carolina gave their votes to fellow Southerners, Pinckney and Jefferson, and New Englanders gave the South Carolinian their backing, "Mr. Pinckney will be elected."[67]

Prior to the early December meeting of the South Carolina state legislature to chose presidential electors, it was not clear whether the Federalists or Republicans would have a majority since some of the newly elected legislators appeared to be uncommitted. The Federalists, however, after some initial optimism about their chances, were stunned when the House of Representatives elected a Republican speaker by a two-to-one margin. The issue was still not clear, however, and the Republican Pinckney (Charles, second cousin to C. C. and Thomas Pinckney) labored mightily to secure his state's votes for Jefferson and Burr and to head off the Federalist plot to distract and divide the Republicans by offering a C. C. Pinckney and Jefferson ticket. Successfully keeping his forces in line, Charles Pinckney was able to fend off the Federalist challenge and South Carolina cast all 8 votes for the Republican candidates.[68]

The election was deadlocked. The Federalists had been defeated, but both Jefferson and Burr had received the identical number of electoral votes, 73, to Adams's 65, Pinckney's 64, and Jay's 1. This meant that the election would be thrown into the House of Representatives for resolution. The vote totals demonstrated more proto-party discipline than in 1796 when Adams and Jefferson obtained 71 and 68, respectively, to Pinckney's 59, Burr's 30, Sam Adams's 15, and Oliver Ellsworth's 11. Additionally in 1796 a total of 22 votes had been scattered among various other candidates.[69]

The balloting in 1800, as might have been anticipated, also clearly exhibited the sectional division of the country. Of Adams's 65 electoral votes, 56, or 86 percent, were from the New England and Middle Atlantic states, while only 9, or 14 percent, were from the South. The South, of course, was a bastion of strength for the Republicans with 53, or 73 percent, of the 73 votes for Jefferson and Burr coming from that section. The Middle Atlantic states of New York and Pennsylvania provided 20, or 27 percent, of the total. Adams received 100 percent of New England's electoral vote, while Jefferson received 85 percent of the South's total.[70]

The South's slave population and the three-fifths clause that counted a slave as three-fifths of a person for allocating representation in Congress as well as levying taxes was the critical margin of victory for Jefferson. For without the three-fifths clause, one historian speculates, the South would have lost 14 electoral votes, and Adams would have won, 63–61.[71]

The presidential election, however, was just one dimension of the political contest. The Republicans also scored a significant victory in

Congress. The House of Representatives that had been elected in 1798–99 had been strongly Federalist, by a 63–to–43 margin. In 1800, however, the Republicans reversed the difference, winning a 65–to–41 edge.[72]

VII

The election was not a *national* political victory for the Republicans.[73] Support for the Republicans and Federalists was strongly sectional as the voting results indicate. The Federalists, centered in New England, feared Virginia's size, wealth, and political strength, while the Republicans, with their Southern orientation, felt an estrangement from New Englanders, who, they believed, had alien cultural values and different political practices and objectives.

Even the impressive congressional victory did not represent a national political victory for the Republicans. Altogether the Federalists lost 22 House seats from 1798 to 1800, with 10 of those seats coming from New England and the Middle Atlantic states. Four of the 10 seats that were transferred to the Republicans came from Massachusetts, where Gerry and his opponent characterized themselves as antiparty, centrist, or, in Formisano's language, "candidates of the Revolutionary Center." The state election was not, according to Formisano, "an organized party battle." Indeed, great confusion accompanied the voting and led one Boston Federalist paper, J. Russell's *Gazette*, to complain: "*All* call themselves Republicans . . . and most say they are Federalists." Adding to the confusion of the very vocal and vociferous antiparty partisanship was the fact that both Gerry and his gubernatorial opponent supported Adams's reelection.[74] Thus, the Republican gains in Congress from Massachusetts represented a victory not so much for Jefferson and the Southern-based Republicans but rather a desperate effort by public men of the "Revolutionary Center" to reach an accommodation between the proto-parties that were threatening to destroy the fruits of the American Revolution.

The majority of the seats the Republicans gained in Congress, 12 of 22, came from the South, 6 from Virginia alone. Thus, although the Republicans made some gains in the Northern states in 1800 in both Congress and the Electoral College, their success should not be regarded as a national victory. The Republicans were, and would continue to be, Southern-based, Southern-oriented, and Southern-led.

To the Republican leadership in December 1800, however, the Federalists, despite their loss in the electoral college, remained a serious threat. The tie between Jefferson and Burr seemed to present them with a golden opportunity to sow dissension among the victorious Republicans or perhaps even prevent their taking power. Mindful of Burr's unhappiness four years earlier when some Southern Republicans had failed to support him, the Republicans had scrupulously avoided offending the New Yorker in 1800 by holding back votes so that Jefferson would be the only winner. But in their eagerness not to cause discord, they had created a deadlock that threatened to snatch away their victory at the very hour of their triumph.

12.

Electoral Gridlock
The Crisis of 1801

With the militia of Massachusetts consisting of 70,000 (*regulars let us call them*) in arms—with those of New Hampshire and Connecticut united almost to a man, with half the number of at least the citizens of eleven other states ranged under the federal banner in support of the constitution, what could Pennsylvania do aided by Virginia—the militia of the latter untrained and farcically performing the manual exercise with cornstalks instead of muskets.

—*WASHINGTON FEDERALIST*, FEBRUARY 12, 1801

The tie vote in the electoral college between Burr and Jefferson precipitated a crisis that stands as one of the two great political and constitutional crises in the history of the republic. From December 1800 until late February 1801, when the election was finally decided in the House of Representatives, the country teetered at the brink of disintegration. The atmosphere was feverish with tension, fear, and confusion. Federalists and Republicans were willing to believe that their opponents were capable of virtually any actions, no matter how treacherous, or violent, in order to gain or retain power. Rumors swept Washington, D.C., which had just become the nation's capital in June of 1800, and the various state capitals about Federalist plots to deny Jefferson the presidency by a usurpation of power or by throwing support to Burr. Talk was rife about militias arming, a possible civil war, and the breakup of the union. There were even reports that Jefferson would be assassinated.

Adding to the anxiety about violence were lingering fears from the Virginia slave conspiracy in the summer of 1800 and the outbreak of two mysterious fires in Washington. The building that housed the War Department burned November 8, while portions of the Treasury Department were damaged by flames on January 20.

The Federalists charged rather weakly that the Republicans had had some hand in the conflagrations. To many Republicans, however, the fires were the frantic acts of a party about to lose its power. The objective of the blazes, the Republicans believed, was to destroy official documents and, thus, to cover up years of corruption and lies. For example, it was charged that the fire in the War Department had destroyed the proof the Republicans needed to substantiate their charges that the government had sent arms to Toussaint in Santo Domingo.[1]

"One thing is admitted by the Anglo-Federalists," asserted one Republican editor, "that the offices of the *War* and *Treasury Departments* were burnt down by design; in this point we most heartily concur with them." The journalist pointedly reminded his readers that innocent men had nothing to hide.[2] And one of Monroe's correspondents wrote after the Treasury fire that "there is no doubt but that every purpose which was intended is answered" by the fire. Every person he had spoken to that day in Washington, he continued, had agreed "that the thing was willful." The letter writer wished that the Virginia legislature "were in possession of those facts" but, since he assumed it had adjourned, he felt that Monroe as governor should be notified.[3]

Samuel Dexter, a Massachusetts Federalist, was secretary of treasury as well as the acting secretary of war at the time of the fires and, therefore, became the target of much Republican abuse. "Mr. *Dexter* has been rather unfortunate in *fire works*," the Republican *General Advertiser* chided.

> He had not been warm in the chair of the war department, before there was a terrible combustion: he was soon after translated to the cold calculating chair of finance, "when lo! there, cometh a *hot wind*" and the treasury office is consumed! It would not be discreet to remove this dexterous secretary to the navy office, lest our navy should follow the path of fire, and the secrets of our state department would, were he to approach them, be erased like certain *acts of the senate*, in the reign of Tiberius, even from the records of the government and of history.[4]

The failed slave conspiracy and the mysterious fires were not the only events contributing to the near hysteria surrounding the election of 1800. In the two-month period between the time when it was discovered in December that Jefferson and Burr were deadlocked to the time set in February for the House of Representatives to begin balloting, newspapers were filled with wild rumors of other violent and illegal actions.

There were, for example, at least two reports of threats to assassinate Jefferson and talk in the Federalist press of civil war.[5] A Connecticut supporter wrote Jefferson that the Republicans were "constantly threatened with bloodshedding and civil war [if we succeed]."[6] Even as early as the first part of December, some Republicans in Philadelphia had organized in an attempt to thwart any Federalist provocation. The citizen militia group, which invited new members to join the company "in order to defend the country against foreign and domestic enemies, and [to] support the laws," called itself the "Republican Blues."[7]

It was the Federalists' aim, one Republican frantically warned, to burn "the constitution at the point of a bayonet," and it was reported that one Federalist was heard to have said "that every democrat should be put to death in order to secure the government in the former hands."[8]

The Federalists were not without their own theories about Republican plots and intrigues, some having to do with the Republicans intending to gain the presidency permanently, backed by the military. The *Salem Federalist* warned that a *"Conspiracy* is mentioned abroad" and that it was "whispered that when the Philosopher [Jefferson] gets into the chair, and a suitable force provided at his back, he is to declare himself permanent!"[9]

It is now clear from a modern day perspective that most of the rumors of plots and conspiracies that gripped the country with fear were born out of a frenzy of suspicion and hostility rather than out of fact.[10] Yet the public men in that winter of 1800–1801 did not have such a perspective. Living in Washington or isolated communities around the country, they had to deal with a political deadlock with imperfect, incomplete, and often false information. And this political gridlock, they were convinced, had the awful potential to destroy the republic and the Constitution.

II

The Constitution provided that in the event of a tie in the electoral college or if any presidential candidate failed to win a majority of the possible electoral votes, the House of Representatives would settle the contest, with each state casting a single vote and the winner needing a majority of the ballots. In 1800, with sixteen states in the union, the winning candidate would need nine or more votes. There is some evidence that the Founders had expected that, after the universally popular Washington had left the presidency, the House would frequently be called upon to elect the president after the electoral college had screened the candidates, since the Constitution provided that if no candidate had a majority of votes, the House would "chuse by Ballot one of them for President . . . from the five highest on the

List."[11] Actually some Federalists might have had this procedure in mind when they nominated Adams and Thomas Pinckney in 1796 and Adams and C. C. Pinckney in 1800, since all men had support for the presidency. Few Republicans, however, outside a few of Burr's strongest admirers, would have presumed that Burr had a legitimate claim to the chief executive's office.

In the winter of 1800–1801, however, it was by no means clear what the results of such balloting in the House of Representatives would be. The Federalists controlled the House but did not control the congressional delegations from a majority of the states. Of the sixteen states, eight could be counted upon to support Jefferson, while six were controlled by the Federalists. The remaining two states were divided.[12] How the House would act would depend on Burr's course of action and on whether the Federalists would support Burr or attempt to keep Jefferson out of office by other means. Exacerbating the potential for a violent or extraconstitutional outcome was the fact that the new republic had few precedents and certainly none for handling an electoral deadlock.

Before the final election returns had come in, at least as early as November of 1800, many Republicans had begun to recognize that the main threat to Jefferson's election would come not from the two Federalist candidates but from their own miscalculation. Sensitive to Burr's suspicion from four years earlier, the Virginia leadership had made no plans to divert votes away from the New Yorker to assure a Jefferson victory. And in November, at least for awhile, there were even fears that Burr, not Jefferson, would receive a greater number of electoral votes than his running mate.[13]

The key variable in any plan to resolve the deadlock, of course, was Aaron Burr himself, an ambitious and cunning politician. His public position was that he "would utterly disclaim all competition" between Jefferson and himself and that the Republicans could be "assured that the federal party can entertain no wish for such an exchange."[14] Nevertheless, despite his disavowals, the tie vote was obviously a tempting opportunity for Burr and posed an awkward and extremely dangerous problem for the Republicans, who were suspicious of Burr's motives.

Jefferson penned a carefully and skillfully drawn letter to Burr, after learning that, while the official tally of the vote was not yet in, "both parties" agreed that "the two Republican candidates stand highest." The letter was the Virginian's attempt to force Burr's hand and to find out what the New Yorker would do when the likely tie vote between them would be sent to the House of Representatives for resolution. Jefferson assured Burr of Southern Republican support and voiced concern that "several of the high-flying federalists have expressed their hope that the two republican tickets may be equal, and their determination in that case to prevent a choice by the H of R, (which they are strong enough to do,)." Jefferson congratulated Burr on the election but cleverly appeared to hold out the promise of a more activist and important position within the administration than that of the vice presidency, which was a perfunctory one and not really considered part of the administration. "While I must congratulate you, my dear Sir, on the issue of this contest," Jefferson wrote, "because it is more honorable, and doubtless more grateful to you than any station within the competence of the chief magistrate, yet for myself, and for the substantial service of the public, I feel most sensibly the loss we sustain of your aid in our new administration." It "leaves a chasm in my arrangements," he continued, "which cannot be adequately filled up."[15]

In response, Burr reassured Jefferson that his supporters were "perfectly informed of . . . [his] Wishes on the subject" and that he would "never think of diverting a single Vote" from Jefferson, even in the event of a tie vote. And should the matter come before the House of Representatives, the New Yorker was confident that Jefferson would have "at least nine States," the needed majority. Rising to Jefferson's bait, Burr offered to "abandon the office of V. P. if it shall be thought that I can be more useful in any Active station."[16]

There was to be no further mention of a more "Active" role for Burr within a Jefferson administration, however. Instead, behind the polite jockeying of the two running mates, there was increasing apprehension on the part of the Republican leaders over the tie vote and what action the Federalists might take.

Most Federalists did not believe Burr's disavowal of presidential ambition and immediately saw it to their advantage to support Burr and at least gain some advantage from their own defeat. A South Carolina Federalist, Robert Goodloe Harper, who had been instrumental in pushing the Alien and Sedition Laws through Congress, wrote Burr shortly after the tie vote became known that the "language of the Democrats is, that you will yield your pretensions to their favorite; and it is whispered that overtures to this end are to be, or are made to you." Harper advised Burr to consider his own interests and "to take no step whatever by which the choice of the house of Representatives can be impeded or embarrassed." Burr was further instructed to be discreet and keep "the game perfectly in . . . [your] hand" and not to answer Harper's letter "or any other that may be written . . . by a federalist; nor write to any of that party."[17]

Harper was a strong advocate for Burr, arguing that the Federalists should give him their support "without asking or expecting any assurances or Explanations respecting his future Administration." One of those Federalists who, according to the Republicans, were "desperados" and who were willing to "go any lengths, to risque every thing in opposition to Mr. Jefferson," Harper believed Jefferson's "Democratic Spirit" and "false Principles of Government" would destroy the country.[18]

The rumor that the Federalists might support Burr was circulating among the Republicans within several days of the disclosure of the vote, causing one Jefferson supporter to fear that the new government would fall "into the hands of Hamilton and his Myrmidons."[19] Ironically, while at least some Republicans suspected collusion between Hamilton and Burr late in 1800, there was none. The relationship between the two was a hostile one and would grow increasingly antagonistic until eventually the New Yorkers would fight a duel in which Hamilton would lose his life.

On December 29, Burr dropped a bombshell by writing Maryland Republican Congressman Samuel Smith that he would be willing to serve as president if chosen by the House.[20] The statement shocked Smith, who was worried that, if such information were made public, it might encourage Burr's Federalist supporters and tempt Republicans from the Middle Atlantic states into supporting him. The congressman was also concerned about a rumor that a New York Federalist, David Ogden, had purportedly been in Washington speaking for Burr and attempting to solicit Republican support for him. In an angry but diplomatic response, Smith tried to discourage any interest Burr might have had in the presidency. Smith assured Burr that Jefferson refused to believe the Federalist rumors and continued to consider Burr a friend and supporter, and he adamantly denied Burr's charge that the Virginians had been "abusing" the New Yorker. "The *feds* will attempt to disunite us," Smith counseled Burr, by tactics such as rumormongering, and thus "we must not believe any thing that comes from them, we must be on our guards." Finally and most importantly, Burr was pointedly advised that when Smith had traveled to Washington he had found "the Democrats" of the eight states united and "*immoveable*," vowing to "continue to the End of the session to vote for Mr. Jefferson."[21]

In response, Burr denied ever having talked to Ogden and further defended himself by referring to an earlier letter he had written assuring the Maryland congressman that he was not in competition with Jefferson for the presidency. Burr had not, he vowed, "said or written to any one a word tending to contravene my letter to you of . . . [December] 16th."[22] And a few weeks later Burr wrote Jefferson denouncing "the most malignant Spirit of slander and intrigue" that was "calculated to disturb our harmony."[23]

Despite the denials, rumors persisted about Burr's apostasy, especially since Burr did not move to withdrew his name or publicly disclaim any interest in the presidency. And the Federalists continued to attempt to persuade Republicans to support Burr based upon the assumption that, if offered the presidency, he would accept it. Smith himself, Edward Livingston of New York, and James Linn of New Jersey were all Republicans whom the Federalists apparently tried to woo. Hamilton, who opposed any effort to elevate Burr to the presidency, reported that the Republicans "as a body prefer Jefferson, but among them are many who will be better suited by the *dashing projecting* spirit of *Burr*" and who after an initial gesture of support for Jefferson "will go over to Mr. Burr." Specifically Livingston, Hamilton advised, "has declared among his friends that his first ballot will be for Jefferson his second for Burr."[24]

III

While the Republicans regarded the Federalist plan to support Burr as a betrayal of the public's intent, another proposal the Federalists considered in December and January was seen as little short of a declaration of war. As early as December 19, 1800, Gouverneur Morris had told Hamilton that some Federalists were proposing "to prevent any Election and thereby throw the Government into the Hands of a President [pro tempore] of the Senate." This was not mere idle conversation, Morris said, for the proponents "even went so far as to cast about for the person."[25]

This scheme, which Jefferson had also mentioned in his December 15 letter to Burr, could be effectuated under the provisions of a 1792 statute that specified that "in case of removal, death, resignation or inability both of the President and Vice President of the United States, the President of the Senate pro Tempore, and in case there shall be no President of the Senate, then the Speaker of the House of Representatives, for the time being shall act as President of the United States until the disability be removed or a President shall be elected."[26] This meant that if the electoral deadlock could be prolonged beyond the expiration of Adams's term on March 4, then the country would be without a president and the provisions of this statute could be invoked. Its invocation then would have led to a Federalist being named acting president since the Federalists controlled both houses of Congress and would continue to do so until the Seventh Congress, elected in 1800, convened in December of 1801.

The idea apparently did not die, for it was later reported that in January "on Friday Night, the 9th instant, a Federal Caucus was held at the city of Washington, for the express object of organizing measures for defeating the election of Mr. Jefferson," or, to use the words of a member present, "of any Election of a President." The caucus, however, failed to agree on a course of action and "broke up without concluding upon any decisive measures."[27]

There seems little doubt that the Federalists were considering, as part of their strategy, attempting to block the election of a president in the House of Representatives.[28] Despite Hamilton's grave misgivings about Jefferson, he was not a proponent of such a plan. Indeed, he warned that although "the Federalists may be disposed to play the game of preventing an election and leaving Executive power in the hands of a future President of the Senate," this, "if it could succeed, [this] would be . . . a most dangerous and unbecoming policy."[29] Hamilton's concern, however, was not shared by President Adams, who was of the opinion that there was "no more danger of a political convulsion, if a President, *pro tempore*, of the Senate, or a Secretary of State, or Speaker of the House, should be made President by Congress, than if Mr. Jefferson or Mr. Burr is declared such."[30]

The Republicans, of course, were prepared to vigorously oppose any Federalist move to bypass the election and confer presidential power on the president pro tempore of the Senate as blatant usurpation. In his diary Jefferson wrote that any such extreme Federalist action would be "a very dangerous experiment" and one bound "to produce resistance by *force*."[31] It would, he warned, bring "a suspension of the federal government, for want of a head" and would open "upon us an abyss, at which every sincere patriot must shudder."[32]

Some Republicans feared that the Federalists would not only usurp power but do so with the force of arms. As the House session approached, the Republican *General Advertiser* charged the Federalists with scheming to renew the Sedition Law, which was to expire in March, and to call to Washington a "considerable . . . portion of the Marines" to aid and enforce their usurpatious attempt to subvert the will of the people and replace Jefferson with their own minion.[33] And at about the same time, Henry Brackenridge of Pennsylvania, writing Jefferson, envisioned Federalist usurpers, possibly led by Hamilton in an Oliver Cromwell-like fashion, as not hesitating to seize forts, arsenals, stores, and arms for use by a volunteer army in order to retain power. He also suggested that Federalists involved in a usurpation effort would most likely be insulated from any legal repercussions because they controlled the judiciary.[34]

Within the Federalists' ranks there was apparently some disagreement over how far to carry the crisis. By early 1801, however, the majority of Federalists seem to have concluded that the more viable and immediate objective should be to push to have Burr elected. Failing that, the other more extreme and dangerous alternative of preventing an election would still be available if they had the stomach for persevering with it. The pursuit of Burr's candidacy in the House of Representatives could, in fact, lead to one or the other of the outcomes, it was reasoned. First, it might force Burr's election by intimidating some Republicans wishing to avoid a constitutional crisis into switching their votes. And second, as the more radical option of last resort, the support of Burr might lead to a deadlock, thus preventing the election of either candidate and placing power in the hands of some Federalist official appointed by Congress.

The task, then, for Burr's Federalist supporters was to convince their colleagues to assist in electing the New Yorker president. To this end the Federalists advanced four main arguments, none of them flattering to Burr. The first was simply that Jefferson because of his obnoxious principles was more dangerous than the opportunistic Burr. Theodore Sedgwick declared that the Virginian had been "hostile to all those great systems of Administration" that formed the basis of "our national prosperity" and had, by his devotion to states' rights, been unceasing in his efforts "to reduce, in *practice*, the administration of this government to the *principles* of the old confederation." Burr, on the other hand, was "a mere matter-of-fact man" who had "no pernicious theories" and whose "very selfishness prevents his entertaining any mischievous predilections for foreign nations." And, even if Burr were unworthy, Sedgwick lamely concluded, "his unworthiness is neither so extensively known, nor so conclusive as that of . . . [Jefferson]." Of the two men, it was asserted, the Federalists would "be more disgraced . . . by assenting to the election of Jefferson."[35]

Second, some Federalists maintained that their support for Burr would seriously divide the Republicans and "sow among them the

seeds of a mortal division."[36] Should "Burr . . . be elected by the federalists against the hearty opposition of the Jacobins," one Federalist
predicted, "the wounds mutually given and received will, probably, be
incurable." And third, if Burr were to win the presidency with Federalist backing, the Federalists would control him for he "must depend on
good men for his support and that support he cannot receive but by a
conformity to their views."[37]

The fourth reason was the Federalists' fear of the power of Virginia. James Bayard, congressman from Delaware who was later to
play a crucial role in the House vote, articulated this sectional antagonism, which was shared by many Northern Federalists. Recognizing
the limitations and weaknesses of both Burr and Jefferson, Bayard
reported that the "State ambition of Virginia as the source of present
Party" was enough to incline him to support the New Yorker. The
"Faction who govern . . . [Virginia] aim to govern the UStates," he
charged, and "Virginia will never be satisfied, but when this state of
things exists." If, on the other hand, "Bur [*sic*] should be the President
they will not govern," and their objectives would be frustrated.[38]

IV

When Hamilton learned of the increasing Federalist support for
Burr, he began a frantic letter-writing campaign to convince his colleagues of their folly in preferring the unscrupulous Burr over the
untrustworthy Jefferson. There was no one of either party in New
York, Hamilton claimed, who did not believe that Burr was the "most
unfit man in the U.S. for the office of President."[39] "His private character is not defended by his most partial friends," Hamilton charged, for
he "is bankrupt beyond redemption except by the plunder of his
country" and, if "he can, he will certainly disturb our institutions to
secure to himself *permanent power* and with it *wealth*."[40] In letter after
letter Hamilton catalogued Burr's defects: Burr was a "profligate; a
voluptuary in the extreme, with uncommon habits of expense;" a
debtor with all "his visible property . . . deeply mortgaged;" and a
man who had "*constantly* sided with the party hostile to federal measures before and since the present constitution."[41]

Hamilton admitted all of the objections to Jefferson—that he was
"crafty and persevering," not "very mindful of truth," and "a contemptible hypocrite"—but in the final analysis "a true estimate of Mr.
J's character warrants the expectation of a temporizing rather than a
violent system." Burr, on the other hand, was a man of "*extreme and*

irregular ambition," a man "far more *cunning* than *wise*, far more *dexterous* than *able*" and "inferior in real ability to Jefferson."[42] If Jefferson were to become president, "the whole responsibility of bad measures will rest with the anti-Federalists," but if Burr were to be elevated to the presidency by the Federalists, "the whole responsibility will rest with them."[43]

"There is no circumstance which has occurred in the course of our political affairs," Hamilton concluded, "that has given me so much pain as the idea that Mr. Burr might be elected to the presidency by the means of the Federalists."[44] For by supporting Burr for president, Hamilton warned, the Federalists would disgrace themselves and become "a disorganized and contemptible party." By contrast, they would become unified and strengthened if they allowed Jefferson to assume the presidency. If the Federalists chose to support Burr, Hamilton would "be obliged to consider . . . [himself] as an *isolated* man," he said, for it would be impossible for him "to reconcile with . . . [his] notions of *honor* or policy, the continuing to be of a Party which . . . will have degraded itself and the country."[45]

Jefferson, however, would have to be made to pay a certain price for the presidency, Hamilton advised. The Federalists would have to extract certain assurances from the Virginian, including his support for "the present fiscal system," an "adherence to the present neutral plan" in foreign affairs, the "preservation and gradual increase of the Navy," and the continuance in office of "all our Federal Friends except in the Great Departments," in which there "and in other matters he ought to be free."[46]

Hamilton was mystified and frustrated over his seeming inability to convince his Federalist colleagues that to support Burr was to court disaster. It was all the more disturbing to him because he had become accustomed to having his views play a predominant role in shaping Federalist policy. No doubt the death of Washington, who had been a strong patron of Hamilton's, served to lessen the New Yorker's influence. But there were also strong indications that after his immoderate public outburst against Adams other party leaders had begun to question his judgment. A close associate of Hamilton's lamented that an "opinion has grown . . . which at present obtains almost universally, that [Hamilton's] character *is radically deficient in discretion,* and therefore the federalists ask, what avail the most preeminent talents—the most distinguished patriotism—without the all important quality of discretion?" Therefore, it was sadly concluded that Hamilton was "considered as an unfit head of the party," and the Federalists were, as a result, "without a rallying point."[47]

Hamilton was not alone among the Federalists in opposing Burr. John Marshall, who had almost "insuperable objections" to Jefferson, concluded that he would support neither his fellow Virginian nor Burr.[48] And John Adams, who, like Hamilton, was becoming increasingly isolated, deplored that "all the old Patriots, all the Splendid Talents, the long experience, both of Feds and Antifeds, must be subjected to the humiliation of seeing this dexterous Gentleman [Burr] rise like a balloon, filled with inflatable air, over their heads." "What a discouragement to all virtuous exertion," Adams lamented, "and what an encouragement to Party intrigue and corruption."[49]

The sentiments of Hamilton, Marshall, and Adams undoubtedly mirrored those of many Federalist and Republican leaders in the winter of 1800–1801 for it must have seemed incredible that a man of Burr's background would be taken as a serious candidate for the presidency. The "old Patriots" with their "Splendid talents" and "long experience" as members of a Whig elite that had led the country through revolution and the tumultuous early years of the republic surely must have been humiliated, as Adams indicated, with Burr's balloon-like rise to prominence.

Burr was not the kind of man that the Founding Fathers had anticipated filling the office of president. Hamilton in *Federalist* 68 had maintained that the electoral college mode of electing a president, with its filtering and screening of candidates by men of prominence and virtue from all the states, would afford "a moral certainty that the office of President will seldom fall to the lot of any man who is not in an eminent degree endowed with the requisite qualifications." While in an individual state, "talents for low intrigue, and little arts of popularity, may alone suffice to elevate a man to the first honors," Hamilton had written, "it will require other talents, and a different kind of merit, to establish him in the esteem and confidence of the whole Union." Thus, it would be virtually guaranteed that the presidency would be "filled by characters pre-eminent for ability and virtue."[50] The president, to use historian Ralph Ketcham's words, was expected to be "a patriotic leader . . . above party . . . [and] to furnish leadership that was fundamentally moral and in accord with a higher law."[51]

Who was Aaron Burr and how could such a man, who fell so short of measuring up to the presidential yardstick as outlined in *Federalist* 68, aspire to the chief executive's office? Obviously, Burr was not of Washington's stature but neither was anyone else in the republic. But Burr was also far from the equal of Adams or Jefferson in terms of his reputation or the role he had played in the nation's public life. Washington, as the soldier who had led the nation's army to victory, and Adams and Jefferson, as statesmen and diplomats, were linked in the public's mind as having been instrumental in the creation of the American republic.

Younger than Washington by twenty-four years, than Adams by twenty-one years, and than Jefferson by thirteen years (and, in fact, nearer in age to the country's fourth and fifth presidents, Madison and Monroe), Burr had served as an officer in the Continental Army until ill health had forced him to resign in 1779, had practiced law in New York, and had held the offices of state attorney general, state assemblyman, and United States senator from New York. But, by 1800 it could not be said, despite his experience and even allowing for his youth, that Burr had had a distinguished public career or could be expected "to furnish leadership that was fundamentally moral and in accord with a higher law." In fact, the public perception of Burr seems to have been that of a man who was a spendthrift, speculator, and profligate. Perhaps John Quincy Adams, in a note in his diary after Burr's death, best summed up the controversial New Yorker's reputation. "Burr's life, take it altogether," Adams wrote, "was such as in any country of sound morals his friends would be desirous of burying in profound oblivion."[52] That such a man was close to being elected president in 1801, therefore, is nothing less than extraordinary.

In part, Burr's ascendancy to political prominence was due to his political acumen and organizing skills. But, perhaps more importantly, it reflected the deep polarization of American politics and the desperation of both Republicans and Federalists. Southern Republicans were desperate to *gain* power. New York and Aaron Burr as vice president, they believed, were their instruments to save the country, republicanism, and the Constitution. The Federalists were just as desperate to *retain* power. Burr, after the tie, appeared to be a means for them to continue in control of the government.

V

In February the House of Representatives would begin balloting to break the deadlock between Burr and Jefferson, and, as the month approached, the Republicans discussed numerous scenarios. Among the possible outcomes were the obvious ones: the election of Jefferson or the election of Burr (the latter of whom would either serve or resign in favor of Jefferson) and the extension of the crisis beyond inauguration day so as to put the chief executive's office into the hands of some Federalist government officer. Other possibilities were also considered, including a call for a new election or a joint Jefferson-Burr request for an early meeting of the next, Republican-dominated, Congress to resolve the crisis.[53]

The Republicans worked to devise strategies so that they would be able to react to all eventualities. Early in January, Madison wrote to Jefferson outlining two possible courses of action in the event the Federalists tried to thwart the election of Jefferson or Burr. Either the Republicans could acquiesce to a Federalist-imposed "suspension or usurpation of the Executive authority" until the next Congress met in December 1801 or Jefferson and Burr could jointly and unofficially agree to convene the new Congress early to settle the dispute. Madison favored joint action by the two Republican presidential contenders, arguing that while the proceedings would not be "strictly regular, the irregularity . . . will lie in form only rather than substance; whereas the other remedies proposed are substantial violations of the will of the people, of the scope of the Constitution, and of the public order and interest."[54]

Albert Gallatin, a powerful leader in the House of Representatives and later Jefferson's secretary of treasury, was the major Republican strategist and tactician for dealing with the Federalist challenges. Upon arriving in Washington in the middle of January 1801, Gallatin found that most public men in the "embryo capital," as it was styled by one early detractor, were, "being all thrown together in a few boarding-houses, without hardly any other society than ourselves . . . not likely to be either very moderate politicians or to think of anything but politics." And while a few "drink, and some gamble . . . the majority drink naught but politics, and by not mixing with men of different or more moderate sentiments, they inflame one another."[55]

Gallatin, himself, was susceptible to this overcharged, highly emotional atmosphere. In his first letter to his wife, he was fairly optimistic for he was convinced that Federalists from Maryland, Delaware, and Vermont were inclined "to an acquiescence in Mr. Jefferson's election."[56] Within a week's time, however, Gallatin changed his mind, becoming more apprehensive and less sanguine about a peaceful and constitutional settlement to the electoral deadlock. "I see some danger in the fate of the election," he related to his wife, "which I had not before contemplated." He was not sure "what are the plans of the New England and other violent Federals . . . but I am certain that if they can prevail on three or four men who hold the balance, they will attempt to defeat the election under pretence of voting for Burr." In other words, Gallatin believed that some Federalists at least were supporting Burr with the real objective of maintaining the impasse and thus making it possible for a usurpation. This, Gallatin declared, would be "most certainly . . . resisted."[57]

As he was being buffeted and influenced by the rumors and gossip in the incestuous and closed Washington society, Gallatin drafted an important memorandum to Jefferson and other party leaders outlining Republican responses to possible Federalist courses of action. This plan, Gallatin reported, which met "with the approbation of our party" and Jefferson's complete approval, maintained that the Federalists had three options: to elect Burr, to prevent the election of either Jefferson or Burr and order a new election, or to block the election and "assume *executive* power during [an] *interregnum*."[58] The latter strategies could be carried out because there would still be a Federalist majority in the House until the next session of Congress, nearly a year away.

Gallatin, confident that Jefferson's eight votes were solid, felt that the Republicans could prevent the election of Burr by standing firm, thus forcing the Federalists to choose between acquiescing to Jefferson's election or initiating some sort of usurpatious action. If the Federalists did resort to the latter and tried to assume executive power, he said, they would have to be "resisted by freemen whenever they have the power of resisting," for to "admit a contrary doctrine would justify submission in every case, and encourage usurpation for ever hereafter." The question, therefore, was *how* to resist such a provocative action by the Federalists.

In answering that question, Gallatin looked to the states as the arenas where the issue would finally be settled. In solidly Republican states, he said, actions taken by a usurper president could be disregarded, whereas in other states Republicans would have to wait it out. In any case, he threatened, a usurper president would be subjected to future punishment "according to law as soon as regular government shall have been established." In the states where the majority of the people and the government "support the usurpation," the Pennsylvanian advised, "the minority may submit for a while, because they are under actual coercion." In other states "where we may act, supported by our State governments, we shall run no risk of civil war by refusing to obey only those acts which may flow from the usurper as President." Thus, federal laws having to do with "collection of duties, payment of debt, etc.," would be scrupulously enforced by Republican-controlled states "either separately or jointly," while all president-initiated actions, especially the calling up of the militia, would be disobeyed or ignored. Gallatin warned against rash responses. The Republicans would have to agree to prevent "every partial insurrection, or even individual act of resistance, except when supported by the laws of the particular State."

The issue of whether or not to acquiesce to a new election in the event the House could not break the deadlock was a source of real concern. Since the Federalists controlled one house of the legislature in New York, Maryland, Pennsylvania, and South Carolina, they could, by refusing to pass implementing legislation, prevent the participation in any new election of these states, which had given 33 Republican electoral votes in 1800. That being the case, Gallatin reasoned, the 49 Federalist-assured electoral votes of New England, New Jersey and Delaware would defeat the 44 Republican-assured votes of Virginia, North Carolina, Georgia, Kentucky, and Tennessee. In addition, a new election would mean the "reanimation of the hopes and exertions of the Federal party in some States, and despair of success on the part of the Republicans" and would raise "the possibility of a dissolution of the Union, if the disfranchised States . . . declare *they* will not submit" to a new election and are supported by the other Republican states.[59]

Despite the strong objections to a new election offered by Gallatin, apparently some Republicans believed that it might be an acceptable alternative. Gallatin even flirted with the idea himself, but in late January he wrote his wife that the Republicans "must consider the election as completed, and under no possible circumstance consent to a new election." However, indicating that there was some controversy among his Republican colleagues over what policy to adopt, Gallatin conceded that his opinion "may be overruled by our friends."[60]

VI

As the Republicans and Federalists were maneuvering and jockeying for position prior to the formal counting of the electoral votes on February 11, the House of Representatives adopted an important resolution. This proposal—brought forth by a House committee of sixteen members, one from each state—recommended that the House go into continuous session until the deadlock was broken.[61] This resolution was of great significance because it made the government a virtual hostage to the presidential balloting since no other business could be undertaken until that was concluded. In addition, it was also a grim reminder to the membership that they were working against an urgent deadline, for with the expiration of Adams's term on March 4, the United States would have no government if the impasse were not resolved.

Both Republicans and Federalists appeared to be intransigent and resolute on the eve of the balloting. The Republicans believed, as Gallatin's discussions about strategy with party leaders had brought out, that, if they stood firm in their support of Jefferson, the Federalists would be forced either to allow Jefferson's election or to be responsible for precipitating a constitutional crisis. This strategy was based upon the Republican assumption that the Federalists were vulnerable to pressure. Federalist moderates from Vermont, Delaware, and Maryland, it was believed, would refuse to push the issue to the brink and would ultimately cast their votes for Jefferson.[62]

The Federalists in the House, for their part, were convinced that they could elect Burr by maintaining the standoff and seducing a few Republicans, mainly from the Middle Atlantic states, to desert Jefferson. Federalist James Bayard of Delaware, who was later to become a pivotal figure in the balloting, was rumored to be offering important government posts to Republicans Samuel Smith of Maryland and Edward Livingston of New York if they would drop Jefferson in favor of Burr.[63] Moreover, there is evidence that if Burr could not be elected president some of the more radical Federalists were still willing to work to maintain the stalemate beyond Adams's term of office, thus forcing the issue and making the president pro tem of the Federalist-dominated Senate the chief executive. Certainly some Republicans believed this to be the case, including one Virginia congressman who wrote Madison about it. Some "Whisper," he said, "that the Senate on their meeting on the 4 of March will appoint a president pro tem who will act as the president of the U.S."[64]

This kind of usurpation would be boldly resisted with *force* by the Republicans, Jefferson advised Governor Monroe in mid-February, and the Federalists had been publicly so warned. The Republicans had declared "openly and firmly," Jefferson related, that if an act were passed placing the government in the hands of some federal officer, thus circumventing the election, "the day such an act passed, the middle States would arm, and that no such usurpation, even for a single day, should be submitted to." This, Jefferson recounted, "shook" the Federalists. In addition, the Federalists were advised that the Republicans were considering calling "a convention to re-organize the government, and to amend it." This was an anathema to the Federalists, Jefferson believed, for the "very word convention gives them the horrors, as in the present democratical spirit of America, they fear they should lose some of the favorite morsels of the constitution." This notion of a convention along with the necessity of arming Virginia was being discussed by a number of Republicans during those crucial weeks from early January to early February of 1801.[65]

VII

The House of Representatives began balloting on February 11 during a snowstorm so severe that it was even difficult for members to travel between the capitol and their nearby rooming houses. As expected Jefferson received the support of eight states: New York, New Jersey, Pennsylvania, Virginia, North Carolina, Kentucky, Georgia, and Tennessee, while Burr received the backing of six: New Hampshire, Massachusetts, Rhode Island, Connecticut, Delaware, and South Carolina. Vermont and Maryland were divided so they cast no votes. And since neither candidate received the necessary nine votes, the House continued to ballot. In a letter written to his wife a day following the beginning of the balloting, Gallatin reported that the voting, which had begun about 1 P.M. the day before, had continued all night uninterrupted until 8 o'clock the next morning, with twenty-seven ballots having been cast without any change in the division.[66]

As the balloting continued, additional threats, counterthreats, and rumors not only of impending civil disorder but also of armed conflict pitting state against state made the political climate even more turbulent. The nation's future seemed to be hanging in the balance. The *Washington Federalist* called the crisis "momentous" and feared that the United States had "arrived at that disastrous period in the life of nations" when *liberty* threatened to destroy the government and its laws. The Federalist paper debunked Republican threats of civil war claiming that "the tumultuous meetings of a set of factious foreigners in Pennsylvania, or a few *fighting* bacchanals of Virginia," did not represent the people of the country. Furthermore, the Republicans were warned, if conflict were to be provoked by Virginia and Pennsylvania forces, which the Federalists ridiculed as incompetent, these forces would be overcome by the government. "With the militia of Massachusetts consisting of 70,000 (*regulars let us call them*) in arms," the paper said defiantly, "with those of New Hampshire and Connecticut united almost to a man, with half the number of at least the citizens of eleven other states ranged under the federal banner in support of the Constitution, what could Pennsylvania do aided by Virginia—the militia of the latter untrained and farcically performing the manual exercise with cornstalks instead of muskets?"[67]

The Republicans, for their part, charged that it was the Federalists, or the "Anglofederalists" as one styled them, who were ready to provoke a military conflict and, thus, cripple or destroy the union. "We have been threatened that we should see one of the leaders of this party," the *General Advertiser* exhorted, "at the head of a victorious army, unless Pinckney should be chosen president." It was the Republicans, the paper continued, who had been bullied and terrorized by threats to burn "the constitution . . . at the point of a bayonet," to assassinate Jefferson, or "to support a usurper" with "70,000 Massachusetts militia."[68]

Republicans in Washington were especially unnerved by a report from Philadelphia, erroneous as it turned out, that "the people had seized the public arms." At 3 A.M. Gallatin wrote a hurried note from the House chamber to A. J. Dallas in Philadelphia deploring the rumors of violent action. "By all means preserve the city quiet," Gallatin implored his colleague. "Anything which could be construed into a commotion would be fatal to us."[69]

John Beckley, Republican campaign strategist, assured Gallatin the Republicans had not yet been involved in any provocative action but were ready to take action if necessary. While the Federalists had removed "several hundred stand of arms and 18 pieces of cannon, heretofore in the hands of the Militia, . . . into the public arsenals of the U.S.," Beckley explained, there had been no Republican violence in Philadelphia and the people were "solemn, calm and deliberate." However, Gallatin was told that the Republicans would not stand for any Federalist provocation. Every Pennsylvania member of Congress, he said, was to receive a letter from Philadelphia Republicans declaring that the day an act of usurpation passed Congress would be "the first day of revolution and Civil War." Republican congressmen were duty bound, in the event such an act were passed, to "solemnly protest against the Act, appeal to their constituents and the World and [to] withdraw from Congress."[70]

How close was the country to armed conflict during the tense days of the winter of 1800–1801? Participants in the events of January and February 1801 clearly saw this as a possible, even probable, outcome. Two Republican governors, Thomas McKean of Pennsylvania and James Monroe of Virginia, in fact, took bold steps under the cloak of secrecy to prepare their states for a possible military confrontation. McKean made arrangements to mobilize his state's militia force in the event of a showdown. Monroe made plans to use the Virginia militia to block the federal government from removing the federal arms stored in a Virginia arsenal and from transporting them out of the state—plans that would have put the Virginia militia in a position to make use of the arms.

Monroe had made efforts the previous July to form an alliance between himself and the Republican governor of the large and powerful Keystone State, second only to Virginia in population. Writing to McKean to congratulate him on his election, Monroe had observed that it signaled the beginning "of a change in our political system, which promised to restore our country to the state it formerly enjoyed" and secure "those liberties we acquired by our revolution, and which ought never to have been put in danger." McKean and Pennsylvania were being counted upon, Monroe urged, "to promote the sacred cause of our country."[71]

During the balloting both governors were in daily contact with Washington correspondents. Monroe, because the "state of things" was "so critical and alarming," established "a chain of expresses" between Richmond and Washington with riders traveling "day and night with the dispatches intrusted to their care."[72] One such dispatch brought Monroe the welcome news that Pennsylvania had 22,000 men "prepared to take up arms in the event of extremities."[73] The governors also kept in close contact with their respective legislatures. In Pennsylvania the Republicans prevented the legislative session from adjourning during the national balloting, and in Virginia Monroe was empowered to convene the state legislature "without delay" should "any plan of usurpation be attempted at the federal town."[74]

Governor McKean, as was indicated by Monroe's correspondent, was ready to take drastic and dramatic steps, including military ones, in the event Jefferson were denied the presidency by an act of usurpation. Indeed, McKean drafted a letter to Jefferson during the height of the crisis reporting that he and the Pennsylvania Republicans were prepared to use force to react to a Federalist usurpation of power. In the draft he later sent to Jefferson, he noted that if it had been necessary the "militia would have been warned to be ready, arms for upwards of twenty thousand were secured, brass field pieces etc. etc. and an order would have been issued for the arresting and bringing to justice every Member of Congress and other persons found in Pennsylvania who should have been concerned in the treason." Furthermore, McKean said he would have issued a proclamation "enjoining obedience on all officers civilian and military and the citizens of this State to you as President and Mr. Burr as Vice President."[75]

The Virginians were also ready to take radical action if necessary, including, it appears, issuing a call to arms. One of Governor Monroe's correspondents, for example, urged that Virginia "provide for an addition[al] number of arms . . . for the militia" as well as for making certain the state forces were well organized and well trained.[76]

Monroe was especially worried that a large stand of arms in a federal arsenal at New London, Virginia, could be used against the state by a usurping, Federalist-controlled government should there be a test of force. And the Virginia governor took steps to block this prospect and to preserve the arms for possible use by the state militia in any future confrontation. As part of this, Monroe sent a loyal Republican militia officer on a covert mission in early 1801 to discover the condition and security of the arms, which, he reported to the governor, included "4000 excellent muskets and bayonets with about 3000 cartridge boxes" as well as "two good brass field pieces with their carriages and a very large quantity of musket cartridges, powder and ball." The firearms, according to the militia officer, had been refurbished since their capture during the Revolution at the surrender at Yorktown.

Monroe's suspicions about the Federalists' interest in the arms were confirmed when the militia officer was told by the federal official in charge of the arsenal that he had received notice that "the arms and stores were shortly to be moved" and that he had been instructed to prepare to transport them immediately. Such a removal, however, Monroe's agent assured the governor, could most likely be intercepted by a loyal Republican "body of Militia Cavalry from the Cities" because it would require "a train of 100 wagons" to move the arms and such a large number of wagons would have to be brought in from the outside.

In order to prevent such a removal, Monroe apparently called out the state's militia to guard the stores. Hoping to remove any suspicion concerning the motive for the action, Monroe's agent had falsely claimed to the federal official on guard at the arsenal that the purpose of the militia mobilization was to protect the arms from "a wicked negro or a madman [who] might blow them up any night and that a militia guard . . . [was] the surest control of the slaves."

The Republican spy also checked out the political sympathies of the local militia officers. To a captain who was "an ardent Republican," Monroe's agent reported that he had "ventured to hint what . . . [he] had heard respecting the removal of the arms shortly and to insinuate the design of disarming the State in order to secure an usurpation."

The captain responded that "if . . . it were attempted he would oppose it by force."[77]

Thus, two Republican governors of key states made plans to deal with a possible military confrontation with the Federalist-controlled federal government. Neither McKean nor Monroe, however, *sought* such a confrontation. Both hoped for a peaceful solution. But each believed that violence was within the realm of possibility and did what he could to *prepare* for that possible eventuality.

VIII

While speculations and rumors were wildly flying about and contingency plans to deal with the crisis were being made in various state capitols, the House of Representatives continued to ballot. The Federalists persisted in their strategy of voting for Burr and attempting to seduce Republicans from their support for Jefferson, reasoning that the "Jeffersonians can acquiesce in Burr with less reproach than the federalists can agree to Jefferson." It was reported to Jefferson that James Bayard of Delaware had offered the post of secretary of the navy to Samuel Smith, if Smith would switch his allegiance to Burr. Smith asked Bayard if he were "authorized to make the offer," and Bayard replied that "he was authorized."[78]

On February 14 or 15, the first weekend after the balloting had begun and after some thirty ballots had been cast, James Bayard dropped a bombshell by announcing to his Federalist colleagues that since "Mr. Burr would not co-operate with us, I [am] determined to end the contest by voting for Mr. Jefferson." The Delaware Congressman argued that since it was impossible to elect Burr, the Federalists risked the union, for "to exclude Jefferson [would be] at the expense of the constitution." Shocked Federalist members of the House of Representatives met two separate times in caucus to discuss Bayard's startling proposal. "The clamour was prodigious" and the "reproaches vehement," Bayard reported about the first meeting, which he said "broke up in confusion." New Englanders, it was maintained, denounced the scheme and "declared they meant to go without a constitution and take the risk of a Civil War." After much agitation and recrimination, however, the Federalists finally decided at a second meeting upon a strategy acquiescing to Jefferson's election.

The plan was put into effect on February 17. To set it in motion the Federalist congressman from Vermont withdrew from the House chamber, which allowed his Republican colleague to cast the state's vote for Jefferson, and Federalists from Maryland did the same, allowing their Republican associates to carry the state for the Virginian. Burr lost Delaware's support when Bayard, as the state's only congressman, voted a blank ballot. South Carolina Federalists, like Bayard, cast blank ballots, thus removing their state from the tally. So, although the Federalist congressmen from four New England states stubbornly persisted in their support of Burr, on the thirty-sixth ballot Jefferson was elected president by the House of Representatives, with ten states voting for him, four for Burr, and two failing to vote.[79]

Why did Bayard and at least some of the other Federalists decide to yield to Jefferson's election? First, it is clear that they feared that to perpetuate the deadlock would bring the country to a constitutional abyss, which clearly risked civil war. Second, Bayard was convinced through his negotiations with leading Republicans, such as John Nicholas of Virginia and Samuel Smith of Maryland, that he had reached some understanding with Jefferson on certain matters of policy —namely that Jefferson would "support . . . the public credit," maintain "the naval system," and not remove "subordinate public officers . . . on the ground of their political character."[80]

However, Jefferson later vehemently denied as "absolutely false" any account that a deal had been struck, insisting that neither Smith "nor any other republican ever uttered the most distant hint to me about submitting to any conditions, or giving any assurances to anybody."[81] Both Bayard and Jefferson were probably right. Gallatin, years later, surmised that Smith, "who was very erroneously and improperly afraid of a defection" on the part of some Republicans, "undertook to act as an intermediary, and confounding his own opinions and wishes with those of Mr. Jefferson, reported the result in such a manner as gave subsequently occasion for very unfounded surmises."[82]

Third, Bayard and his colleagues finally despaired in their support of Burr because of the New Yorker's apparent unwillingness to actively seek the presidency. *"Had Burr done any thing for himself, he would long ere this have been president,"* one disappointed Federalist wrote.[83] Bayard, who had only reluctantly come to support the New Yorker anyway, denounced Burr as having "acted a miserable paltry part" and having done nothing when the "election was in his power."[84] It had been possible to elect Burr, he said, but it would have "required his cooperation." Burr, Bayard concluded, would "never have another chance of being President of the U. states and the little use he has made of the one which has occurred gives me but a humble opinion of the talents of an unprincipled man."[85]

Why did Burr not seize the opportunity and actively seek his own election? One historian has concluded that Burr followed a course of "watchful waiting."[86] Another recent, and more sympathetic, biographer argues that the New Yorker was too "proud to renounce his Presidential pretensions, lest that action be construed as an admission of inadequacy," and "too timid or gentlemanly, or both, to exploit the situation." Thus he "sat out the tie election."[87]

Despite these assessments, Burr's role throughout the deadlock has remained an enigma. The prize of the presidency clearly tempted him. And he had no great loyalty to Jefferson and the Virginia Republicans who he felt were quite capable of betraying him as they had done earlier. If Burr were the shrewd and masterful politician he was purported to be, he, no doubt, had a well-informed and carefully calculated appraisal of his chances to win the presidency. Perhaps in the final analysis, he concluded that the cost of election with Federalist support was too high. Or perhaps he had a failure of nerve or made a strategic miscalculation.

Possibly, too, Burr's political acumen has been overrated. Flattered by Federalist courting and deeply coveting the presidency, Burr perhaps allowed himself to be drawn into the intrigue without knowing how to extricate himself. Not willing to give up his chance for the presidency, but also not wanting to break with Jefferson, he may have decided to play a noncommittal role in an effort not to burn his bridges with either Federalists or Republicans. As it turned out, this course of action was disastrous. It brought him the condemnation of both.

IX

Conducted in an atmosphere of animus and political polarization, the election of 1800 represents a critical turning point in the history the United States. It marks the first time that political power in the country was transferred from one political group to another. And such a transference stands as an important milestone in republican government, according to political scientists. As one scholar has said, "the voluntary, peaceful transfer of vast powers from one set of committed leaders to another who by definition are adversaries" is "one of the most complex and mysterious phenomena in political life."[88]

However, the historical conventional wisdom that holds that the Republicans and Federalists were the "first national parties" and, as such, that they "brought new order into the conduct of government"[89] simply fails to appreciate the severity of the crisis. The Federalists and

Republicans were sectionally based proto-parties who—in a time characterized by a terrible anxiety about the future—regarded the holding of national power by adversaries as intolerable.

Nor did the transfer of power from the Federalists to the Republicans mark a stage in the maturation of political parties or indicate that parties had "come of age."[90] Clearly this was not the way the participants perceived the transfer of power. For political parties to have "come of age" in 1800 would have required a general acceptance and toleration of an opposition party on the national level. This had not been established by 1800 and indeed evolved only gradually over the next few decades. It was not until the Jacksonian party system was fully established that we can say with certainty that parties had taken on most of their modern characteristics, including continuity of organization, appeal to a mass electorate, and general acceptance of the idea of a loyal opposition.

During those critical days in late 1800 and early 1801, public men considered violence and the destruction of the union as distinct and even likely possibilities.[91] Both Federalists and Republicans seemed willing to go to the brink to secure an electoral victory.

An exchange of letters between Jefferson and McKean reveals that the Virginian was delighted to hear of Pennsylvania's pledge of armed support during the darkest days of the crisis. On the day that McKean learned of Jefferson's election by the House of Representatives, the Pennsylvania governor wrote the president-elect congratulating him and advising him that upon hearing of the successful election he had burned a long letter he had written to Jefferson. In that letter McKean said, he had "detailed . . . [his] intended operations in case of a certain unfortunate event in the decision of the House of Representatives."[92]

After his inauguration, Jefferson responded to McKean's letter, assuring the governor that although every Republican would have acquiesced in Burr's election because that would have been in "keeping with the constitution," any usurpation would have to have been resisted, presumably by force. "In the event of an usurpation," Jefferson said

> I was decidedly with those who were determined not to permit it. Because that precedent once set, would be artificially reproduced and end soon in a dictator. Virginia was bristling up as I believe. I shall know the particulars from Gov. Monroe whom I expect to meet in a short visit I must make home. . . . I am sorry you committed to the flames the communication of details you mention to have been preparing for me. They would have been highly acceptable, and would now be very encouraging, as shouldered on two such

massive columns as Pensva and Virga, nothing could be feared. If it were not too troublesome I would still solicit the communication at some leisure moment.[93]

Near the end of his life and almost half a century after the electoral crisis of 1801, Gallatin wrote a long letter downplaying Republican actions. Apparently reacting to charges that the Republicans had threatened to disrupt the union or had proposed changes in the Constitution, Gallatin reminisced that it had been the Republicans who had been "the most sincere and zealous supporters of the Constitution" and that this had "constituted their real strength." To this end, Gallatin discounted Jefferson's more belligerent remarks. He disclaimed the idea that Jefferson had mentioned calling a convention to amend the Constitution. In addition, he argued that even if the rumor had been true that 1500 men from Maryland and Virginia had planned to march on Washington, inauguration day, March 4, 1801, to put "to death . . . [a] usurping pretended President," a loyal Republican governor, McKean, had in readiness the Pennsylvania militia who were ready to march to Washington "for the purpose not of promoting, but of preventing civil war and the shedding of a single drop of blood."[94]

Gallatin's recollection was faulty, as evidenced by McKean's letter to Jefferson. McKean was prepared to act, not to prevent violence, as Gallatin was to have it, but to assure Jefferson the presidency.[95] When he was out of power in later life, Gallatin, like Madison, was embarrassed by the radical and disunionist sentiments that had been expressed by some Republicans in 1800 and 1801. After 1820, for example, the use of the doctrine of states' rights as a defense for particularistic ends and for slavery tarnished it in the eyes of Gallatin and other early Republicans. Thus, consciously or unconsciously, they mentally reconstructed the past to fit their later vision of reality.[96]

There was a peaceful transition of power from the Federalists to the Republicans in 1801, but the potential for violence was real. The country was in as much peril then as in any other era in American history with the single exception of the Civil War.

There was no violence, but the threat of violence, like Macbeth's torment by Banquo's ghost, haunted and preoccupied Americans of that era. There was no way for the public men closeted in the House of Representatives for ballot after ballot and other citizens throughout the nation anxiously awaiting news from the capital to have known that there would be a peaceful resolution to a grave and seemingly insolvable political deadlock and crisis. They hoped for the best but made plans to deal with the worst.

Epilogue

The "revolution of 1800 . . . was as real a revolution in the principles of our government as that of 1776 was in its form." —THOMAS JEFFERSON

Jefferson's inauguration and the Republican victory in 1801 were not simply the temporary triumph of one political party over another. Nor did they signal the acceptance of the idea of a loyal opposition by the public men of the era. Nor did they herald the coming of age of a national two-party political system. Instead, these events were the triumph of Virginia-led and Southern-centered Republicans who saw themselves as having saved republicanism, the Constitution, and the republic and as having given birth to the permanent ascendancy of a Republican hegemony.

Furthermore, although the Republicans in 1801 were living in an increasingly complex, market-oriented society divided into a patchwork of economic, social, and ethnic interests, Republican political theory remained rooted in classical republican ideas, which did not embrace this diversity. Jefferson and the Republicans did not abandon classical republicanism, with its expectations of civic harmony and consensus concerning a national public good, even though the ideology was becoming less and less relevant to the social, demographic, and economic *reality* of the United States at the beginning of the nineteenth century. Instead, they unconsciously interpreted political events in such a way as to reshape their understanding of the public good along *sectional* and *partisan* lines. Thus, with great conviction and great sincerity they could believe that the Republicans and their policies *alone* reflected and served the national public good.

Jefferson was convinced that the Federalists, or at least their leaders, did not share with the Republicans a fundamental commitment to republican principles. Indeed, he denounced government under Federalist management as a "travestie." But, at the same time, he did not look at the Federalist domination of national politics in the 1790s as evidence that the American people had abandoned republican principles, but as evidence rather that the people had been *temporarily* misled by unscrupulous leaders outside the republican consensus, leaders who had been animated by crass, self-interested, and partisan objectives. Thus, the Republican victory in 1801, Jefferson believed, represented a repudiation of the Federalists' abuse of the people's trust and foreshadowed "the new establishment of republicanism" in the United States.[1]

In many respects Jefferson and the Republicans regarded their election in 1800 as equivalent to the ratification of the Constitution in 1788. The Federalists would, it was presumed, as had the Antifederalists in 1788, be discredited by their having been vanquished and disappear from the political scene. Years later Jefferson revealed his conception of the historical significance of his election when he wrote that the "revolution of 1800 . . . was as real a revolution in the principles of our government as that of 1776 was in its form."[2]

In his inaugural address in 1801 Jefferson appealed for national unity, urging his "fellow citizens" to "unite with one heart and one mind" and to join with him in restoring "to social intercourse that harmony and affection without which liberty and even life itself are but dreary things." Pointing a finger at the Federalists for their bigotry and fanaticism in sponsoring the Alien and Sedition Laws, he lectured his countrymen "that having [by the Revolution] banished from our land that religious intolerance under which mankind so long bled and suffered, we have yet gained little if we countenance a political intolerance as despotic, as wicked, and capable of as bitter and bloody persecutions."

In his effort to unite the country, Jefferson asserted that while party names had been used to distract and mislead Americans in the past, they were now meaningless as the victorious Republicans were the political embodiment of a broad-based republican consensus. "We have called by different names brethren of the same principle," Jefferson exclaimed, but we "are all republicans—we are federalists."[3]

And any future political division, if there were to be one, would be between "republican and monarchist," Jefferson avowed, envisioning "that the body of the nation, even that part which French excesses forced over to the federal side," would "rejoin the republicans, leaving only those who were pure monarchists, and who will be too few to form a sect."[4] Thus, all who supported republican government under the Constitution would now be both republicans and Republicans, he believed.

For Jefferson and the Republicans, therefore, preservation of republicanism and the Constitution, depended upon their own continued political ascendancy. This is shown in a letter Jefferson wrote to his youngest daughter in those tense days before the House of Representatives finally elected him to the presidency. In it, he expressed confidence that, if he were elected, the government would be "brought back to its republican principles" and that it would be "so established as that when I retire, it may be under full security that we are to continue free and happy."[5] Later, attempting to bring unity to a group of feuding Republicans, Jefferson asserted that the Republicans were far more than a political party. Such a designation, he considered demeaning. "The Republicans," he declared, echoing a strong civic humanist theme, "are the *nation*."[6]

The Republican victory in 1801, *did*, in fact, usher in an extended period of Republican and Virginia domination of the federal government. Through 1825 the presidency would remain in the hands of Republican leaders from the state of Virginia, which in 1800 was the predominant state in terms of wealth and power, having a population a third greater than Pennsylvania, the next largest state. The Virginia dynasty of Jefferson, Madison, and Monroe so totally controlled national politics that in 1820 Monroe was unopposed for his second term.

This ascendancy of the Virginians had been the Federalists' worst nightmare in the 1790s and continued to be a cause for Federalist despair down to their disappearance as a political force after the War of 1812. In 1799, Hamilton, in an obvious reference to Virginia, had suggested that "the subdivision of the great states is indispensable to the security of the General Government and with it of the Union."[7] This concern about Virginia's power was also publicly expressed in 1814 near the end of the divisive and unpopular war with Great Britain. Then, the New England Federalists, desperate and bitter over the Republicans' conduct of the war, gathered in convention in Hartford and denounced the Virginia and Southern domination of American politics and the political system that allowed "popular leaders in one section of the Union, the controul of public affairs in perpetual succession." The crisis could only be resolved, these Federalists believed, by adopting several constitutional amendments, including one reducing Southern representation in the House of Representatives by eliminating the three-fifths clause that allowed slave states to include their slaves as counting toward representation. In addition, the Federalists called for prohibiting a president from succeeding himself and forbidding a president from being "elected from the same state two terms in succession."[8] However, the conclusion of the war and the withering away of Federalist influence, at least outside of New England, ended the discussion of amendments aimed at limiting Virginia's influence.

II

For Jefferson, Republican hegemony after 1801 was synonymous with the preservation of the Constitution and republicanism. And this explains the often fierce, often intractable, apparently unseemly partisanship exhibited by the Virginian as president—a partisanship that has often been misinterpreted by historians as simply a betrayal of his earlier principles.

Jefferson's handling of domestic issues such as his battle with the Federalist-dominated judiciary, the threat of Burr's Western conspiracy, and the increasing rift within the ranks of the Republicans between the agrarian-minded Old Republicans, as they were called, and their more nationalist and commercial-minded brethren stirred up an intense partisanship. But as controversial as Jefferson's actions involving domestic problems were, it was the steps he took in response to foreign policy questions in order to maintain Republican hegemony that have most often resulted in a misunderstanding of his motives.

As the great war between Great Britain and France continued, the United States, as in the earlier decade, found it difficult to protect its neutral commerce. And in reaction the Jefferson administration enacted a drastic embargo policy that prohibited American ships from leaving their ports to engage in foreign trade. The unpopular embargo was widely opposed and violated and, thus, the Jefferson administration moved to impose Draconian enforcement practices that were then and have continued to be seen as repressive and anti-libertarian.

The apparent discrepancy between Jefferson the opposition leader and Jefferson the president, Jefferson the civil libertarian and Jefferson the ruthless enforcer of the embargo has caused considerable debate among historians. Was Jefferson a hypocrite who professed one thing but did another, as some hold, or was he the suffering idealist whose ideals were tried and tested by the demands of power, as others contend?

Henry Adams, who has a not unsubstantial axe to grind in defending the reputation of his great-grandfather, John Adams, was perhaps the first historian to accuse Jefferson of hypocrisy and of betraying his principles by his actions as a president. The Virginia leader, Adams maintains, had undertaken to create a government which should interfere in no way with private action, and he had created one which interfered directly in the concerns of every private citizen in the land. He had come into power as the champion of State rights, and had driven States to the verge of armed resistance. He had begun by claiming credit for stern economy, and ended by exceeding the expenditure of his predecessors. He had invented a policy of peace, and his invention resulted in the necessity of fighting at once the two greatest Powers in the world.

As a result, Adams charges, Jefferson "left office as strongly and almost as generally disliked as the least popular President who preceded or followed him."[9]

Historian Leonard Levy's more modern indictment of Jefferson's hypocrisy is as severe as Adams's. Jefferson, writes Levy, "had the mentality and passion of a true believer, certain that he was absolutely right," and conducted himself as a "doctrinaire 'tinged with fanaticism.'" While president he exercised power ruthlessly, "was not averse to the most devious and harsh tactics to achieve his ends," and was a "party to many abridgments of personal and public liberty."[10]

Especially troubling to Levy was Jefferson's apparent lack of self-doubt or his failure to be "tormented by conscience when he so readily used the army to enforce the embargo and recklessly disregarded the injunctions of the Fourth Amendment." In fact Levy sees the enforcement effort as the single "most repressive and unconstitutional legislation ever enacted by Congress in time of peace." Its adoption, he suggests, represents "the only time in American history that the President was empowered to use the army for routine or day-by-day execution of the laws."[11] Jefferson, to be sure, Levy concludes, was "a libertarian, and American civil liberties were deeply in his debt. But he was scarcely the *constantly faithful* libertarian and rarely, if ever, the *courageous* one."[12]

The charges that Jefferson abandoned his principles upon assuming the powers of the presidency and that he violated civil liberties have been vigorously contested by a number of historians, none more eloquently than Dumas Malone. Malone's Jefferson is depicted as having been trapped by nearly impossible circumstances that forced him to choose between imposing a cruel and harsh embargo upon American commerce or drawing the country into the great war between Britain and France. And faced with the widespread evasion of the provisions of the embargo, Jefferson is seen as having only by absolute necessity urged the passage of a sweeping enforcement measure that gave him and his agents in the ports extensive and arbitrary powers to seize goods and confiscate vessels that seemed suspicious and appeared to be conspiring to violate the embargo.[13]

Malone attempts to distance Jefferson—who, he says, was then in his "period of passivity"—from the brutal enforcement of the law. As "far as the record goes," he claims, "the initiative in this matter was taken by Senator [William Branch] Giles, and the recommendations by which this legislation was guided were those of Gallatin." Furthermore, Malone argues that the Jefferson administration, unlike the High Federalists of 1798, passed no sedition law and "freedom of opinion was unimpaired and the right of opposition was maintained." Finally, despite the similarity between the New England Federalists' rhetoric denouncing the embargo and the Kentucky and Virginia Resolutions, Malone insists that there was a fundamental distinction in the character of the polemics. Whereas the Kentucky and Virginia Resolutions were concerned with protecting free speech and the right of opposition, members of the New England Federalist opposition were merely protesting infringements upon "economic freedom."[14]

These two views of Jefferson, although seemingly divergent, can be reconciled. The major reason that historians have so fundamentally differed over Jefferson's actions as president is that they have shared a misconception about the nature of politics in the early republic as *understood* by Jefferson as well as by other Republicans and Federalists.

If Jefferson acted as a "true believer, certain that he was absolutely right," or appeared to be a man not "tormented by conscience," as characterized by Leonard Levy, it is because Jefferson innocently and sincerely believed that the election of the Republicans in 1800 had saved the republic that had been given birth to in 1776. And further, he was convinced that every effort had to be made after 1800 to ensure that the Federalists, who had betrayed the Revolution and the Constitution during their stewardship of power in the 1790s, would never be permitted to exercise power again. And despite Malone's assertion that "the right of opposition was maintained," Jefferson's words and deeds belie that he or his Republican colleagues ever viewed the Federalists as a loyal opposition. Instead the Federalists were seen as a treacherous menace. Under such circumstances, toleration of an opposition, an opposition that by definition threatened Republican hegemony and thus the national public good, was out of the question.

It is not surprising, therefore, that Jefferson regarded Massachusetts' opposition to the embargo as amounting to "almost . . . rebellion and treason"[15] or that Jefferson's secretary of war was so apprehensive about the loyalty of the New England Federalists that he believed they could not be trusted with military commissions.[16] Thus, in the view of the Republicans, the New England Federalists' opposition was not an opposition within the boundaries of a commonly agreed upon consensus. Rather, it was seen as outside the widespread commitment to republicanism and the Constitution.

In the years since Jefferson's presidency, other highly esteemed presidents have had to balance their devotion to civil liberties with their vows to protect the republic. Abraham Lincoln's suspension of habeas corpus during the Civil War, the abridgement of civil liberties by the Woodrow Wilson administration during World War I, and the internment of the Japanese during World War II by the Franklin Delano Roosevelt administration, to name a few, were all highly questionable and troublesome actions taken or endorsed by popular and effective presidents. In each case the president acted on the belief that the preservation of the republic justified the use of antilibertarian means.

Yet, Jefferson's case is not quite analogous to those of his successors since the republic during his administration was in a particularly precarious position as it struggled to maintain its independence and sovereignty in a world polarized between England and France. In addition, there was at that time no acceptance of the idea of a loyal opposition, nor was there a tradition of political parties sharing and alternating in power. Thus, the circumstances surrounding Jefferson's actions were unique and occurred within a historical context quite different from that of those who came after him.

For Jefferson and the Republicans their victory had signaled the opening of a new era in American politics. With the national government in the Republicans' hands, power that would have been *dangerously* wielded by the Federalists could now be *safely* administered by men who were unquestionably committed to the nation's greater public good. Thus, Jefferson's harsh and rigorous enforcement of the embargo, including the routine use of the army against smugglers and others who sought to evade its restrictions,[17] can best be understood as the conduct of a man who believed that the alternatives to arbitrary actions against individual civil liberties were even worse. In other words, Jefferson was willing to take actions that were contrary to many of his instincts and basic beliefs because he feared that not doing so would risk the country's becoming involved in a crushing and devastating war with either France or England. And, unlike his successors, Jefferson could not find solace in a Constitution and a union that had weathered many challenges or an established two-party system that had brokered out many disputes. Indeed, the newness and apparent fragility of the union, the largely untried Constitution, and the lack of historical momentum only served to heighten the sense of vulnerability felt by those in the early republic.

The intense and uncompromising nature of politics in those early years, according to historian Roger Brown, even goes a long way toward explaining the later decision of the Madison administration to go to war in 1812. The Republicans, Brown argues, feared "above all else" that submission to England's humiliating restrictions on American commerce and insults to the American flag would revitalize Federalism and threaten Republican "control of the nation's political life and draw odium down upon republican government."[18]

III

Ironically, maintenance of Republican hegemony, especially after the Federalist threat virtually disappeared after 1815, was more troubled by *internal* divisions within the increasingly successful but also increasingly diverse Republican party than by *external* ones. The Virginia-led and Southern-dominated Republican coalition that came to power in 1801 was an uneasy alliance that could be maintained only as long as the Federalists could be perceived as offering a credible threat. And almost from the beginning of Jefferson's administration the Republicans tended to divide into two rival camps—the radicals (or Old Republicans) and the moderates (or nationalists)—each of whom viewed the other as unfaithful to the principles of the "Revolution of 1800."

The Old Republicans, who championed states' rights and strict construction of the Constitution and celebrated the principles of 1798 as enunciated in the Kentucky and Virginia resolutions, tended to be more democratic, hostile to any accommodation with the Federalists, suspicious of banking, and agrarian-minded. The moderates, on the other hand, were nationalists who embraced positive federal action and supported tariffs, internal improvements, and banks as a means of facilitating commercial expansion and economic growth. By the end of James Madison's administration in 1817, as historian Richard Ellis shows, the moderates, having incorporated the moderate wing of the Federalist party, had prevailed.[19]

In 1807, near the end of his second administration, Jefferson noted that he had anticipated this division within the Republicans. He had expected, he wrote, that "when the republicans should have put all things under their feet, they would schismatize among themselves." And "whatever names the parties might bear," he argued, "the real division would be into moderate and ardent republicanism." This split, however, would pose "no great danger," Jefferson was confident, and should be "considered as apostasy only when they [Republicans] purchase the votes of federalists, with a participation in honor and power."[20]

The Panic of 1819 and the Missouri Compromise of 1819–1820 so profoundly exacerbated economic and sectional divisions within the party, however, that these divisions became virtually irreconcilable. Coming after a brief period of postwar prosperity, the Panic cruelly dashed Americans' optimistic hopes and brought to a sudden end the nationalism and speculative mania of the postwar period. In addition to inflaming always present sectional jealousies, the financial collapse reinvigorated the Old Republican wing of the party because the bank failures and widespread economic dislocation seemed to validate their critique of the economic nationalism of the moderate Republicans.

The Missouri Compromise, which ostensibly solved the issue of slavery in the Louisiana Territory by forbidding it north of 36° 30′ latitude, rekindled Southerners' deep fears about the safety of their peculiar institution and threatened to split the party along sectional lines. John Quincy Adams saw the political crisis arising from the issue as revolutionizing American politics and dividing the country into pro and antislavery parties. In the future, he predicted, it would provide the foundation "for a new organization of parties . . . [and the formation of] a new party . . . terrible to the whole Union, but portentously terrible to the South—threatening in its progress the emancipation of all their slaves, threatening in its immediate effect that Southern domination which has swayed the Union for the last twenty years."[21] Jefferson also recognized the terrible potential of the Missouri question, calling it in 1820 "the knell of the Union" and likening it to "a fire-bell in the night" that "awakened and filled . . . [me] with terror."[22]

Thus, the Panic of 1819 and the Missouri Compromise, as they exacerbated the bitter ideological divisions between nationalists and Old Republicans and intensified suspicions between the sections, seemed to portend the destruction of Republican hegemony. And this hegemony was further endangered by the personal ambitions of and jealousies among the various Republican leaders as they scrambled to become the successor to James Monroe, the last Virginia president. So, by the 1820s, the Republican party, with the demise of its Federalist opposition, had become bloated and shapeless. And in 1824 it fielded no fewer than five candidates for president, each representing not only his own pretensions for the office but also the aspirations of some sectional or other constituency. Massachusetts resident John Quincy Adams was eventually sent to the White House, but only after the deadlocked election was finally resolved in the House of Representatives. Nonetheless, Adams's sectional identification with New England along with his nationalist views alienated many Southerners as well as other Old Republicans who regarded Adams as no more than a Federalist in Republican clothing.

In an effort to salvage the tottering Republican party in the mid-1820s, Martin Van Buren of New York and Thomas Ritchie of Virginia resurrected the old Jeffersonian alliance between their two states by attempting to rebuild and reconstitute the party of Jefferson.[23] This partnership between the "planters of the South and plain Republicans of the North," was intended, Van Buren promised, to silence former Federalists and some Northern Republicans who were clamoring "against Southern influence and African slavery."[24]

Monroe, in Van Buren's view, had made a fundamental error during his administration in pursuing an amalgamationist, nonpartisan policy, and this had dramatically reversed the fiercely partisan politics of Jefferson and Madison. By abandoning a politics driven by sharp ideological differences for one of impartiality, moderation, and noncombativeness, Van Buren believed Monroe had put the Republicans on a disastrous course and one that had led to the victory of the neo-Federalist Adams in 1824.[25]

Van Buren's celebration of the virtues of partisan conflict and political parties represents a sharp break with civic humanism, which preached virtue, selflessness, and nonpartisanship as essential attributes of public men seeking to legislate for the public good. Unlike the Founding Fathers, Van Buren argued that the partisanship of political parties did not *threaten* republicanism but rather made a *positive,* if not *essential,* contribution to the American political system. Political parties, Van Buren insisted, were valuable institutions in that they organized "strife within manageable limits," cemented "civic loyalty," and helped to create "institutional cohesion." And in direct contradiction to the older generation of public men who held civic humanism as an ideal, Van Buren asserted that an organized opposition, far from being dangerous, had a powerful, beneficial role in forcing the majority party to seek unity and cohesion in order to escape defeat.[26]

Van Buren's analysis, while astute in its insights into American two-party politics *as it was to become,* badly misreads the political history of the early republic and in so doing has misled historians. Van Buren is wrong in believing that Monroe's nonpartisanship or policy of amalgamation *contradicted* that of his predecessors. Instead, both Jefferson and Madison viewed their party as a temporary instrument to attain hegemony and this hegemony, once attained, as the embodiment of a public consensus upon the general good. They also expected the proto-party distinctions forged in the 1790s to wither away eventually. So Van Buren, in reconstituting the Republican party in the 1820s, was trying to restore what had never been—competitive party politics between balanced, ideologically divided parties that accepted the idea of a loyal opposition.

But if Van Buren's history was faulty, his political organizing skills were not. The party fashioned by the New Yorker and Thomas Ritchie around the candidacy of Andrew Jackson in the 1820s was a durable one. Based upon Old Republican principles of states' rights and strict construction of the Constitution, the embryonic Democratic party became a successful coalition that dominated American politics from 1828 down to the Civil War, holding the presidency for twenty-four of the thirty-two years. Its success was largely built upon appealing to the anticommercial instincts of many Americans and avoiding the issues of sectionalism and slavery.[27]

Indeed, the Democratic party—the alliance that Van Buren had promised between the "planters of the South and plain republicans of the North"—like its predecessor, the Jeffersonian Republican party, was, by and large, the instrument through which the South dominated the federal government.[28] Of the federal officers that served from the ratification of the Constitution down to the Civil War, as historian James McPherson reminds us, a Southerner was president more than two-thirds of the time and a Southerner was speaker of the House of Representatives 64 percent of the time. The Supreme Court was also dominated by the South with "with twenty of the thirty-five justices to 1861" coming from the slave states.[29]

IV

In retrospect, it is clear that the election of 1800 settled once and for all the question of presidential succession and the transference of power from one party to another. But the participants themselves failed to appreciate this great truth about American politics. It was only later that the historian, in an effort to impose order, to impose meaning on chaos, invented the notion of a first party system. To the victorious men of 1800 and their immediate successors, a "band of patriots"—the Republicans—had saved the nation from the excesses of party, excesses that were embodied in Federalism. And it was up to the Republicans to insure that the Federalists were never handed the reins of power again. Well into the Jacksonian period, the terms *Federalist* and *Federalism* were used as epithets to blacken the names of political opponents.

Furthermore, the political universe of Andrew Jackson in the 1820s and 1830s was shaped by memories of the absolutist nature of the earlier political struggle between Republican and Federalist. As late as 1835, the Old Hero asserted that "it was only by preserving the identity of the Republican party as embodied and characterized by the principles introduced by Mr. Jefferson that the original rights of the states and the people could be maintained." It was for this, he explained, that he had "labored to reconstruct this great Party" in order to preserve "its permanent ascendancy."[30] Not only does Jackson's statement indicate the Old Hero's intense partisanship, but, more importantly, it reveals the residue of certain assumptions shaped at the end of the eighteenth century about the permanency of victory.

The ideas that parties might alternate in power and that there might be such a thing as a loyal opposition were slow to gain acceptance. For it was not until the election of 1844 that a political party was able to regain the presidency once it had been lost.[31] Before this, political parties that had lost power had also lost their legitimacy, so to speak, to represent the public's articulation of the national will. This was true of the Federalists as well as the National Republicans of John Quincy Adams. Thus it was not until James K. Polk's victory, coming four years after fellow Democrat Martin Van Buren had failed to win the presidency, that it could be said that a balanced, resilient, and mature party system had finally come of age.

As the memory of the 1790s and the election of 1800 grew dimmer and dimmer, the assumptions that informed the politics of Jackson and other men of his generation became less influential and no longer evoked the great passion or conviction they once had. By the 1830s and certainly the 1840s, political parties—an anathema at the time the Constitution was adopted—had become accepted by most Americans as a vital part of the political process. But this acceptance came gradually and without fanfare or even the critical awareness of the participants themselves. Republicans became National Republicans, or Democrats, or Whigs, or Lincoln Republicans—or even Antimasons, Liberty party men, or Free Soilers.

But Jeffersonian Republicanism was the root branch of all the succeeding parties. Federalism had been routed and discredited by its defeat in 1800 and its gestures toward disunion during the War of 1812. The new political national consensus was embodied in the Jeffersonian Republicans. And it was they who gave the mantle of legitimacy to the federal government. In time this would change. The Constitution and the Supreme Court would eventually become the final arbiters of the limits of national power and authority. But until this occurred, Republicanism was the embodiment of the will of the American people. "The Republicans," as Jefferson had declared in 1810, were "the *nation*."[32]

Notes

INTRODUCTION

1. Wood, "Ideology and the Origins of Liberal America," 633.

2. Washington to the Secretary of War, Nov. 17, 1799, in Fitzpatrick, ed., *Washington*, 37, 428. Morgan (*Inventing the People*, 276) writes, "It is difficult at this time to capture the sense felt by Madison and others like him that a United States government would be contending with forces that might prove too much for it. . . . The future of republican government did hang in the balance."

3. Young, *Washington Community*, 110–42, 250–54, and Huntington, *Political Order*, 93–139.

4. My own analysis has benefited from the rich and insightful historical literature published in the past twenty years. The interest in republicanism dates from the publication of three extraordinarily influential works: Bailyn, *Ideological Origins* and *Origins of American Politics*; Wood, *Creation of the American Republic*. The extensive literature is cited and discussed in Kloppenberg's excellent article, "Virtues of Liberalism;" Lienesch's, *New Order of the Ages*, 3–14; and Matthews, *Radical Politics of Jefferson*, 1–18. See also Shalhope, "Toward a Republican Synthesis," and "Republicanism and Early American Historiography;" and Kelley, "Ideology and Political Culture. Also McDonald, *Novus Ordo Seclorum*.

5. For a discussion of the civic humanist tradition in classical and Renaissance times and its influence in Anglo-American thought, see Pocock, "Civic Humanism," 87. This civic humanism, a number of historians have contended, shaped a Court-versus-Country conflict, first in eighteenth-century British opposition politics and then later in the United States. See Breen, *Tobacco Culture*; Hutson, "Country, Court, and Constitution," 356–58; Murrin, "Great Inversion," 407; and Banning, *Jeffersonian Persuasion*. Appleby criticizes Banning and by implication other historians who subscribe to the Court-versus-Country thesis. She points out that Banning assumes but does not prove that "eighteenth-century British opposition ideas acted as the 'structured medium through which Americans continued to perceive their world and give expression to their hopes and discontents'" ("What Is Still American in the Political Philosophy of Jefferson?" 303). Wills (*Explaining America,* 38) also criticizes the applicability of the Court-versus-Country thesis to explain the conflict between the Republicans and Federalists in the 1790s. He points out that since David Hume, who had such a profound influence on Madison, was an "enemy" of Country ideology and indeed "made the best case for Walpolism," it is difficult to reconcile Madison with Country philosophy.

6. Rossiter, ed., *Federalist Papers*, 82.

7. Pocock, "Civic Humanism," 87.

8. See Wood's brilliant new book, *Radicalism of the American Revolution.* He argues that "if we measure the radicalism by the amount of social change that actually took place—by transformations in the relationships that bound people to each other—then the American Revolution was not conservative at all; on the contrary: it was as radical and as revolutionary as any in history" (5). See also Bailyn, *Ideological Origins*, 283, 302–5, 318; Ryerson, *Revolution Is Now Begun*, 247–56.

9. For a discussion of liberal republicanism, see Appleby, *Capitalism and a New Social Order*, 94, 22. McCoy (*Elusive Republic*, 236–37, 8–11) attempts to accommodate liberal and classical republicanism, holding that eighteenth-century republicanism meant reconciling and adapting classical republican-ism to the more liberal and pluralistic forces in the early republic. See also Kramnick, *Republicanism and Bourgeois Radicalism.*

10. Wood, "Ideology and the Origins of Liberal America," 635. See also Lienesch, *New Order of the Ages*, 6.

11. Morgan, *Inventing the People*, quotations from 286 and 256; see also 235–306.

12. As quoted in Wood, *Creation of the American Republic*, 373–74. A sim-ilar sentiment was expressed by Jeremy Belknap of New Hampshire, who asserted, "Let it be stated as a principle that government originates from the people; but let the people be taught . . . that they are not able to govern themselves" (see Karsky, "Agrarian Radicalism," 87).

13. Robbins, "'Discordant Parties,'" 511, 505–29.

14. Apter, "Reflections on the Role of a Political Opposition," 154, 165. Apter argues that the idea of opposition has not often been questioned in the West. Although this may well be true enough as a generalization across time, it was not true in the 1790s. Rather, many of Apter's generalizations about the problems faced by an opposition in a postrevolutionary society can be applied to the United States in the 1790s.

15. Huntington, *Political Order*, 5–8. Hartz, in his *Liberal Tradition in America*, provides the best statement of the persuasiveness and pervasiveness of a Lockean-derived ideology that mitigates and tempers conflict and channels it harmlessly within the restrictive boundaries of American liberalism.

16. Butterfield, *Whig Interpretation*, 12, 30. Hatch (*Sacred Cause of Liberty*, 3) makes a similar point: "We have placed a high priority on questions framed by our own climate of opinion and neglected that which . . . [is] the first goal of the historian: to enter in some degree into minds that are unlike our own."

17. Stone, "Charles Homer Haskins Lecture," 21–22. Kloppenberg ("Vir-tues of Liberalism," 30) warns that "we must avoid reading back into the struggles of the eighteenth century contending forces that did not appear until later."

18. Benson, *Toward a Scientific Study of History*, 206.

19. Gutman ("Work, Culture, and Society," 580) quotes Fernand Braudel as reminding him that "'victorious events come about as the result of many

possibilities,' and that 'for one possibility which actually is realized, innumerable others have drowned.' Usually these others leave 'little trace for the historian.' 'And yet,' Braudel adds, 'it is necessary to give them their place because the losing movements are forces which have at every moment affected the final outcome.'"

20. The proponents of this view are numerous: Hoadley argues: "When it became clear that the opposition was concerned only with specific policy alternatives within the existing constitutional system, it was far easier for such opposition to be tolerated. Once the legitimacy of opposition was established, the acceptance of parties followed. . . . The peaceful transfer of power in 1801 reflected the growing acceptance of the legitimacy of opposition and the idea of party" (*Origins of American Political Parties,* 191). Kelley (*Cultural Pattern in American Politics,* 93) has maintained that the stage was set with the meeting of the first Congress and that "mass political parties would soon appear for the first time in world history." Risjord (*Chesapeake Politics,* 521) talks of the "mature party system, 1793–1800." Cunningham (*Jeffersonian Republicans,* 261) maintains that "between the inaugurations of Washington and Jefferson, the two-party system became rooted in American politics." Goodman ("First Party System," 64) concludes that the Republicans and the Federalists "organized conflict and in doing so intensified it, but they also instituted an orderly means of settling differences without resorting to violence" and "offered hope to the threatened or discouraged that the next election would bring a change in fortune and the restoration of virtue to the seats of power." See also Ryan, "Party Formation in Congress," 531; Miller, *Federalist Era,* 101; Bell, *Party and Faction,* 3, 15, 187–88; Charles, *Origins of the Party System,* 83, 90; and Chambers, *Political Parties,* 122, 126. There are, of course, exceptions to the above generalization. Kerber (*Federalists in Dissent,* 195) although primarily interested in the cultural divisions between Federalists and Republicans, astutely notes "that for a long time it was unclear that the nation had a two-party destiny. Until Jefferson's election, many continued to indulge the hope that a permanent party division could be avoided." Formisano ("Deferential-Participant Politics," 473–87) also attacks the notion that a two-party system was established in the 1790s: "The era from Washington to 'Tippecanoe and Tyler Too' should be thought of primarily as a transitional phase of political culture in which the passage from a traditional, notable-oriented and deferential politics on the one hand to a party, electorate-oriented and egalitarian style of politics on the other, did not come about abruptly" (473).

21. Duverger (*Political Parties,* 418) has argued that "in the United States the two parties are rival teams, one occupying office, the other seeking to dislodge it. It is a struggle between the ins and outs, which may never become fanatical, and creates no deep cleavage in the country."

22. Hofstadter, *American Political Tradition,* viii.

23. Hofstadter, *Idea of a Party System,* 74–75.

24. Ibid., 85–86.

25. I use the term *men* recognizing that politics of that era, was, for the most part, restricted to adult, white males. See Heller, "'Fiery Frenchified

Dames,'" who very ably describes the role women were playing in the politics of the 1790s.

26. Bolingbroke, *Idea of a Patriot King,* as quoted by Hofstadter, *Idea of a Party System,* 10.

27. Jefferson to Francis Hopkinson, Mar. 13, 1789, in Boyd, ed., *Jefferson,* 14: 649–50.

28. Morgan, in his *Inventing the People,* brilliantly makes the point about the illusiveness of public opinion when sovereignty resides in the people.

29. The words are Banning's (*Jeffersonian Persuasion,* 149), but the sentiment is widely shared by others.

30. The "almost unchallenged rule of the Virginia Dynasty and the Democratic-Republican Party served to legitimate national authority and democratic rights. . . . By the time the nation divided again into two broad warring factions which appealed for mass support, the country had existed for forty years, the Constitution had been glorified, and the authority of the courts had been accepted as definitive" (Lipset, *First New Nation,* 45).

31. Andrews, *Colonial Background of the Revolution,* 220.

CHAPTER 1

1. Good descriptions of the inaugural celebration are in Griswold, *Republican Court,* 137–46, and in Flexner, *Washington,* 3, 182–91.

2. Washington to the Acting Secretary of War, Apr. 1, 1789, in Fitzpatrick, ed., *Washington,* 30: 268.

3. See Griswold, *Republican Court,* 113–36.

4. Elias Boudinot to his wife, date unknown, as quoted, ibid., 130–32.

5. Jensen and Becker, eds., *Documentary History of the First Federal Elections,* 1, vii–xii.

6. Madison to Jefferson, June 30, 1789, in Boyd, ed., *Jefferson,* 15: 224.

7. Geertz, "Integrative Revolution," 120, 120–21n. I am grateful to Professor Norman Kutcher of Syracuse University for this citation.

8. Lipset, *First New Nation,* 16.

9. See Ryerson, *Revolution Is Now Begun,* 247–56, for an excellent summary of the impact of the Revolution on American politics.

10. Huntington, *Political Order,* 30.

11. Ibid., 9–10.

12. Ibid.

13. Adams, *History of the United States,* 1: 16.

14. S. Comte de Volney quoted by Brown, *Mirror for Americans,* 25.

15. Meyer, *History of Transportation,* 3–64; Brown, *Mirror for Americans,* 43–48, see especially map on rates of travel in 1800, 272; Nettles, *Emergence of a National Economy,* 159–62; Philbrick, *Rise of the West,* 303–21; for accounts of travel on the Wilderness Road; Gephart, *Transportation and Industrial Development,* 20–56; Ambler, *History of Transportation,* 17–80, for a discussion of water transportation in the early West.

16. Kenyon, ed., *Antifederalists,* xli.

17. See Gross, *Minutemen and Their World*, 14, 66. See also Formisano, *Transformation of Political Culture*, 26–27; and Zuckerman, *Peaceable Kingdoms*, 136–38.

18. Wood, *Creation of the American Republic*, 188.

19. See Kelley, "Ideology and Political Culture," 536–40. See Maier, *Old Revolutionaries*, 272–75, for a discussion of the republicanism of Revolutionary New England.

20. See Sydnor, *Development of Southern Sectionalism*, 34–43, for a discussion of the county court and local government in the South. Freehling (*Road to Disunion*, chap. 3) gives an excellent account of how deference politics worked in the South.

21. Kelley, "Ideology and Political Culture," 536–40.

22. Peterson, ed., *Portable Jefferson*, 124–25. Isaac (*Transformation of Virginia*, 321) points out that republicanism did not necessarily create a political consensus, but rather was a cause for instability. Republicanism was "launched at first by the gentry as a means of regenerating traditional authority," but in the period after ratification of the Constitution, "it had become a vehicle of popular assertion" and added an element of considerable instability with its legitimacy being derived "from an idealization of individual autonomy."

23. See Morgan, *American Slavery, American Freedom*, 380–81, 385. For a somewhat different view that points out the "discrepancies between ideal and fact" in using race to bond elite and non-elite whites in the South, see Freehling, *Road to Disunion*, 42–43.

24. Kenyon, ed., *Antifederalists*, 132–34, and the excellent introduction on Antifederalist thought, xxi–lxvi.

25. Sam Adams to Richard Henry Lee, Dec, 13, 1787, in Cushing, ed., *Sam Adams*, 4: 324–25.

26. Young (*Washington Community*, 55, 60, and 152) notes that the public men of the early republic had "a nagging doubt about the moral legitimacy" of being a politician and power holder.

27. See Kelley's insightful article, "Ideology and Political Culture," 531–62, especially pp. 536–40. Lienesch (*New Order of the Ages*, 12) makes the same point: "While virtually all Americans of the time could consider themselves to be republicans, they often held startlingly dissimilar notions of the meaning of republicanism itself."

28. My understanding of the Antifederalists has greatly benefited from Cornell, "Aristocracy Assailed," 1148–72.

29. As quoted in Kenyon, ed., *Antifederalists*, L.

30. See Morgan (*Inventing the People*, 267–87) for an excellent discussion of the debate between Federalists and Antifederalists over representation.

31. This reference to representatives possessing "the same interests, feelings, opinions, and views, which the people themselves would possess, were they all assembled" is very close to Madison's language in *Federalist* 10, although the two men would disagree about the maximum feasible size of the constituency.

32. Storing, *Complete Anti-Federalist*, 3: 158.

33. Ibid., 376–78

34. Rossiter, ed., *Federalist Papers*, 325, 82. Morgan (*Inventing the People*, 286–87) points out that Madison's representation scheme had assumed "an existing social structure in which the people would know and recognize and defer to their natural leaders," but that, with the exception of the Revolution, the people had only "granted this deference . . . on a local level."

35. Wood, for example, (*Creation of the American Republic*, 606, 499–518, 614–15) suggests that the ratification of the Constitution "represented both the climax and the finale of the American enlightenment, both the fulfillment and the end of the belief that the endless variety and perplexity of society could be reduced to a single and harmonious system." In departing from many of the ideas of the "classical Whig world of 1776," Wood believes, the Federalist proponents of the Constitution rejected the notion of an organic wholeness of society. Rather, Wood argues, the Federalists characterized society as "an agglomeration of hostile individuals coming together for their mutual benefit." See also Appleby's, *Capitalism and a New Social Order*.

36. Main, *Antifederalists*, 254n; Flexner, *Washington*, 3, 141.

37. Lipset, *First New Nation*, 18.

38. Cunliffe, *Washington*, 20–21.

39. Jefferson to David Humphreys, Mar. 18, 1789, in Boyd, ed., *Jefferson*, 14: 676–78. See also, McDonald, *Washington*, 25.

40. Washington, "The First Inaugural Address," Apr. 30, 1789, in Fitzpatrick, ed., *Washington*, 30: 294.

41. See Madison to Richard Peters, Aug. 19, 1789, Madison Papers.

42. Storing, *Complete Anti-Federalist*, 3: 136.

43. Tench Coxe to Madison, Jan. 27, 1789, and Madison to unknown, Feb. 16, 1789, Madison Papers.

44. Saint John de Crevecoeur to Jefferson, Jan. 5, 1789; Jefferson to William Short, Feb. 9, 1789; and James Monroe to Jefferson, Feb. 15, 1789, all in Boyd, ed., *Jefferson*, 14: 414–16, 529, 557–58.

45. Madison to Jefferson, Mar. 29, 1789, ibid., 15: 5–8.

46. Wood, *Creation of the American Republic*, 538.

47. Richard Henry Lee to Edmund Randolph, Oct. 16, 1787, in Ballagh, ed., *Richard Henry Lee*, 2: 452–53. See also Sam Adams to Elbridge Gerry, Aug. 22, 1789, in Cushing, ed., *Sam Adams*, 4: 330–32.

48. Morgan (*Inventing the People*, 282–83) points out that the Federalists believed that "if subjects and rulers were the same, if government was by the people, it was a contradiction in terms for them to make concessions to themselves."

49. See Rutland, *Birth of the Bill of Rights*, chaps. 7–9, for a full discussion of the adoption of the amendments.

50. Miller, *Federalist Era*, 20–24.

51. Madison to Richard Peters, Aug. 19, 1789, Madison Papers.

52. But Madison's course itself was not without its potential political pitfalls. The Antifederalists, as Madison rightly suspected, had schemed to use the amendment process to alter the original meaning of the Constitution

completely. Richard Henry Lee, for example, had written the arch Antifeder-alist, Patrick Henry, that even though the amendments did not go as far as he and others would have liked, "by getting as much as we can at different times, we may at last come to obtain the greatest part of our wishes." See Richard Henry Lee to Patrick Henry, June 10, 1790, in Ballagh, ed., *Richard Henry Lee,* 2: 524–25.

53. Ellis ("Persistence of Antifederalism after 1789," 295–314) argues per-suasively that the principles of antifederalism, democracy, agrarianism, and states' rights, continued to influence American politics down to the Jacksonian era.

CHAPTER 2

1. Griswold, *Republican Court,* 114–23.

2. Compiled from Lightfoot, "State Delegations in Congress."

3. Bureau of the Census, *Historical Statistics,* 13.

4. Madison to Jefferson, May 27, 1789, Jefferson to Madison, Aug. 28, 1789, Washington to Jefferson, Oct. 13, 1789, in Boyd, ed., *Jefferson,* 15: 153, 369, 519.

5. Madison to Jefferson, Oct. 8, 1789, ibid., 509–10.

6. Jefferson to Washington, Dec. 15, 1789, ibid., 16: 34–35.

7. Washington to Jefferson, Jan. 21, 1790, ibid., 116–17.

8. Miller, *Hamilton,* 225.

9. Farrand, ed., *Records of the Convention,* 1: 282–93.

10. Hamilton to Gouverneur Morris, Feb. 27, 1802, as quoted in Stourzh, *Hamilton,* 39.

11. Madison to Jefferson, May 9, and May 27, 1789, in Boyd, ed., *Jefferson* 15: 114–15, 153–54.

12. Syrett, ed., *Hamilton,* 6: 86.

13. Madison to Jefferson, Jan. 24, 1790, as quoted by Malone, *Jefferson and the Rights of Man,* 290–91.

14. Ferguson, *Power of the Purse,* 297–301; Miller, *Hamilton,* 239–40.

15. Henry Lee to Madison, Mar. 13, 1790, Madison Papers.

16. Henry Lee to Madison, Mar. 4, 1790, ibid.

17. As quoted in Ammon, *James Monroe,* 86.

18. Henry Lee to Madison, Apr. 3, 1790, and Edmund Randolph to Madi-son, May 20, 1790, Madison Papers.

19. Ferguson, *Power of the Purse,* 306–11; Cooke, "Compromise of 1790," 526.

20. Cooke, "Compromise of 1790," 527.

21. Charles, *Origins of the Party System,* 23.

22. See Ford, ed., *Jefferson,* 1: 162–64, for Jefferson's later account of the bargain.

23. On the consummation of the deal, see Cooke, "Compromise of 1790," 523–25, 540–43, and on Jefferson's belief, see ibid., 545.

24. Madison to Henry Lee, Oct. 7, 1787 [1789], Madison Papers.

25. Jefferson to Thomas Mann Randolph, June 20, 1790, and Jefferson to Monroe, June 20, 1790, in Boyd, ed., *Jefferson*, 16: 536–40. See also Madison to James Madison, Sr., July 31, 1790, in Hunt, ed., *Madison*, 6: 19–20.

26. Cooke, "Compromise of 1790," 543.

27. Monroe to Jefferson, July 18, 1790, in Boyd, ed., *Jefferson*, 16: 231–33.

28. Miller, *Federalist Era*, 52; Rose, *Prologue to Democracy*, 10–12. Malone (*Jefferson and the Rights of Man*, 337) argues that Jefferson was suspicious of the motives of those (especially Patrick Henry) who continued to press their opposition to assumption and thus was indifferent to the Virginia House of Delegates' vote.

29. John Brown to Harry Innes, July 10, 1790, Harry Innes Papers.

30. For the excise tax, see Flexner, *Washington*, 277–78; Malone, *Jefferson and the Rights of Man*, 338–39. For Hamilton's, "Report on a National Bank," see Syrett, ed., *Hamilton*, 7: 306, 309, 310.

31. Madison's speech, Feb. 2, 1791, in Hunt, ed., *Madison*, 6: 19–36; See also the speech of Feb. 8, 1791, 36–42.

32. As quoted by Hammond, *Banks and Politics in America*, 116.

33. Charles, *Origins of the Party System*, 23; Bell, *Party and Faction*, 128–29.

34. Jefferson's "Opinion of the Constitutionality of a National Bank," Feb. 15, 1791, in Boyd, ed., *Jefferson*, 19: 275–80; Flexner, *Washington*, 278–82; and Malone, *Jefferson and the Rights of Man*, 342–45.

35. Hamilton, "Opinion on the Constitutionality of an Act to Establish a Bank," Feb. 23, 1791, in Syrett, ed., *Hamilton*, 8: 107.

36. Flexner, *Washington*, 278–82; Malone, *Jefferson and the Rights of Man*, 342–50.

37. Madison to Jefferson, July 10, 1791, in Hunt, ed., *Madison*, 6: 54–55.

38. Here, of course, I am at odds with Appleby's ("Commercial Farming," 849) argument that "what was distinctive about the Jeffersonian economic policy was not an anticommercial bias, but a commitment to growth through the unimpeded exertions of individuals whose access to economic opportunity was both protected and facilitated by government." Almost from the time the Republicans took power in 1801 down to the 1820s it is clear that they were divided into two competing ideologies and factions: one the Old Republican, agrarian, states' rights wing, and the other the more nationalistic and commercial wing. See Ellis, "Persistence of Antifederalism after 1789," and my *Jacksonians versus the Banks*, where I argue that a Jeffersonian antibank, anticommercial bias was a major force in shaping the Jackson party.

39. Breen, *Tobacco Culture*, xii–xiii, 142.

40. Peterson, ed., *Portable Jefferson*, 217.

41. Breen, *Tobacco Culture*, xii–xiii, 142.

42. There was a major expansion of the wheat producing area from New York and Pennsylvania into Virginia and Maryland. See Henretta, "Families and Farms," 17.

43. Jefferson, *Notes on Virginia*, as quoted in Breen, *Tobacco Culture*, 206; see also 204–6.

44. Isaac, *Transformation of Virginia*, 319–20.

45. Goodman, "First Party System," 64.

46. See McCoy, *Elusive Republic*, 151; also 48–75, 136–65.

47. Murrin, "Great Inversion," 407.

48. Jefferson to T. M. Randolph, May 15, 1791, in Ford, ed., *Jefferson* 5: 335–37.

49. Jefferson to Philip Freneau, Feb. 28, 1791, and Jefferson to Madison, July 21, 1791, both in Jefferson Papers. Also Madison to Jefferson, May 1, 1791, in Hunt, ed., *Madison*, 6: 45–50; and Madison to Jefferson, July 24, 1791, in Boyd, ed., *Jefferson*, 20: 667–68. Also see Malone, *Jefferson and the Rights of Man*, xxviii.

50. *National Gazette*, Dec. 5, 1791, and *General Advertiser*, Dec. 26, 1791.

51. Jefferson to Archibald Stuart, Dec. 23, 1791, in Boyd, ed., *Jefferson*, 22: 435–37.

52. *National Gazette*, Jan. 30 and Jan. 19, 1792.

53. Rossiter, ed., *Federalist Papers*, 314–17. See also Wills (*Explaining America*, 24–33) for a discussion of No. 49 and Hume's influence on Madison.

54. *National Gazette*, Feb. 6 and Apr. 5, 1792. See also Jan. 26, Mar. 15, Mar. 19, Aug. 18, Sept. 12, and Dec. 12, 1792.

55. Rossiter, ed., *Federalist Papers*, 84.

56. I have used Madison's term *party* instead of *proto-party* in my discussion of his essay on "parties," in order to avoid confusion. As mentioned earlier, I prefer *proto-party* which I believe more accurately describes these premodern institutions that lacked most of the essential characteristics of modern parties.

57. Madison, "Candid State of Parties," in Hunt, ed., *Madison*, 6: 106–19.

58. Malone, *Jefferson and the Rights of Man*, 436. See McCoy (*Elusive Republic*, 136–65) for a discussion of Madison's and Hamilton's competing political economics. For the beginnings of the feud between Hamilton and Jefferson, see McDonald, *Hamilton*, 237–61.

59. See Jefferson to Washington, May 23, 1792, in Boyd, ed., *Jefferson*, 23: 535–40, and Jefferson's memorandum of a conversation with Washington, July 10, 1792, Jefferson Papers.

60. Hamilton to Edward Carrington, May 26, 1792, in Syrett, ed., *Hamilton*, 11: 426–45.

61. "T. L. No. III," Aug. 11, 1792, ibid., 12: 193–94; and "Metellus," Oct. 24, 1792, ibid., 613–17.

62. Washington to Hamilton, July 29, 1792, ibid., 129–34.

63. Hamilton to Washington, Aug. 18, 1792, ibid., 228–58; quotation on page 253.

64. Washington to Jefferson and to Hamilton, Aug. 23 and 26, 1792, in Fitzpatrick, ed., *Washington*, 32: 128–34.

65. Jefferson to Washington, Sept. 9, 1792, in Ford, ed., *Jefferson*, 6: 101–9. Jefferson reiterated his promise to Washington in a conversation he reported in his diary, Feb. 7, 1793, in Sawvel, ed., *Anas of Jefferson*, 103–5.

66. See Malone (*Jefferson and the Rights of Man*, 14–36) for a defense of Jefferson, which argues that he did play a more detached and disengaged role after he promised Washington he would. For a contrary view, see Ford, ed.,

Jefferson, 6: 168–71, for Jefferson's draft of the resolutions condemning Hamilton alongside the ones Giles introduced. See also Anderson, *Giles*, 20–25.

CHAPTER 3

1. Taylor, *An Enquiry*, 49–55.
2. Jefferson to Nicholas Lewis, Feb. 9, 1791, Jefferson Papers.
3. Jackson and Twobig, eds., *Diaries of Washington*, 6: 96.
4. Washington to David Humphreys, July 20, 1791, as quoted by Rose, *Prologue to Democracy*, 28.
5. *National Gazette*, June 8, 1792. Also see Henry Lee's correspondence with James Madison for a growing disillusionment with Washington: Jan. 8 and Jan. 29, 1792, Madison Papers.
6. Jefferson's memorandum, "Conversations with the President," Mar. 1, 1792, Jefferson Papers.
7. Fitzpatrick, ed., *Washington*, 32: 45–49. See Madison to Washington, June 21, 1792, in Hunt, ed., *Madison*, 6: 111–16, for Madison's reply.
8. Jefferson's memorandum, "A Conversation with Washington," July 10, 1792, Jefferson Papers.
9. Jefferson to Washington, May 23, 1792, in Ford, ed., *Jefferson*, 6: 1–6.
10. Madison's memorandum of a conversation with Washington, May 5, 1792, in Hunt, ed., *Madison*, 6: 106–10.
11. *National Gazette*, Oct. 13, 1792. See also Apr. 2, June 18, and July 25, 1792; and Hunt, ed., *Madison*, 6: 104–5.
12. *National Gazette*, Sept. 1 and Aug. 8, 1792, where it was suggested "that no such party as the antifederal exists."
13. Ibid., Dec. 8 and July 7, 1792.
14. For a good account of George Clinton in New York, the disputed gubernatorial election of 1792, and Clinton's vice presidential candidacy in 1792, see Young, *Democratic Republicans*, 277–341. See also Cunningham, *Jefferson Republicans*, 45–49.
15. Jefferson to Madison, June 21, 1792, and Jefferson to Monroe, June 23, 1792, in Ford, ed., *Jefferson*, 6: 89–91, 93–95.
16. Monroe to Jefferson, July 17, 1792, Jefferson Papers.
17. John Nicholson to Madison, Oct. 3, 1792, Madison Papers.
18. Monroe to Madison, Oct. 9, 1792, in Hamilton, ed., *Monroe*, 1: 242–45; Madison to Monroe, [undated letter], Madison Papers. See also Monroe and Madison to Melancton Smith and Marinus Willet, Oct. 19, 1792, Monroe Papers.
19. Cunningham, *Jeffersonian Republicans*, 48, 46–49.
20. *National Gazette*, Dec. 8, 1, 5, and 19, 1792.
21. Cunningham, *Jeffersonian Republicans*, 49n.; Dauer, *Adams Federalists*, 87.
22. Cunningham, *Jeffersonian Republicans*, 49.
23. Ibid., 44–45.
24. Young, *Democratic Republicans*, 340.

25. Formisano, *Transformation of Political Culture*, 30–31.

26. Risjord, *Chesapeake Politics*, 408. Bell (*Party and Faction*, 254–55) lists a fourteen-to-five division in Virginia.

27. As quoted in Beeman, *Old Dominion*, 110, and 108–13.

28. Bell, *Party and Faction*, 185.

29. Bell (ibid., 8) says 34 percent, whereas Nelson M. Polsby in his "Institutionalization of the U.S. House," 146, says 56.5 percent of the first-term members did not return.

30. Jefferson to Thomas Pinckney, Dec. 3, 1792, in Ford, ed., *Jefferson*, 6: 143–44. See also Jefferson to Thomas Pinckney, Apr. 12, 1793, Jefferson Papers.

31. Taylor to Madison, May 11 and June 20, 1793, Dodd, ed., "John Taylor Correspondence," 253–54, 254–60. See also Monroe to Madison, May 18, 1793, in Hamilton, ed., *Monroe*, 1: 254–55.

32. Madison to Taylor, Sept. 30, 1793, Madison Papers. Madison referred to Jefferson as our "distant friend." Although Jefferson suggested a mid-November publication date, the pamphlet apparently was not published until early 1794.

33. Taylor, *An Enquiry*, 6.

34. Taylor, *An Examination*, 5. Here Taylor is taking the opposition position Madison had taken at the Convention, arguing in favor of large constituencies. See Morgan, *Inventing the People*, 274–77.

35. Taylor, *Definition of Parties*, 14.

36. *National Gazette*, Mar. 19, 1793.

37. Taylor, *An Enquiry*, 56–57, 47, and 7.

38. Ibid., 49, 54–55.

39. Monroe to Jefferson, July 17, 1792, Jefferson Papers.

40. Taylor, *An Enquiry*, 55.

41. This is the meaning of the word at least after the mid-seventeenth century and certainly is the meaning Taylor uses. See the *Oxford Universal Dictionary on Historical Principles*, 1440.

42. Taylor, *Definition of Parties*, 2.

43. Taylor, *An Enquiry*, 85. Taylor's choice of words, "a band of patriots" was probably influenced by his reading of Bolingbroke. See Foord (*His Majesty's Opposition*, 145–51) and Ketcham (*Presidents above Party*, 57–66) for discussions of Bolingbroke's political beliefs.

44. Rossiter, ed., *Federalist Papers*, 82.

45. Jefferson's memorandum of a conversation with Washington, Feb. 7, 1793, Jefferson Papers.

46. For a vivid description of this political system, see Sydnor, *American Revolutionaries in the Making*.

47. See Morgan, *American Slavery, American Freedom*, 380–81, 385.

48. Peterson, *Jefferson and the New Nation*, 37.

49. *National Gazette*, Aug. 15, 22, and Oct. 3, 1792, and May 1, 1793.

50. Cunningham, *Jeffersonian Republicans*, 38–45.

51. *National Gazette*, Aug. 11, 15, and 22, 1792.

52. Hartford, Conn., *American Mercury*, Apr. 1, 1793, as reprinted in the *National Gazette*, Apr. 17, 1793.

53. For a discussion of the democratization of American politics during and after the Revolution, see Main, *Political Parties*; Ryerson, *Revolution Is Now Begun*; and Gross, *Minutemen and Their World*. For a recent summary of the historiographical conflict over the meaning of democracy and the battle over ratification, see Hutson, "Country, Court, and Constitution."

CHAPTER 4

1. See Stinchcombe, *American Revolution*, 208–9. See also Ketcham, "France and American Politics," 198–223, and Banner, "France and the Origins of American Political Culture," 651–70.

2. As quoted by Hatch, *Sacred Cause of Liberty* 156. See also 155 for a discussion of the development of civil millennialism in the writings of the New England clergy. See Bloch (*Visionary Republic,* 75–93) for a somewhat different emphasis.

3. Paine, *Common Sense* as quoted by Commanger and Morris, ed., *Spirit of 'Seventy-Six*, 1: 290–91.

4. See Bloch (*Visionary Republic,* 150–231) for a discussion of how the French Revolution reinforced American millennialism.

5. *Boston Gazette*, Sept. 7, 1789, as quoted in Hazen, *American Opinion of the French Revolution,* 142.

6. Ibid.

7. George Tuberville to Madison, Jan. 28, 1793, Madison Papers.

8. Madison to George Nicholas, Mar. 15, 1793, as quoted in Ketcham, "France and American Politics," 220–21.

9. Tagg, "Bache," 224. The author generously sent me parts of this manuscript, which was in press at the University of Pennsylvania Press at the time.

10. I have discussed this point at some length in an unpublished paper, "American Reaction to Threats against the Third Republic, 1870–1900."

11. *General Advertiser,* July 26, 1793, as quoted in Tagg, "Bache," 222.

12. Madison to George Nicholas, Mar. 15, 1793, as quoted in Ketcham, "France and American Politics," 220–21.

13. Jefferson to Jean Pierre Brissot De Warville, May 8, 1793, in Ford, ed., *Jefferson,* 6: 248–49.

14. *Boston Gazette and County Register,* Sept. 26, 1791, and *New York Journal, and Weekly Register,* Jan. 28, 1792, as quoted by Newman, in " '*Principles* and Not *Men*,' " 12. I am very grateful to Professor Newman sharing with me this as well as other parts of his dissertation, "American Popular Culture."

15. Malone, *Jefferson and the Ordeal of Liberty,* 45–47.

16. Jefferson to William Short, Jan. 3, 1793, in Ford, ed., *Jefferson,* 6: 153–57.

17. See Palmer (*Age of the Democratic Revolution,* 2: 518–46) for a discussion of politics in the United States after the "revolutionizing" of the French Revolution in 1792. See especially p. 525 for a discussion of the Federalist and

Republican perception of their own position in relationship to France. See also Kaplan (*Jefferson and France,* chap. 3) and DeConde (*Entangling Alliance,* 86–87) for an analysis of the impact of the French Revolution after 1793. Jones (*America and French Culture*) discusses the American reception to various aspects of French culture.

18. Chauncey Goodrich to Oliver Wolcott, Feb. 17, 1793, in Gibbs, ed., *Memoirs,* 1: 88.

19. Nash, "American Clergy," 395, 399. See also Wood ("Conspiracy and the Paranoid Style, 401–41) for a discussion of how events were often seen and explained in conspiratorial terms by eighteenth-century Americans.

20. Oliver Wolcott, Sr., to Oliver Wolcott, Mar. 25, 1793, and Chauncey Goodrich to Oliver Wolcott, Mar. 24, 1793, in Gibbs, ed., *Memoirs,* 1: 90–91.

21. Washington to Hamilton, Jefferson, Knox, and Randolph, Apr. 18, 1793, in Syrett, ed., *Hamilton,* 14: 326–27.

22. The proclamation issued Apr. 22, 1793, may be found in Fitzpatrick, ed., *Washington,* 32: 430–31. Jefferson's position may be found in two letters to Madison, June 23 and June 29, 1793, in Ford, ed., *Jefferson,* 6: 315–16 and 325–28 as well as in two memorandums of Apr. 18 and Nov. 8, 1793, in Sawvel, ed., *Anas of Jefferson,* 118–20 and 174–78. The best secondary account of Jefferson's position is in Malone, *Jefferson and the Ordeal of Liberty,* 68–89. See also Ammon, *Genet,* 47–51.

23. Hamilton and Henry Knox to Washington, May 2, 1793, in Syrett, ed., *Hamilton,* 14: 367–96; Malone, *Jefferson and the Ordeal of Liberty,* 74–76; Ammon, *Genet,* 47–53; and Combs, *Jay Treaty,* 108–9. See also McDonald (*Hamilton,* 263–83) where he believes Hamilton "understood European affairs better" (265).

24. "Opinion on French Treaties," Apr. 28, 1793, in Ford, ed., *Jefferson,* 6: 219–31.

25. Jay's Treaty will be dealt with in chapter 6. The above paragraphs are drawn from DeConde, *Entangling Alliance,* 91–100.

26. *National Gazette,* May 15 and July 27, 1793, as quoted in Newlin, *Hugh Henry Brackenridge,* 132–33. Also *National Gazette,* May 8, 1793, and *General Advertiser,* Dec. 14, 1793.

27. Monroe to Jefferson, May 28, 1793, in Hamilton, ed., *Monroe,* 1: 256–59.

28. Tagg, "Bache," 238–39.

29. Madison to Jefferson, June 19, 1793, Madison Papers, and Madison to Jefferson, June 13, 1793, in Hunt, ed., *Madison,* 6: 130–33.

30. Jefferson to Madison, May 19, June 2, June 23, and Aug. 11, 1793, in Ford, ed., *Jefferson,* 6: 259–62, 315–16, and 367–70.

31. "Pacificus No. 1," in Syrett, ed., *Hamilton,* 15: 33–43. See also McDonald, *Hamilton,* 278–79.

32. Jefferson to Madison, July 7, 1793, in Ford, ed., *Jefferson,* 6: 338–39. See also Madison to Jefferson, June 19, 1793, Madison Papers.

33. "Helvidius" letters, in Hunt, ed., *Madison,* 6: 138–88.

34. See Ammon (*Genet,* 1–31) for Genet's background.

35. John Steele to Hamilton, Apr. 30, 1793, as quoted in Bowman, *Struggle for Neutrality,* 56–57.

36. Tagg, "Bache," 239.

37. For a discussion of Genet's arrival in the United States and his instructions, see DeConde, *Entangling Alliance,* 180–85, 198–201; Thomas, *American Neutrality,* 77–90; Ammon, *Genet,* 22–29; Malone, *Jefferson and the Ordeal of Liberty,* 90–98; McDonald, *Hamilton,* 272; and Bowman, *Struggle for Neutrality,* 56–75.

38. Jefferson to Madison, May 19, 1793, in Ford, ed., *Jefferson,* 6: 259–62.

39. For an excellent discussion of the rather knotty problem of neutrality, see Thomas, *American Neutrality,* specifically pp. 118–64 for the conflicting interpretations concerning privateers. See also Ammon, *Genet;* DeConde, *Entangling Alliance,* 204–33; and Bowman, *Struggle for Neutrality,* 56–98.

40. Jefferson to the French Minister, June 5, 1793, in Ford, ed., *Jefferson,* 6: 282–83.

41. The above account is drawn from DeConde, *Entangling Alliance,* 217–23; Thomas, *American Neutrality,* 137–43; and Bowman, *Struggle for Neutrality,* 73–75.

42. Jefferson to Monroe, June 28, 1793, in Ford, ed., *Jefferson,* 6: 321–24.

43. Memorandum of Jefferson, Aug. 1 and Aug. 2, 1793, in Sawvel, ed., *Anas of Jefferson,* 156–61; Thomas, *American Neutrality,* 226–32; Ammon, *Genet,* 101–9; DeConde, *Entangling Alliance,* 296–300; and Malone, *Jefferson and the Ordeal of Liberty,* 124–28.

44. Malone, *Jefferson and the Ordeal of Liberty,* 129–31. Genet's successor, Joseph Fauchet, was ordered to arrest Genet and send him back to France for punishment. American officials, however, declined to assist the French, and Genet remained in the United States and eventually married the daughter of Governor George Clinton of New York.

45. Samuel Higgenson to Hamilton, Aug. 24, 1793, in Syrett, ed., *Hamilton,* 15: 273–76.

46. *General Advertiser,* July 2, 1793, as quoted in Tagg, "Bache," 247. See also pp. 245–47.

47. *National Gazette,* June 5 and 12, 1793.

48. Sawvel, ed., *Anas of Jefferson,* 158–59.

49. Ibid., 148–51.

50. Ibid., 162–63.

51. Jefferson to Madison, Aug. 3, 1793, and "Notes on Party Policy," Feb. 1793, in Ford, ed., *Jefferson,* 6: 361–62 and 171–72; and Jefferson to Madison, Aug. 11, 1793, Jefferson Papers.

52. Ammon, *Genet,* 134–40; and Ammon, "Genet Mission," 725–41.

53. Two of Hamilton's confidants, John Jay and Rufus King, informed the public by a letter to the press that Genet had threatened to "appeal from the President to the people." For an excellent account of this controversy, see the long editorial note accompanying the letter from Hamilton to Rufus King, Aug. 13, 1793, in Syrett, ed., *Hamilton,* 15: 233–42.

54. Ammon ("Genet Mission," 725–41) points out the central role the

Genet Affair had in forcing the Federalists and the Republicans to broaden their support through publicly endorsed resolutions.

55. Madison to Archibald Stuart, Sept. 1, 1793, in Hunt, ed., *Madison*, 6: 188–90.

56. Ibid.; Madison to Jefferson, Aug. 27 and Sept. 2, 1793, Madison to Monroe, Sept. 15, 1793, ibid., 178–79, 191–92, and 197–98. See Monroe to Jefferson, Sept. 3 and Oct. 14, 1793, and Monroe to Madison, Sept. 25, 1793, in Hamilton, *Monroe*, 1: 273–76, 278–79, and 276–77. For the resolutions passed in Richmond and Caroline County see the *General Advertiser*, Dec. 17 and 18, 1793.

57. As quoted in Risjord, *Chesapeake Politics*, 429. See also pp. 428–29 and Tagg, "Bache," 248.

58. The words are Madison's as expressed in a number of letters in the late summer and fall of 1793. See notes 55 and 56.

59. Link, *Democratic Republican Societies*, 19–35; Foner, ed., *Democratic Republican Societies*, 4.

60. *General Advertiser*, May 16, 1794.

61. Link, *Democratic Republican Societies*, 13–15.

62. Foner, *Democratic Republican Societies*, 9.

63. Link, *Democratic Republican Societies*, 72–73.

64. Foner, *Democratic Republican Societies*, 8.

65. Young, *Democratic Republicans*, 394–95.

66. Coward, *Kentucky in the New Republic*, 99–101.

67. *General Advertiser*, Jan. 18, 1794.

68. As quoted in Link, *Democratic Republican Societies*, 6–7. See also the *National Gazette*, July 13, 1793, for the declaration of principles of the Democratic Society of Pennsylvania.

69. *General Advertiser*, Feb. 28, 1795.

70. Wood's *Newark Gazette*, Dec. 31, 1794, as quoted by Link, *Democratic Republican Societies*, 106.

71. *Boston Gazette*, Jan. 20, 1794, as quoted by Link, *Democratic Republican Societies*, 106.

72. David Ross to Hamilton, July 23, 1793, in Syrett, ed., *Hamilton*, 15: 121–22.

73. For rumors of meetings with French representatives, see Sawvel, ed., *Anas of Jefferson*, 150.

74. "No Jacobin NO. VII," in Syrett, ed., *Hamilton*, 15: 268–70.

75. Sawvel, ed., *Anas of Jefferson*, 157–59. See also Jefferson to Madison, Aug. 11, 1793, Jefferson Papers.

76. Link, *Democratic Republican Societies*, 149.

77. Tinkcom, *Republicans and Federalists in Pennsylvania*, 82; and Young, *Democratic Republicans*, 395–96, 410–12, 559–60, and 575–76.

78. Cunningham, *Jeffersonian Republicans*, 63–66.

79. Countryman, *People in Revolution*, 140–43, 145, 294–95.

80. In contrast to my interpretation is Kramnick's "Republican Revisionism Revisited," 629–64, and Appleby's "Commercial Farming," 833–49.

81. Jefferson to Madison, June 9, 1793, in Ford, ed., *Jefferson*, 6: 290–94.

82. Jefferson to the president, July 31, 1793, in Ford, ed., *Jefferson*, 6: 360–61; and memo, Aug. 6, 1793, Jefferson Papers.

83. Morgan, *Inventing the People*, 277.

CHAPTER 5

1. A version of this section appeared as my "Whiskey Rebellion," 119–33. See also Miller, "Democratic Societies," 324–49.

2. For an excellent recent account of the Whiskey Rebellion, see Slaughter, *Whiskey Rebellion*, esp. 95–105 for a discussion of the Excise Bill in Congress. See also the various essays in Boyd, ed., *Whiskey Rebellion*.

3. Baldwin, *Whiskey Rebels*, 71–72.

4. Opposition to the excise was not confined to western Pennsylvania. See Tachau, "Whiskey Rebellion in Kentucky," 239–59; Crow, "Whiskey Rebellion in North Carolina," 1–28; and Slaughter, *Whiskey Rebellion*, 117–20.

5. Barber, "Among the Most '*Techy Articles of Civil Police*,'" 60–61. See also Slaughter, *Whiskey Rebellion*, 12–27.

6. Slaughter, *Whiskey Rebellion*, 73. See also Gibbs, ed., *Memoirs*, 1: 146–47; Brackenridge, *History of the Western Insurrection*, 17. Cooke ("Whiskey Insurrection," 316–46) downplays the economic factors as motives for the insurrection. The point should be made, however, that the excise was, in many ways symbolic—to many it symbolized the section's political impotence and reaffirmed the fears that the section would be not only neglected (as apparently born out by the government's inaction on the Mississippi question), but also discriminated against. The excise further reflected the difficulty, if not the impossibility, at least in the minds of western Pennsylvanians, of Congress being able to legislate for the general good.

7. Baldwin, *Whiskey Rebels*, 71–72.

8. Slaughter, *Whiskey Rebellion*, 109–24.

9. Resolution in Syrett, ed., *Hamilton* 12: 308–9n. Also see Gibbs, ed., *Memoirs*, 1: 146–48. The emphasis in the quotation is mine.

10. Hamilton to Washington and to John Jay, Sept. 1 and Sept. 3, 1792, in Syrett, ed., *Hamilton*, 12: 311–12 and 316–17; Slaughter, *Whiskey Rebellion*, 120.

11. For an excellent account of the Washington administration's eventual decision to use force against the Whiskey Rebels, see Kohn, "Washington Administration's Decision," 567–84.

12. As quoted in Slaughter, *Whiskey Rebellion*, 123.

13. Ibid., 120.

14. Ibid., 175–89.

15. Ibid. See also Brackenridge, *History of the Western Insurrection*, 79–151; Baldwin, *Whiskey Rebels*, 129–71; Miller, *Federalist Era*, 157.

16. Kohn, "Washington Administration's Decision," 571–72.

17. Dallas, ed. *A. J. Dallas*, 150.

18. Kohn, "Washington's Administration's Decision," 575–76; Baldwin, *Whiskey Rebels*, 185.

19. As quoted in Baldwin, *Whiskey Rebels*, 198.

20. *General Advertiser*, Nov. 1, 1794; Kohn, "Washington Administration's Decision," 578.

21. Hamilton to Angelica Church, Oct. 23, 1794, in Syrett, ed., *Hamilton*, 17: 340.

22. *General Advertiser*, Nov. 1 and Nov. 8, 1794. Also Slaughter, *Whiskey Rebellion*, 206–21; Baldwin, *Whiskey Rebels*, 234–35 and 262–64.

23. Maier, *From Resistance to Revolution*, 4–5.

24. Slaughter, *Whiskey Rebellion*, 227; also see 223–28 and 12–27.

25. See Pitkin, *Concept of Representation*, for an excellent discussion of the concept of representation. See also Morgan, *Inventing the People*.

26. Morgan, *Inventing the People*, 51.

27. Foner, ed., *Democratic Republican Societies*, 29. See also Link, *Democratic-Republican Societies*, 145–48. Slaughter (*Whiskey Rebellion*, 165) says that "no evidence links the societies to violent protest against the excise. It is possible, however, that they unwittingly contributed to an existing atmosphere of opposition, providing a forum for reinforcement of local concerns."

28. Jefferson also opposed the excise and argued in 1793 that it should be repealed in favor of a state tax. See Cunningham, *Jeffersonian Republicans*, 53.

29. Foner, ed., *Democratic Republican Societies*, 88–89.

30. The quoted phrase is from Wood, *Creation of the American Republic*, 615. For a discussion of the views of representation as expressed in *The Federalist Papers*, see Wills, *Explaining America*, 179–264, and Morgan, *Inventing the People*, 263–87.

31. "Declaration of the Committees of Fayette County," Sept. 1794, in Adams, ed., *Gallatin*, 1: 6.

32. Sixth annual address to Congress, Nov. 19, 1794, in Fitzpatrick, ed., *Washington*, 34: 29.

33. Washington to Edmund Randolph, Oct. 16, 1794, ibid., 2–4. See also Miller, "Democratic Societies," 334–36.

34. Wiebe, *Opening of American Society*, 73–74.

35. *Annals of the Congress of the United States*, 1793–1795, 3d Congress, 899–906; Madison to Jefferson, Nov. 30, 1794, Madison Papers; Madison to Monroe, Dec. 4, 1794, in Hunt, ed., *Madison*, 6: 219–27.

36. *Annals of the Congress of the United States*, 1793–1795, 3d Congress, 906–7.

37. Ibid., 913–14.

38. Ibid., 921–32. The emphasis in the quotation is mine.

39. Ibid., 911–12, 934–35.

40. Ibid., 947. See Madison to Jefferson, Nov. 30, 1794, Madison Papers, for a report on the debate and vote in the House.

41. Jefferson to Madison, Dec. 28, 1794, in Ford, ed., *Jefferson*, 6: 516–19; Madison to Jefferson, Nov. 30, 1794, Madison Papers; Madison to Monroe, Dec. 4, 1794, in Hunt, ed., *Madison*, 6: 219–27.

42. *General Advertiser*, Feb. 28, 1795.

43. Ibid., Dec. 27, 1794.

44. Link, *Democratic-Republican Societies*, 196–202.

45. Whitaker, *Spanish-American Frontier*, 95–96. See also John Breckinridge's "Remonstrance to Congress and Press," Breckinridge Family Papers.

46. Whitaker, *Spanish-American Frontier*, 95–96.

47. DeConde, *Entangling Alliance*, 243–44; Bemis, *Pinckney's Treaty*, chaps. 1–5.

48. Whitaker, *Spanish-American Frontier*, 93–102, 118. See also Bemis, *Pinckney's Treaty*, chaps. 6 and 7; Harrison, *Breckinridge*, 52–53; Watlington, *Partisan Spirit*, 79–187. Coward (*Kentucky in the New Republic*, 8–9) suggests that threats of secession may have also been used to bring pressure on Congress to admit Kentucky as a separate and independent state.

49. Clark to the French Minister, Feb. 5, 1793, in Turner, ed., "Correspondence between Clark and Genet," 967–71; Turner, "Origins of Genet's Projected Attack," 665; Lowitt, "Activities of Citizen Genet," 252–54; Harrison, *Breckinridge*, 55–56.

50. As quoted in DeConde, *Entangling Alliance*, 236; see also 235–48.

51. Jefferson's memorandum, July 5, 1793, in Sawvel, ed., *Anas of Jefferson*, 129–31. See also Lowitt, "Activities of Citizen Genet," 256–57; Turner, "Origin of Genet's Projected Attack," 668–69.

52. Washington's Proclamation, Mar. 24, 1794, in Fitzpatrick, *Washington* 33: 304–5; DeConde, *Entangling Alliance*, 249–50. See Breckinridge's highly sarcastic public reply to the President's proclamation, May 6, 1794, in the Breckinridge Family Papers.

53. Lowitt, "Activities of Citizen Genet," 255–65, and DeConde, *Entangling Alliance*, 250. Also R. Breckinridge and Jas. Brown to Gov. Isaac Shelby of Kentucky, Jan. 10 and Feb. 16, 1794, in Turner, ed., "Correspondence between Clark and Genet," 1032–33, 1040–41.

54. Coward (*Kentucky in the New Republic*, 99) says that three societies were organized in the state.

55. "Old Fashioned Republican," [undated and unsigned], Breckinridge Family Papers. See also Coulter, "Democratic Societies," 384; Harrison, *Breckinridge*, 56–57.

56. "Remonstrance to Congress and Press," [1793], Breckinridge Family Papers. The Remonstrance is reprinted in Foner, ed., *Democratic Republican Societies*, 366–68.

57. *General Advertiser*, Dec. 18, 1793, contains a list of resolutions passed by the Democratic Society in Lexington on September 16. See also Coulter, "Democratic Societies," 381–82, and Harrison, *Breckinridge*, 54–55.

58. Coulter, "Democratic Societies," 378–79; Harrison, *Breckinridge*, 56–57.

59. Edmund Randolph to Jefferson, Aug. 28, 1794, Jefferson Papers; Coulter, "Democratic Societies," 388. See also J. Brown to Monroe, Dec. 5, 1794, Monroe Papers; Harrison, *Breckinridge*, 60–61.

60. DeConde, *Entangling Alliance*, 251; Whitaker, *Spanish-American Frontier*, 196–222; Miller, *Federalist Era*, 188–89; and Bemis, *Pinckney's Treaty*, 198–314.

61. Taylor memorandum to Madison, May 11, 1794, in Hunt, ed., *Disunion Sentiment*, [23].

62. See Morgan (*Inventing the People*, 275–77) for Madison's views at the time the Constitution was ratified.

CHAPTER 6

1. Jefferson to Thomas Pinckney, Dec. 3, 1792, in Ford, ed., *Jefferson*, 6: 143–44, and William Branch Giles to Jefferson, Dec. 9, 1795, Jefferson Papers. See also Bell (*Party and Faction*, 254–56) where he contends the split between the Federalists and the Republicans was, respectively, 53 to 57 in the Third Congress and 57 to 58 in the Fourth Congress.

2. Breen, *Tobacco Culture*, 206–7.

3. An excellent summary of this American foreign policy conflict can be found in Combs, *Jay Treaty*, 31–51; and DeConde, *Entangling Alliance*, 73–78.

4. Jefferson's "Report," in Ford, ed., *Jefferson*, 6: 470–84. See also Combs, *Jay Treaty*, 116–17.

5. Madison's resolutions, in Hunt, ed., *Madison*, 6: 203–8. See also Combs, *Jay's Treaty*, 117–20.

6. Combs, *Jay Treaty*, 117–20.

7. Bemis, *Jay's Treaty*, 183–252.

8. Ibid., 253–78, and Combs, *Jay Treaty*, 120–22.

9. Bemis, *Jay's Treaty*, 271, and Combs, *Jay Treaty*, 120–22. Spencer Roane to Monroe, Feb. 24, 1794, Monroe Papers; Madison to Jefferson, Mar. 2 and Apr. 14, 1794, Madison Papers.

10. Madison to Jefferson, May 11, 1794, Madison Papers; Jefferson to Monroe and to Madison, Apr. 24 and May 15, 1794, in Ford, ed., *Jefferson*, 6: 503–7 and 510–12.

11. Madison to Jefferson, May 25, 1794, in Hunt, ed., *Madison*, 6: 215–18.

12. John Edwards to John Breckinridge, Mar. 16, 1794, Breckinridge Family Papers.

13. Ibid., May 24, 1792, for the burning of an effigy of John Jay.

14. Bemis, *Jay's Treaty*, 268–69; Miller, *Federalist Era*, 150–51.

15. Monroe to Jefferson, Mar. 16, 1794, in Hamilton, ed., *Monroe*, 1: 285–89; Combs, *Jay Treaty*, 122–23.

16. R. R. Livingston to Madison, Jan. 30, 1795, and Madison to Jefferson, Feb. 15, 1795, Madison Papers.

17. Combs, *Jay Treaty*, 137–58; Perkins, *First Rapproachment*, 1–6; Bemis, *Jay's Treaty*, esp. 318–73.

18. As quoted by Bemis, *Jay's Treaty*, 372. Combs (*Jay Treaty*, 116–17) says that the United States exported nearly twice as much to Great Britain as to France and imported nearly seven times as much. The tonnage of *American ships* involved in the French trade, however, was double that of ships trading with Great Britain.

19. Pierce Butler to Madison, June 12, 1795, and Henry Tazewell to Madison, June 26, 1795, Madison Papers; R. R. Livingston to Monroe, July 10, 1795, S. T. Mason to Monroe, June 29, 1795, and Henry Tazewell to Monroe,

June 27, 1795, Monroe Papers; *General Advertiser,* June 16, June 20, and July 10, 1795; Combs, *Jay Treaty,* 161–62.

20. S. T. Mason to Monroe, June 29, 1795, and R. R. Livingston to Monroe, July 10, 1795, Monroe Papers; Rose, *Prologue to Democracy,* 93; Combs, *Jay Treaty,* 161; DeConde, *Entangling Alliance,* 112; and Miller, *Federalist Era,* 167.

21. Bemis, *Jay's Treaty,* xiii–xiv.

22. Miller, *Federalist Era,* 168–69.

23. Madison to R. R. Livingston, Aug. 10, 1795, in Hunt, ed., *Madison* 6: 234–38; Madison to Jefferson, Aug. 6, 1795, Madison Papers; *General Advertiser,* July 18 and 29, 1795.

24. Farnham, "Virginia Amendments of 1795," 81–82.

25. *General Advertiser,* July 22, 1795; G. Cabot to Rufus King, July 27, 1795, in King, ed., *Rufus King,* 2: 18–20; Combs, *Jay Treaty,* 162–63. Also Jefferson to Madison, Aug. 3, 1795, Madison Papers.

26. R. King to C. Gore, July 24, 1795; G. Cabot to R. King, Aug. 14, 1795; C. Gore to R. King, Aug. 7, 1795; C. Gore to R. King, Sept. 13, 1795; G. Cabot to R. King, July 25, 1795, all in King, ed., *Rufus King,* 2: 16–32.

27. *General Advertiser,* Aug. 4, 1795.

28. "Defense No. 1," in Syrett, ed., *Hamilton,* 18: 475–89.

29. Ibid., 477.

30. Jefferson to Madison, Sept. 21, 1795, in Ford, ed., *Jefferson,* 7: 31–33.

31. Madison to unknown, Aug. 23, 1795, in Hunt, ed., *Madison,* 6: 238–57.

32. Combs, *Jay Treaty,* 164–69, and Miller, *Federalist Era,* 169–71. See Tachau, "George Washington and the Reputation of Edmund Randolph," 15–34, for a good account of the Randolph-Fauchet affair. See also DeConde, *Entangling Alliance,* 122–25; Malone, *Jefferson and the Ordeal of Liberty,* 262–63; and Peterson, *Jefferson and the New Nation,* 549.

33. Fitzpatrick, ed., *Washington,* 34: 254n.

34. Washington to Hamilton, July 25, 1795, ibid., 262–64. In the same letter, Washington, although he was not supposed to have known of the Randolph-Fauchet intrigue at this time, questioned anxiously: "To what *length* their [the French] policy may induce them to carry matters, is too much in embryo at this moment to decide: but I predict much embarrassment to the government therefrom." See also Combs, *Jay Treaty,* 166–68. It is almost too much of a coincidence that the Fauchet revelations followed almost immediately, but there is no direct evidence that Washington learned of these until he returned to Philadelphia early in August.

35. Jefferson to Madison, Sept. 21, 1795, in Ford, ed., *Jefferson* 7: 31–33; John Beckley to Monroe, Sept. 23, 1795, Monroe Papers.

36. Madison to Jefferson, Feb. 29, 1796, Madison Papers. See Newman ("'*Principles* and *Not Men*'") for a discussion of the politics of Washington's birthday celebrations.

37. *General Advertiser,* Sept. 4, 1795.

38. Ibid.

39. Rossiter, ed., *Federalist Papers,* 314. Madison had warned that "frequent appeals [to the people] would, in great measure, deprive the government of

that veneration which time bestows on everything, and without which perhaps the wisest and freest governments would not possess the requisite stability."

40. *General Advertiser,* Sept. 10 and 12, 1795.

41. Pole, *Political Representation,* 243.

42. *General Advertiser,* Sept. 14, 1795.

43. *Petersburg Intelligencer,* as quoted, ibid., Oct. 16, 1795.

44. Even the gloomy Fisher Ames had concluded that despite the fact that "Faction" ruled the House of Representatives, the "friends of order" had the presidency and Senate, and that the opposition would "not impeach the President." See Ames to Thomas Dwight, Dec. 30, 1795, in Ames, ed., *Ames,* 1: 180–81.

45. *General Advertiser,* Nov. 26, 1795.

46. Robert Simons to unknown [undated, probably Dec. 1795], and Madison to Simons, [undated, probably Dec. 1795], Madison Papers. See also essay by Robert Simmons [probably the same as above although the spelling was different] in the South Carolina *State Gazette* as reprinted in the *General Advertiser,* Nov. 12, 1795.

47. Risjord, *Chesapeake Politics,* 457–58; Kurtz, *Presidency of John Adams,* 24; DeConde, *Entangling Alliance,* 135; and Farnham, "Virginia Amendments of 1795," 84–85.

48. Farnham, "Virginia Amendments of 1795," 84–88. In South Carolina the state's lower house passed a motion "declaring the agreement to be highly injurious to the interests of the United States," but elsewhere, despite acrimonious debates, proponents of the treaty managed to keep legislation against it from being adopted.

49. Giles to Jefferson, Dec. 9, 1795, Jefferson Papers.

50. Giles to Jefferson, Dec. 20, 1795, ibid.; Madison to Jefferson, Dec. 13 and Dec. 27, 1795, Madison Papers; and Madison to Monroe, Dec. 20, 1795, in Hunt, ed., *Madison,* 6: 257–63.

51. Giles to Jefferson, Dec. 9, 1795, Jefferson Papers.

52. Ames to Thomas Dwight, Mar. 9, 1796, in Ames, ed., *Ames,* 1: 187–88.

53. Madison to Jefferson, Mar. 6, 1796, Madison Papers.

54. Madison to Monroe, Apr. 18, 1796, ibid.; Combs, *Jay Treaty,* 175–77.

55. Message to the House, Mar. 30, 1796, in Fitzpatrick, ed., *Washington,* 35: 2–5.

56. Madison to Jefferson, Apr. 4 and 18, 1796, Madison Papers.

57. *General Advertiser,* Apr. 2 and 4, 1796.

58. Madison's Speech on Jay's Treaty, Apr. 6, 1796, in Hunt, ed., *Madison,* 6: 263–300. See also *Annals of the Congress of the United States, 1795–1796,* 4th Congress, 1st Session, 771–83; Combs, *The Jay Treaty,* 177; and Madison to Jefferson, Apr. 11, 1796, Madison Papers. See also Giles to Jefferson, Mar. 31, 1796, Jefferson Papers, where he proposed that the proper course for the House to adopt was to refuse to appropriate the funds until the president capitulated, but he warned that this would "require nerves."

59. Gallatin to Alexander Addison, May 13, 1796, Gallatin Papers.

60. Chauncey Goodrich to Wolcott, Apr. 12, 1796, in Gibbs, ed., *Memoirs*, 1: 326; Kurtz, *Presidency of John Adams*, 51–2; Combs, *Jay Treaty*, 180–81.

61. Chauncey Goodrich to Oliver Wolcott, Sen., Apr. 20, 1796, in Gibbs, ed., *Memoirs*, 1: 330–31.

62. Kurtz, *Presidency of John Adams*, 66.

63. As quoted in Combs, *Jay Treaty*, 184.

64. *Annals of the Congress of the United States, 1795–1796*, 4th Congress, 1st Session, 1258–59.

65. DeConde, *Entangling Alliance*, 139; Miller, *Federalist Era*, 175–76; and Kurtz, *Presidency of John Adams*, 70–72.

66. Madison to Jefferson, Apr. 23, May 1, and May 22, 1796, and Madison to his father, Apr. 25, 1796, Madison Papers; Madison to Monroe, May 14, 1796, in Hunt, ed., *Madison*, 6: 301–2; Alexander Addison to Gallatin, May 4, 1796, and Gallatin to Addison, May 13, 1796, Gallatin Papers; *Annals of the Congress of the United States, 1795–1796*, 4th Congress, 1st Session, 1279–91; and Combs, *Jay Treaty*, 185–87.

67. Bell, *Party and Faction*, 24, 25.

68. I have calculated the percentages from figures in Kurtz, *Presidency of John Adams*, 72–73. See also Bell, *Party and Faction*, 54, 147–49. I have included Delaware as part of the Middle Atlantic States for my calculations, since Delaware was historically, economically, and culturally tied to Pennsylvania. See Munroe, *Federalist Delaware*, 165–70, 200–206.

69. "Notes on Prof. Ebeling's Letter of July 30, 1795," in Ford, ed., *Jefferson*, 7: 44–49. This letter was just a draft and there is no evidence that a final letter was sent. See Malone, *Jefferson and the Ordeal of Liberty*, 264–65n.

70. Giles to Jefferson, Dec. 9, 1795, Jefferson Papers.

71. Bell, *Party and Faction*, 8. This was about average for Congresses in the 1790s.

72. Rossiter, ed., *Federalist Papers*, 319.

73. Bell, *Party and Faction*, 191.

74. Jefferson to Giles, Dec. 31, 1795, in Ford, ed., *Jefferson*, 7: 41–44.

75. Ames to Thomas Dwight, Apr. 18, 1796, in Ames, ed., *Ames*, 1: 192; and John Stuart to Francis Preston, May 20, 1796, Campbell-Preston Family Papers.

76. "Notes on Prof. Ebeling's Letter of July 30, 1795," in Ford, ed., *Jefferson*, 7: 44–49.

77. Malone, *Jefferson and the Ordeal of Liberty*, 264. Malone dismisses such rhetoric as "partisan exaggeration which may and often should be discounted," and "more like a stump speech than the calm utterance of a retired statesman." But in so doing he misreads the very special nature of the politics of the 1790s. By labeling Jefferson's strong rhetoric as "partisan exaggeration" and scolding him for acting like a political boss instead of a statesman, he imposes a standard of behavior established in a later time.

CHAPTER 7

1. Washington to Hamilton, June 26, 1796, in Fitzpatrick, ed., *Washington,* 35: 101–4.

2. Hamilton to Washington, July 5, 1796, in Syrett, ed., *Hamilton,* 20: 246–47.

3. For the speech as Hamilton's work, see Note, Hamilton to Washington, May 10, 1796, ibid., 169–73.

4. Farewell Address, in Fitzpatrick, ed., *Washington,* 35: 231.

5. Ibid., 221.

6. Ibid., 224–25.

7. Ibid., 227–28.

8. See Pocock "Civic Humanism," 80–103.

9. John Adams to Abigail Adams, Jan. 1, Jan. 20, Mar. 1, and Apr. 1, 1796, in Adams, ed., *John Adams,* 1: 483–90. Fisher Ames to Thomas Dwight, May 19, 1796, in Ames, ed., *Ames,* 1: 193–94; Chauncey Goodrich to Oliver Wolcott, Sen., May 6, 1796, in Gibbs, ed., *Memoirs,* 1: 336–37; William Smith to Ralph Izard, May 18, 1796, in Phillips, ed., "South Carolina Federalists Correspondence," 781.

10. John Adams to Abigail Adams, Feb. 15, 1796, Adams Papers.

11. John Adams to Abigail Adams, Feb. 27, 1796, ibid.

12. Jefferson to Madison, June 9, 1793, in Ford, ed., *Jefferson,* 6: 290–94.

13. Jefferson to Madison, Apr. 3, 1794, ibid., 501–3.

14. Jefferson to Mann Page, Aug. 30, 1795, ibid., 7: 23–25.

15. Jefferson to Giles, Apr. 27, 1795, Jefferson Papers; and Malone, *Jefferson and the Ordeal of Liberty,* 295.

16. Jefferson to Madison, Dec. 28, 1794, in Ford, ed., *Jefferson,* 6: 516–19.

17. Jefferson to Madison, Apr. 27, 1795, Madison Papers. This very significant letter has been seriously distorted. Paul Leicester Ford, the editor of the widely used compilation of Jefferson's writings, *The Writings of Thomas Jefferson,* made a serious error in transcribing the letter. In Ford's work, Jefferson is quoted as writing that he wants to prevent "any division or loss of votes, which might be fatal to the Republican interest." (*Jefferson,* 7: 8–11.) The original letter, however, which is in the Madison Papers in the Library of Congress, uses the phrase "Southern interest." In the copy of the letter, in the Jefferson Papers at the Library of Congress, the word "Southern" has been crossed out and "Republican" written in above. Ford's error might be understandable if he had used the copy in the Jefferson Papers, but he cites the original in the Madison Papers. A number of interesting questions arise: when was the change made in Jefferson's copy of the letter? Was it made by Jefferson? If so, was it made within a short time of the writing of the letter, or did he correct it much later when a reference to "Southern" interest would have been politically embarrassing? Or was the change made by someone after Jefferson's death? See my "Unraveling the Mystery of Jefferson's Letter."

18. Madison to Monroe, Feb. 26, 1796, Madison Papers; and Madison to Monroe, Sept. 19, 1796, as quoted in Malone, *Jefferson and the Ordeal of Liberty*, 276; and Peterson, *Jefferson and the New Nation*, 553.

19. Schachner, *Jefferson*, 2, 577.

20. Malone, *Jefferson and the Ordeal of Liberty*, 275–76. Peterson agrees with Malone saying that Jefferson became a candidate "in spite of himself," and that it "was a *fait accompli* before he had knowledge of it" (*Jefferson and the New Nation*, 543–44).

21. See Peterson, *Jefferson and the New Nation*, 238–39, for an assessment of Jefferson's conduct as war governor, and Malone, *Jefferson and the Ordeal of Liberty*, 280, for the Federalists' uses of the charges in 1796.

22. Jefferson to Maria Jefferson Eppes, Mar. 3, 1802, as quoted by Brodie, *Jefferson*, 282, 284–85. For the same sentiment, see Jefferson to Monroe, Feb. 8, 1798, in Ford, ed., *Jefferson*, 7: 197–99.

23. Brodie, *Jefferson*, 284–85.

24. Jefferson to Edward Rutledge, Dec. 27, 1796, in Ford, ed., *Jefferson*, 7: 93–95.

25. See Pious, *American Presidency*, 26–29.

26. Jefferson to Wilson Nicholas, Oct. 19, 1795, Jefferson Papers. Also Malone, *Jefferson and the Ordeal of Liberty*, 276–77.

27. William Smith to Ralph Izard, May 18 and Nov. 8, 1796, in Phillips, ed., "South Carolina Federalist Correspondence," 784–85; Oliver Wolcott to Wolcott Sen., Oct. 17, 1796, and to Jonathan Dayton, Sept. 15, 1796, in Gibbs, ed., *Memoirs*, 1: 386–88, 383–84. See also Cunningham, *Jeffersonian Republicans*, 91–92; Malone, *Jefferson and the Ordeal of Liberty*, 277–78; Kurtz, *Presidency of John Adams*, 93–94. Oliver Wolcott, the secretary of treasury, as late as September 1796, was making inquiries among his colleagues about who would run with Jefferson. See Jonathan Dayton to Wolcott, Sept. 15, 1796, in Gibbs, ed., *Memoirs*, 1: 383–84.

28. Sedgwick to Hamilton, Nov. 19, 1796, with enclosures (Jonathan Dayton to Sedgwick, Nov. 12 and Nov. 13, 1796; Sedgwick to Dayton, Nov. 19, 1796) in Syrett, ed., *Hamilton*, 20: 402–7.

29. King to Hamilton, May 2, 1796; John Marshall to King, Apr. 19, 1796; Hamilton to King, May 4, 1796; all ibid., 151–53, 158.

30. Chauncey Goodrich to Wolcott, Sen., Dec. 17, 1796, in Gibbs, ed., *Memoirs*, 1: 411–13; Dauer, *Adams Federalists*, 96–97.

31. Harper to Ralph Izard, Nov. 4, 1796, in Phillips, ed., "South Carolina Federalist Correspondence," 782–84; and Harper to Hamilton, Nov. 4, 1796, in Syrett, ed., *Hamilton*, 20: 369–72.

32. Wolcott to Wolcott, Sen., Oct. 17, Nov. 19, and Nov. 27, 1796, in Gibbs, ed., *Memoirs*, 1: 386–88, 396–97, 400–403.

33. Wolcott to Hamilton, Nov. 6, 1796, ibid., 375–76.

34. Hamilton to unknown, Nov. 8, 1796, Hamilton to Wolcott, Nov. 9, 1796, in Syrett, ed., *Hamilton*, 20: 376–78; Robert Troup to Rufus King, Nov. 16, 1796, in King, ed., *King*, 2: 110.

35. See Kurtz, *Presidency of John Adams*, 110–13. Kurtz reported that after

the election Robert Troup wrote Rufus King that, despite warnings from friends, Hamilton publicly supported Pinckney's election over Adams.

36. Ames to Wolcott, Sept. 26, 1796, in Gibbs, ed., *Memoirs*, 1: 384–85.

37. As quoted in Stourzh, *Hamilton*, 112, 109.

38. Richardson, ed., *Compilation of Messages and Papers*, 1: 207–10. The emphasis is Washington/Hamilton's.

39. Wolcott, Sen., to Wolcott, Oct. 3, 1796; Wolcott to Hamilton, Apr. 29, 1796; and Wolcott to William Heth, June 19, 1796, all in Gibbs, ed., *Memoirs*, 1: 334–35, 385–86, 361–62.

40. Kurtz, *Presidency of John Adams*, 114–30; Malone, *Jefferson and the Ordeal of Liberty*, 284–88; Cunningham, *Jeffersonian Republicans*, 101; and DeConde, "Washington's Farewell," 641–58.

41. Malone, *Jefferson and the Ordeal of Liberty*, 284–85, and Bowman, *Struggle for Neutrality*, 172–96 and 228–78.

42. Malone, *Jefferson and the Ordeal of Liberty*, 287. Clarfield, however, (*Timothy Pickering and the American Republic*, 176–77) argues, in opposition to Malone, that Adet's interference could "explain the razor-thin victory that gave the Jeffersonians all but one of the state's [Pennsylvania's] electoral votes."

43. Madison to Jefferson, Dec. 5, 1796, Madison Papers.

44. Hamilton to Wolcott, Nov. 22, 1796; Wolcott to Wolcott, Sen., Nov. 27, 1796; both in Gibbs, ed., *Memoirs*, 1,:398–403.

45. Jefferson to Philip Mazzei, Apr. 24, 1796, in Ford, ed., *Jefferson*, 7: 72–8. Malone (*Jefferson and the Ordeal of LIberty*, 267–68, 306–7) attempts to downplay Jefferson's reference to Washington, while Peterson (*Jefferson and the New Nation*, 571–73) appears to accept the interpretation that Jefferson was referring to Washington.

46. *General Advertiser*, Oct. 5, 6, and 28, 1796.

47. Taylor to Daniel Carroll Brent, Oct. 9, 1796, in Dodd, ed., "John Taylor Correspondence," 260–68.

48. *General Advertiser*, Oct. 22, 1796.

49. Taylor's report of a conversation he had with Adams in Taylor to Brent, Oct. 9, 1796, in Dodd, ed., "John Taylor Correspondence," 260–68.

50. See Dauer, *Adams Federalists*, 106, for 1796 electoral results. Also Kurtz, *Presidency of John Adams*, 412–14.

51. Kurtz, *Presidency of John Adams*, 409, and Cunningham, *Jeffersonian Republicans*, 94n, differ somewhat on how the states chose the electors. I have followed *Historical Statistics of U.S.*, 681.

52. Kurtz, *Presidency of John Adams*, 147; Cunningham, *Jeffersonian Republicans*, 114–15; Goodman, *Democratic-Republicans*, 204, Formisano, *Transformation of Political Culture*, 30–33.

53. Risjord, *Chesapeake Politics*, 508. For the Yazoo scandal, see Rose, *Prologue to Democracy*, 85, 90–99.

54. Rose, *Prologue to Democracy*, 138.

55. Kurtz, *Presidency of John Adams*, 177–87.

56. Young, *Democratic Republicans*, 575–78.

57. See my Introduction for a discussion of some of those works.

58. Chambers, *Political Parties in a New Nation*, 122, 126, 137. For Chambers the Jay Treaty controversy had been an earlier major political milestone because it had transformed "the Republican movement into a Republican Party," with the resulting coordination of activity between leaders in Philadelphia and leaders and followers at the state and local levels. Hoadley (*Origins of American Political Parties*, 137) argues that the debate over Jay's Treaty "marked one of the first organized attempts by an opposition group to defeat an important administration proposal" and that "this effort did mark a significant step in the development of the Republican party."

59. Cunningham, *Jeffersonian Republicans*, 94, 114.

60. Kelley, "Ideology and Political Culture," 539.

61. Goodman, "First Party System," 64.

62. As quoted in Cunningham, *Jeffersonian Republicans*, 108–9.

63. Kurtz, *Presidency of John Adams*, 143–44.

64. Kelley, "Ideology and Political Culture," 538–40; Kelley, *Cultural Pattern in American Politics*; and Shalhope, "Republicanism and Early American Historiography," 342. Howe, although he recognizes the "peculiarly violent character of American political life," during the 1790s, emphasizes, as does Kelley, the consensual nature of republicanism. Despite the violent rhetoric, the men of the 1790s "shared a common body of assumptions about republican political society—the problems involved in its establishment and the prerequisites for its maintenance and survival." See Howe's "Republican Thought," 147, 153. Kerber (*Federalists in Dissent*, 4) gives an excellent analysis of the Federalist culture.

65. Benson (*Turner and Beard*, 212–17, 228) was one of the first historians to conceptualize political conflict in the early national period in terms of two conflicting views of the Good Society: one, agrarian-minded; the other, commercial-minded. See McCoy's *Elusive Republic* for an analysis of the accommodation of the Republican agrarian vision to the nineteenth-century reality of a expanding market economy.

66. As quoted in Dauer, *Adams Federalists*, 102.

67. Jefferson to Madison, Apr. 27, 1795, Madison Papers.

68. Adams to Knox, Mar. 30, 1797, in Adams, ed., *John Adams*, 8: 535–36.

69. Adams to his wife, Dec. 12, 1796, ibid., 1: 495–96.

70. Stephen Higginson to Hamilton, Jan. 12, 1797, in Syrett, ed., *Hamilton*, 20: 465–66.

71. Kerber, *Federalists in Dissent*, 195.

72. Adams to wife, Dec. 12, 1796, in Adams, ed., *John Adams*, 1: 495–96.

73. Gerry to Adams, Jan. 30, 1797, Gerry Papers.

74. Adams had been highly offended by a published remark made by Jefferson in 1791 critical of "political heresies," which Adams had assumed had been directed at him. To follow the controversy, see Jefferson to Adams, July 17, July 29, and Aug. 30, 1791, in Cappon, ed., *Adams-Jefferson Letters*, 1: 245–46, 247–50, and 250–52.

75. Adams to Tristram Dalton, Jan. 19, 1797, and Adams to Gerry, Feb. 20, 1797, Adams Papers.

76. Chauncey Goodrich to Wolcott, Sen., Jan. 9, 1797, in Gibbs, ed., *Memoirs*, 1: 417–18. Bache's the *General Advertiser* or *Aurora* had become the chief organ of the Republican opposition.

77. Hamilton to King, Feb. 15, 1797, in Syrett, ed., *Hamilton*, 20: 515–16.

78. Madison to Jefferson, Dec. 5, 1796, Madison Papers; Jefferson to Madison, Dec. 17, 1796, in Ford, ed., *Jefferson*, 7: 91–3.

79. Madison to Jefferson, Dec. 19, 1796, in Hunt, ed., *Madison*, 6: 296–302.

80. Jefferson to Madison, Jan. 1, 1797, in Ford, ed., *Jefferson*, 7: 98–100; Jefferson to Adams, Dec. 28, 1796, in Cappon, ed., *Adams-Jefferson Letters*, 1: 262–63; Madison to Jefferson, Jan. 15, 1797, in Hunt, ed., *Madison*, 6: 302–5; and Jefferson to Madison, Jan. 30, 1797, in Ford, ed., *Jefferson*, 7: 115–16.

81. *General Advertiser*, Mar. 11, 13, and 14, 1797.

82. Smith to King, Apr. 3, 1797, as quoted in Kurtz, *Presidency of John Adams*, 208.

CHAPTER 8

1. For Britain's greater threat to American independence, see Malone, *Jefferson and the Ordeal of Liberty*, 313–14, 374.

2. Cunningham maintains that the Federalists held a margin of 56 to 50 in the Fifth Congress, *Jeffersonian Republicans*, 134; while Bell (*Party and Faction*, 256–57) claims that the Federalist advantage was 64 to 53.

3. DeConde, *Quasi-War*, 16–17.

4. As early as Jan. 1797, Madison reported hearing that he was to be appointed to go to France. See Madison to Jefferson, Jan. 22, 1797, Madison Papers and Jefferson's note, Mar. 2, 1797, in Sawvel, ed., *Anas of Jefferson*, 184–85. See letter 13 of the *Boston Patriot* series written by Adams in 1809 in Adams, ed., *John Adams*, 9: 284–85, for Adams's version of the meeting. See also Adams to Gerry, Apr. 6, 1797, ibid., 8: 538–40.

5. Knox to Adams, Mar. 19, 1797, in Adams, ed., *John Adams*, 8: 532–34, and Hamilton to Pickering, Mar. 29, 1797, in Syrett, ed., *Hamilton*, 20: 556–57. Also Hamilton to Washington, Jan. 25–31, 1797, 480–82; Hamilton to Sedgwick, Feb. 26, 1797, 521–23; Hamilton to Pickering, Mar. 22, 1797, 545–46.

6. Letter 13 of the *Boston Patriot* Series of 1809, in Adams, ed., *John Adams*, 9: 285–86.

7. Wolcott to Hamilton, Mar. 31, 1797, in Gibbs, ed., *Memoirs*, 1: 485–88; and Pickering to Hamilton, Mar. 26, 1797, in Syrett, ed., *Hamilton*, 20: 548–49.

8. Stinchcombe, "John Adams' Peace Policy." See also Adams to Gerry, June 20, 1797, in Adams, ed., *John Adams*, 8: 546.

9. Jefferson's note, Mar. 2, 1797, in Sawvel, ed., *Anas of Jefferson*, 184–85.

10. Ibid.

11. Adams's Letter 13 of the *Boston Patriot*'s series of 1809, in Adams, ed., *John Adams*, 9: 285.

12. Kurtz, *Presidency of John Adams*, 222.

13. Jefferson to Gerry, May 13, 1797, in Ford, ed., *Jefferson*, 7: 119–24.

14. Sedgwick to King, Mar. 12, 1797, and George Cabot to King, Mar. 19, 1797, in King, ed., *King*, 2: 156–59, 161.

15. Jefferson to Gerry, May 13, 1797, in Ford, ed., *Jefferson*, 7: 119–24.

16. Wolcott, Sen., to Wolcott, Mar. 20, 1797, in Gibbs, ed., *Memoirs*, 1: 475–77.

17. Uriah Tracy to Hamilton, Apr. 6, 1797, in Syrett, ed., *Hamilton*, 20: 24–26.

18. Adams's "Special Session Message," May 16, 1797, in Richardson, ed., *Compilation of Messages and Papers*, 1: 223–29.

19. Hamilton to Smith, Apr. 10, 1797, in Syrett, ed., *Hamilton*, 20: 29–41, 38n. Even though Hamilton held no official position, he was in constant contact with members of Adams's cabinet, receiving privileged information and giving advice. See the exchange of letters between McHenry, Pickering, and Hamilton throughout Apr. and early May 1797 (ibid., 48–84).

20. DeConde, *Quasi-War*, 31.

21. Kurtz, *Presidency of John Adams*, 231–32; John Dawson to Madison, May 18, 1797, Madison Papers.

22. Jefferson to Peregrine Fitzhugh, June 4, 1797, in Ford, ed., *Jefferson*, 7: 134–38.

23. Jefferson to Edward Rutledge, June 24, 1797, ibid., 152–55.

24. Jefferson to Burr, June 17, 1797, ibid., 145–49.

25. Ibid.

26. Burr to Jefferson, June 21, 1797, as quoted in Kurtz, *Presidency of John Adams*, 234–35.

27. Malone, *Jefferson and the Ordeal of Liberty*, 324.

28. "Petition," Aug. 1797, in Ford, ed., *Jefferson*, 7: 158–64. See also Malone, *Jefferson and the Ordeal of Liberty*, 334–37; and Koch and Ammon, "Virginia and Kentucky Resolutions," 152–53.

29. Jefferson to Monroe, Sept. 7, 1797, in Ford, ed., *Jefferson*, 7: 171–74.

30. Koch and Ammon, "Virginia and Kentucky Resolutions," 153–54. The following year, Jefferson drafted yet another petition suggesting means to correct the problem. Reasoning that since the Federalists dominated the federal courts, jurors should be chosen not by the courts, but by the people. If this procedure were followed, he hoped, juries were more likely to be made up of men of sound republican principles. See Malone, *Jefferson and the Ordeal of Liberty*, 335–37.

31. "Petition," Aug. 1797, in Ford, ed., *Jefferson*, 7: 158–64.

32. For my discussion of the XYZ affair, I have relied on DeConde's *Quasi-War*, 36–73, and on Stinchcombe's "Talleyrand," 575–90, and his *XYZ Affair*, passim.

33. Adams to Heads of Departments, Jan. 24, 1798, in Adams, ed., *John Adams*, 8: 561–62.

34. Gallatin to wife, Jan. 19, 1798, Gallatin Papers.

35. Sedgwick to unknown, Mar. 7, 1798, as quoted by Smith, *Freedom's Fetters*, 21; Hamilton to Pickering, Mar. 27, 1798, in Syrett, ed., *Hamilton*, 21: 384.

36. Jefferson to Madison, to Edmund Pendleton, to Peter Carr, Mar. 15, Apr. 2, Apr. 12, 1798, in Ford, ed. *Jefferson*, 7: 216–18, 227–30, 238–40. Also Madison to Jefferson, Apr. 2, 1798, in Hunt, ed., *Madison*, 6: 311–16; J. Dawson to Madison, Mar. 29, 1798, Madison Papers.

37. Note to Department Heads, in Adams, ed., *John Adams*, 8: 568–69.

38. DeConde, *Quasi-War*, 67–68.

39. "Message," Mar. 19, 1798, in Adams, ed., *John Adams*, 9: 156–57.

40. "Stand No. 1," Mar. 30, 1798, in Syrett, ed., *Hamilton*, 21: 384.

41. Jefferson to Monroe and to Madison, Mar. 21, 1798, in Ford, ed., *Jefferson*, 7: 218–22.

42. Jefferson to John Wise, Feb. 12, 1798, as quoted by Malone, *Jefferson and the Ordeal of Liberty*, 364–65.

43. Both Gallatin and Giles opposed the request for the documents, with Giles warning: "You are doing wrong to call for those dispatches. They will injure us." As quoted in DeConde, *Quasi-War*, 72 and 70–73 for a discussion of Congress's decision to call for the dispatches. Also Malone, *Jefferson and the Ordeal of Liberty*, 370–72.

44. Jefferson to Madison, Apr. 12, 1798, in Ford, ed., *Jefferson*, 7: 236–38.

45. Jefferson to Madison, to James Lewis, Jr., and to Archibald Stuart, Apr. 19, May 9, and June 8, 1798, ibid., 242–50, 269–72.

46. Jefferson to Madison, May 10 and 17, 1798, ibid., 251–54.

47. Abigail Adams to Mary Cranch, Apr. 26, 1798, as quoted in Smith, *Freedom's Fetters*, 9.

48. Jefferson to Madison, June 21, 1798, in Ford, ed., *Jefferson*, 7: 272–75.

49. Jefferson said his name was "running through all the city as detected in criminal correspondence with the French directory." See Jefferson to Monroe and Madison, Apr. 5, 1798, ibid., 230–34.

50. Jefferson to Madison, June 21, 1798, ibid., 272–75.

51. *Porcupine's Gazette*, June 18, 1798, as quoted in Smith's *Freedom's Fetters*, 101–2.

52. Jefferson to Madison, June 21, 1798, in Ford, ed., *Jefferson*, 7: 272–75.

53. William Bingham to King, June 5, 1798, in King, ed., *King*, 2: 331; Hamilton to King, June 6, 1798, in Syrett, ed., *Hamilton*, 21: 490–91.

54. The best discussion of the Alien and Sedition Laws and the Congressional debate is in Smith, *Freedom's Fetters*.

55. Jefferson to Randolph, May 9, 1798, Jefferson Papers, and to Madison, May 3, 1798, in Ford, ed., *Jefferson*, 7: 246–49.

56. For texts of the laws, see Smith, *Freedom's Fetters*, 435–42.

57. Hamilton to Pickering, and to Wolcott, June 7 and 29, 1798, in Syrett, ed., *Hamilton*, 21: 494–95, 522.

58. *Annals of the Congress of the United States, 1797–1799*, 5th Congress, 1991–92.

59. Ibid., 2093–94.

60. Ibid., 2024; Palmer, *Age of the Democratic Revolution*, 2: 482.

61. Speech in Congress, *Annals of the Congress of the United States, 1797–1799*, 5th Congress, 2110.

62. As quoted in Helms, "Nathaniel Macon," 147–48.

63. Adams's addresses of May 2, 8, 10, and 27, 1798, in Adams, ed., *John Adams*, 9: 186–87, 191–95.

64. Madison to Jefferson, May 20, 1798, in Hunt, ed., *Madison*, 6: 320–22.

65. James Lloyd to Washington, July 4, 1798, as quoted by Dauer, *Adams Federalists*, 199.

66. Sedgwick to King, July 1, 1798, in King, ed., *King*, 2: 352–53.

67. Mason Stephens Thompson to Jefferson, July 6, 1798, and Henry Tazewell to Jefferson, July 5, 1798, Jefferson Papers.

68. Troup to King, June 10 and July 10, 1798, in King, ed., *King*, 2: 344–46, 362–64.

69. For a very good discussion of the differences between the Regular Army, Additional Army, Provisional Army, and Eventual Army, see editor's note, in Syrett, ed., *Hamilton*, 22: 383–90, and Kohn, *Eagle and Sword*, 229.

70. To follow the controversy over Hamilton's appointment, see Hamilton to Washington, July 29–Aug. 1, 1798, in Syrett, ed., *Hamilton*, 22: 36–40; see esp. the introductory note, 4–21. Also see Cabot to King, Nov. 16, 1798, in King, ed., *King*, 2: 468.

71. Kohn, *Eagle and Sword*, 230–38.

72. Washington to McHenry, Sept. 30, 1798, as quoted in ibid., 243–44. See Syrett, ed., *Hamilton*, 22: 87–146, 270–313, 316–39, for the elaborate lists of candidates' names and the comments about each of them.

73. Hamilton to Otis, Dec. 27, 1798, and Hamilton to Sedgwick, Feb. 2, 1799, in Syrett, ed., *Hamilton*, 22: 393–94, 452–54.

74. Hamilton to McHenry, Feb. 6, 1799, ibid., 466–67.

75. Kohn, *Eagle and Sword*, 244. See Malone, *Jefferson the President: Second Term*, 518, for Republican's fears about the army's political reliability.

76. Jefferson to Madison, to Pendleton, to Peter Carr, Mar. 15, Apr. 2, and Apr. 12, 1798, in Ford, ed., *Jefferson*, 7: 216–18, 227–30, 238–40; Madison to Jefferson, Apr. 2, 1798, in Hunt, ed., *Madison*, 6: 311–16; Dawson to Madison, Mar. 29, 1798, Madison Papers.

77. Jefferson to Pendleton and to Carr, Apr. 2 and Apr. 12, 1798, in Ford, ed., *Jefferson*, 7: 227–30, 238–40. He told Carr that he expected "some favorable changes in the representatives from . . . [the Eastern] quarter."

78. Monroe to Jefferson, to Madison, and to Jefferson, Apr. 8, June 24, and June [no date], 1798, in Hamilton, ed., *Monroe*, 3: 116–18, 129–39.

79. Jefferson to Madison and to Monroe, Apr. 19, 1798, in Ford, ed., *Jefferson*, 7: 240–44. Troup to King, June 10, 1798, in King, ed., *King*, 2: 344–46.

80. Jefferson to Madison, Apr. 19, May 10, June 7, 1798, in Ford, ed., *Jefferson*, 7: 242–44, 251–52, 266–69.

81. Madison to Jefferson, May 20, 1798, in Hunt, ed., *Madison*, 6: 320–22.

CHAPTER 9

1. Hamilton to Sedgwick, Feb. 2, 1799, in Syrett, ed., *Hamilton,* 22: 452–54.

2. Taylor to Monroe, Mar. 25, 1798, in Dodd, ed., "John Taylor Correspondence," 268–70; Taylor to Jefferson, May 13, 1798, Jefferson Papers.

3. Jefferson to Taylor, June 1, 1798, in Ford, ed., *Jefferson,* 7: 263–66. These words are Jefferson's paraphrase of a Taylor letter, presumably destroyed, to a third party. In a note to the letter, Ford states that George Tucker, in the *Southern Literary Messenger* for May 1838, argued that the faded letter-press copy of Jefferson's letter was misread and the true rendition was "it is not *usual* now." The internal evidence of the letter does not support Tucker's view. One may only surmise that Tucker's efforts reflect the same desire of the unknown person who changed Jefferson's 1795 letter to Madison from "Southern interest" to "Republican interest." In both instances they attempt to sanitize the ideas of the Republican opposition and downplay any hint of sectionalism and secessionist sentiment.

4. Jefferson to Monroe, Sept. 7, 1797, ibid., 171–74.

5. Jefferson to John Taylor, June 1, 1798, ibid., 263–66.

6. Among others, Cunningham, *Jeffersonian Republicans,* 142, and Hofstadter, *Idea of a Party System,* 114–17.

7. Jefferson to John Wise, Feb. 12, 1798, as reported in Malone, *Jefferson and the Ordeal of Liberty,* 364–65.

8. Taylor to Jefferson, June 25, 1798, in Dodd, ed., "John Taylor Correspondence," 271–76.

9. Ibid.

10. Ibid.

11. Taylor to Monroe, Mar. 25, 1798, ibid., 268–70; Taylor to Jefferson, May 13, 1798, Jefferson Papers.

12. John Taylor to Jefferson, June 25, 1798, in Dodd, ed., "John Taylor Correspondence," 271–76.

13. Ibid.

14. Ibid.

15. Jefferson to Madison, Sept. 6, 1789, in Peterson, ed., *Jefferson,* 444–51.

16. Taylor to Jefferson, June 25, 1798, in Dodd, ed., "John Taylor Correspondence," 271–76.

17. John Page to Jefferson, June 21, 1798, Jefferson Papers.

18. Pocock, "Civic Humanism," 87.

19. John Page to Jefferson, June 21, 1798, Jefferson Papers.

20. Jefferson to John Cabel Breckenridge, Dec. 11, 1821, in Ford, ed., *Jefferson,* 7: 290–91n. Koch and Ammon, in their "Virginia and Kentucky Resolutions," 149–50, call into question the reliability of Jefferson's memory on some specific points in this letter. For a question of general strategy, however, I see no reason to doubt Jefferson's recollection.

21. Koch and Ammon, "Virginia and Kentucky Resolutions," 151–53;

Taylor to Jefferson, June 25, 1798, in Dodd, ed., "John Taylor Correspondence," 271–76.

22. Dawson to Monroe, July 29, 1798, Monroe Papers.

23. Jefferson to Archibald Hamilton Rowan, Sept. 26, 1798, in Ford, ed., *Jefferson*, 7: 280–81.

24. Jefferson to Samuel Smith, Aug. 22, 1798, ibid., 275–80.

25. "Drafts of the Kentucky Resolutions of 1798," ibid., 289–309.

26. The following summer, Jefferson made his most extreme threat to secede; to Madison, Aug. 23, 1799, Madison Papers.

27. Jefferson to Madison, Nov. 17, 1798, in Ford, ed., *Jefferson*, 7: 288.

28. Jefferson to Taylor, Nov. 26, 1798, ibid., 309–12.

29. Wilson Cary Nicholas to Jefferson, Oct. 4, 1798, Jefferson Papers, and Jefferson to Nicholas, Oct. 5, 1798, in Ford, ed., *Jefferson*, 7: 281–82. For a later letter and a somewhat imperfect recollection of events, see Jefferson to Breckinridge, Dec. 11, 1821, ibid., 290–91n. Also see Koch and Ammon, "Virginia and Kentucky Resolutions," 147–56.

30. Smith, "Grass Roots of Kentucky Resolutions," 221–45, and Koch and Ammon, "Kentucky and Virginia Resolutions," 156–58.

31. Coward, *Kentucky in the New Republic*, 113.

32. Jefferson to Wilson Cary Nicholas, Nov. 29, 1798, in Ford, ed., *Jefferson*, 7: 312–13.

33. As quoted by Beeman, *Old Dominion*, 191.

34. As quoted by ibid., 192–93.

35. See the discussion of Gabriel's Plot in chapter 11.

36. "Resolutions," Dec. 21, 1798, in Hunt, ed., *Madison*, 6: 326–31.

37. Beeman, *Old Dominion*, 194.

38. Koch and Ammon, "Virginia and Kentucky Resolutions," 161.

39. Madison to Jefferson Dec. 29, 1798, in Hunt, ed., *Madison*, 6: 327–29n.

40. Taylor to Jefferson, Dec. 11, 1798, Jefferson Papers. Pole (*Political Representation*, 238–39) argues that the conventions called by Massachusetts dissidents during Shay's Rebellion were "an old way of meeting new problems" and represented the "lack of effective instruments in the hands of a gravely discontented section of the people."

41. Banning, *Jeffersonian Persuasion*, 265, and Risjord, *Chesapeake Politics*, 540–41.

42. Virginia *Journal of the Senate*, Jan. 24, 1799, 103, 111–12.

43. Anderson, "Contemporary Opinion," 46–47, 58–59.

44. Ibid., 57.

45. See ibid. (Jan. 1900), 235–37.

46. *Observations on a Letter from George Nicholas of Kentucky to his Friend in Virginia*, as quoted, ibid. (Jan. 1900), 237–38.

47. Jefferson to Madison, Jan. 30, 1799, in Ford, ed., *Jefferson*, 7: 338–39.

48. Fries Rebellion will be discussed in chapter 10.

49. Jefferson to Edmund Pendleton and to Archibald Stuart, Feb. 14 and Feb. 13, 1799, in Ford, ed., *Jefferson*, 7: 350–60.

50. Taylor to Jefferson, May 6, 1799, and Taylor to Monroe, Mar. 25, 1798, in Dodd, ed., "John Taylor Correspondence," 281–82, 268–70.

51. Taylor to Harry Innes, Apr. 25, 1799, Innes Papers.

52. Taylor to Creed Taylor, Apr. 10, 1799, as quoted in Cunningham, *Jeffersonian Republicans,* 135.

53. Taylor to Harry Innes, Apr. 25, 1799, Innes Papers.

54. Taylor to Jefferson, Feb. 15, 1799, in Dodd, ed., "John Taylor Correspondence," 278–81.

55. Samuel Hopkins to John Breckinridge, July 15, 1799, Breckinridge Family Papers.

56. See chapter 10 for a discussion of the Federalists' reports and fears about the stockpiling of arms in Virginia.

57. Koch and Ammon, "Virginia and Kentucky Resolutions," 163, 163n. See also Beeman, *Old Dominion,* 202.

58. General Davie to James Iredell, June 17, 1799, as quoted in Koch and Ammon, "Virginia and Kentucky Resolutions," 164–65.

59. William Heath to Hamilton, Jan. 14 and Jan. 18, 1799, in Syrett, ed., *Hamilton,* 22: 413–16, 422–24, and Sedgwick to King, Nov. 15, 1799, in King, ed., *King,* 3: 145–48.

60. As quoted in Davidson, "Virginia and the Alien and Sedition Laws," 337.

61. Giles had resigned his seat in Congress to become a member of the Virginia General Assembly in the fall of 1798.

62. Giles, *Political Miscellanies,* as quoted in Anderson, *Giles,* 69–70.

63. Davidson, in his "Virginia and the Alien and Sedition Laws," points to these factors in challenging a number of nineteenth- and early twentieth-century historians who had argued that Virginia was preparing for armed resistance to the enforcement of the Alien and Sedition Laws. Koch and Ammon, in their "Virginia and Kentucky Resolutions," 163, 163n., follow Davidson, as, for the most part, does Richard Beeman in his *Old Dominion,* 202–3.

64. And the Federalists did move that any purchase of arms be suspended for a year, but the motion was defeated (Beeman, *Old Dominion,* 203–4). See Virginia, *Journal of the Senate,* Jan. 1799, for the various defensive measures passed by the legislature.

65. As quoted in Beeman, *Old Dominion,* 203. Historian Richard H. Kohn believes that the Virginians were prepared to "resist the Alien and Sedition Acts with force," and they would have been well aware how the passage of defensive measures "would look, and that the timing of such legislation, so soon after the Virginia Resolutions, would be peculiar" (Kohn, *Eagle and Sword,* 399n.).

66. See Peterson, *Jefferson Image,* 443, 457, for a brilliant discussion of "the Jefferson Image [that] was constantly evolving" throughout American history. He points out that although the Kentucky and Virginia Resolutions "served the reactionary cause of Southern segregationists, they performed a greater service, one authenticated by the latest historical judgment, in directly

connecting Jefferson to the champions of freedom in an analogous situation a century and a half later."

67. A remarkable note from the editors of the *William and Mary Quarterly* published in 1948 as a preface to Koch and Ammon's "Virginia and Kentucky Resolutions" is a good illustration of the point. The editors wrote that they "take special pleasure in publishing this article at this time because of its bearing on the fierce political controversy now raging within the Democratic Party over 'the Rights reserved to the States' by the Tenth Amendment to the Constitution, and because of the light it throws on the appeal to history now being made by the 'Southern rebels' in that party." They pointed out that the Koch and Ammon article demonstrated that Jefferson and Madison "in advancing *their* theory of States' Rights were not defending the abstract authority of the states as an end in itself, but as a practical means to protect the civil rights of living persons." And it was these states rights doctrines, the editors announced, that "provided the unifying element in the great North-South intersectional alliance" and the basis for making "the Virginians the outstanding national leaders of American liberalism." See note from the editors, Koch and Ammon, "Virginia and Kentucky Resolutions," 145–46.

CHAPTER 10

1. Kohn (*Eagle and Sword*, 194–95) argues that "Federalists as a group had decided by 1798 that the greatest danger was dissent and disunion, which made the Republicans the chief enemy, and that the greatest military menace was internal revolt timed to coincide with an invasion by a French expeditionary force." Many Federalists, he maintains, "had honestly concluded, after five years of increasing tension and violent political strife, that the Republicans were dedicated agents of the French, bent on overturning the Constitution, and furthermore Federalists had good cause for these fears—not proof, but enough evidence for honest, balanced men logically to reach such conclusions."

2. William Heath to Hamilton, Jan. 14 and Jan. 18, 1799, in Syrett, ed., *Hamilton*, 22: 413–16, 422–24.

3. Sedgwick to King, Jan. 20 and Mar. 20, 1799, Pickering to King, May 4, 1799, in King, ed., *King* 2: 514–18, 579–83, and 3: 12–13. Wood ("Conspiracy and the Paranoid Style," 433) concludes that the "climax in America of the late eighteenth century's frenzy of plots and counterplots came in 1798 with the most serious crisis the young nation had yet faced." And it was this "crisis" that "brought the country close to civil war and led, in New England at least, to Federalist accusations that the Republican party was in league with an international Jacobinical conspiracy."

4. I have followed Peter Levine's excellent article, "Fries Rebellion," 241–58, and Davis, *Fries Rebellion.*

5. Davis, *Fries Rebellion,* 33.

6. Report, Fall 1799, in Gibbs, ed., *Memoirs,* 2: 298–306.

7. Hamilton to McHenry, Mar. 18, 1799, in Syrett, ed., *Hamilton,* 22: 552–53.

8. Miller, *Federalist Era*, 247–48.

9. Levine, "Fries Rebellion," 244–45.

10. DeConde, *Quasi War*, 162–66; Bowman, *Struggle for Neutrality*, 362–66.

11. DeConde, *Quasi War*, 174–76.

12. Sedgwick to Hamilton, Feb. 7, 1799, in Syrett, ed., *Hamilton*, 22: 469–72.

13. Kohn, *Eagle and Sword*, 257–58.

14. Deconde, *Quasi War*, 178–79; Sedgwick and Pickering to Hamilton, Feb. 19 and Feb. 25, 1799, in Syrett, ed., *Hamilton*, 22: 487–90, 500–503. See also Adams to Washington, Feb. 19, 1799, in Adams, ed., *John Adams*, 8: 624–26, where Adams explains his decision to Washington.

15. Hamilton to Sedgwick, Feb. 21, 1799, and Sedgwick to Hamilton, Feb. 22 and Feb. 25, 1799, in Syrett, ed., *Hamilton*, 22: 493–95 and 503–5. See also DeConde, *Quasi War*, 184–87, and Shaw, *Character of Adams*, 260–61. Oliver Ellsworth, chief justice of the Supreme Court, and (after Patrick Henry refused) William Richardson Davie, a Federalist governor of North Carolina, were chosen to join Murray in Europe to begin the discussions with the French.

16. Shaw, *Character of Adams*, 260–61.

17. Troup to King, June 5, 1799, in King, ed., *King*, 3: 33–35.

18. George Cabot to King, Oct. 6, 1799, ibid., 113–14.

19. DeConde, *Quasi-War*, 215–16, and Kurtz, *Presidency of John Adams*, 387–88. See also, Miller, *Hamilton*, 501–2.

20. Adams's letter to the *Patriot* as quoted in Gibbs, ed., *Memoirs*, 2: 271; Adams to Pickering, Oct. 16, 1799, in Adams, ed., *John Adams*, 9: 39; and DeConde, *Quasi-War*, 215–22. See also, Miller, *Hamilton*, 501–2; and Shaw, *Character of Adams*, 260–65. Shaw makes a persuasive case that Adams's actions in the fall of 1799 stemmed more from a threat to "his executive prerogative" rather than from his sudden discovery of cabinet machinations against him. Shaw argues that the Adams presidency was characterized by the president's repeated failure to follow up his actions with the appropriate administrative measures and oversight. Of Adams's decision to send the envoys, Shaw writes: "The decision was admirable—in its sacrifice of party support no less than in its successful outcome. But it hardly deserved Adams's later description of it as part of the 'Steady pursuit of a Uniform regular Plan,' any more than his sporadic campaign for Dutch recognition. . . . Soon after issuing the order he again dropped the initiative" (265).

21. Morse to Olcott, Nov. 8, 1799, in Gibbs, ed., *Memoirs*, 2: 287.

22. Presumably this would be a congressional committee.

23. Hamilton to Otis, Dec. 27, 1798, and Hamilton to Sedgwick, Feb. 2, 1799, in Syrett, ed., *Hamilton*, 22: 393–94, 452–54.

24. Ernst, *Rufus King*, 265.

25. Hamilton to King and to Miranda, Aug. 22, 1798, in Syrett, ed., *Hamilton*, 22: 154–56.

26. King to Hamilton, Jan. 21, 1799, in King, ed., *King*, 2: 519.

27. Hamilton to Otis, Jan. 26, 1799, in Syrett, ed., *Hamilton*, 22: 440–41.

28. Hamilton to Jonathan Dayton, [Oct.–Nov. 1799], in Syrett, ed., *Hamilton,* 23: 599–604.

29. Hamilton to Jonathan Dayton, [Oct.–Nov. 1799], in Syrett, ed., *Hamilton,* 23: 599–604. Like Hamilton, Sedgwick noted the sinister implications of Virginia's rendering "its militia as formidable as possible" and supplying "its arsenals and magazines" (Sedgwick to King, Nov. 15, 1799, in King, ed., *King,* 3: 145–48). The ideas, sentiments, and in some cases the language of the Sedgwick and Hamilton letters are quite similar. It seems obvious that they represented the considered conclusions of the Hamiltonian wing of Federalism.

30. Stewart (*Opposition Press,* 3–33) claims that both the Federalists and Republicans believed that the newspapers were responsible for the Republican victory in 1800.

31. Smith, *Freedom's Fetters,* 188–204, 204–20, 247–57, 359–73, 373–84, 385–90, and 398–417.

32. Ibid., 334–58, as quoted, 345.

33. Stewart (*Opposition Press,* 610) estimates that its circulation in 1800 was 1,700.

34. Ibid., 611.

35. For an excellent discussion of the Federalist prosecution of Duane, see Smith, *Freedom's Fetters,* chap. 13.

36. Pickering to Adams, July 24, 1799, in Adams, ed., *John Adams,* 9: 3–4.

37. Adams to Pickering, Aug. 1, 1799, ibid., 5.

38. Smith, *Freedom's Fetters,* 285–88.

39. Ibid., 288–89, 300.

40. Madison to Jefferson, Mar. 15, 1800, in Hunt, ed., *Madison,* 6: 406–7. See also Jefferson to Monroe, Feb. 16 and Mar. 4, 1800, Jefferson Papers; and S. T. Mason to Madison, Mar. 7, 1800, Madison Papers; and Smith, *Freedom's Fetters,* 288–94.

41. *Aurora,* Mar. 17, 18, 21, and 24, 1800, as quoted by Smith, *Freedom's Fetters,* 296. See also J. D. Dawson to Madison, Mar. 30, 1800, and S. T. Mason to Madison, Apr. 2, 1800, Madison Papers; and Jefferson to Randolph, Apr. 4, 1800, Jefferson Papers. Duane eluded a warrant served by the Senate but was indicted under the Sedition Law on Oct. 17, 1800. The case remained unresolved, however, until Jefferson assumed the presidency and dismissed the case. See Smith, *Freedom's Fetters,* 300–306.

42. Monroe to Jefferson, Apr. 23, 1800, in Hamilton, ed., *Monroe,* 3: 173–74.

43. Hamilton to Washington, May 19, 1798, in Syrett, ed., *Hamilton,* 21: 466–68.

44. Rose, *Prologue to Democracy,* 206–7, 216–18.

45. Sedgwick to King, July 26 and Dec. 29, 1799, in King, ed., *King,* 3: 69–71, 162–63.

46. *Norfolk Herald,* Mar. 19, 1799, as quoted in Rose, *Prologue to Democracy,* 219.

47. Ibid., 219–23.

48. Taylor was responding to Jefferson's suggestion that Monroe be put up

to replace the recently deceased Henry Tazewell in the United States Senate. Taylor to Jefferson, Feb. 15, 1799, Jefferson Papers; Jefferson to Taylor, Jan. 24, 1799, in Ford, ed., *Jefferson*, 7: 322–23; and John Guerrant to Monroe, Oct. 14, 1799, Monroe Papers. Taylor's suggestion was followed and Monroe served as governor at a critical time, from 1799–1802.

49. Taylor to Madison, Mar. 4, 1799, as quoted in Koch and Ammon, "Virginia and Kentucky Resolutions," 163–64.

50. Walter Jones and others to Madison, Feb. 7, 1799, Madison Papers. Monroe was asked to intercede with his friend by Spencer Roane to Monroe, Mar. 24, 1799, Monroe Papers.

51. Jefferson to Madison, Apr. 19, 1798 [misdated, 1799], in Ford, ed., *Jefferson*, 7: 242–44.

52. Ibid.

53. See Risjord, *Chesapeake Politics*, 546–47; Beeman, *Old Dominion*, 204–11; Rose, *Prologue to Democracy*, 220–28; and Bell, *Party and Faction*, 258–59. There is some disagreement over the results of the election. Rose says that the Federalists had 8 out of 23 congressional seats, while Risjord says 6 of 18; Beeman 8 of 19; and Bell 8 of 20.

54. Rose, *Prologue to Democracy*, 222, 227–28. Although the Federalists did make gains, Rose notes that "despite the emergence of an active, though still small, Federalist interest in Virginia during the latter half of 1799, the political composition of the General Assembly when it met in December was difficult to assess in terms of party preference" (227). See also Risjord, *Chesapeake Politics*, 546–47, who argues that there was little change in the relative strength of the legislature after the election, and Beeman, *Old Dominion*, 204–11.

55. Miller, *Federalist Era*, 255; Bell, *Party and Faction*, 256–59. Miller and Bell differ on the split in North Carolina, with Bell claiming both Federalists and Republicans held 5 seats, whereas Miller maintains that there was a 7 to 3 split in favor of the Federalists. Dauer, *Adams Federalists*, 273.

56. Jefferson to Madison, Aug. 23, 1799, Madison Papers.

57. Ibid.

58. Jefferson to Wilson C. Nicholas, Sept. 5, 1799, in Ford, ed., *Jefferson*, 7: 389–92. See also Koch and Ammon, "Virginia and Kentucky and Resolutions," 115–18, for a discussion of Jefferson's change of position.

59. Breckinridge to Jefferson, Dec. 13, 1799, Jefferson Papers, and Koch and Ammon, "Virginia and Kentucky Resolutions," 169.

60. Koch and Ammon, "Virginia and Kentucky Resolutions," 171–73.

61. Madison to Jefferson, Dec. 29, 1799, in Hunt, ed., *Madison*, 6: 342–44n.

62. Jefferson to Madison, Nov. 26, 1799, as quoted in Koch and Ammon, "Virginia and Kentucky Resolutions," 170.

CHAPTER 11

1. Gerry to——Eliot, June 21, 1800, Gerry Papers.

2. Monroe to Thomas McKean, July 12, 1800, in Hamilton, ed., *Monroe*, 3: 194.

3. *Connecticut Courant,* Sept. 2, 1800, as quoted in Lerche, "Jefferson and the Election of 1800," 480.

4. Miller, *Federalist Era,* 255; Bell, *Party and Faction,* 256–59.

5. As quoted in Dauer, *Adams Federalists,* 241.

6. Hamilton to King, Jan. 5, 1800, in King, ed., *King,* 3: 173–74.

7. Kurtz, *Presidency of John Adams,* 392.

8. Sedgwick to King, May 11, 1800, in King, ed., *King,* 3: 236–39. See Hamilton to Sedgwick, May 4, 1800, for much the same language, in Syrett, ed., *Hamilton,* 24: 452–53.

9. Jefferson to Gideon Granger, Aug. 13, 1800, in Ford, ed., *Jefferson,* 7: 138–41. Jefferson said, however, that even if the Republicans did win the election there, it would be a hollow victory and that their tenure in New England would "be a very uneasy one."

10. Jefferson to Gerry, Jan. 26, 1799, Jefferson to Gideon Granger, Aug. 13, 1800, also Jefferson to Samuel Adams, Feb. 26, 1800, ibid., 15–26, 450–53, 114–15.

11. Gerry to——Wendall, June 13, 1800, Gerry Papers. See also Goodman, *Democratic-Republicans,* 104–5.

12. Formisano, *Transformation of Political Culture,* 72.

13. Ibid., 88.

14. As quoted by ibid., 73–74.

15. See Formisano's discussion of Gerry for a somewhat different interpretation, ibid., 72–76.

16. McCormick, *Presidential Game,* 226–28.

17. Jefferson to Monroe, Mar. 26 and Apr. 13, 1800, Monroe Papers. Jefferson traveled through Richmond on his way home but stayed out of the public eye. See Malone, *Jefferson and the Ordeal of Liberty,* 477.

18. As quoted by Lomask, *Burr,* 1: 244.

19. Matthew L. Davis to Gallatin, Mar. 29, 1800, and George J. Warner to Gallatin, May 2, 1800, Gallatin Papers, and Lomask, *Burr,* 1: 236–46.

20. John Dawson to Madison, Dec. 12, 1799, Madison Papers.

21. Matthew Davis to Gallatin, May 5, 1800, Gallatin Papers.

22. Gallatin to Hannah Gallatin, May 6, 1800, ibid; Cunningham, *Jeffersonian Republicans,* 162–64.

23. Letter of John Nicholson, Dec. 26, 1803, *American Historical Review* 8 (1902–03): 511–13; James Nicholson to Gallatin, May 7, 1800, Mrs. Albert Gallatin to her husband, May 7, 1800, and Albert Gallatin to his wife, May 12, 1800, in Adams, *Life of Gallatin,* 242, 243. Lomask, *Burr,* 1: 247–55, argues that Clinton wanted the vice presidential nomination in 1800 and later believed that "Burr had tricked him out of it."

24. Hamilton to Jay, May 7, 1800, and Hamilton to Sedgwick, May 4, 1800, in Syrett, ed., *Hamilton,* 24: 464–67, 444–53. Also Pickering and C. Gore to King, May 7 and May 5, 1800, in King, ed., *King,* 3: 232–33.

25. Miller, *Federalist Era,* 258–59.

26. Adams to Pickering, May 10, 1800, Pickering to Adams, May 12, 1800, and Adams to Pickering, May 12, 1800, in Adams, ed., *John Adams,* 9: 53–55.

Abigail Adams as quoted in Clarfield, *Pickering and American Diplomacy*, 212.

27. James McHenry to John McHenry, Jr., May 20, 1800, enclosed with Hamilton from McHenry, May 20, 1800, in Syrett, ed., *Hamilton*, 24: 506–12. Kohn, *Eagle and Sword*, 240–43, is more sympathetic to McHenry.

28. McHenry to Adams, May 31, 1800, enclosed with McHenry to Hamilton, June 2, 1800, in Syrett, ed., *Hamilton*, 24: 550–65.

29. Sedgwick to Hamilton, May 13, 1800, and Hamilton to McHenry, June 6, 1800, ibid., 582–86, 573.

30. *The [Trenton] Federalist; or New-Jersey Gazette,* June 2, 1800, as quoted, ibid., 482–86n.

31. See ibid. and Hamilton to McHenry, June 6, 1800, ibid., 573.

32. Hamilton to Sedgwick, May 10, 1800, ibid., 474–75.

33. Ames to Goodrich, June 12, 1800, in Gibbs, ed., *Memoirs,* 2: 366–67.

34. Cabot to King, Aug. 9, 1800, in King, ed., *King,* 3: 291–92.

35. Ames to Wolcott, June 12, 1800, in Gibbs, ed. *Memoirs,* 2: 367–70.

36. Wolcott to Ames, Aug. 10, 1800, ibid., 400–405.

37. Ibid.

38. Letter 17 to the *Boston Patriot,* in Adams, ed., *John Adams,* 9: 300–301.

39. Abigail Adams to Thomas Boylston Adams, July 12, 1800, as quoted in Syrett, ed., *Hamilton,* 24: 574–77n.

40. Sedgwick to Hamilton, May 7, 1800, ibid., 467–68.

41. For an excellent discussion of the Federalists during the spring and summer of 1800, see Kohn, *Eagle and Sword,* chap. 13.

42. *Letter,* in Syrett, ed., *Hamilton,* 25: 186–234. For discussions of Hamilton's letter, see Cabot to Hamilton, Aug. 21, 1800, Wolcott to Hamilton, Sept. 3, 1800, Hamilton to Wolcott, Sept. 26, 1800, and Wolcott to Hamilton, Oct. 2, 1800, in Gibbs, ed., *Memoirs,* 2: 407–8, 416–18, 421–22, and 430–31, and Ames to Hamilton, Aug. 26, 1800, in Ames, ed., *Ames,* 1: 280–82.

43. Cunningham, *Jeffersonian Republicans,* 229–30.

44. Syrett, ed., *Hamilton,* 25: 176–77; Smith, *Freedom's Fetters,* 373.

45. Callender to Jefferson, Sept. 13, 1800, Jefferson Papers; John Randolph to Joseph H. Nicholson, Sept. 26, 1800, Nicholson Papers. Also Egerton, "Gabriel's Conspiracy," 207; Aptheker, *Slave Revolts,* 219–28; and Jordan, *White over Black,* 393–96.

46. Jefferson to Monroe, July 14, 1793, as quoted in Aptheker, *Slave Revolts,* 42; see also 41–42.

47. Jefferson to S. George Tucker, Aug. 28, 1797, as quoted in Jordan, *White over Black,* 386.

48. *Gazette of the United States,* Sept. 13, 1800, as quoted in Aptheker, *Slave Revolts,* 150.

49. *Virginia Herald,* Sept. 23, 1800, as quoted in Jordan, *White over Black,* 396.

50. Murray to Adams, Dec. 9, 1800, as quoted in Aptheker, *Slave Revolts,* 227.

51. Egerton, "Gabriel's Conspiracy."

52. Aptheker, *Slave Revolts*, 396, 377, 386.

53. Pole, *Political Representation*, 544–64, gives some turnout figures for Massachusetts, Connecticut, New Hampshire, Pennsylvania, Maryland, Virginia, and North Carolina, but they are sketchy and inconclusive.

54. Editor's note in Syrett, ed., *Hamilton*, 24: 444–53.

55. Ibid. Also Jefferson to Philip Norborne Nicholas, Apr. 7, 1800, in Ford, ed., *Jefferson*, 7: 439–40; Charles Polk and G. Duvall to Madison, June 20 and June 6, 1800, Madison Papers.

56. Jefferson to Madison, Mar. 4, 1800, in Ford, ed., *Jefferson*, 7: 429–34.

57. Dawson to Madison, May 4, 1800, Madison Papers; Mason to Monroe, May 15 and May 23, 1800, Monroe Papers.

58. Formisano, *Transformation of Political Culture*, 73; *American Mercury*, Sept. 4, 1800, as quoted in Cunningham, *Jeffersonian-Republicans*, 219; also 200–201, 204–10, and 217–18. And editor's note in Syrett, ed., *Hamilton*, 24: 444–53.

59. Editor's note in Syrett, ed., *Hamilton*, 24: 444–53.

60. Ibid., and Cunningham, *Jeffersonian Republicans*, 158, 230–31. See also Prince, *New Jersey's Jeffersonian Republicans*, 41–68, for an excellent discussion of New Jersey.

61. Wolcott to Ames, Aug. 10, 1800, in Gibbs, ed., *Memoirs*, 2: 400–405. See also Cunningham, *Jeffersonian Republicans*, 189–91.

62. McHenry to Wolcott, Nov. 9, 1800, in Gibbs, ed., *Memoirs* 2: 445.

63. Editor's note in Syrett, ed., *Hamilton*, 24: 444–53; Dawson to Madison, Dec. 12, 1799, and Feb. 1, 1800, Madison Papers; Jefferson to Monroe, Jan. 12, 1800, in Ford, ed., *Jefferson*, 7: 401–3.

64. Risjord, *Chesapeake Politics*, 556.

65. Broussard, *Southern Federalists*, 30.

66. Jefferson to Thomas Mann Randolph, Nov. 30, 1800, as quoted by Cunningham, *Jeffersonian Republicans*, 231.

67. Pickering to William Loughton Smith, May 7, 1800, as quoted in editor's note in Syrett, ed., *Hamilton*, 24: 444–53.

68. Broussard, *Southern Federalists*, 30–31; Charles Pinckney to Jefferson, Nov. 22, 1800, in Hamilton, ed., *Monroe*, 3: 244–46n. See letters of Peter Freneau from Columbia, South Carolina, in late Nov. and early Dec. 1800, Miscellaneous Papers. Also, Miller, *Federalist Era*, 267; Cunningham, *Jeffersonian Republicans*, 188–89, 231–36; and Syrett, ed., *Hamilton*, 24: 452.

69. Dauer, *Adams Federalists*, 106.

70. Ibid., 106, 257.

71. Freehling, *Road to Disunion*, 147. Jefferson would have lost 12 and Adams 2.

72. Dauer, *Adams' Federalists*, 273–74. See Bell, *Party and Faction*, 258–59, for the Sixth Congress, and Cunningham, *Jeffersonian Republicans*, 247, for the Seventh. Cunningham warns that the figures are "only approximate."

73. I am at odds here with Cunningham, who, in his effort to show the national dimensions of the Republican victory, denies that the victory of the Republicans in 1800 was merely "the transference of the twelve electoral votes

of New York from Adams to Jefferson." In other words, he argues that only looking at the presidential election and the addition of middle state support to Jefferson's solidly southern base distorts the true significance of the overall election. What Cunningham sees as more important was the "impressive," broadly based Republican showing in the congressional races where the Republicans scored "a much wider margin of victory . . . than in the presidential contest." See Cunningham, *Jeffersonian Republicans*, 247–48.

74. Formisano, *Transformation of Political Culture*, 108.

CHAPTER 12

1. *General Advertiser*, Jan. 27, 1801, for reports on the fire. Also M. Clay to Monroe, Jan. 21, 1801, Monroe Papers.

2. *General Advertiser*, Jan. 27, 1801.

3. M. Clay to Monroe, Jan. 21, 1801, Monroe Papers.

4. *General Advertiser*, Jan. 26, 1801. That February, while balloting for the Presidency was taking place, the House of Representatives appointed a committee to investigate the fires. After examining the testimony of a number of witnesses, the committee members found no evidence that the fire at the War Department was the result of "negligence or design," but they were unable to form any conclusions about the Treasury fire. See Gibbs, ed., *Memoirs*, 2: 478–81.

5. *General Advertiser*, Dec. 17, 1800, and Jan. 3, 1801.

6. Granger to Jefferson, Oct. 18, 1800, Jefferson Papers.

7. *General Advertiser*, Dec. 11, 1800.

8. Ibid., Jan. 7, Jan. 10, and Feb. 3, 1801.

9. *Salem Federalist*, as quoted, ibid., Jan. 29, 1801.

10. See Wood, "Conspiracy and the Paranoid Style," for an excellent discussion of an eighteenth-century view of causality.

11. For evidence that the Founders expected the House to elect the president, see See Pious, *American Presidency*, 28–29.

12. Jefferson to Madison, Dec. 19, 1800, in Ford, ed., *Jefferson*, 7: 470–72; Cunningham, *Jeffersonian Republicans*, 240–41; Miller, *Federalist Era*, 269.

13. Hugh Williamson to Monroe, Nov. 6, 1800, and Madison to Monroe, Nov. 10, 1800, Monroe Papers. See Madison to Jefferson, Oct. 21, 1800, in Hunt, ed., *Madison*, 6: 409–10, where Madison relays the concern from Burr's supporters that the Southern states will fail to give their support to Burr.

14. Burr to Samuel Smith, Dec. 16, 1800, in Kline, ed., *Burr* 1: 471.

15. Jefferson to Burr, Dec. 15, 1800, ibid., 469–70. Lomask (*Burr*, 1: 273) argues that Jefferson "was not interested in giving Burr an 'active station' in the government, only in wringing from him an avowal of disinterest in the Presidency."

16. Burr to Jefferson, Dec. 23, 1800, Jefferson Papers.

17. Harper to Burr, Dec. 24, 1800, in Kline, ed., *Burr*, 1: 474–75.

18. George W. Erving to Monroe, Jan. 25, 1801, and Diary of Gouverneur Morris, Dec. 27, 1800, ibid., 475n.

19. G. W. Erving to Monroe, Dec. 17, 1800, Monroe Papers. See also Dawson to Madison, Dec. 18, 1800, Madison Papers.

20. Burr to Smith, Dec. 29, 1800, in Kline, ed., *Burr*, 1: 478–79.

21. Smith to Burr, Jan. 11, 1800 [misdated, 1801], ibid., 487–89.

22. Burr to Samuel Smith, Jan. 16, 1801, ibid., 493.

23. Burr to Jefferson, Feb. 12, 1801, ibid., 501.

24. Editor's notes, ibid., 490, 92–93; Jefferson's note, Feb. 12, 1801, in Sawvel, ed., *Anas of Jefferson*, 209–10; Hamilton to Gouverneur Morris, Jan. 9, 1801, in Syrett, ed., *Hamilton*, 25: 304–5.

25. Morris to Hamilton, Dec. 1, 1800, in Syrett, ed., *Hamilton*, 25: 266–68.

26. As quoted, ibid., 268–69n. Also Jefferson to Burr, Dec. 15, 1800, in Kline, ed., *Burr*, 1: 469–70.

27. *General Advertiser*, Jan. 16, 1801, as quoted, ibid., 302–3n.

28. Some early historians, however, have vigorously rejected the notion that the Federalists "contemplated preventing any choice of President, and by force of their majority in Congress placing the office in commission" (Gibbs, ed., *Memoirs*, 2: 489).

29. Hamilton to Gouverneur Morris, Jan. 9, 1801, in Syrett, ed., *Hamilton*, 25: 304.

30. Adams to Gerry, Feb. 7, 1801, in Adams, ed., *John Adams*, 9: 97–98. Adams did say that such congressional action should "be followed by another election, and Mr. Jefferson would be chosen; I should, in that case, decline the election."

31. Jefferson's diary entry of Apr. 15, 1806, in Sawvel, ed., *Anas of Jefferson*, 237–41. My emphasis added.

32. Jefferson to John Breckenridge, Dec. 18, 1800, to Madison, Dec. 19 and Dec. 26, 1800, and to Tench Coxe, Dec. 31, 1800, in Ford, ed., *Jefferson*, 7: 468–69, 474–75, 157–63; Caesar Rodney to Jefferson, Dec. 28, 1800, Jefferson Papers.

33. *General Advertiser*, Jan. 7, Jan. 10, and Feb. 3, 1801.

34. Brackenridge to Jefferson, Jan. 19, 1801, Jefferson Papers.

35. Sedgwick to Hamilton, Jan. 10, 1801, in Syrett, ed., *Hamilton*, 25: 310–13.

36. Harrison Gray Otis to Hamilton, Dec. 17, 1800, ibid., 259.

37. Sedgwick to Hamilton, Jan. 10, 1801, ibid., 310–13.

38. Bayard to Hamilton, Jan. 7, 1801, ibid., 299–303. Bayard reported that the Federalists would "meet on friday for the purposes of forming a resolution as to their line of conduct," but he had "not the least doubt of their agreeing to support Bur [*sic*]." Bayard, himself, however, was undecided and asserted that the Federalist decision would "not bind me," even though "it might cost me a painful struggle to disappoint the views and wishes of many gentlemen with whom I have been accustomed to act." Also Gouverneur Morris to Hamilton, Jan. 26, 1801, and John Rutledge, Jr., to Hamilton, Jan. 10, 1801, ibid., 329–30, 308–10.

39. Hamilton to Bayard, Dec. 27, 1800, ibid., 275–77.

40. Hamilton to Wolcott, Dec. 16, 1800, ibid., 257.

41. Hamilton to John Rutledge, Jr., Jan. 4, 1801, ibid., 293–98.

42. Hamilton to Bayard, Jan. 16, 1801, ibid., 319–24.

43. Hamilton to Wolcott, Dec. 17, 1800, in Gibbs, ed., *Memoirs*, 2: 458–60. Curiously, this letter was omitted from Syrett, ed., *Hamilton*, 25: 263, where the editor states that the "Letter of December 17 [was] not found."

44. Hamilton to Wolcott, Dec. 17, 1800, in Gibbs, ed., *Memoirs*, 2: 458–60.

45. Hamilton to Bayard, Jan. 16, 1801, ibid., 319–24.

46. Hamilton to James McHenry, Jan. 4, 1801, ibid., 292–93. See also Hamilton to Wolcott, Dec., 1800, ibid., 286–88. These conditions by which the Federalists would allow the election of Jefferson were almost identical to those that James Bayard believed he had negotiated for the following February.

47. R. Troup to King, Dec. 31, 1800, in King, ed., *King*, 3: 358. See also Troup to King, Feb. 12, 1801, ibid., 390–91.

48. Marshall to Hamilton, Jan. 1, 1801, in Syrett, ed., *Hamilton*, 25: 290–91.

49. Adams to Gerry, Dec. 30, 1800, Gerry Papers.

50. Rossiter, ed., *Federalist Papers*, 414.

51. Ketcham, *Presidents above Party*, 228.

52. As quoted in Lomask, *Burr*, xi.

53. A discussion of the various rumors and possible Republican responses can be found in the letters written by Albert Gallatin to his wife, Hannah, in Jan. and Feb. 1801, in the Gallatin Papers. Also see the editor's note in Kline, ed., *Burr*, 1: 481–87.

54. Madison to Jefferson, Jan. 10, 1801, in Hunt, ed., *Madison*, 6: 410–16.

55. Young, *Washington Community*, 41; Gallatin to his wife, Jan. 22, 1801, in Adams, *Life of Gallatin*, 255.

56. Gallatin to his wife, Jan. 15, 1801, in Adams, *Life of Gallatin*, 254–55.

57. Gallatin to his wife, Jan. 22, 1801, ibid., 255.

58. Gallatin to Henry A. Muhlenberg, May 8, 1848, ibid., 248–51.

59. "Plan," in Adams, ed., *Gallatin*, 1: 18–23. Although the memorandum was not dated, it was apparently written sometime during Jan. 1801, for many of the arguments made were repeated in letters to his wife, Hannah, during the same period. See also many of the ideas discussed in Gallatin's letters to Hannah, Jan. 15, Jan. 22, and Jan. 29, 1801, Gallatin Papers. Gallatin's math was faulty because the states of Virginia, North Carolina, Georgia, Kentucky, and Tennessee combined for only 40 electoral votes, while New York, Maryland, Pennsylvania, and South Carolina had given the Jefferson-Burr ticket 33 votes in 1800. See the totals in Dauer, *Adams Federalists*, 257.

60. Gallatin to Hannah, Jan. 22, 1801, Gallatin Papers.

61. Gallatin, in a letter to his wife dated Feb. 5, 1801 (Adams, *Life of Gallatin*, 259–60), says that "Bayard has proposed, and a committee of sixteen members, one from each State, have agreed, that on the 11th February, the day fixed by law for counting the votes, if it shall appear, as is expected, that the two persons highest in vote (Jef. and Burr) have an equality, the House shall immediately proceed (in their own chamber) to choose by ballot the President, and *shall not adjourn until a choice is made*." Bayard, however, in a

letter to Richard Bassett, Feb. 6, 1801, reports that "a Committee consisting of a member from every State has determined and reported accordingly that the election shall be completed without adjournment. This is against my opinion and I shall oppose it, in the House" (Donnan, ed., *Bayard,* 123).

62. Gallatin to his wife, Jan. 15, 1801, in Adams, *Life of Gallatin,* 252–55; Dawson to Madison, Feb. 12, 1801, Madison Papers.

63. Jefferson's diary entry of Feb. 12, 1801, in Sawvel, ed., *Anas of Jefferson,* 209–10. Livingston's role was a rather shadowy one. Bayard, later in a legal deposition, claimed that Livingston "was the confidential agent for Mr. Burr" (Davis, ed., *Memoirs of Burr,* 2: 125). Hamilton evidently felt the same about Livingston; see editor's note in Kline, ed., *Burr,* 1: 492–93.

64. Bayard implies as much in his legal deposition; see Davis, ed., *Memoirs of Burr,* 2: 122–37. See also Dawson to Madison, Feb. 12, 1801, Madison Papers.

65. Jefferson to Monroe, Feb. 15, 1801, in Ford, ed., *Jefferson,* 7: 490–91. Also Judge Tucker to Monroe, Jan. 7 and Jan. 23, 1801, and George W. Erving to Monroe, Jan. 25, 1801, Monroe Papers; and Monroe to Jefferson, Jan. 6, 1801, in Hamilton, ed., *Monroe,* 3: 253–55.

66. Gallatin to his wife, Feb. 12, 1801, and to James Nicholson, Feb. 14, 1801, in Adams, *Life of Gallatin,* 260–62. See also Jefferson to Monroe, Feb. 12, 1801, Monroe Papers; and Samuel W. Dana to Wolcott, Feb. 11, 1801, in Gibbs, ed., *Memoirs,* 2: 489–90.

67. *Washington Federalist,* Feb. 12, 1801, as quoted in the *General Advertiser,* Feb. 17, 1801.

68. *Washington Federalist* as quoted in the *General Advertiser,* Feb. 19, 1801.

69. Dallas, *A. J. Dallas,* 112–13. One letter from the capital expressed the hope that the report was not true, for every "moderate man should exert himself to prevent so improper a step and every thing violent." He reassured his readers that, "when constitutional means fail us, it will then be time enough to resort to extremities" (*General Advertiser,* Feb. 16, 1801).

70. Beckley to Gallatin, Feb. 15, 1801, Gallatin Papers.

71. Monroe to McKean, July 12, 1800, McKean Papers.

72. Monroe to John Hoomes, Feb. 14, 1801, in Hamilton, ed., *Monroe,* 3: 258–59; McKean to Jefferson, Feb. 20, 1801, Jefferson Papers.

73. J. Tyler to Monroe, Feb. 11, 1801, Monroe Papers.

74. McKean to Jefferson, Feb. 20, 1801, Jefferson Papers; Monroe to Jefferson, Jan. 20, 1801, in Hamilton, ed., *Monroe,* 3: 257.

75. McKean to Jefferson, Mar. 19, 1801, McKean Papers. This is a re-creation of an earlier letter that McKean had destroyed once hearing of Jefferson's election. Jefferson requested the re-created draft in his letter to McKean, Mar. 9, 1801, ibid.

76. Judge Tucker to Monroe, Jan. 7 and Jan. 23, 1801; George W. Erving to Monroe, Jan. 25, 1801, Monroe Papers. See also Monroe to Jefferson, Jan. 6, 1801, in Hamilton, ed., *Monroe,* 3: 253–55.

77. Major T. M. Randolph to Monroe, Feb. 14, 1801, Monroe Papers.

78. Samuel W. Dana to Wolcott, Feb. 11, 1801, in Gibbs, ed., *Memoirs,* 2:

489–90. See Jefferson's note of Feb. 12, 1801, in Sawvel, ed., *Anas of Jefferson,* 209–10. For the best account of Bayard's role in resolving the deadlock, see Borden, *Bayard,* 86–95. Also Lomask, *Burr,* 1: 280, 289–94.

79. Bayard to McLane, Feb. 17, 1801, Jefferson Papers; Bayard to Samuel Bayard, Feb. 22, 1801, in Donnan, ed., *Bayard,* 131–32; Borden, *Bayard,* 89–90; Davis, *Memoirs of Burr,* 127–28; and editor's note in Kline, ed., *Burr,* 1: 486–87. Also George W. Erving to Monroe, Feb. 17, 1801, Monroe Papers; Thomas Mason to John Breckinridge, Feb. 19, 1801, Breckinridge Family Papers; Gallatin to James Nicholson, Feb. 16, 1801, and to his wife, Feb. 17, 1801, Gallatin Papers.

80. Deposition of Bayard, Apr. 3, 1806, in Davis, ed., *Memoirs of Burr,* 2: 129–33. Bayard, at the time, was convinced that he had firm assurances from Jefferson. He wrote McLane, a Federalist officeholder, that "I have taken good care of you, and think if prudent, you are safe" (Bayard to McLane, Feb. 17, 1801, Jefferson Papers). Bayard's demands on Jefferson were the very same ones Hamilton had called for in December. See Hamilton to Wolcott, Dec. 17, 1800, in Gibbs, ed., *Memoirs,* 2: 458–60.

81. Jefferson's diary account, Apr. 15, 1806, in Sawvel, ed., *Anas of Jefferson,* 237–41. This controversy may best be followed in Davis, ed., *Memoirs of Burr,* 2: 112–37; and Borden, *Bayard,* 89–95.

82. This is the opinion of Gallatin writing many years later. Gallatin to Henry A. Muhlenberg, May 8, 1848, in Adams, *Life of Gallatin,* 248–51, and is followed by Borden, *Bayard,* 91–93.

83. William Cooper to Thomas Morris, Feb. 13, 1801, in Davis, ed., *Memoirs of Burr,* 2: 113.

84. Bayard to Hamilton, Jan. 7, 1801, in Syrett, ed., *Hamilton,* 25: 299–303.

85. Bayard to Richard Bassett, Feb. 16, 1801, in Donnan, ed., *Bayard,* 126–27; Bayard to Hamilton, Mar. 8, 1801, in Syrett, ed., *Hamilton* 25: 344–46.

86. Borden, *Bayard,* 82.

87. Lomask, *Burr,* 1: 294–95.

88. Grodzins, "Political Parties and the Crisis of Succession," 317. Grodzins, to my knowledge, was one of the first scholars to note the critical nature of the election of 1800.

89. Chambers, *Political Parties,* foreword. Chambers's conclusions about the pluralist nature and consensus-seeking and conflict-resolving abilities of American political parties is shared by most scholars. I do not believe, as I have argued, that this was true of the proto-parties of the early republic, and I think that many scholars, in addition to Chambers, have mistakenly attempted to impose these later characteristics of American party politics on the events of the 1790s.

90. Noble Cunningham represents the view of many historians when he argues that "this transferring of political power from one party to another" in 1801 was "full proof that political parties had come of age." See Cunningham, *Jeffersonian Republicans,* 248, as well as McCormick, *Presidential Game,* 69–75, and Rose, *Prologue to Democracy,* 283, who maintains that the "establishment of the first American party system was accomplished substantially by the close of the elections of 1800."

91. In contrast to this conclusion, see Richard Hofstadter, who has written that the "central significance" of the election of 1800 was that *"violent resistance was never, at any time, discussed,"* nor "was disunion discussed as a serious immediate possibility in 1801" (Hofstadter, *Idea of a Party System*, 129–30, emphasis his). In a footnote, however, he maintains that although "Federalists did not discuss violent resistance, some Republicans talked of such action if the Federalists, in plain violation of the popular will, persisted in snatching the prize from Jefferson."

92. McKean to Jefferson, Feb. 20, 1801, Jefferson Papers.

93. Jefferson to McKean, Mar. 9, 1801, McKean Papers. For the response, see McKean to Jefferson, Mar. 19, 1801, ibid.

94. Gallatin to Henry Muhlenberg, May 8, 1848, in Adams, *Life of Gallatin*, 248–51.

95. McKean to Jefferson, Mar. 19, 1801, McKean Papers.

96. See my "Unraveling the Mystery," 411–18.

EPILOGUE

1. Jefferson to Robert R. Livingston, Dec. 14, 1800, in Ford, ed., *Jefferson*, 7: 462–66. The theme that a small group of Federalist leaders had misled the American people ran throughout Jefferson's correspondence in 1801. See Jefferson to Thomas Mann Randolph and Thomas Lomax, Feb. 19 and Feb. 25, 1801, ibid., 497–98, 500. Also Monroe to Jefferson, Mar. 3 and Mar. 18, 1801, in Hamilton, ed., *Monroe*, 3: 261–64 and 268–74.

2. Jefferson to Spencer Roane, Sept. 6, 1819, in Peterson, ed., *Portable Jefferson*, 562.

3. Inaugural Address, Mar. 4, 1801, Koch and Peden, eds., *Jefferson*, 321–22.

4. Jefferson to Benjamin Smith Barton, Feb. 14, 1801, in Ford, ed., *Jefferson*, 7: 489–90.

5. Jefferson to Maria Eppes, Feb. 15, 1801, Jefferson Papers, University of Virginia.

6. As quoted by Peterson, *Jefferson and the New Nation*, 931.

7. Hamilton to Jonathan Dayton, [Oct.-Nov. 1799], in Syrett, ed., *Hamilton*, 23: 599–604.

8. Commager, ed., *Documents of American History*, 209–11.

9. Adams, *History of the United States*, 4: 454–55.

10. Levy, *Jefferson and Civil Liberties*, 163, 165, 162, 161, 160.

11. Ibid., 166, 138, 139.

12. Ibid., 160. The emphasis in the quotation is mine.

13. Malone, *Jefferson the President: Second Term*, 636–57.

14. Ibid., 654–55.

15. As quoted, ibid., 639.

16. Ibid., 517–18.

17. A good discussion of the tough choices Jefferson had to make as president during his second term can be found in Peterson, *Jefferson and the*

New Nation, 801–921. See also Levy, *Jefferson and Civil Liberties,* for a more critical treatment of Jefferson's actions.

18. Brown, *Republic in Peril,* 73. For the War of 1812's impact on "the making of liberal America," see Watts, *Republic Reborn.*

19. See Ellis (*Jefferson Crisis,* 267–84, 277–78) who argues that the decline of Federalist power after 1800 "only served to heighten the differences between radicals and moderates within the Republican party" and that the "real meaning of Jeffersonian Democracy . . . is to be found in the political triumph of the moderate Republicans and their eventual amalgamation with the moderate wing of the Federalist party."

20. Jefferson to Cooper, July 9, 1807, as quoted in Dangerfield, *Era of Good Feelings,* 99–100.

21. As quoted by Brown, "Missouri Crisis," 65, 57.

22. Jefferson to John Holmes, Apr. 22, 1820, Koch and Peden, eds., *Jefferson,* 698. Also see Freehling, *Road to Disunion,* 144–61, for an excellent discussion of the Missouri controversy in which the author analyzes the different attitudes toward slavery in the upper and lower South.

23. Brown, "Missouri Crisis," 63.

24. As quoted by Remini, *Election of Jackson,* 57. Remini's book is an excellent account of the foundation of the Jackson or Democratic Party.

25. Van Buren, *Autobiography,* 123, 192–93.

26. For a discussion of Van Buren's views about political parties see Hofstadter, *Idea of a Party System,* 212–52. See also Cole's discussion of Van Buren's early party views in his *Van Buren,* 127, 125. Cole argues that Van Buren rejected "Monroe's amalgamation of parties" and believed that the very "continuance of the old party division" was at stake in the 1820s.

27. On Americans' anticommercialism, see my *Jacksonians versus the Banks.*

28. This point is ably made by Brown, "Missouri Crisis." See also Freehling, *Road to Disunion,* 560, where he argues that "Jacksonianism began and largely remained strongest in the South and in the southern half of both sections."

29. McPherson, *Battlecry of Freedom,* 859–60. In the sixty years between the inauguration of Jefferson and the inauguration of Lincoln, non-Republican and non-Democratic presidents, including J. Q. Adams, served for only twelve years.

30. Jackson to Joseph Conn Guild, Apr. 24, 1835, as quoted by Latner, *Presidency of Jackson,* 127.

31. Sharp, *Jacksonians versus the Banks,* 327.

32. As quoted by Peterson, *Jefferson and the New Nation,* 931.

Bibliography

MANUSCRIPT COLLECTIONS

Adams Papers. Massachusetts Historical Society (microfilm).
Breckinridge Family Papers. Library of Congress.
Campbell-Preston Family Papers. Library of Congress.
Gallatin, Albert. Papers. New-York Historical Society Collection.
Gerry, Elbridge. Papers. Library of Congress.
Innes, Harry. Papers. Library of Congress.
Jefferson, Thomas. Papers. Library of Congress.
McKean, Thomas. Papers. Historical Society of Pennsylvania.
Madison, James. Papers. Library of Congress.
Miscellaneous Papers. Library of Congress.
Monroe, James. Papers. Library of Congress.
Nicholson, J. H. Papers. Library of Congress.

PUBLISHED CORRESPONDENCE

Adams, Charles Francis, ed. *The Works of John Adams, 2nd President of the United States.* 10 vols. (Boston, 1850–56).
Adams, Henry, ed. *The Writings of Albert Gallatin.* 3 vols. (Philadelphia, 1879).
Ames, Seth, ed. *Works of Fisher Ames.* 2 vols. (Boston, 1854).
Ballagh, James Curtis, ed. *The Letters of Richard Henry Lee.* 2 vols. (New York, 1970).
Boyd, Julian P., ed. *The Papers of Thomas Jefferson.* 23 vols. (Princeton, 1950–).
Cappon, Lester J., ed. *The Adams-Jefferson Letters: The Complete Correspondence between Thomas Jefferson and Abigail and John Adams.* 2 vols. (Chapel Hill, N.C., 1959).
Commager, Henry Steele, ed. *Documents of American History.* 9th ed. (Englewood Cliffs, N.J., 1973)
Cushing, Henry Alanzo, ed. *The Writings of Sam Adams.* 4 vols. (New York, 1904–1908).
Dallas, George M., ed. *Life and Writings of A. J. Dallas* (Philadelphia, 1871).
Davis, Matthew L., ed. *Memoirs of Aaron Burr.* 2 vols. (New York, 1836–37).
Dodd, William E., ed. "John Taylor Correspondence." *The John P. Branch Historical Papers of Randolph-Macon College* 2 (June 1908): 253–353.
Donnan, Elizabeth, ed., *Papers of James A. Bayard* (Washington, D.C., 1915).
Fitzpatrick, John C., ed. *The Writings of George Washington.* 39 vols. (Washington, D.C., 1931–44).

Ford, Paul Leicester, ed. *The Writings of Thomas Jefferson.* 10 vols. (New York, 1892–99).

Gibbs, George, ed. *Memoirs of the Administrations of Washington and John Adams.* 2 vols. (New York, 1846).

Hamilton, Stanislaus Murray, ed. *The Writings of James Monroe.* 7 vols. (New York, 1898–1903).

Hunt, Gaillard, ed. *Disunion Sentiment in Congress in 1794* (Washington, D.C., 1904).

———, ed. *The Writings of James Madison.* 9 vols. (New York, 1900–10).

Jackson, Donald, and Dorothy Twobig, eds. *Diaries of George Washington.* 6 vols. (Charlottesville, 1976–79).

Kenyon, Cecelia M., ed. *The Antifederalists* (Indianapolis, 1966).

King, Charles R., ed. *The Life and Correspondence of Rufus King.* 6 vols. (New York, 1894–1900).

Kline, Mary-Jo, ed. *Political Correspondence and Public Papers of Aaron Burr.* 2 vols. (Princeton, 1983).

Koch, Adrienne, and William Peden, eds. *The Life and Selected Writings of Thomas Jefferson* (New York, 1944).

Letter of John Nicholson, Dec. 26, 1803. *American Historical Review* 8 (Apr. 1903): 511–13.

Peterson, Merrill D., ed. *The Portable Thomas Jefferson* (New York, 1975).

Phillips, U. B., ed. "South Carolina Federalist Correspondence, 1789–1797." *American Historical Review* 14 (July 1909): 731–43.

Rossiter, Clinton, ed. *The Federalist Papers* (New York, 1961).

Sawvel, Franklin ed. *The Anas of Thomas Jefferson* (New York, 1903).

Storing, Herbert J., ed. *The Complete Anti-Federalist.* 7 vols. (Chicago, 1981).

Syrett, Harold C., ed. *The Papers of Alexander Hamilton.* 27 vols. (New York, 1961–87).

Turner, Frederick Jackson, ed. "Correspondence between Clark and Genet." In American Historical Association, *Report of the Historical Manuscripts Commission of the American Historical Association, 1896* (Washington, D.C., 1897).

Van Buren, Martin. *The Autobiography of Martin Van Buren* (Washington, D.C., 1920).

DOCUMENTS

Annals of the Congress of the United States, 1793–1799. 3rd, 4th, and 5th Congresses (Washington, D.C., 1847–51).

Commager, Henry Steele, and Richard B. Morris, eds. *The Spirit of 'Seventy-Six, The Story of the American Revolution as told by Participants.* 2 vols. (Indianapolis, 1958).

Farrand, Max, ed. *The Records of the Federal Convention of 1787.* 4 vols. (New Haven, 1966).

Foner, Philip S., ed. *The Democratic Republican Societies, 1790–1800, a Documentary Sourcebook of Constitutions, Declarations, Addresses, Resolutions, and Toasts* (Westport, Conn., 1976).

Jensen, Merrill, and Robert A. Becker, eds. *The Documentary History of the First Federal Elections, 1788–1790.* vol. 1 (Madison, Wis., 1976).

Richardson, James D., ed. *A Compilation of the Messages and Papers of the Presidents.* 10 vols. (Washington, D.C., 1911).

U.S. Department of Commerce, Bureau of the Census. *Historical Statistics of the United States, Colonial Times to 1957* (Washington, D.C., 1961).

Virginia. *Journal of the Senate, 1799.*

NEWSPAPERS AND PAMPHLETS

Philadelphia *General Advertiser.*

Philadelphia *National Gazette.*

Taylor, John. *A Definition of Parties; or the Political Effects of the Paper System* (Philadelphia, 1794).

———. *An Enquiry into the Principles and Tendency of Certain Public Measures* (Philadelphia, 1794).

———. *An Examination of the Late Proceedings in Congress respecting the Official Conduct of the Secretary of Treasury* (1793).

BOOKS AND ARTICLES

Adams, Henry. *History of the United States of America during the First Administration of Thomas Jefferson.* 9 vols. (New York, 1962).

———. *The Life of Albert Gallatin* (New York, 1943).

Ambler, Charles Henry. *A History of Transportation in the Ohio Valley* (Glendale, Calif., 1909).

Ammon, Harry. *The Genet Mission* (New York, 1973).

———. "The Genet Mission and the Development of American Political Parties." *Journal of American History* 52 (Mar. 1966): 725–41.

———. *James Monroe: The Quest for National Identity* (New York, 1971).

Anderson, Dice Robins. *William Branch Giles: A Biography* (Menasha, Wis., 1915).

Anderson, Frank Maloy. "Contemporary Opinion of the Virginia and Kentucky Resolutions." *American Historical Review* 5 (Oct. 1899 and Jan. 1900): 45–63, 225–52.

Andrews, Charles M. *The Colonial Background of the American Revolution* (New Haven, 1967).

Appleby, Joyce. *Capitalism and a New Social Order: The Republican Vision of the 1790s* (New York, 1984).

———. "Commercial Farming and the 'Agrarian Myth' in the Early Republic." *Journal of American History* 68 (Mar. 1982): 833–49.

———. "What Is Still American in the Political Philosophy of Thomas Jefferson?" *William and Mary Quarterly* 39 (Apr. 1982): 287–309.

Apter, D. E., "Some Reflections on the Role of a Political Opposition in New Nations." *Comparative Studies in Society and History* 4 (1961–62): 154–68.

Aptheker, Herbert. *American Negro Slave Revolts* (New York, 1963).

Bailyn, Bernard. *The Ideological Origins of the American Revolution* (Cambridge, Mass., 1967).

———. *The Origins of American Politics* (New York, 1967).

Baldwin, Leland D. *Whiskey Rebels: The Story of a Frontier Uprising* (Pittsburgh, 1939).

Banner, James M., Jr. "France and the Origins of American Political Culture." *Virginia Quarterly Review* 64 (Autumn 1988): 651–70.

Banning, Lance. *The Jeffersonian Persuasion: Evolution of a Party Ideology* (Ithaca, N.Y., 1978).

Barber, William D. "'Among the Most *Techy Articles of Civil Police*': Federal Taxation and the Adoption of the Whiskey Excise." *William and Mary Quarterly* 25 (Jan. 1968): 58–84.

Beeman, Richard R. *The Old Dominion and the New Nation, 1788–1801* (Lexington, Ky., 1972).

Bell, Rudolph M. *Party and Faction in American Politics: The House of Representatives, 1789–1801* (Westport, Conn., 1973).

Bemis, Samuel Flagg. *Pinckney's Treaty: America's Advantage from Europe's Distress* (New Haven, 1960).

———. *Jay's Treaty: A Study in Commerce and Diplomacy,* rev. ed. (New Haven, 1962).

Benson, Lee. *Toward a Scientific Study of History: Selected Essays* (Philadelphia, 1972).

———. *Turner and Beard: American Historical Writing Reconsidered* (Glencoe, Ill., 1960).

Bloch, Ruth H. *Visionary Republic: Millennial Themes in American Thought, 1756–1800* (New York, 1985).

Borden, Morton. *The Federalism of James A. Bayard* (New York, 1955).

Bowman, Albert Hall. *The Struggle for Neutrality: Franco-American Diplomacy during the Federalist Era* (Knoxville, Tenn., 1974).

Boyd, Steven R., ed. *The Whiskey Rebellion: Past and Present Perspectives* (Westport, Conn., 1985).

Brackenridge, Henry W. *History of the Western Insurrection in Western Pennsylvania Commonly Called the Whiskey Insurrection, 1794* (Pittsburgh, 1859).

Breen, T. H. *Tobacco Culture: The Mentality of the Great Tidewater Planters on the Eve of the Revolution* (Princeton, 1985).

Brodie, Fawn M. *Thomas Jefferson: An Intimate History* (New York, 1974).

Broussard, James H. *The Southern Federalists, 1800–1816* (Baton Rouge, 1978).

Brown, Ralph H. *Mirror for Americans: Likeness of the Eastern Seaboard, 1810* (New York, 1943).

Brown, Richard H. "The Missouri Crisis, Slavery, and the Politics of Jacksonianism." *South Atlantic Quarterly* 65 (Winter 1966): 55–72.

Brown, Roger H. *The Republic in Peril: 1812* (New York, 1964).

Butterfield, Herbert. *The Whig Interpretation of History* (New York, 1965).

Chambers, William Nisbet. *Political Parties in a New Nation: the American Experience, 1776–1809* (New York, 1963).

Charles, Joseph. *The Origins of the American Party System* (New York, 1961).

Clarfield, Gerard H. *Timothy Pickering and American Diplomacy, 1795–1800* (Columbia, Mo., 1969).

———. *Timothy Pickering and the American Republic* (Pittsburgh, 1980).

Cole, Donald B. *Martin Van Buren and the American Political System* (Princeton, 1984).

Combs, Jerald A. *The Jay Treaty: Political Background of the Founding Fathers* (Berkeley, 1970).

Cooke, Jacob E. "The Compromise of 1790." *William and Mary Quarterly* 27 (Oct. 1970): 523–45.

———. "The Whiskey Insurrection: A Re-evaluation." *Pennsylvania History* 3 (July 1963): 316–46.

Cornell, Saul. "Aristocracy Assailed: The Ideology of Backcountry Anti-Federalism." *Journal of American History* 76 (Mar. 1990): 1148–72.

Coulter, E. Merton. "The Efforts of the Democratic Societies of the West to Open Navigation of the Mississippi." *Mississippi Valley Historical Review* 11 (Dec. 1924): 376–89.

Countryman, Edward. *A People in Revolution: the American Revolution and Political Society in New York, 1760–1790* (Baltimore, 1981).

Coward, Joan Wells. *Kentucky in the New Republic: The Process of Constitution Making* (Lexington, Ky., 1979).

"The Creation of the American Republic, 1776–1787: A Symposium of Views and Reviews." *William and Mary Quarterly* 44 (July 1987): 549–640.

Crow, Jeffrey J. "The Whiskey Rebellion in North Carolina" *North Carolina Historical Review* 66 (Jan. 1989).

Cunliffe, Marcus. *George Washington, Man and Monument* (New York, 1960).

Cunningham, Noble. *The Jeffersonian Republicans: The Formation of Party Organization, 1789–1801* (Chapel Hill, N.C., 1957).

Dangerfield, George. *The Era of Good Feelings* (London, 1953).

Davidson, Philip G. "Virginia and the Alien and Sedition Laws." *American Historical Review* 36 (Jan. 1931): 336–42.

Davis, William W. H. *The Fries Rebellion, 1798–1799* (New York, 1969).

Dauer, Manning J. *The Adams Federalists* (Baltimore, 1968).

DeConde, Alexander. *Entangling Alliance: Politics and Diplomacy under George Washington* (Durham, N.C., 1958).

———. *The Quasi-War: the Politics and Diplomacy of the Undeclared War with France, 1797–1801* (New York, 1966).

———. "Washington's Farewell, the French Alliance, and the Election of 1796." *Mississippi Valley Historical Review* 43 (Mar. 1957): 641–58.

Duverger, Maurice. *Political Parties: Their Organization and Activity in the Modern State* (London, 1962).

Egerton, Douglas R. "Gabriel's Conspiracy and the Election of 1800." *Journal of Southern History* 56 (May 1990): 191–214.

Ellis, Richard E. *The Jefferson Crisis: Courts and Politics in the Young Republic* (New York, 1971).

———. "The Persistence of Antifederalism after 1789." In Richard Beeman, et al., eds. *Beyond Confederation:Origins of the Constitution and American National Identity* (Chapel Hill, N.C., 1987).

Ernst, Robert. *Rufus King, American Federalist* (Chapel Hill, N.C., 1968).

Farnham, Thomas J. "The Virginia Amendments of 1795: An Episode in the Opposition to Jay's Treaty." *Virginia Magazine of History and Biography* 75 (Jan. 1967): 75–88.

Ferguson, E. James. *The Power of the Purse: A History of American Public Finance, 1776–1790* (Chapel Hill, N.C., 1961).

Flexner, James Thomas. *George Washington and the New Nation, 1783–1793* (Boston, 1970).

Foord, Archibald S. *His Majesty's Opposition, 1714–1830* (Oxford, Eng., 1964).

Formisano, Ronald P. "Deferential-Participant Politics: The Early Republic's Political Culture, 1789–1840." *American Political Science Review* 68 (1974): 473–87.

———. *The Transformation of Political Culture: Massachusetts Parties, 1790s–1840s* (New York, 1983).

Freehling, William W. *The Road to Disunion: Secesssionists at Bay, 1776–1854* (New York, 1990).

Geertz, Clifford. "The Integrative Revolution, Primordial Sentiments and Civil Politics in New States." In Clifford Geertz, ed., *Old Societies and New States: The Quest for Modernity in Asia and Africa* (New York, 1967).

Gephart, William Franklin. *Transportation and Industrial Development in the Middle West* (New York, 1909).

Goodman, Paul. *The Democratic-Republicans of Massachusetts: Politics in a Young Republic* (Cambridge, Mass., 1964).

———. "The First American Party System." In William Nisbet Chambers and Walter Dean Burnham, eds. *The American Party System: Stages of Political Development* (New York, 1967).

Griswold, Rufus Wilmont. *The Republican Court; or American Society in the Days of Washington* (New York, 1867).

Grodzins, Morton. "Political Parties and the Crisis of Succession in the United States: The Case of 1800." In Joseph LaPalombara and Myron Weiner, eds., *Political Parties and Political Development* (Princeton, 1966).

Gross, Robert A. *The Minutemen and Their World* (New York, 1976).

Gutman, Herbert. "Work, Culture, and Society in Industrializing America, 1815–1919." *American Historical Review* 78 (June 1973): 531–88.

Hammond, Bray. *Banks and Politics in America, from the Revolution to the Civil War* (Princeton, 1957).

Harrison, Lowell H. *John Breckinridge: Jeffersonian Republican* (Louisville, Ky., 1969).

Hartz, Louis. *The Liberal Tradition in America: An Interpretation of American Political Thought since the Revolution* (New York, 1955).

Hatch, Nathan O. *The Sacred Cause of Liberty: Republican Thought and the Millennium in Revolutionary New England* (New Haven, 1977).

Hazen, Charles D. *Contemporary American Opinion of the French Revolution* (Baltimore, 1897).

Heller, Susan Branson. "'Fiery Frenchified Dames': American Women and the French Revolution." Paper presented at the annual meeting of the American Historical Association, Chicago, Dec. 1991.

Helms, James. "Early Career of Nathaniel Macon." (Ph.D.diss., University of Virginia, 1962).

Henretta, James A. "Families and Farms: *Mentalite* in Pre-Industrial America." *William and Mary Quarterly* 35 (Jan. 1978): 3–32.

Hoadley, John F. *Origins of American Political Parties, 1789–1803* (Lexington, Ky., 1986).

Hofstadter, Richard *The American Political Tradition and the Men Who Made It* (New York, 1948).

———. *The Idea of a Party System: the Rise of Legitimate Opposition in the United States, 1780–1840* (Berkeley, 1969).

Howe, John R., Jr. "Republican Thought and the Political Violence of the 1790s." *American Quarterly* 19 (Summer 1967): 148–65.

Huntington, Samuel P. *Political Order in Changing Societies* (New Haven, 1975).

Hutson, James H. "Country, Court, and Constitution: Antifederalism and the Historians." *William and Mary Quarterly* 38 (July 1981): 337–68.

Isaac, Rhys. *The Transformation of Virginia, 1740–1790* (Chapel Hill, N.C., 1982).

Jones, Howard Mumford. *America and French Culture, 1750–1848* (Chapel Hill, N.C., 1927).

Jordan, Winthrop D. *White over Black: American Attitudes toward the Negro, 1550–1812* (Chapel Hill, N.C., 1968).

Kaplan, Lawrence S. *Jefferson and France: An Essay on Politics and Political Ideas* (New Haven, 1967).

Karsky, Barbara. "Agrarian Radicalism in the Late Revolutionary Period (1780–1795)." In Erich Angermann, et al., eds. *New Wine in Old Skins: A Comparative View of Socio-Political Structures and Values Affecting the American Revolution* (Stuttgart, 1976).

Kelley, Robert. *The Cultural Pattern in American Politics: The First Century* (Washington, D.C., 1979).

———. "Ideology and Political Culture from Jefferson to Nixon." *American Historical Review* 82 (June 1977): 531–62.

Kerber, Linda K. *Federalists in Dissent: Imagery and Ideology in Jeffersonian America* (Ithaca, N.Y., 1970).

Ketcham, Ralph. "France and American Politics." *Political Science Quarterly* 78 (June 1963): 198–223.

———. *Presidents above Party: The First American Presidency, 1789–1829* (Chapel Hill, N.C., 1984).

Kloppenberg, James T. "The Virtues of Liberalism: Christianity, Republicanism, and Ethics in Early American Political Discourse." *Journal of American History* 74 (June 1987) 9–33.

Koch, Adrienne, and Harry Ammon. "The Virginia and Kentucky Resolutions: An Episode in Jefferson's and Madison's Defense of Civil Liberties." *William and Mary Quarterly* 5 (Apr. 1948): 145–76.

Kohn, Richard H. *Eagle and Sword: the Federalists and the Creation of the Military Establishment in America, 1783–1802* (New York, 1975).

———. "The Washington Administration's Decision to Crush the Whiskey Rebellion." *Journal of American History* 59 (Dec. 1972): 567–84.

Kramnick, Isaac. "Republican Revisionism Revisited." *American Historical Review* 87 (June 1982): 629–64.

———. *Republicanism and Bourgeois Radicalism: Political Ideology in Late Eighteenth-Century England and America* (Ithaca, N.Y., 1990).

Kurtz, Stephen G. *The Presidency of John Adams: The Collapse of Federalism, 1795–1800* (New York, 1961).

Latner, Richard B. *The Presidency of Andrew Jackson: White House Politics, 1829–1837* (Athens, Ga., 1979).

Lerche, Charles D., Jr. "Jefferson and the Election of 1800: A Case Study in the Political Smear." *William and Mary Quarterly* 5 (Oct. 1948): 467–91.

Levine, Peter. "The Fries Rebellion: Social Violence and the Politics of the New Nation." *Pennsylvania History* 40 (July 1973).

Levy, Leonard. *Jefferson and Civil Liberties, the Darker Side* (Cambridge, Mass., 1963).

Lienesch, Michael. *New Order of the Ages: Time, the Constitution, and the Making of Modern American Political Thought* (Princeton, 1988).

Lightfoot, Billy Bob. "The State Delegations in the Congress of the United States, 1789–1801." (Ph.D. diss., University of Texas, 1958).

Link, Eugene Perry. *Democratic Republican Societies, 1790–1800* (New York, 1942).

Lipset, Seymour Martin. *The First New Nation: The United States in Historical Perspective* (New York, 1963).

Lomask, Milton. *Aaron Burr.* 2 vols. (New York, 1979).

Lowitt, Richard. "Activities of Citizen Genet in Kentucky in 1793–1794." *Filson Club Historical Quarterly* 22 (Oct. 1948): 252–67.

McCormick, Richard P. *The Presidential Game: The Origins of American Presidential Politics* (New York, 1982).

McCoy, Drew R. *The Elusive Republic: Political Economy in Jeffersonian America* (Chapel Hill, N.C., 1980).

McDonald, Forrest. *Alexander Hamilton: A Biography* (New York, 1979).

———. *Novus Ordo Seclorum: The Intellectual Origins of the Constitution* (Lawrence, Kan., 1985).

———. *The Presidency of George Washington* (Lawrence, Ks., 1974).

McPherson, James M. *Battlecry of Freedom: The Civil War Era* (New York, 1988).

Maier, Pauline. *From Resistance to Revolution: Colonial Radicals and the Development of American Opposition to Britain, 1765–1776* (New York, 1972).

———. *The Old Revolutionaries: Political Lives in the Age of Sam Adams* (New York, 1982).

Main, Jackson Turner. *The Antifederalists: Critics of the Constitution, 1787–1788* (Chapel Hill, N.C., 1961).

———. *Political Parties before the Constitution* (Chapel Hill, N.C., 1973).

Malone, Dumas. *Jefferson and the Ordeal of Liberty* (Boston, 1962).

———. *Jefferson the President: Second Term, 1805–1809* (Boston, 1974).

———. *Jefferson and the Rights of Man* (Boston, 1951).

Matthews, Richard K. *The Radical Politics of Thomas Jefferson: A Revisionist View* (Lawrence, Ks., 1984).

Meyer, Balthasar Henry. *History of Transportation in the United States before 1860* (Gloucester, Mass., 1948).

Miller, John C. *Alexander Hamilton, Portrait in Paradox* (New York, 1959).

———. *The Federalist Era, 1789–1801* (New York, 1963).

Miller, William. "The Democratic Societies and the Whiskey Insurrection." *Pennsylvania Magazine of History and Biography* 62 (July 1938): 324–49.

Morgan, Edmund. *American Slavery, American Freedom: The Ordeal of Colonial Virginia* (New York, 1975).

———. *Inventing the People: The Rise of Popular Sovereignty in England and America* (New York, 1989).

Munroe, John A. *Federalist Delaware, 1775–1815* (New Brunswick, 1954).

Murrin, John M. "The Great Inversion, or Court Versus Country: A Comparison of the Revolution Settlements in England (1688–1721) and America (1776–1816)." In J. G. A.Pocock, ed., *Three British Revolutions: 1641, 1688, 1776* (Princeton, 1980).

Nash, Gary B. "The American Clergy and the French Revolution." *William and Mary Quarterly* 22 (July 1965): 392–412.

Newlin, Claude Milton. *The Life and Writings of Hugh Henry Brackenridge* (Mamaroneck, N.J., 1971).

Nettles, Curtis P. *The Emergence of a National Economy, 1775–1815* (New York, 1962).

Newman, Simon P.. "American Popular Culture in the Age of the French Revolution." (Ph.D. diss., Princeton University, 1991).

———. "'*Principles* and not *Men*': The Political Culture of Leadership in the 1790s." Paper presented to the Philadelphia Center for Early American Studies, May 4, 1990.

Palmer, R. R. *The Age of the Democratic Revolution:A Political History of Europe and America, 1760–1800.* 2 vols. (Princeton, 1964).

Perkins, Bradford. *The First Rapproachment: England and the United States, 1755–1805* (Philadelphia, 1955).

Peterson, Merrill D. *The Jefferson Image in the American Mind* (New York, 1962).

———. *Thomas Jefferson and the New Nation, a Biography* (New York, 1970).

Philbrick, Francis S. *The Rise of the West, 1754–1830* (New York, 1965).

Pious, Richard M. *The American Presidency* (New York, 1979).

Pitkin, Hanna Fenichel. *Concept of Representation* (Los Angeles, 1967).

Pocock, J. G. A. "Civic Humanism and Its Role in Anglo-American Thought." *Politics, Language and Time:Essays on Political Thought and History* (New York, 1971).

Pole, J. R. *Political Representation in England and the Origins of the American Republic* (London, 1966).

Polsby, Nelson M. "The Institutionalization of the U.S.House of Representatives." *American Political Science Review* 62 (March 1968): 144–65.

Prince, Carl E. *New Jersey's Jeffersonian Republicans: The Genesis of an Early Party Machine, 1789–1817* (Chapel Hill, N.C., 1967).

Remini, Robert V. *The Election of Andrew Jackson* (Philadelphia, 1963).

Risjord, Norman K. *Chesapeake Politics, 1781–1800* (New York, 1978).

Robbins, Caroline. "'Discordant Parties': A Study of the Acceptance of Party by Englishmen." *Political Science Quarterly* 73 (Dec.1958): 505–29.

Rose, Lisle A. *Prologue to Democracy: The Federalists in the South, 1789–1800* (Lexington, 1968).

Rutland, Robert Allen. *The Birth of the Bill of Rights, 1776–1791* (New York, 1962).

Ryan, Mary P. "Party Formation in the United States Congress, 1789–1796: A Quantitative Analysis." *William and Mary Quarterly,* 3d ser., 18 (Oct.1971): 523–42.

Ryerson, Richard Alan. *The Revolution Is Now Begun: The Radical Committees of Philadelphia, 1765–1776* (Philadelphia, 1978).

Schachner, Nathan. *Thomas Jefferson: A Biography.* 2 vols. (New York, 1951).

Shalhope, Robert E.. "Republicanism and Early American Historiography." *William and Mary Quarterly* 39 (Apr. 1982): 334–56.

———. "Toward a Republican Synthesis: The Emergence of an Understanding of Republicanism in American Historiography." *William and Mary Quarterly* 29 (Jan. 1972): 49–80.

Sharp, James Roger. "American Reactions to Threats against the Third Republic." Unpublished paper.

———.*The Jacksonians versus the Banks: Politics in the States after the Panic of 1837* (New York, 1970).

———. "Unraveling the Mystery of Jefferson's Letter of April 27, 1795." *Journal of the Early Republic* 6 (Winter 1986): 411–18.

———. "The Whiskey Rebellion and the Question of Representation." In Steven R. Boyd, ed., *The Whiskey Rebellion: Past and Present Perspectives* (Westport, Conn., 1985).

Shaw, Peter. *The Character of John Adams* (Chapel Hill, N.C., 1976).

Slaughter, Thomas P. *The Whiskey Rebellion: Frontier Epilogue to the American Revolution* (New York, 1986).

Smith, James Morton. *Freedom's Fetters: The Alien and Sedition Laws and American Civil Liberties* (Ithaca, N.Y., 1966).

———. "The Grass Roots Origin of the Kentucky Resolutions." *William and Mary Quarterly* 27 (Apr. 1970): 221–45.

Stewart, Donald H. *The Opposition Press of the Federalist Period* (Albany, N.Y., 1969).

Stinchcombe, William. *The American Revolution and the French Alliance* (Syracuse, N.Y., 1969).

———. "John Adams' Peace Policy." Unpublished paper.

———. "Talleyrand and the American Negotiations of 1797–1798." *Journal of American History* 62 (Dec. 1975): 575–90.

———. *The XYZ Affair* (Westport, Conn., 1980).

Stone, Lawrence. "The Charles Homer Haskins Lecture: A Life of Learning."

American Council of Learned Societies Newsletter 36 (Winter/Spring 1985): 3–22.

Stourzh, Gerald. *Alexander Hamilton and the Idea of Republican Government* (Stanford, Calif., 1970).

Syndor, Charles S. *American Revolutionaries in the Making: Politial Practices in Washington's Virginia* (New York, 1962).

———. *The Development of Southern Sectionalism, 1819–1848* (Baton Rouge, La., 1948).

Tachau, Mary K. Bonsteel. "George Washington and the Reputation of Edmund Randolph." *Journal of American History* 73 (June 1986): 15–34.

———. "The Whiskey Rebellion in Kentucky." *Journal of the Early Republic* 2 (Fall 1982): 239–59.

Tagg, James. *Benjamin Franklin Bache and the Philadelphia Aurora* (Philadelphia, 1991).

Thomas, Charles Marion. *American Neutrality in 1793: A Study in Cabinet Government* (New York, 1931).

Tinkcom, Harry M. *The Republicans and Federalists in Pennsylvania, 1790–1801* (Philadelphia, 1950).

Turner, Frederick Jackson. "The Origins of Genet's Projected Attack on Louisiana and the Floridas." *American Historical Review* 3 (July 1898): 650–71.

Watlington, Patricia. *The Partisan Spirit: Kentucky Politics, 1779–1792* (New York, 1972).

Watts, Steven. *The Republic Reborn: War and the Making of Liberal America, 1790–1820* (Baltimore, Md., 1987).

Whitaker, Arthur Preston. *The Spanish-American Frontier, 1783–1795: The Western Movement and the Spanish Retreat in the Mississippi Valley* (Boston, 1927).

Wiebe, Robert H. *The Opening of American Society: From the Adoption of the Constitution to the Eve of Disunion* (New York, 1985).

Wills, Garry. *Explaining America: The Federalist* (New York, 1982).

Wood, Gordon S.. "Conspiracy and the Paranoid Style: Causality and Deceit in the Eighteenth Century." *William and Mary Quarterly* 39 (July 1982): 401–441.

———. *The Creation of the American Republic, 1776–1787* (Chapel Hill, N.C., 1969).

———. "Ideology and the Origins of Liberal America." *William and Mary Quarterly* 44 (July 1987): 628–40.

———. *The Radicalism of the American Revolution* (New York, 1992).

Young, Alfred F. *The Democratic Republicans of New York: The Origins, 1763–1797* (Chapel Hill, N.C., 1967).

Young, James Sterling. *The Washington Community, 1800–1828* (New York, 1966).

Zuckerman, Michael. *Peaceable Kingdoms: New England Towns in the Eighteenth Century* (New York, 1970).

Index